The Enemy

The Enemy
An Intellectual Portrait of Carl Schmitt

GOPAL BALAKRISHNAN

VERSO
London • New York

to Perry

First published by Verso 2000
© Gopal Balakrishnan 2000

Verso
UK: 6 Meard Street, London W1V 3HR
US: 180 Varick Street, New York, NY 10014–4606

Verso is the imprint of New Left Books

ISBN 978-1-85984-359-8

British Library Cataloguing in Publication Data
A catalogue record for this book is available from the British Library

Library of Congress Cataloging-in-Publication Data
Balakrishnan, Gopal.
 The enemy : an intellectual portrait of Carl Schmitt / Gopal Balakrishnan.
  p. cm.
 Includes bibliographical references and index.
 ISBN 1-85984-760-9 (cloth)
 1. Schmitt, Carl, 1888—Contributions in political science. I. Schmitt, Carl,
1888– II. Title.

JC263.S34 B33 2000
320.53'3'092—dc21
                                                                    00–039922

Typeset in 10/12½pt ITC New Baskerville by
SetSystems Ltd, Saffron Walden, Essex
Printed by Biddles Ltd, Guildford and King's Lynn

Contents

Acknowledgements

I would like to thank Perry Anderson, first and foremost, for his role in bringing this project to completion. His detailed commentaries on every draft are now so intertwined with my own formulations that in many places I can no longer say where my thought ends and his begins. Michael Mann read nearly every draft, and provided me with one of the central motifs of the book: that Schmitt's work mirrored the breakdown of traditional European conservatism. Robert Brenner read an earlier draft as well as numerous introductions and conclusions; his comments compelled me to think about the overarching strategic vision running through Schmitt's work. All three encouraged me to further improve this work in ways which I never ultimately pulled off.

I would also like to acknowledge Benedict Anderson, Peter Baldwin, Rogers Brubaker, Casiano Hacker-Cordon, Peter Gowan, Saul Friedlander, Mark McGurl, Dylan Riley, and George Yin. All of them provided acute criticisms of various chapters which compelled me to repeatedly write new drafts. A very special thanks to Gillian Beaumont and Judith Habermas for their thorough editing of the manuscript.

I would like to thank my mother and father for providing me with a very supportive atmosphere as I wrote this work in three successive summers at their house in Maine.

Finally, special acknowledgements are due to Tom Mertes and Grace Ryu who helped me at every stage and in every way.

'All the talk is of the minimizing of Evil, the prevention of violence: nothing but security. This is the condescending and depressive power of good intentions, a power that can dream of nothing except rectitude in the world, that refuses even to consider a bending of Evil, or an intelligence of Evil.'

Jean Baudrillard, *The Transparency of Evil*

Introduction

[The writings of Carl Schmitt form what is arguably the most disconcerting, original and yet still unfamiliar body of twentieth-century political thought. In the English-speaking world he is *terra incognita*, a name redolent of Nazism, the author of a largely untranslated *oeuvre* of short texts forming no system, coming to us from a disturbing place and time in the form of scrambled fragments.] Contextualization, demystification and unscrambling: an intellectual portrait of Carl Schmitt poses these challenges in a uniquely intense form.

Even before these problems are laid out and confronted, I would like to attempt a preliminary estimation of Schmitt's stature, as it will not be entirely obvious that the subject of this study was one of the great minds of this century. Readers are justified in approaching such a claim with suspicion, and those who know Schmitt only through some portion of the now rapidly growing secondary literature are perhaps doubly justified: there is simply no consensus as to whether he is historically significant and intellectually relevant enough to read with diligence.

There are probably few modern political thinkers whose reputation has fluctuated so wildly across time and space: a classic in one country, a nonentity in another; near the epicentre of intellectual contention in one era, a disturbing manifestation of an extinct *Zeitgeist* in the next. Those who are familiar with modern European intellectual history will perhaps have come across his name as a respected point of reference, an adversary or interlocutor in the writings of figures such as Georg Lukács, Walter Benjamin, Karl Mannheim, Leo Strauss, Friederich Hayek, Norberto Bobbio and Jürgen Habermas, to mention only a few, more familiar and perhaps more sympathetic names. A study of Carl Schmitt's thought has to be able to explain his role in key episodes of twentieth-century European intellectual history, and to provide compelling reasons for taking him seriously. The reader should form his or her own – unprompted – judgements, and it is in this spirit that I offer the findings of this study. Those who still insist on adopting the role of either prosecutor or defence attorney in discussing Schmitt can, I hope, be convinced that there are far more interesting issues involved.

Carl Schmitt identified the inadequacies of traditional conceptions of the state in a historical context in which it was no longer plausible to think of the German state as either an impartial power standing above society or a fully sovereign entity in the international community. The Weimar Republic was hovering on the brink of collapse: a liberal democracy whose centre of gravity was an unstable system of corporatist bargaining, antithetical to older norms of government by discussion; the geopolitical shell of a recently defeated Great Power, locked into a precarious new world order rigged to limit the sovereignty of rogue states (Germany and Soviet Russia) with reparations, sanctions and police action. Schmitt tracked the postwar erosion of Westphalian interstate conventions of war and peace, and explored the ways in which it was intertwined with the fiscal and legitimation crisis of European state form. He argued that the shattering of the walls separating a zone of war and diplomacy from the stateless regions of civil society had generated a decentred political system in which power politics, international financial flows, highly adversarial competition between political parties, and an ongoing class struggle between employers and workers were linked in constantly shifting configurations. The European state of early modern origin was losing its monopoly of legitimate violence, and Schmitt argued that as a result, the terrain of political battle could no longer be adequately mapped by classical state-centred theories.

Schmitt's writings probe the effects of this transformation in the nature of statehood on other fundamental categories of political and social theory. In a tradition which links Hegel to Weber, the legal-rational state is portrayed as the culmination of a long-term process of civilization in the occidental world. Schmitt claimed that war and revolution had brought this civilizing process to an end. A new era of permanent civil war was at hand in which the categories of friend and enemy would come to structure the entire field of social vision. Clearly, Schmitt's ideas took shape at a time when liberal democracy was more fragile and menaced than it is today, but I believe that as a theory of the hollowing out of parliamentary government and the nature of war and peace in a chronically precarious new world order, his writings can help us to frame more sharply the outlines of these problems in our own time. I will attempt to approach this problem of what is living and what is dead in his thought – implicitly in the body of this intellectual portrait, explicitly in its concluding chapter, and with the intent to convince.

Only a small fraction of Carl Schmitt's writings have been translated into English, and this has made a fair appraisal of his work difficult for those who do not read German. The language barrier has created a situation where most people are overly reliant on a secondary literature which often has idiosyncratic concerns. To pinpoint the singularity of this study, I would say that it is a comprehensive intertextual reconstruction and analysis of almost his entire work – a project never previously attempted. My objective is to reconstruct the main lines of his thought from 1919 to 1950 by identifying the problems he was addressing in context. For those looking for a fuller portrait of Schmitt the man, this study may seem incomplete. In presenting the biographical details of his life, I am indebted to the work of others. More materials will soon become available, which will permit a more finely graded portrait of the man. The study of Carl Schmitt's life is in an incipient stage; the only claim I make for this book is that it is the first, provisional framework for the comprehensive and critical evaluation of his thought.

The main objective of an intellectual portrait is to resolve a series of problems posed by the relationship between the textual and biographical planes of a career; the justification for such a study is that this interposition of planes brings to light otherwise difficult to discern, illocutionary dimensions of the texts. Precisely along this axis the case of Schmitt presents a set of highly specific and unusual problems which, I will argue, can be resolved only in the form of diachronic contextualization. Before one can discuss the 'ideas of Carl Schmitt', one must be able to identify them, and this is far more difficult than is generally assumed, for the following reasons: (a) because his writings are difficult to situate in the contemporary grid of academic specialization; (b) because there is a flux and discontinuity of political position running through his entire work; and finally (c) because there is no consensus on how to evaluate his support for Nazism as one episode within a far longer career. Let me address these problems in this order.

An intertextual reconstruction has to span an intellectual career that confounds our contemporary disciplinary expectations, especially in Anglo-Saxon cultures. While many of those who have written on Schmitt have recognized the range of his work, critical evaluation of its content is often impeded by an inability to enter into unfamiliar intellectual terrains. There are two particular problems here:

1. The exceptional position of law in the Weimar Republic, where the historic importance of theoretical jurisprudence in a Roman-based legal culture was suddenly and massively overdetermined by the ramshackle nature of the Constitution itself, the fruit of deliberate evasion and *arrière-pensée*, which left wide areas open to interpretative strife. Schmitt became a peculiarly central figure in Weimar Germany as politics came to revolve around conflicts over an open-ended constitution.

This may be an unfamiliar landscape for a US or UK reader. To understand the degree of difficulty here, one need only consider the radically different position of the Constitution in US political life – widely held to be a sacrosanct document, supposedly closed for all time in its basic principles. Or in Britain, where there is an unwritten consensus around legally unlimited Cabinet government, and the formulas of native constitutionalism date from a pre-democratic age. More generally, one can say that in Anglo-Saxon countries, native common-law traditions of legal thought do not overlap with a canon of political theory focused on problems of the meaning and locus of sovereignty, and the division between public and private. The idioms and agendas of Schmitt's legal theory are embedded in what are often historically remote and intellectually alien contexts.

But although Carl Schmitt was by vocation a professor of constitutional law, anyone who has even a cursory familiarity with his work knows that his texts cover a wider intellectual terrain, one which is equally – if not more – unfamiliar. This generates another interdisciplinary obstacle to the proper understanding of his work.

2. It is often very difficult to reconstruct imaginatively the discursive space in which a particular intervention by Schmitt is occurring, and this is not just a problem for Anglo-Americans. The themes he explored, the idioms he employed and the range of his references defy – even wilfully transgress – the disciplinary classifications of even the transitional era in which he lived, let alone those of contemporary *Homo academicus*. In his view, the discipline of jurisprudence was intellectually moribund, and needed to look for sources of renewal in both the classical traditions of political thought and modern social theory. Schmitt lived and wrote on the other side of that great transformation in the intellectual division of labour which unfolded over the long interval between the late nineteenth and mid-twentieth century. The social space for his kind of boundary-transgressing intellectual practice began to open up with the reconfiguration of the disciplinary map brought about by the emergence of new disciplines. Although a post-classical academic economics had been universally institutionalized, sociology was only beginning to emerge as a discipline in its own right, and political science was in an even more inchoate phase. Carl Schmitt was a product of the last period before the consolidation of the social sciences as an institutional complex in the postwar world. The division between the social sciences and the humanities was not nearly as sharply drawn as it is today. Indeed, the humanities occupied much of the space of what would become the social sciences, and was experienced as a unitary multinational cultural space which still exercised an enormous, albeit declining, force. The result is that on the one hand Schmittt's writing is often closer to

political theory or sociology than to law as we would understand it; on the other, it roams freely on to the terrain of theology, aesthetics and history, where we would not expect a legal academic to venture.

There are two reasons why Schmitt was able to capitalize on the possibilities opening up in these shifting intellectual fields. The first is an extraordinarily diversified endowment of cultural capital. Intimately familiar with contemporary intellectual production in several European languages, he had horizons of reference and perspective incomparably broader than those whose thought was circumscribed by national disciplinary traditions. The second is an attitude, more difficult to specify, stemming from a Catholic, petty-bourgeois and provincial background. Carl Schmitt was an outsider in the Wilhelmine social world, and readily turned his back on the 'good old days' of prewar Germany. His formative political moment came with the realization that the age of traditional conservative–liberal politics was at an end, and that new approaches to the problem of legitimacy were required to hold the fort against the discontents of civilization. The First World War and its revolutionary aftermath had remorselessly devalued and shattered the stock of intellectual traditions dating from the nineteenth century. Schmitt, a man without conventional allegiances or sentimentalities, could pick up selected pieces, innovate, improvise and recombine. As a renewer, defender and enemy in the world of ideas, he worked like a *bricoleur*.

I will demonstrate in this study that, in addition to these problems of intellectual cartography, there is a perpetual flux of political positions across Schmitt's work. Compared to cases where a thinker is built 'all of a piece' out of a formative episode which crystallizes into a system that is subsequently filled out over the remainder of a career, here we are confronted with a figure who is moulting with astonishing frequency. In the former cases, a thorough abstraction of thought from the existence behind it is normal, and reasonably warranted. Here one thinks of figures like Immanuel Kant or John Rawls. Schmitt is almost the typological paradigm of the extreme opposite type of intellectual, one whose work consists overwhelmingly of interventionist texts. The consequence is that while his works exhibit flashes of sharp political self-definition in relation to recurring targets, there is an alarming discontinuity in the positions he adopted as these targets shifted, or came into his field of vision from a different direction. When his work is reconstructed in a chronological sequence, a pattern emerges in which he repeatedly returned to the same problems, while continually oscillating between ultimately irreconcilable stances when it came to solutions. Although some of these shifts have been noted in the secondary literature, the full scope of the intertextual conundrums which arise under close scrutiny has never been adequately grasped. The resolution of these conundrums requires that the arguments of each text be presented in a narrative sequence, because the meaning of arguments in individual texts can be fully understood only when they are seen as modifications or inversions of positions previously staked out. Since these transformations involve Schmitt redefining his relationship to other currents of thought, this dynamic has to be identified in order to retrieve the intertwining of intention and premises in the relationship of text to context.

What is the significance of this pattern of flux and discontinuity for an overall estimation of Schmitt as a political thinker? I would argue that many of his ideas are not so firmly ensconced on the right side of the political spectrum. In the gallery of the intransigent Right, dominated by figures like Nietzsche, Hayek and Strauss, Schmitt stands out. His mind was focused neither on the remorseless logic of the market nor on unalterable natural inequalities, nor even on the degeneration of culture under the impact of modernity – the three thematic prongs of the Right in the twentieth century. Indeed, Schmitt revelled in ironic inversions of liberal and left-wing themes, taking as his motto a phrase from the Young Hegelian Bruno Bauer: 'Only he who knows his prey better than it knows itself can conquer.'

Finally, when one considers the difficulties that stand in the way of an objective appraisal of Schmitt's thought, the spectre of his relationship to Nazism, and Fascism more generally, looms large. His high-profile, conspicuous support for the Nazis after they had come to power continues to evoke supercharged partisan judgements of how to evaluate this episode in terms of what he wrote and did before and, to a lesser extent, after. Here again, there is a general and a specific problem.

1. The general problem is posed by the very large number of European intellectuals who favoured or collaborated with Fascism before and during the war, and continued to be regarded as thinkers of importance or distinction after it: Heidegger, Gehlen, De Mann (both the uncle and the nephew), Benn, Céline, Jünger, Gentile, Croce, Della Volpe; in the world of English literature there was Eliot, Pound, Yeats and Lewis. Clearly, in any intelligent discussion about what is unique about Schmitt's case, one would need to situate him in a more detailed collective biography of this Fascist-sympathizing/collaborating constellation in the European intellectual aristocracy of the interwar era. When one focuses on any of these often very different cases, the question always arises: how are such episodes to be judged within the whole career of the person – that is to say, what weight do we give

them? Almost always, the issue is whether the option for Fascism was opportunism, a logical culmination of a pre-Fascist trajectory, or an episodic aberration.

2. In the specific case of Schmitt, the problem is more acute, since he alone, of the high intelligentsia which opted for Fascism, was a political thinker of the first rank (that is to say, he was not a philosopher, novelist, poet, critic, historian, etc.), and he was more institutionally complicitous than any of the others in this constellation with the exception of Gentile – who was not really a political theorist and, moreover, did not survive the war. Carl Schmitt is not, then, the typical case of an intellectual flirting with Fascism, then leaving behind a legacy of controversy about the significance of this episode in the interpretation of his work. His writings as a legal adviser to Papen, Schleicher and Goering were interventions with consequences reverberating far outside the community of scholars.

For many people, the explicitly political context and concerns of Schmitt's work seem to impose the requirement that first, one must determine the motives and extent of his relationship to National Socialism, and then, on the basis of this verdict, interpret his work. The problem with this is that his notoriety brings to mind so many associations, that it is very easy to read his writings in a spirit of familiarity, coasting along until we come across something which fits our preconceived notions.

This raises the issue of how to situate the preoccupations of the contemporary reception of Schmitt's thought in a long, nationally diverse history of commentary and critique. The breadth and longevity of this reception are impressive. In different European national contexts and at different historical moments – going back all the way to the 1920s – Schmitt has periodically appeared as a figure to be seriously reckoned with by Left, Right and Centre. For some, the most surprising – not to say scandalous – aspect of this reception is the ongoing relationships to figures and intellectual traditions of the Left. Intelligent connoisseur of Marx, astute observer of Bolshevism, academic adviser to Kirchheimer and Neumann, admired by Benjamin, and – more begrudgingly – by Lukács, Schmitt wanted to know and be known by his adversaries. But this relationship between Schmitt and the Left was not limited to the *Querverbindungen* of the Weimar era. The elder statesman of Italian political thought, the liberal socialist Norberto Bobbio, has for decades been engaged with Schmitt's work. A younger Habermas offered a severe indictment of the hollowing out of the liberal-democratic order in *The Structural Transformation of the Public Sphere*, a work conspicuously influenced by Schmitt's essay on the crisis of parliamentarianism. In the late 1960s, small circles of the far Left in

Germany and Italy cautiously appropriated ideas from this same essay in developing their extraparliamentary agendas. More recently, defenders of Schmitt can be found in the USA writing in the once left-wing journal *Telos*.

Yet arguably, the main impetus behind the contemporary renaissance of interest in Schmitt's thought is a shift to the Right in German intellectual life. His postwar presence in the conservative academic culture of the Federal Republic was always pervasive, but it was only ever partly acknowledged – for discretion's sake. In the 1980s a young conservative coterie writing for the *Frankfurter Allgemeine Zeitung* exhumed a recently deceased Schmitt, adding an element of scandalous intellectual glamour to a rather conventional late-twentieth century right-wing agenda. Irreverence towards a left-liberal academic establishment in the world of literary journalism is part of a larger sea change in which idioms from a buried theoretical continent are resurfacing. After a long postwar career on the fringe of mainstream respectability, Carl Schmitt has become a clear and distinct point of reference in the major zones of German intellectual contention – the legacy of the Nazi past, constitutional law, national reunification, immigration, and Europe.

The persisting lacunae in the secondary literature are all the more noteworthy considering the duration, national diversity and political range of the Schmitt reception. Even in Germany, decades after he acquired a national reputation, the outlines of some of the major problems he was addressing are often only casually traced in the secondary literature. The reception of Schmitt's work in various national contexts has always been filtered through political agendas which have brought attention to certain dimensions of his thought while obscuring others. Astonishingly, there is still not even a tentative consensus as to what his main ideas were – that is to say, what weight should be given to particular texts, to particular formulations within texts over against others, in a coherent system of weights and measures. Because he at no point attempted to integrate his far-ranging intellectual interventions into a finished system, commentary on his writings often takes its cue from the powerful symbolic associations which his name continues to evoke. These associations crystallize around one or another of the arcane-sounding formulations which are conspicuous in his writings, giving rise to a great number of small interpretative prisms. Everyone is, of course, entitled to take what they want from Schmitt's writings, but let us not confuse this kind of appropriation with the business of interpreting him. He is already protean enough; reading him against the grain, when the grain is still unrecognizable, simply postpones the day of intellectual reckoning.

There are many contrasting stances that those who write on Schmitt have traditionally adopted. Unsympathetic commentators denounce him as a Fascist or an opportunist; sympathetic commentators either present neatly sanitized, apologetic accounts of the relationship between his writings and his political allegiances, or – worse – portray him as someone with dark, arcane insights into 'the political'. What is common to all these approaches is that they treat Schmitt as an affectively charged symbol, not as someone whose thought could be understood through a comprehensive and systematic study.

A restructuring of the whole field of Schmitt commentary and critique is about to take place as masses of new documentation appears. This should concentrate and refine our judgements. Two important biographies have recently appeared in German: one by Paul Noack, the other by Andreas Koenen, supplementing the materials provided by the American Joseph Bendersky, who wrote the first biography of Schmitt to appear in any language. I have drawn on all three of these very helpful works in designing and assembling the biographical architecture of this study. Although they do not attempt to provide a comprehensive overview and critical evaluation of his thought, without the foundations and layout provided by these earlier studies, my own attempts at synthesis would have been far more difficult. Archival research is still at an incipient stage, and mountains of material remain unstudied: several diaries, 17,000 letters written to and by Schmitt, annotations and more. Here I have relied on the work of others. Portraying the man whose presence is disseminated over this mass of material involves shrewd guesswork, and I offer my own sketches tentatively. But Schmitt's fame and significance rest on his published work, and this is the focus of my study, and the basis upon which it should be judged.

Although I have emphasized the centrality of context, ideas taking shape in real historical time, this is not just an intellectual history. The legacy of Carl Schmitt is too disconcerting for our own political universe for him to be treated as a period piece. I will return to this issue of his contemporary relevance in the Conclusion. My view is that his writings are like the still unexplored contents of a time capsule.

Carl Schmitt is a difficult figure. But even people of diametrically opposite political allegiances can profit intellectually from taking him seriously, and not just with the intention of refuting everything he has to say. One of Schmitt's undeniable intellectual virtues was a willingness to read and engage seriously with the arguments of people at the other end of the political spectrum. I have tried to write this book in a similar spirit.

1

The Young Carl Schmitt

The earliest years of the life of Carl Schmitt are shrouded in obscurity, and only faintly discernible from some small biographical fragments. The attempt to identify formative influences from childhood and adolescence is perhaps always a precarious enterprise, one which invariably succumbs to the illusions of retrospection. Certain lives are easier to portray in this biographical mode, as the intimate features of the subject bear the unmistakable marks of a social background, a generation and a national character. But world wars and revolutions are often solvents of these inherited identities, erasing, scrambling and recombining the relevant details from the past. Out of such experiences, people who in more normal circumstances might have passed through life unnoticed emerge out of the catastrophic grinding up of backgrounds, generations and national characters with rather unfamiliar features. Carl Schmitt was one of these emergent figures. The early years of his life are sketched here to suggest how initial biographical co-ordinates may have been concealed and negated by the acquisition of later roles. The objective is to portray the origins of a disconcertingly unsettled, protean mind, one which would later be attuned to all the contradictions of an age of war and revolution.

The Schmitt family, with branches extending into Lorraine, had come down the Mosel as Catholic migrants to the small, largely Protestant town of Plettenberg in the Rhineland. Although the Rhineland was a long way from Berlin, it had been ruled as a part of the Prussian state since the end of the Napoleonic Wars, and over the course of the nineteenth century it became Prussia's most industrially advanced region. The local Prussian administration had for a long time worked with the Catholic Church in securing the traditional *ancien régime* priorities of public order, tax and tithe collection. This uneasy partnership was broken during Bismarck's *Kulturkampf* as Prussia, now the core of a modern German nation-state, sought to wrest control over education and social welfare away from the Church. Beyond its tactical significance for Bismarck, the *Kulturkampf* emerged from the convergence of National Liberalism and administrative centralization in a historically Protestant state; progressive and bigoted in equal measure,

it provoked a full-scale mobilization of the region's Catholics, creating
a bitter legacy of mistrust on their part towards the priorities of the
new nation-state.

Many of Schmitt's relatives were prominent local members of the
Catholic Centre Party which, like the Social Democratic Party, was
enormously strengthened by the experience of repression under Bismarck. The Schmitt family was on the very lowest rung of the petty-
bourgeoisie; the father, Johann, worked at the local railway station.
Participation in the affairs of the Church gave such people some claim
to social respectability, if only in the eyes of fellow Catholics. Most
poor, small-town Catholics lived in a world closed off from a hostile,
increasingly secular society, a world in which the local priest was a
revered authority in matters of politics and morality. Although there
was a Catholic majority in the region, tiny Plettenberg was an evangelical community. The hostilities of the *Kulturkampf* were still hanging in
the air in this obscure backwater of the Sauerland.[1] Schmitt was born
in 1888, the year in which the young Wilhelm II ascended to the throne
of the recently established Prusso-German Reich. It is unlikely that the
Imperial coronation in far-off Berlin generated much enthusiasm in
the Schmitt household.

In his childhood certain opportunities opened up for Schmitt which
exposed him to the society outside this cloistered world. Recognized as
exceptionally gifted, he was given a scholarship to study at the local
Gymnasium in nearby Attendorn. Bookish Catholic children were
usually singled out as potential candidates for the priesthood, and
would not typically have been exposed to the full course of studies at
such a Gymnasium. The fact that he was allowed to continue his studies
at Attendorn suggests that his family placed more value on a secular
education than was typical of their kind. Many of his relatives were
French-speakers, from the provinces annexed by Prussia in the Franco–
Prussian War, and he distinguished himself by an early fluency in that
language. At school he learned Latin, Greek and a number of modern
languages, including Spanish and Italian. From an early age he was
fascinated by the expressive potentials and limitations of different
languages, and much of the distinctive style of his later writing betrays
an intimate familiarity with the stylistic norms of Latin and French.[2]

At the Gymnasium Schmitt was exposed to a humanistic curriculum
which had an unsettling effect on his relationship to Catholic dogma.[3]
Even if he never fully embraced the world-views of German Idealism,
Charles Darwin, or liberal Protestant biblical critics, these influences
had irreparably corrosive effects on that simple, unquestioning belief
which distinguishes the devout from those intellectuals who, even when
they are unwilling to accept any modern secular ideology, no longer
believe in the literal tenets of their faith.

Upon graduation, Schmitt decided to attend the Friedrich-Wilhelm University of Berlin, the pinnacle of the German university system and thus one of the greatest universities in the world. Although he had considered studying philology, the stern advice of a rich uncle from Lorraine pointed him in the more practical direction of jurisprudence.[4] Such were the contingent beginnings of a remarkable and controversial career. Berlin was the veritable antithesis of the world in which he had grown up: a giant metropolis of power, money and modern culture, it was alien to his native sensibilities in both scale and atmosphere; not only North-German-Protestant but, at least in the popular imagination, in some way Jewish as well. From this point on he would always have a deeply ambivalent relationship to the city, finding it both fascinating and disturbing. The feeling of being an outsider in the exclusive *fin-de-siècle* world of Berlin's elites comes across in a later recollection:

> I was an obscure young man of modest descent. . . . Neither the ruling strata nor the opposition included me. . . . That meant that I, standing entirely in the dark, out of the darkness looked into a brightly lit room. . . . The feeling of sadness which filled me made me more distant and awoke in others mistrust and antipathy. The ruling strata experienced anybody who was not thrilled to be involved with them as heterogeneous. It put before him the choice to adapt or to withdraw. So I remained outside.[5]

In the last years of the Weimar Republic Schmitt would return to Berlin, and be welcomed into these circles. But his initial experience was too overwhelming, and he retreated after two semesters to the less abrasive environment of Munich; and then, after only one semester, he departed again for the even more congenial Strasbourg.

What was going on in the world of German academic law when Schmitt was a student? Since the 1870s, 'legal positivism' had come to dominate the discipline. 'Positive' in this context meant the opposite of what, by the late nineteenth century, had increasingly come to be seen as the chimerical norms of 'natural' law. Modern legal positivism, as formulated by Laband and Gerber in the 1870s, had sought to eliminate all traces of natural-law language – indeed, political and moral commentary of any kind – from the study of law. The positivist project was to make the formal analysis of the meaning of legal terms in statutes the exclusive focus of jurisprudence, and treat the entire body of law as if it formed a seamless system of norms.

While the older legacy of Savigny's Historical School of Law had made it possible for Laband to justify this assumption in terms of the 'organic unity' of German legal culture, the *Volksgeist* might have seemed too nebulous a thing for those who wanted a more incontrovertibly scientific foundation. The formalism of Marburg neo-Kantianism provided an alternative justification for conceiving of the legal system as a unified system: unity, it was argued, was simply the transcendental condition of legal judgement. But the fortunes of legal positivism did not ultimately depend upon philosophical fashion; positivism became the intellectual common sense of this academically trained legal establishment because it seemed to meet the demand for more uniformity and predictability in the legal process. The turn-of-the-century codification of a German civil law code was its crowning intellectual achievement, and provided a seemingly convincing demonstration that the totality of private legal relations could be conceptualized within a self-contained system. The unity of private law was now no longer just an assumption; it had been secured by legislative enactment.

As we shall see, the situation was different when it came to constitutional law. Here the intellectual achievements of prewar legal positivists were considerably less impressive. The constitutional settlement inherited from Bismarck kept fundamental questions like the locus of sovereignty and control over the budget within the Reich unresolved. The constitutional commentary of the *Kaiserreich*, taking its cue from Laband, sought to conceal the inherently political nature of these unresolved problems with compromise formulas, masquerading as objective legal reasoning. It was not until after the war, when some of the inhibitions about exploring these problems were overcome, that constitutional law took off as the most dynamic branch of academic jurisprudence.

But even before the war, German jurisprudence was showing signs of intellectual crisis. From the turn of the century, serious challenges to the theoretical hegemony of legal positivism were emerging. The leading figures of the so-called 'Free Law movement' – Kantorowicz, Ehrlich and Fuchs – sought to demolish the stereotypical image of a judge as an automaton who mechanically applies legal norms to come up with a technically correct ruling. These scholars emphasized – and, indeed, celebrated, often in a fashionably Nietzschean mode – the creative role played by 'irrational' ethical sentiments in judicial decisions.

Schmitt's prewar legal writings are extensive commentaries on the issues which these criticisms of legal positivism had opened up. In his dissertation on criminal law entitled *Über Schuld und Schuldarten* ('On Guilt and Degrees of Guilt')[6] he argued that the discretionary prerogative of a judge to determine a sentence highlighted the moment of decision as a free-floating element in the legal process. Perhaps this aspect of criminal law appealed to Schmitt's incipient, temperamental 'decisionism'. Another work, *Gesetz und Urteil* ('Statute and Judgement')[7] expanded on the implications of this open, ungrounded moment in the legal process, and argued that the meaning of a norm was entirely embedded in the ultimately arbitrary conventions of interpretation within the legal community: 'A judicial decision is now correct when it can be assumed that another judge would have come to the same judgement.' 'Another judge' here means the empirical type of a modern legally trained jurist.[8]

Even as Schmitt underscored the indeterminacies of legal interpretation, he took for granted positivism's purely statutory conception of law, albeit with a certain amorphous ambivalence. The terminology of his Habilitation text, completed in 1914 and entitled *Der Wert des Staates und die Bedeutung des Individuums* ('The Value of the State and the Significance of the Individual'),[9] often suggests a certain sympathy for neo-Thomist natural law, a 'higher law' which the state has the duty to 'realize' in the form of positive law. But many of the substantive conclusions of this work were in fact stringently positivist – indeed, nearly the opposite of the views he would develop after the war: 'The state is a legal structure whose significance resides entirely in the task of realizing law.'[10] This 'higher law' which the state translates into positive law was so indeterminate, as Schmitt conceived it, that it could be known only through the decisions of the state; in other words, it was a logical fiction with no relation to the ethical precepts of the Catholic natural-law tradition.[11] But invoking an indeterminate 'higher law' led to an ultimately inconsequential critique of legal positivism. Indeed, very similar formulations could be found in the writings of Hans Kelsen, the most brilliant and most extreme representative of legal positivism. According to Schmitt, one of the central problems of natural-law doctrine – the legitimacy of a title to power, and the conditions of obedience to those who have it – was simply not an issue for jurisprudence: 'The question of how to help the empirical individual is no longer one of legal philosophy, just as little as the question of how the holder of power can be made to stick to the law.'[12] In later works he would attempt to reframe this problem, by extracting it from the natural-law tradition in which it was embedded.

These prewar legal writings suggest that Schmitt had hardly developed a coherent critique of legal positivism, let alone an alternative vision of law. To all appearances he seemed to be at home in the politically complacent world of *belle-époque* academia. The oppositional sentiments he cultivated in the last years of the *Kaiserreich* did not find an outlet in his legal work but, rather, in satirical polemics against the luminaries of German *Kultur*: Friedrich Nietzsche, Thomas Mann and Walter Rathenau.[13] While these writings bear the marks of juvenalia, they reveal a counter-cultural literary sensibility which would indirectly influence his later political development. Even though he was never fully Bohemian, his social intercourse with Munich's avant-garde contributed to neutralizing the appeal of a literary propaganda campaign which portrayed Germany as fighting for an apolitical, 'higher' *Kultur*.

⌐ Carl Schmitt, twenty-six years old at the beginning of the First World
War, did not share the initial belligerent enthusiasm of his countrymen.⌐
One should pause and reflect on this fact, if only because it suggests
how detached he was from the defining experience of his generation;
nothing he wrote at the time even hints at Germany's 'mission' in this
war, nor is there any evidence that it had any 'world-historical' significance for him. Why was he so emotionally detached from the national
cause? A professed lack of interest in politics cannot be the explanation, since this 'unpolitical' stance was – as in the case of Thomas Mann
– easily compatible with ultra-patriotism. ⌐Perhaps reservations stemming from his Catholic background kept him from wholeheartedly
believing that 'Prussia' was fighting the just war.⌐ Many educated
German Catholics were swept up in the wave of patriotism which
washed over the country, but Schmitt was not from this kind of
background. The local Catholic priest in Plettenberg, unlike his more
enthusiastic Protestant counterpart, probably counselled his parish-
ioners to serve honourably, but to pray for peace. ⌐However great his
intellectual distance from this petty-bourgeois, Catholic and regional
subculture had become, Schmitt's residual allegiances to it pulled him
away from the nationalist obsessions of academic Germany. Perhaps his
family connections in Lorraine, where the local population often
harboured historical sympathies for the French, played a role here. In
any case, he was far too Latin to see the French as the representatives
of a soulless 'civilization' at war with German '*Kultur*'.⌐

Having passed the assessor's examination in Berlin, Schmitt volun-
teered for the reserve infantry. While he was in basic training he
claimed to have sustained a back injury, and a month later he was
transferred to the General Command of Army Corps 1 in Munich. In
this non-combat capacity he was promoted to lance corporal, and later
to sergeant, and in this rank he served in the censorship section of the
regional martial law administration.

Schmitt did not socialize only with the military, legal and academic
establishment in the city. Indeed, he was an *habitué* of the city's still
dynamic – if now fading – café culture, frequented at the time by some
of the leading figures of German Expressionism.

> Before the war Munich had been a cultural centre in many respects superior
> to Berlin; drinking a cup of coffee in the Café Luitpold or Stefanie one
> could meet within an hour almost everyone who was anyone among the
> leading painters of both the older and the younger generation, not to
> mention a great many writers and composers.[14]

Since his student days in Strasbourg he had actively sought out such
company.[15] ⌐It was in this setting that Schmitt experienced the *Sturm
und Drang* of a somewhat belated young adulthood, entering into ill-

fated wedlock with his first wife, a woman who claimed to be a Serbian noblewoman. At the time Serbia was an enemy nation.⏋

Although this Bohemian milieu was hardly 'leftist', the patriotism of the local population – 'the boors', as they were called by Munich's Left Bank – was altogether too conventional to take seriously. There were indeed some who struck bellicose, even apocalyptic notes in the poetry they recited at happenings, but in these cases it is arguable that the medium was the message. In any event, Schmitt does not seem to have identified with this aestheticized bellicosity, and was in fact on good terms, even after the war, with some of those artists who eventually fled Germany for Swiss exile, many of whom, like the Dadaist Hugo Ball,[16] were not only antiwar but also extreme antipatriots. While it is somewhat unlikely that Schmitt ever identified with the views of such *outré* figures, these associations suggest an almost abnormal indifference to the national cause for an academic, and for someone who was neither on the Left nor a pacifist.[17]

Such nonchalance towards the stakes and course of the war suggests that the crystallization of Schmitt's later political outlook was not predetermined by his background. During the war none of his conflicting identities – a semi-Bohemian Catholic antimodernist military functionary working for the martial law administration – became the basis of a determinate political outlook, even if they provided the raw materials of a later synthesis. This raises the question of whether he could have gone in another political direction; was the abrupt shift to the Right which took place in the early Weimar years, as he awoke to political consciousness, somehow natural in the light of his past? Even if his social and religious background, intellectual style and self-conception prevented him from ever making the better-known transition from Romantic to left-wing revolutionary,[18] this does not mean that he was fated to move far in the opposite direction. In the absence of any deeper insights into his psychology, one is tempted to say that a rather unformed character made a decision explicable in terms of his background, but not reducible to it.

The military defeat of Germany in 1918 led to the rapid disintegration of the old monarchic order. Shortly after the panicked abdication of Kaiser Wilhelm II, on 18 November, came the formal proclamation of a republic. A wave of pent-up popular discontent was rolling over the country, and power briefly fell into the lap of councils made up of radicalized workers and soldiers. Although it was later maligned as treasonous and incompetent, the council network effectively prevented the total collapse of distribution and supply during the Allied blockade and subsequent demobilization.[19] While defeat, mutiny and the spectre of social revolution had temporarily incapacitated the coercive machinery of the state, irregular counter-revolutionary squads rapidly formed

to take back this usurped power violently. These squads, the so-called
Freikorps, consisted mainly of demobilized officers and soldiers, with
auxiliary roles for able-bodied students, professionals and property-
owners. On 13 January 1919 the *Freikorps* declared martial law in Berlin,
summarily executing armed workers in a frenzied hunt for revolutionary, 'Spartacist' ringleaders. Two days later, a mounted rifle guard
division, led by Captain Waldemar Pabst, abducted and executed Rosa
Luxemburg and Karl Liebknecht.

The Russian Revolution had changed the nature of these civil
disturbances by giving all the contending parties a glimpse of what
kind of upheavals and transformations a revolution might bring to
Germany. Although the Bolshevik message was sympathetically received
by millions, this was a diffuse sentiment, and was not in the least shared
by the leadership of the Social Democratic Party (SPD). During the war
the party's leaders, Ebert and Noske, had successfully brought the party
and unions into a smooth working relationship with the state apparatus,
and they recoiled from the idea that all these gains might be thrown
away in a fit of revolutionary provocation. Noske, as provisional Defence
Minister of the new republic, gave the green light for the elimination
of the soldiers' councils. Indeed, the leadership of the Majority Social
Democrats self-consciously acted as the shield of a demoralized old
regime, a service which was only grudgingly acknowledged by the
military and *Freikorps*.

The political parties which worked with the military to restore law
and order – the Social Democrats, the Catholic Centre, and the so-
called Left Liberals in the newly formed Democratic Party – had been
politically marginalized under the monarchy. Despite their radically
different views on a number of issues, together they formed what was
called the Weimar coalition. Even though this Left–Centre coalition
held power only intermittently at the federal ('Reich') level, it contin-
uously controlled the state government of Prussia, the bulwark of the
whole Weimar system until the last years of the Republic. The Social
Democrats and the rest of the Weimar coalition sought to stabilize the
new Republic by suppressing the revolutionary Left, to be found at first
in the Minority Social Democrat and then in the Communist Party, in
order to win over the Right. But the Right refused the gesture, and
continued to see the Republic as the embodiment of national defeat,
economic ruin and cultural decadence. For those parties which had
strongly identified with the deposed monarchy, the National Liberals
and the Conservatives – rechristened, respectively, the German People's
Party (DVP) and the German National People's Party (DNVP) – the
establishment of the Republic was a bitter reversal of fortune. Hatred
for Weimar and everything it stood for was the official stance of the
DNVP; while the DVP, representing business interests with a large stake

in stability, adopted a more pragmatic stance towards the Republic. After a brief flirtation with the Left-Liberal Democrats, the educated, Protestant middle classes divided their votes between these two parties until the final years of the Republic, when they began voting National Socialist in large numbers.

The basic framework of the Weimar Republic and its Constitution reflected the precarious and unfinished nature of the German Revolution. This uneasy balance of power was reflected and reproduced in the corporatist agreement between the trade unions and the major employers enshrined in the Stinnes–Legien covenant and the National Service law, recognizing union representation, collective bargaining and compulsory arbitration procedures. Indeed, the basic framework of the Weimar Republic can be said to have crystallized around the alliance between the Majority Social Democrats and the *Freikorps* and Army, the *deténte* between industry and unions, and finally the republican government's decision to accept the terms of the victors in the Treaty of Versailles, and to enshrine compliance with it into the Constitution itself.[20]

Most of these compromises were sealed with the defeat and exclusion of the revolutionary Left, by an alliance of the Weimar coalition with forces further to the right. The postwar collision between the revolutionary Left and this 'Party of Order' unfolded somewhat differently in Berlin, with its large, concentrated working classes confronting a much more intact state apparatus than in Munich, where the local state briefly lost its backbone in the face of vociferous urban crowds. In Munich military defeat blended into a social revolution in which intellectuals played an unusually prominent role. On 7 November 1918 Kurt Eisner, a famous local author and member of the antiwar Minority Socialists, was swept up by a crowd of demonstrators and asked to declare Bavaria's Wittelsbach monarchy officially deposed, and to head a Provisional Government of Workers', Soldiers' and Peasants' Councils. Eisner and those around him were unlikely revolutionaries – indecisive intellectuals who gave the ill-fated revolution its improvisational, amateurish appearance. Moreover, its leadership seemed conspicuously Jewish and counter-cultural, providing numerous stereotypical targets for reactionary *enragés*. Eisner was so discouraged by the course of events and the ensuing deadlock that on 21 February 1919 he was actually attempting to resign as he was shot down by a young, mentally unbalanced right-wing aristocrat, Count Arco-Valley.

The response from the Left was now more determined, and the second phase of the revolution began on 7 April 1919 with the declaration of the so-called Bavarian Soviet Republic. When the Munich garrison attempted to overthrow this 'regime', two foreign Communist leaders, Eugen Levine and Max Levien, took the leadership of the local revolution into their own hands, temporarily buoyed up by the brief revolutionary adventure in Hungary. A flurry of ineffectual measures could not conceal the fact that these were not 'professional revolutionaries' but panicked and disorientated amateurs. Desperate to salvage the situation, the Expressionist playwright Ernst Toller forced the unpopular and isolated Levine and Levien to resign, but was unable to stave off the approaching counter-revolutionary rampage. On 2 May the *Freikorps* entered Munich and, in revenge for the slaying of a hostage, slaughtered six hundred people in two days. The suppression of the Bavarian Soviet Republic and the far Left in Leipzig brought an end to the initial phase of revolutionary upheaval. The German worker now faced a Party of Order which had prevailed through an intransigent class-war politics, creating an ominous precedent for dealing with the social question.[21]

Until 1918, neither the war for European supremacy nor the growing domestic political tension seems to have made a deep intellectual impression on Schmitt. In 1918, Central Europe was beginning to feel the sea change brought about by the Russian Revolution and US President Woodrow Wilson's diplomacy, and it is probable that in this context of sudden and intense politicization Schmitt began to sense that conflict, beyond a certain level of intensity, directly determined the fate of even those who sought to stay on the sidelines. During the postwar revolutionary turmoil he experienced at first hand the tension and insecurity generated by the political polarization of the city when his office was broken into by a band of revolutionaries, and an officer at a nearby table was shot.[22] Such experiences gelled into an abiding fear of civil wars, but also a fascination for the political and moral atmosphere they generated; this fear and fascination were to shape his whole political outlook.

Schmitt's precise attitudes towards the contending parties in Munich's brief civil war are not known. While this was an irreversibly politicizing experience, his antipathy towards the revolutionaries does not seem to have hurtled him very far to the right. Although his relationship to Munich's beleaguered Bohemian milieu was becoming more critical, he was still unlikely to have thought much of the ridiculous and sinister representatives of local patriotism. The gritty panic lurking in the air of civil-war Munich comes across in a marginal entry from Thomas Mann's diary dated 11 August 1918, one day after the flight of the king and the beginning of the revolution: 'Munich, like Bavaria, ruled by Jewish literati.'[23] Although few traces of Schmitt's life in Munich from 1915 to 1921 remain, it is improbable that this was how he would have put it at the time. The victorious counter-revolution had destroyed the rhythm of life of the Munich he had known.

Considering his later reputation as intellectual soldier of the intransigent Right, the absence of any note of obsessive anti-Marxism in any of
his writings from this period is quite simply puzzling. Violent
expressions of fear and hatred against the Left were commonplace
even among otherwise apolitical German liberals and conservatives.
Schmitt, by contrast, maintained a certain *sang-froid*, and there is an
oddly controlled intensity to his published formulations.

Perhaps Schmitt found in the public appearances of Max Weber,
who was teaching in Munich at the time, a pole of political orientation.[24] He would later characterize Weber as 'a revanchist, the most
radical of all revanchism towards Weimar, that I had ever experienced
– at least in the force of his phrases'.[25] In *Politics as a Vocation* and
Science as a Vocation, Weber passionately denounced the fashionable
mysticism of the younger generation, and the related retreat from a
politics of responsibility. These were indirectly some of the themes of
Schmitt's first major work, a polemical intellectual history published
early in 1919 entitled *Politische Romantik* ('Political Romanticism').[26]

Schmitt's interest in Adam Müller's political writings probably went
back more than a few years, and it is very probable that he had
previously found this conservative aesthete and convert to Catholicism
a sympathetic figure. But in the aftermath of what was perhaps a
sudden volte-face, he penned a savagely unflattering portrait of a
charlatan, in his judgement the *primus inter pares* in the chameleon-like
milieu of early-nineteenth-century German Romanticism. After this
work was completed, he would write very little on aesthetic subjects;
just as the young Karl Marx had written *The German Ideology* to put to
rest his erstwhile philosophical consciousness, one could say that
Schmitt wrote *Politische Romantik* to break the clammy grip of aestheti-
cism on his imagination and style.

Schmitt began this work by denying that there was any point in trying
to attribute any coherent political ideology to the German Romantics.
Their quicksilver eloquence could be alternately revolutionary or reactionary, militarist or pacifist, heathen or Christian. At the centre of this
web of phrases and poses was a conservative, reactive habitus desperate
to avoid the mental discipline of political commitment. The ironical
detachment of the German Romantics stemmed from their essentially
voyeuristic relationship to the conflicts rocking the world around
them.[27]

Romantic writings on political themes exuded a spirit of nonchalance, which concealed a true horror of political commitment. Their
style was their ideology. Müller, Novalis and the Schlegel brothers
were masters of capturing certain obscure moods with lyrical phrases;
words, concepts and images were formally grouped together to form

oppositions which, with the help of rhythm and acoustical effect, could sound suggestive and profound. This was a kind of quasi-reasoning based on the affective association around words.[28]

Schmitt piled on citations to demonstrate that the political Romantics saw life as an 'endless conversation', where no one ever has to take sides because there is nothing worth fighting for. Even those who expressed a love of adventure and chaos were accumulating 'experiences'; in an unmistakable allusion to the *Gesinnungspolitik* of the time, he claimed that even when radical postures were adopted, inherent to such political theatre was a secret desire that the external order of things should remain intact.[29] Perhaps thinking of many of those he knew in the cafés and salons of Munich – perhaps even of himself not so long before – he wrote: 'Even the greatest external events, a revolution and a world war is, in itself, of no consequence to him; the process first becomes meaningful when it has become the occasion of a great experience: a brilliant aperçu, or some romantic creation.'[30]

The temporal idiom which best expresses this private aesthetic experience of the world is the 'occasion'. Schmitt argued that political Romanticism, then and now, was a subjective version of a metaphysical occasionalism, in which the world is seen as a series of opportunities for the Romantic subject to reveal his nature. It is a product of the expansion of the aesthetic to embrace a mode of living, an attitude to the world based on the ungrounded, fragmentary experiences of private life.[31] The Romantic subject, however Bohemian or gentrified, is a quintessentially bourgeois figure, in that he conceives of his own existence as co-ordinated by an anonymous, invisible hand. Schmitt contrasted this conception of time as an endless series of fragmentary experiences to time as a finite historical process defined by an all-encompassing struggle, in which individuals are compelled to take sides.

What makes *Politische Romantik* such an unusual work is the fact that it is almost impossible to determine its political tendency in Left–Right terms. Most of those who write about Schmitt assume that from the beginning of the Weimar Republic he was a conservative, Catholic nationalist whose ideas were rooted in a German tradition of anti-liberal thought.[32] Such generic labels do not adequately capture the form and content of Schmitt's ideas. The polemical animus behind this relentless evisceration of German Romanticism cannot be so easily stereotyped: not only was Romanticism one of the central traditions of German conservatism, its anti-revolutionary medievalism had a distinctively Catholic flavour.[33] And Schmitt was entirely aware of these affinities, pointing out that 'political Romanticism in Germany is tied to the Restoration, feudalism, and anti-revolutionary estatist ideals'[34]:

For the young revolutionaries, the French Revolution was the expression of
the free spirit, Romanticism, a spiritless naturalism, a substance which had
not stepped forward into self-consciousness; thus the efforts of the political
Romantics to present the ideal of the plant or the animal to the state, to
recommend the imitation of the growth of the plant or the unarbitrary
movement of the animal organism.[35]

In Germany, Romanticism was the heritage and property of the Right,
and nearly all the well-known native critiques of Romanticism had been
written by Left Hegelians. Schmitt's sympathy for these radical polemics
against the reactionary, 'organic' jargon of the Restoration underscores
the difficulties of discerning the intellectual-political allegiances of this
work. Before one subsumes Schmitt's thought under some neat label,
it is worth considering that he was willing to draw extensively on these
critiques, including those of the young Karl Marx, in order to make his
argument.[36]

Politische Romantik represents a considerable contribution to the
intellectual history of early-nineteenth century Germany because it
sharply distinguished post-Kantian German Idealism, the line from
Fichte to Hegel, from the Romanticism which was its contemporary. By
the late nineteenth century it had become a commonplace to group
the whole of post-Kantian Idealism with an anti-Enlightenment and
anti-revolutionary Romanticism – a misconception which is widespread
even today. Schmitt disputed the claim that the conservative literati of
the Restoration were the pioneers of new historical sensibility; in his
opinion, one could not actually ascribe to the German Romantics any
real sense of history at all. On this point he cited a line that could have
been written by Karl Marx to the effect that Schlegel's ideal state lay
not so much in the actual Middle Ages as in the contemporary Middle
Ages – that is to say, in the German petty absolutism of his time.[37]

Schmitt described Müller and the Schlegel brothers as North
German parvenus migrating southwards through high society in search
of handouts from the arch-reactionary court in Vienna, contrasting
them to Fichte and Hegel, south-westerners drawn to the Berlin of the
reform era, epicentre of an intellectual revolution. One of the major
themes running through all of Georg Lukács's later intellectual histor-
ies of this period in Germany is the distinction between the development of a critical and increasingly objective Idealism culminating in
Hegel, linked to the embryonic progressive aspirations of the middle
classes; and a reactionary, aesthetic subjectivism which begins with the
Romantics, anticipating and typifying their subsequent political impotence and 'feudalization'. Although Lukács could draw upon Marxist
sources to make this point, he was probably influenced by the argument
in Politische Romantik. In any event, he was impressed enough to write a
very favourable review of it.[38]

But no clear political message can be discerned from this apparently improbable sympathy for the Young Hegelian critique, because Schmitt simultaneously drew on the works of the counter-revolutionary Ultras of the same period to attack Romanticism from the diametrically opposite perspective. All the major figures of this counter-revolutionary tradition were Latin Europeans, and in his view there was no exact German equivalent to it. Germany, the land of failed and half-revolutions, had yet to contribute anything to this Latin tradition of counter-revolutionary thought, and had in its stead only a flaccid and apolitical conservatism to its name.[39] The leitmotiv of this Romantic conservatism was the state as a work of art; Schmitt's professed hostility towards the aestheticization of politics distinguishes him sharply from those of his contemporaries on the Right, the so-called 'conservative revolutionaries', with whom he is often associated.[40]

The reason why it is so difficult to discern Schmitt's political allegiance in this text is that he was able to stand simultaneously in two national-intellectual fields: a German one, in which Romanticism was identified with the Restoration; and a contemporary French one, in which Romanticism was identified with Rousseau and the Revolution. While he was fully aware that this national difference explained why the term 'Romantic' was so difficult to define impartially, he did not attempt to adjudicate between the two opposed lines of attack:

> The uncertainty is largely based on the fact that the [German] spokesmen of the coming revolution of 1848 admired Rousseau and the French Revolution, and saw there a great model which they could call upon. In Germany they therefore had to dispute that Romanticism had any relation to the spirit of the Revolution. French writers, by contrast, increasingly emphasized this relationship, and finally equated the Revolution and Romanticism.[41]

This latter equation had become one of the commonplace tropes of the French Right, even among those who otherwise had very little in common with counter-revolutionaries like De Maistre or Bonald. In a not entirely coherent play of binary oppositions, this went hand in hand with a tendency to identify Germany as a whole with Romanticism, while France, in contrast, was portrayed as the land of 'classical' form.[42] The political imagination of one of Schmitt's contemporaries on the French Right, Charles Maurras, was fixated on the identity of the terms of three oppositions: revolution/counter-revolution, Germany/France, Romanticism/classicism. Together these formed the matrix of Maurras's vehemently Germanophobic, counter-revolutionary conception of 'classicism'. Schmitt was a sympathetic reader of Maurras's journal *Action Française*, and he appropriated the terms of these oppositions in formulating his own polemic. But the result of this appropriation generated what – at least for the modern reader – might be an entirely unexpected result: while German left- and French right-wing polemics against Romanticism are impartially balanced, his sympathy for *French* classicism over *German* Romanticism comes out in bold relief. For Schmitt, German Romanticism was the stylistic condensation of the mentality of a politically subaltern, 'feudalized' bourgeoisie,[43] and he would repeatedly recommend the lucid and dispassionate pessimism of the French *esprit classique* as an antidote to it.[44]

Schmitt was, of course, aware that Romanticism was a broad, Europe-wide intellectual phenomenon, not a purely German development. When he shifted his focus away from what was characteristically German in political Romanticism, he tended to identify it with two other targets which periodically appear in this work: the liberal bourgeois and the Bohemian as nineteenth-century European social types, foolish and inconsequential characters in the drama of a class struggle which pitted the Party of Order against the Revolution. But the multiplication of targets in this book only adds to the difficulty of identifying its ultimate political tendency. Schmitt conceded near the end that the very term Romantic might simply be too inherently polemical to define impartially.[45] The evasive political identity of the Romantic as a polemical target could be said to reflect his own perception of the not yet clearly distinguished yet sharply conflicting possibilities of the political moment in which the Weimar Republic was born.

In attacking the principal representatives of early-nineteenth-century political Romanticism, Schmitt was hardly beating a dead horse: despite the intellectual stir which this multifarious polemic generated, Müller and Novalis were 'rediscovered' and sympathetically discussed in numerous works from across the Weimar political spectrum. The great Romanist Ernst Robertus Curtius, a friend and later colleague of Schmitt, in epistolary correspondence vigorously defended Adam Müller's conception of German culture and style.[46] In *Politische Romantik*, 'classical' rigour was the implied antithesis of German Romanticism. In Schmitt's next major work, *Die Diktatur: von den Anfängen des modernen Souveränitätsgedankens bis zum proletarischen Klassenkamp* ('The Dictatorship: From the Beginnings of the Modern Conception of Sovereignty to the Proletarian Class Struggle'),[47] the 'classical' was found in discourses on the Roman institution of dictatorship, which addressed the disturbing necessities of civil-war politics, in a language foreign to the apolitical German middle classes. The Schmitt–Curtius correspondence is illuminating because it reveals how un-German Schmitt could be in Curtius's eyes:

It is enjoyable to see how dictator and Romantic act as counterparts in your intellectual world. . . . In fact there is no German dictator. A corollary of the proposition that the German is unpolitical. Of course in the evaluation . . . we differ. Since for me – and in this I am truly German – the political is no supreme value and its absolutization I find grandiose, but antipathetic.[48]

Curtius was Weimar Germany's foremost commentator on contemporary French literature and an eloquent defender of a cosmopolitan vision of German culture; the fact that he considered Schmitt's intellectual tastes temperamentally 'un-German' suggests that atavistic nationalism was not part of Schmitt's belief system. Thomas Mann, wartime literary defender of an apolitical, monarchist German *Kultur* against – among other things – Anglo-Saxon and French civilization, had, after the war, moved away from this refined bigotry, and come to accept the Republic. In his speech 'The German Republic', he invoked Novalis as a figure whose writings synthesized conservative and progressive German traditions.[49] Karl Mannheim's Habilitation text *Adam Müller and Old Conservatism* (1925) was a sympathetic account not so much of Müller's writings as of an opportunistic 'free-floating' mind, effortlessly adapting its discourses to the changing tune of polished society, in search of an ersatz social identity.[50] For Mannheim, Müller's life typified the existential condition of modern intellectuals, forming no coherent social class themselves and lacking any organic connection to other, more substantial social classes. These very different evaluations of political Romanticism came from figures on both the moderate Right and the moderate Left, who were by and large more content with the framework of the German Republic than Schmitt was; if Müller and Novalis embodied its constitutional spirit, for Schmitt this could only mean that the new state was based on stale, unprincipled and ultimately unstable compromises.

Intellectually speaking, Schmitt had very little in common with Weimar's so-called 'Conservative Revolutionaries'. The purest specimen of this milieu was one Moeller van den Bruck, a man unabashedly of the political Romantic type. Moeller legitimately saw in Adam Müller an intellectual predecessor, and indeed, in substance and style he was much closer to Müller than was Curtius, Mann or Mannheim. The vices which, for Schmitt, characterized the political Romantic were to be found in abundance in the ranks of Weimar's right-wing writers, who added to the original score only a harsh note of extremism. For this reason, most of Schmitt's later friends from these circles ignored, rejected or misunderstood his attack on the core traditions of German conservatism.

By contrast, it would be far easier to situate this work within the contemporary French intellectual scene.[51] In fact, many of the themes which can be found in *Politische Romantik* also appeared in Julien Benda's *Belphégor*, published in the same year. *Belphégor* was:

an attack on a long list of things its author felt had poisoned the age: the cult of sensation and feeling, art as a mystic union with the phenomenon of life, the present 'hatred of intelligence', the vertiginous descent of the intellect to a world of fluidity and mobility, the 'effeminacy' of thought, the disappearance of all mental distinctions.[52]

Politische Romantik was the only one of Schmitt's works to be translated into French in the 1920s, having attracted the admiring attention of those who thought that the Bergsonian *élan vital* was corrupting the rigorous classical style of the French mind.

Schmitt was not nearly as familiar with contemporary developments in English literature, yet his political temperament and intellectual form could at this stage perhaps be best described with the same words with which T.S. Eliot depicted his prewar mentor T.E. Hulme. Hulme, like Schmitt, was drawn to both Charles Maurras and Georges Sorel, and saw in the doctrine of original sin a vivid expression of the pessimism of the 'classical' world-view:

> [He] appears as the forerunner of a new attitude of mind, which should be the twentieth century mind, if the twentieth century is to have a mind of its own. Hulme is classical, reactionary and revolutionary; he is the antipodes of the eclectic, tolerant and democratic mind of the end of the last century.[53]

Here Eliot depicted an emerging reactionary modernism, prone to calling itself 'classical' and its soft-minded enemies 'Romantic'. In a preface to *Politische Romantik* published in 1924, Schmitt claimed that contemporary varieties of political Romanticism were an outgrowth of the crisis and dissolution of the European state form. The atmosphere of this interwar cultural crisis is captured in the following passage:

> An era that produces no great form and no representation based on its own presuppositions must succumb to such states of mind and regard everything that is formal and official as a fraud. . . . If it does not succeed in finding its own form, then it grasps for thousands of surrogates in the genuine forms of other times and other peoples, only to repudiate the surrogate immediately as a sham.[54]

Although the picture Schmitt had in his mind's eye of the political solution to this legitimation crisis was unfocused and fluid, he felt that by returning to older, pre-nineteenth-century traditions of political thought, he could get a more defined image of the problems. *Politische Romantik* is undoubtedly a clarion call for an intellectual rearmament, but because the political alignments of the conjuncture in which it was written were so unfamiliar and fluid, it is not clear who was to be rearmed, and against what. Therein lies the significance of the 'classical' stance adopted by Schmitt in this work: it is a label signifying an intuitive negation of an as yet undefined enemy.

2

Dictatorship Sovereign and Commissarial

Although Schmitt was not sentimentally attached to the recently deposed old regime, and – like most in the mainstream of German Catholicism – adopted a pragmatic attitude towards the new Republic, military defeat had affected his career prospects rather adversely. The University of Strasbourg, where he had expected to find employment after being released from military service in July 1919, was now, with the reannexation of Alsace-Lorraine, in the hands of the French. Temperamentally Francophile and from a family with French-speaking relatives from the contested provinces, he might not even have considered this, in itself, any great injustice. But one thing was no doubt more apparent to him now: that the fate of an individual, even one who considered himself cosmopolitan and European, might ultimately depend upon the power position of the nation-state to which he belonged.

In August 1919 Schmitt was offered a position in Berlin in the new Reich Finance Ministry headed by Mathias Erzberger, leader of the Centre Party and symbol of Catholic collaboration with and prominence within the new Republic.[1] This he turned down – probably because he was unwilling to forgo the possibility of a future as a scholar but also, perhaps, owing to a lack of enthusiasm for the Centre and its leader. Hostility to Erzberger was widespread in the right wing of the Centre Party after 1917, and Schmitt might have shared the distaste for this consummate party politician. But there can be no doubt that Schmitt was considerably further away from the feverishly reactionary views of those who would murder Erzberger two years later.

His expected career path blocked, Schmitt was fortunate to receive a temporary lectureship at the Munich Handelshochschule (College of Business Administration) through the offices of Moritz Julius Bonn. In addition to the stress of these attempts to secure stable employment, his wartime marriage to a colourful Bohemian con artist of purported Serbian descent was disintegrating; she had absconded with many of his books, he had lost contact with her, and was now struggling unsuccessfully to keep up appearances. As a Catholic he was compelled to seek an annulment, and his later failure to receive it would have fateful consequences for his relations with the Church.

Traces of these personal and political tribulations can be detected in the sprawling and discontinuous structure of his next major work, *Die Diktatur*, a history of the theory and practice of emergency powers from early modern Europe to the present. The shocking course of class warfare in Munich had also left its mark on the text, giving it flashes of intensity and focus which might have been absent from a work written under less extraordinary circumstances. But Munich was only one theatre in a nationwide conflict between the revolutionary Left and nearly everyone else on the political spectrum, from the moderate Left to the extreme Right. If we are to gain some insight into Schmitt's perception of the historical stakes involved in this showdown, the larger national context, the shifting balance of power between parties and classes, has to be understood.

The brief phase of exclusive Social Democratic leadership of the Republic had come to an end in March 1919, putting power in the hands of the pro-republican Weimar coalition consisting of the Social Democrats, the Catholic Centre, and the Democrats. This shift to the right was merely the first harbinger of a Red scare which was threatening to overwhelm the new Republic. Although emergency legislation allowed a succession of coalition governments to ban radical presses, suppress strikes and demonstrations, and take scores into 'protective custody', the army was clamouring for the establishment of a nationwide system of justice by courts martial. The objective of certain circles in the officer corps was to have the parties of the radical Left – or least their presses – banned, and ultimately to break up the Weimar coalition by drawing the Catholic Centre into an alliance with the ultra-conservative German National People's Party (DNVP).[2]

The order from the government to dissolve Captain Herman Eckhardt's Navy Brigade, in accordance with Allied demands, set in motion an attempted *coup d'état* against the new Republic. The arch-conservative bureaucrat Wolfgang Kapp and his ally, General Walter von Lüttwitz, forced the Ebert government to flee Berlin, expecting wide support for a restoration of the monarchy. Although many in the government, including some Social Democrats, had resigned themselves to a negotiated solution, the coup rapidly unravelled in the face of a general strike and the counter-mobilization of 50,000 armed workers in the Ruhr. The failure of this so-called Kapp putsch turned out to be a decisive setback for the military, and after April 1920 its subordination to civilian government was total.

Struggling to regain its wartime hegemony, the army sought to exploit the emergency provisions of the new Constitution.[3] During the war, Article 68 of the old Imperial Constitution had provided a loose legal framework for a rather far-ranging martial law. Article 68 gave the Kaiser the right not only to declare war, but also to confer open-ended state-of-siege powers on the military, in his capacity as commander-in-chief. These provisions were modelled on the Prussian state-of-siege law (1851), enacted after and in response to the revolutionary crisis of 1848–49. According to the 1851 Prussian law, in the event of a state of siege, the highest-ranking local officer gained direct control of the local civilian administration, and with it the right to issue decrees, suspend basic rights and, for certain crimes, create special courts.[4] But while the wording and the traditional interpretation of the state-of-siege law specified the rights which could be suspended, the increasingly relentless wartime mobilization resulted in an administrative practice which regularly overstepped these boundaries. The courts – which anyhow had very limited powers of review within the legal tradition of the Kaiserreich – were inclined to interpret the state-of-siege law in the broadest conceivable way, sanctioning the transfer of what were in effect legislative powers to the martial law administration.

Schmitt had been fascinated by the historical implications of these developments. In 1916 he had published an article entitled 'Diktatur und Belagerungszustand' ('Dictatorship and State of Siege')[5] in which he posed the question of whether the contemporary German wartime practice of military administration represented a break with the division-of-powers scheme of the European *Rechtsstaat*. Local military commanders were increasingly becoming *de facto* legislators on anything that involved 'national security', but if the military was now no longer simply executing laws, or even acting within the limits specified by them, in what sense was it still the 'executive'? Schmitt suggested that these new forms of rule by decree represented a return to the historically original form which state power assumed prior to the nineteenth-century evolution of the division-of-powers framework. In his opinion this historical priority revealed that executive power is the essence of statehood, while justice and legislation are derivative, limiting forms.

But he insisted that the return to this historically original form of state power did not entail, strictly speaking, dictatorship – a term which, in this article, was almost exclusively associated with the Jacobin Reign of Terror from 1793 to 1794. Schmitt maintained that the distinguishing characteristic of this dictatorship was that it was authorized by a legislative assembly, executing its own laws. The seemingly improbable implication of this claim was that since the German martial law administration was not being exercised by a Jacobin-style legislature, it was not a 'dictatorship'. In 1916 this term had uniformly negative connotations, and Schmitt, a functionary of the local martial law administration, understandably did not wish to call his superiors dictators. These inhibitions would suddenly dissolve in the civil-war context in which he completed *Die Diktatur*.

By the end of the war there was widespread hostility to martial law, and the first measure of the revolutionary workers' and soldiers' councils had been to lift it. Scholars like Max Weber and Hugo Preuss, who took a leading role in shaping the new Constitution, believed that even if government was now to be based on a parliamentary majority, the office of President had to be strong enough to counterbalance a potentially divided and incapacitated – or simply too left-leaning – Reichstag. As Preuss put it, one had to avoid the dangers of a 'parliamentary absolutism'.

Article 48 of the new Constitution not only gave the President the power to break such deadlocks, but his signature also permitted the Cabinet to exercise draconian emergency powers against almost any threat to public safety. The main difference between the powers granted under this article and the old state-of-siege articles was that the military was now to be subordinated to civilian government.[6] If we are to understand the controversies surrounding Article 48 of the Weimar Constitution, it should be cited in its entirety. One does not have to be a trained jurist to understand that this provision was a dangerously open-ended authorization, an invitation to abuse:

Paragraph 1: If a federal state does not fulfil the duties imposed on it by the Constitution of the Reich or by the law of the Reich, the President can ensure with the help of the armed forces that these duties are carried out.

Paragraph 2: If the public safety and order of the German Reich is seriously disturbed or endangered, the President may take the measures necessary for the restoration of public safety and order, and may intervene if necessary with the help of armed force. To this end he may temporarily revoke in whole or in part the fundamental rights contained in Article 114 [inviolability of personal liberty], 115 [inviolability of home], 117 [privacy of mail, telegraph, and telephone], 118 [freedom of opinion and press], 123 [freedom of assembly], 124 [freedom of association] and 153 [inviolability of private property].

Paragraph 3: The President must inform the Reichstag immediately of all measures taken on the basis of paragraphs 1 and 2. On demand of the Reichstag, the measures are revoked. In a case of immediate danger, a state government may take interim measures in its territory of the kind set out in paragraph 2. These measures must be revoked on demand of the President or the Reichstag.

Paragraph 4: A Reichstag law will determine the details [of permissible measures taken in accordance with this article].[7]

When Schmitt began the research that eventually went into *Die Diktatur*, an intellectual history of controversies surrounding the legitimacy of emergency powers, he could not have anticipated the all-consuming importance which these paragraphs would very rapidly assume in postwar constitutional life. Article 48 is mentioned only in a few pages near the end of the book, in a very brief discussion of the contemporary situation. By the time he was nearing completion he might have wanted to expand on this, but under pressure to finish he concluded rather abruptly with only a few allusions to the contemporary civil war.

While *Politische Romantik* was difficult to situate in Left/Right terms, the politics of *Die Diktatur* is unmistakably on the Right. In this and other works from the early 1920s, the enemy Schmitt had in his mind's eye was 'the proletariat'. But this hard-right crystallization of his political outlook in no way entailed anti-republicanism; in fact, one of the central claims of this work is that a commissarial dictator was essential for maintaining republican institutions.

The contrast between a conservative, 'commissarial dictatorship', which defends the traditional constitutional order, and a revolutionary, 'sovereign dictatorship' – a provisional, legislative assembly acting in the name of the people which dissolves an old constitution and establishes a new one – is the central organizing opposition of *Die Diktatur*. The term 'dictator' originally referred to an extraordinary magistrate in the Roman Republic commissioned for the duration of a political emergency, usually war or sedition, to restore order by suspending normal legal procedure. This is what Schmitt meant by 'commissarial dictatorship'. It was an office that was instituted around 500 BC and lasted until the end of the third century. Although Schmitt referred at the beginning of *Die Diktatur* to Machiavelli's defence of this institution, he did not quote the passage in the *Discourses* where Machiavelli explicitly argued that dictatorship, far from being the gravedigger of republican liberty, was essential to its defence:

> The dictator was made to be temporary and not permanent and only in order to remedy the reason for his creation; and his authority included the power to decide for himself remedies to that pressing danger, to act without consultation and to punish without appeal; but he could not do anything that would reduce the authority of the Senate or the People, to unmake the old orders of the city and make new ones.[8]

Following Machiavelli, Schmitt defined commissarial dictatorship as the discretionary enforcement of exceptional measures whose aim is to restore public safety. In this older, more limited sense, it was unleashed as a terrible instrument of last resort, when public safety could not be restored through the normal channels of legal authority. It was therefore in the nature of a dictatorship, properly understood, to render itself superfluous. This traditional commissarial conception of dictatorial powers presupposed a clear distinction between normal and emergency conditions of the validity and application of the law. Drawing this distinction, according to Schmitt, actually preserved the integrity of the normal legal order, as it kept the law of the land on a different and higher footing from improvised and temporary measures.

Schmitt presented a history of the theory and practice of dictatorship from the early modern period to the nineteenth century, with scattered references to the contemporary class struggle. The point of departure for his study was the propaganda war over the legitimacy of *jura extraordinaria* set in motion by the growth in the power of early modern royal courts at the expense of the traditional legal rights of the political community. While such developments were Western European in scope, for Schmitt, sixteenth-century controversies surrounding the King of France's prerogative to suspend the customary law of the land provided a particularly illustrative historical case study.

Three distinct positions can be discerned from Schmitt's overview of the contending interpretations of the nature of royal justice during the Renaissance. The first can be described as quintessentially *ex parte principis*, a 'Machiavellian' legitimation of the arcana of force and fraud, distilled into the cold maxims of *raison d'état*, justifying the circumvention of the traditional rights and privileges of the estates. The early modern state machine was based and built up on the widening scope of emergency powers exercised by the Prince, acting in the name of *raison d'état* (in German: *Staatsräson*): 'The state, shaken by the struggle of the estates, is, according to its constitution, in an ongoing state of emergency, and its law is down to its last cell, emergency law.'[9]

But a purely technical analysis of the laws of political survival and expansion left little room for a distinction between the ordinary and the exceptional prerogatives of sovereignty. Diametrically opposed to this 'Machiavellian' position were the Monarchomachists – the 'king-killers', predominantly Huguenot defenders of the traditional estates against the encroachments of an amoral statecraft. The Monarchomachist case was defended in an essay entitled *Vindiciae contra tyrannos*, by an author writing under the pseudonym Junius Brutus. It was written in the aftermath of the St Bartholomew's Day massacre of Huguenots by conspirators at court, enamoured of Machiavelli's prescriptions. The essay is a defence of the right of resistance by lower magistrates acting against an impious monarch, thus a tyrant, entailing even a defence of assassination when necessary. A prince ruled only by virtue of a pact with the people, who had only conditionally consented to submit. A prince who ruled by decree, introducing abusive innovations, shunting aside his natural partners, infrequently and manipulatively convoking the estates of the realm, was a tyrant who forfeited his right to rule. His subordinate magistrates were no longer obliged to obey him; in fact they were obliged to vindicate the people by deposing him.[10]

Junius Brutus did not care to distinguish between tyranny and other forms of rule untrammelled by laws. In Schmitt's representation of the political spectrum, between Machiavellian court conspiracy and an archaic and inflexible legalism, lay the moderate position of the *politicien* Jean Bodin. His doctrine of sovereignty, while it was a vigorous defence of royal prerogative, assumed during times of peace the validity of an ancient estates constitution. Schmitt found Bodin's argument in *The Six Books of the Republic* appealing not because of the unprecedented royal power superimposed upon the traditional legal–political structure, but because of his insistence that the Prince's right to transgress these limits and rule by decree was limited to scenarios of political necessity; and even during such exceptional situations, a natural law pertaining to persons and property, and a divine law of revealed truths, continued to hold: 'As for the natural and divine laws, all the princes of the earth are subjected to them, and it is not in their power to transgress them unless they want to make themselves guilty of divine *lèse majesté*.'[11]

Bodin's importance lay in his attempt to pose the question of who has the right to decide that an 'exceptional' situation has arisen, and suspend the laws. But Schmitt claimed that it was only in the framework of an established constitutional order that the proper role of this kind of commissarial dictator could be understood. For Bodin the dictator was not the sovereign, but a commissarial agent of the sovereign's will bound by strict instruction to expedite measures beyond what is specified by the law; upon completion of this specific task, the commission was terminated. Bodin's work was significant for Schmitt in that it identified the proper role of a commissarial dictator within the limits of the early modern *Rechtstaat*, the *Ständestaat*:

> His state, despite his concept of sovereignty, is a *Rechtsstaat*, whose laws are not only the expression of power, issued in any old way and revoked like mere commands. . . . Although he fought the Monarchomachists, he simultaneously saw in Machiavelli's instrumentalization of the law something ruinous, a wicked atheism, which he rejected as unworthy.[12]

Because of this professed hostility to an instrumentalized law, Hobbes – who in later works would be esteemed more highly – appeared here as a secondary figure. For Hobbes, the commonwealth perpetually hovers on the brink of dissolution, the war of all against all, and the peace which is established with the covenant of submission is only a respite. Accordingly, there can be no legal guarantees in this commonwealth. The sovereign, who decides when the legal exception exists, and the dictator, who is commissioned to bring it to an end – these were roles distinguished by Bodin, but fused by Hobbes. The proto-

'Absolutist estates monarchy of Bodin's day was more legalistic than the monstrous Leviathan, spawn of the more remorseless civil war which Hobbes had experienced:

> [Bodin's] distinction between two kinds of state office presupposed a clear opposition of law and ordinance, and had to become irrelevant with the further development of absolutism, because in absolutist state theory, any expression of power essentially and indiscriminately is based on the will of the Prince. The important insight of Bodin was thereby lost, even though his concept of sovereignty enjoyed a well-known success.[13]

The relationship between the terms 'dictator' and 'sovereign' is ambivalent throughout the text, but by and large dictatorship was associated with temporary measures *hors-la-loi*, while sovereignty was associated with authority untrammelled by law. This explicit criticism of untrammelled sovereignty generated tacit oppositions running through the work which reveal its politically moderate pretensions: Hobbes and Rousseau on the one side; Bodin and Montesquieu on the other:

> One can first speak of Absolutism when this kind of natural law and religious limitation fall away, and the state as such becomes the absolute instance, the final judge of good and evil. Theoretically this appears for the first time in Hobbes's political theory. The classical culmination can be found in Rousseau's Social Contract, according to which the state, while established by the voluntary agreement of the citizens, having emerged, relentlessly encompasses all domains of human life.[14]

In fact, for Schmitt, Montesquieu formed a positive point of contrast to both earlier Absolutist and later Enlightenment political theories. Montesquieu was presented as the inheritor of Bodin's moderate stance between a state-destroying legalism and an absolutism which, through the untrammelled will of the sovereign, also destroys the state; and Schmitt cited him to convey a sense of moderation and limits on the issue of emergency powers: 'Under the pretext of restoring order, a limitless power is exercised, and what was previously called freedom is now called rebellion and disorder.'[15] Even more striking than Schmitt's cool attitude towards Hobbes was his sympathy for a figure who represents the antithesis of political 'decisionism'. Again, this suggests that there was something in the Hobbesian doctrine of sovereignty which troubled him: its purely instrumental concept of the law could be seen as the direct ancestor of modern legal positivism.

Until the eighteenth century, the dictator had been an emergency commissar appointed by and acting for the defence of the state. But Schmitt argued that the traditional meaning of the office was lost when the goal of emergency powers was no longer the rescue but the replacement of the traditional political order. To the old figure of the commissarial dictator was now added a new form of European dictator-

ship, which he called 'sovereign dictatorship', identifying it with the
pouvoir constituant – the provisional legislator acting directly in the
name of the sovereign people to enact a new constitution. In arguing
that the sovereign people, and the provisional legislative power acting
in its name, was free to frame a new constitution at will, Schmitt took a
surprisingly clear position: affirming the legitimacy of the Weimar
Republic, explicitly rejecting monarchist arguments that the new
regime was illegal because it had not come into being through a
procedure legally sanctioned by the old Constitution:

> One is supposed to believe that such an enterprise withdraws itself from any
> legal consideration, since the state can only be legally conceptualized as its
> constitution and the total negation of the existing constitution has to
> renounce any legal justification, because the constitution to be implemented,
> according to its own premises, does not yet exist. But this is not the case if a
> power is assumed, without itself being constitutionally established, which
> stands in relation to any existing constitution as the founding power, even if
> it is never encompassed by any constitution [which it founds]. As a conse-
> quence, it [the founding power] cannot be negated even as it negates a
> constitution. This is the meaning of the *pouvoir constituant*.[16]

Schmitt coined the term 'sovereign dictatorship' to designate the
provisional legislative authority, exercised in the name of the sovereign
people, which dissolves an old constitution and enacts a new one. This
sort of revolutionary political authority is usually called a 'constitutional
convention', 'constituent assembly', or '*pouvoir constituant*' – so why did
Schmitt call it a 'sovereign dictatorship'? The answer lies in a political
context in which fear of a social, not just political, revolution was
widespread. At the height of the brief postwar revolutionary wave,
Schmitt became convinced that it was necessary to explore the radical
consequences of an unattenuated popular sovereignty; a modern political order was one which would have continually to confront the
potentially subversive implications of this principle. The tendency of a
permanently assembled people to call into question the rights of
property, and the legitimacy of myriad forms of inequality – this was
the line which led from popular sovereignty to something far more
deadly: the so-called 'dictatorship of the proletariat'. Schmitt's term
'sovereign dictatorship' is a hybrid of the terms 'popular sovereignty'
and the 'dictatorship of the proletariat', and represents an attempt to
capture the moment of potential transition from the first term into the
second.

Karl Marx famously depicted this transitional scenario in *The Eighteenth Brumaire*:

> The parliamentary regime lives by discussion; how shall it forbid discussion?
> Every interest, every social institution, is here transformed into general ideas,

debated as ideas; how shall any interest, any institution, sustain itself above thought and impose itself as an article of faith? The struggle of the orators on the platform evokes the struggle of the scribblers of the press; the debating club in the parliament is necessarily supplemented by debating clubs in the salons and pothouses; the representatives who constantly appeal to public opinion, give public opinion the right to speak its real mind in petitions. The parliamentary regime leaves everything to the decision of majorities; how shall the great majorities outside of parliament not want to decide? When you play the fiddle at the top of the state what else is to be expected than that those down below dance?[17]

Despite its revolutionary origins, Schmitt maintained that popular sovereignty could be subject to constitutional limitation, provided that this provisional legislative power, claiming to act in the name of the people and empowered to change the Constitution, existed only during a defined interregnum and then dissolved itself. The problem with a constitution deriving its legitimacy from popular sovereignty was that even after it had been established, the 'people' continued to exist as a legitimating point of reference outside the established forms in which it was represented. This Rousseauian 'remainder' prevented any inviolable closure of the Constitution's political form, and blurred the distinction between the ordinary and extraordinary conditions of political life. Schmitt believed that this was because the absolute sovereignty of the people could not easily be reconciled with a system of tacit limits placed on the powers of government which defined the liberal constitutional norms of the European *Rechtsstaat*. At the heart of his discourse on popular sovereignty was an image, concocted out of fascination and fear, of the rawest democracy: 'Out of its endless, elusive, groundless power emerges ever new forms, which it can at any time shatter, never limiting itself.'[18]

Schmitt ended *Die Diktatur* by suggesting that nineteenth-century liberalism's hostile attitude to the emergency powers of the executive was based on the assumption that its struggles against the court, army and bureaucracy would never take on a life-and-death character. Nineteenth-century liberals believed that if emergency powers occasionally had to be used against the rabble, then only specific individual liberties would need to be suspended for the duration of the civil unrest, certainly not the entire Constitution:

In Roman law as well as in the natural-law literature, in particular with that unconditional defender of the *Rechtsstaat*, Locke, the most important manifestation of an unlimited authorization is always the right over life and death. But when dictatorship was spoken of in the nineteenth century, it was understood in terms of the so-called 'fictive state of siege'; and when legal treatment of dictatorship was undertaken, it was a matter of press freedom and the like, not of the countless numbers who, on both sides of a civil war, really, not just fictionally, lose their lives.[19]

For Schmitt, one of the central arguments for the viability of liberalism
was undermined by the advent of modern class struggle. Even before
the era of liberalism, Condorcet had articulated its no longer viable
historical premisse: 'We no longer live in an age where there are
powerful groups and classes [estates] within the state. . . . The *associations puissantes* have disappeared.'[20] The point of this citation was that
as long as isolated individuals, and the occasional crowd, confronted
the state, there was no need for hard, emergency government. Schmitt
suggested that after 1848 the proletariat was no longer an episodic
threat to public order but its quasi-permanent enemy, and any limits
placed on the duration and scope of emergency powers had become
dangerous luxuries. Because of the conversion of the European working class to radical and socialist ideas, very dangerous '*associations
puissantes*' had arisen in the midst of European states:

> In the years between 1832 and 1848, which are the most important dates for
> the evolution of the state of siege as a legal institution, the question arose as
> to whether the political organization of the proletariat created an entirely
> new condition, and thus new constitutional concepts.[21]

For Schmitt, the year 1848 was a turning point in modern European
history. The most famous account of this period is, of course, Marx's
masterpiece *Class Struggles in France: 1848–1851*, and Schmitt knew this
work well. The class struggles of 1848 in France, culminating in the
savage repression of the June uprising of the Parisian working class by
National Guard forces under the Republican General Cavaignac, were
events which decisively shaped the whole language of French and
European civil wars. Those who banded together in the Party of Order,
from the moderate Left to the monarchist Right, to crush the insurgent
proletariat saw Cavaignac's dictatorship as the salvation of society; while
beleaguered and defamed revolutionaries defiantly called for a dictatorship of the proletariat. At the end of the month, having massacred
many thousands of proletarians, Cavaignac handed back the powers
which had been delegated to him by the National Assembly. Cavaignac's counter-revolutionary reign of terror exemplified Schmitt's conception of a 'commissarial dictator': an extraordinary magistrate who is
temporarily authorized to suspend normal legal procedure while crushing enemies of the state. At the time, this would have been a rather
vivid allusion for an educated Central European.

But for Schmitt, the opposition of commissarial and sovereign,
restraint and revolution, Right and Left, would not involve simply a
conservative strategy of pitting the first term against the second. He
recognized that the European Right would now be forced to operate
on a political terrain historically occupied by the Left; it even occurred

to him that the old Europe might be able to get the upper hand on its enemies, if it understood their revolutionary doctrines.

The Preface of *Die Diktatur* suggests that the author was more interested in the then ongoing debate about the nature of the dictatorship of the proletariat between the Social Democratic theorist Karl Kautsky on the one side and Lenin and Trotsky on the other than in the Weimar Constitution. The complete title of the book, translated into English, was *The Dictatorship: From the Beginnings of the Modern Conception of Sovereignty to the Proletarian Class Struggle* – that is to say, the history of an idea from Bodin to Lenin. Schmitt's interest in the October Revolution and the seriousness with which he took its leadership come out clearly in the Preface. He claimed that while Kautsky adhered to the modern bourgeois view which saw dictatorship as the rule of a small minority or an individual, the Bolshevik conception, by contrast, had captured its authentic, classical meaning by emphasizing the provisional nature of a dictatorship:

> According to the nature of the case, it can be useful to work with one or another method, in any case the essential thing is the transition to the communist end goal, for which the implementation of the dictatorship of the proletariat is only a technical instrument. . . . This proletarian state does not seek to be definitive; rather, it is a transition. The essential factor thereby once again receives its meaning, which had receded in the bourgeois literature. . . . The communist argumentation makes it clear that it [dictatorship], because it is, in theory, a transition, should be introduced only by way of exception, and only under the compulsion of circumstances. That also belongs to its concept, and it then depends on what makes an exception.[22]

But the Bolsheviks had not just restored an older doctrine; they had dialectically transformed it into its opposite. In Lenin's theory of history, every state was a dictatorship of a social class – that is, in the last instance, emergency rule by armed bodies of men, untrammelled by laws. As Walter Benjamin would put it later in *Theses on History*, in a formulation influenced by both Lenin and Schmitt, all of class history is in a state of emergency, but only the dictatorship of the proletariat brings about the real state of emergency; because this provisional organization of the victorious toiler is the last dictatorship of human history, a temporary regime union brings an end to history as a permanent state of emergency. Marxism, for Schmitt, was a philosophy of history in which legality was a mere instrument to accomplish the historically necessary – and therefore legitimate – goal of social revolution. It had passed a historical death sentence on the bourgeoisie. In this work and in others written during the early Weimar period, Schmitt, haunted by the spectre of social revolution, explored several possible responses to this verdict.

The Weimar Constitution was drafted in a situation in which the final form the state would assume had still not been determined, owing to the lack of any unequivocal popular mandate with clear and distinct legitimating principles. The fluid nature of the political situation was reflected in the ambivalence of Schmitt's text on the issue of whether the emergency measures adopted by the Reich government were those of a commissarial or sovereign dictatorship.[23] But even later he would sometimes define presidential powers in a way which suggested the tenuous nature of the distinction. He was not unaware of the significance of this dissolving boundary: he noted that near the end of the late Republican period in Rome, commissarial dictatorship became the lever by which the old constitution was overturned.[24]

But Schmitt acknowledged that the 'unprecedented authorization' which the President had even as a commissarial dictator posed some serious problems of accountability and limitation. This authorization was prevented from overstepping the boundaries of this commission, and of the Constitution itself, by being limited to issuing temporary measures. Such measures had to be sharply distinguished from laws which always require a qualified legislative majority: 'These are measures which, if this unlimited authorization is not supposed to mean the dissolution of the entire legal order, are only measures of a concrete nature and, as such, can become neither acts of legislation nor the administration of justice.'[25] Schmitt argued that if a sharp distinction was not made between laws and measures, the Constitution would become a provisional document entirely at the disposal of the President and any legislative majority, as bearers of the *pouvoir constituant*. If the Reichstag was a defined power *in* the Constitution, not a power *over* it, it could not authorize the President to act in a legislative capacity, or could do so only by imposing strict limits of duration. But until these powers were subject to statutory limitation as anticipated in the last paragraph of Article 48, he suggested that presidential emergency powers 'would work like the residue of the sovereign dictatorship of the National Assembly'.[26]

In a statement on the subject at a legal conference in Jena in 1924, Schmitt more clearly related the exercise of emergency powers to an interpretation of Article 48, and thus to the underlying principles of the Weimar Constitution:

> A sovereign dictatorship is irreconcilable with the constitution of a *Rechtsstaat*. A republican constitution . . . would be entirely provisional and precarious in the hands of a sovereign dictator, who would, by virtue of his extraordinary authority, always have the power to improvise new organizations alongside those in accordance with the Constitution. Despite all those phrases like 'unfettered authority' and '*plein pouvoir*' which have been used to describe the discretion of the President under Article 48, Paragraph 2, it would be impossible for him to exercise a sovereign dictatorship on the basis of this

constitutional provision, even if this were done only in conjunction with the counter-signature of the government. Either sovereign dictatorship or constitution; the one excludes the other.[27]

Because the Weimar Constitution was now more firmly in place, Schmitt could more categorically claim that although the ultimate source of its legitimacy was the will of the people, this will was exercised within the safe limits of a *Rechtsstaat*. Sovereign dictatorship and *Rechtsstaat* were mutually exclusive, so the emergency measures issued on the basis of Article 48 were perforce of a commissarial nature, and thus to be sharply distinguished from laws. The Revolution was now over, he thought, and the framework of a concrete constitutional order which could permit such distinctions to be made seemed to be in place.

The problem with which Schmitt was grappling – and thought he had resolved in 1924 – was how the most radical spectres of popular sovereignty could be definitively exorcized. Between 1921 and 1924 he explored a number of alternatives. The first was the ultra-authoritarian view that the Revolution haunting European society needed to be violently exorcized by a counter-revolutionary dictatorship in an eschatologically conceived civil war. The second was the very different idea that the Catholic Church could help to stabilize the postwar situation because, as the last significant embodiment of a common West European political civilization, it was uniquely able to play the role of mediator in national and class conflicts; the Roman Church was a bulwark of the European state form, protecting it against the full, politically radical consequences of modernity. The third was, again, another entirely different position: the legitimation crisis of the post-liberal state would be solved not by trying to hold back the rise of the masses but, rather, by the plebiscitary integration of the masses into a 'homogeneous' national democracy.

3

The State of Emergency

Schmitt's precarious professional situation was stabilized when he was given a professorship at the law faculty of the University of Greifswald in 1921. But despite this improvement on the professional front, Greifswald was a particularly alienating environment for Schmitt: the university at the bottom of the hierarchy of German universities, the town a dreary and inclement cultural backwater. From his correspondence with Ernst Robertus Curtius, it is easy to discern that Schmitt was in a despairing mood during his brief stay, not knowing how brief it would be: 'I keenly sympathize with your Greifswald situation. . . . That you will be buried there seems highly unlikely. For both of us it is a matter of a short-term evil. . . .'[1]

While he actually had to stay there only for the winter semester of 1921, this period constituted a significant episode in Schmitt's intellectual development. It was here, in this rather bleak environment, that he looked to Catholicism for a language which could express both his pessimism about the direction in which the world around him was moving, and his vision of institutions which could save Europe from the seemingly unending convulsions of permanent war and revolution. His later reputation as a Catholic thinker is based almost entirely on the feverish intellectual production of these months.

Although Schmitt's perspective on political developments was coloured by the view from Greifswald, national defeat, civil war and economic collapse had generated an apocalyptic atmosphere in broad swathes of German society. Oswald Spengler's book *The Decline of the West* had capitalized on this mood, and became a major success. The idea that modern European society was experiencing the end of an era in world history comes across in several of Schmitt's writings. Schmitt would often use various 'epochal' frames of reference to interpret the significance of a contemporary political problem: depending upon the problem, the age could be defined as beginning in 1848, in the early modern centuries of civil and religious warfare, or even at the onset of the Christian era in history. The idea that the Christian era in history was coming to an end is a theme upon which Schmitt could draw to give his political diagnoses an eschatological focus and intensity.

Although this is not a mere literary affectation, the occasional resort to this theme is highly characteristic of his deep intellectual style.

This style took shape in a very receptive intellectual context. Out of the upheavals of war and revolution had emerged an often startling new theological language which challenged the secular schemes of historical interpretation inherited from the nineteenth century. The first major work in this genre was Karl Barth's *Der Römerbrief*, published in 1918. This was an attack on an entire tradition of German critical theology which had begun in the early nineteenth century with David Strauss's *Life of Jesus*, a work which had effectively demolished the credibility of Scriptural testimony. Following Hegel's lead, liberal Protestant theology held that faith and reason could be reconciled in a progressive historical process. Breaking with this legacy, the new dialectical theology took its cue from Kierkegaard in its emphasis on the radical cleavage between authentic faith and an all-too-human intellect, unable to grasp the parodoxes of revelation.

But the theological avant-gardism of the Weimar period was not only a Protestant phenomenon: Martin Buber was one of several heterodox Jewish scholars who inaugurated a radical reinterpretation of religious tradition by attempting to restore the integrity of marginalized mystical currents. Even outside the theological community, the appearance of a work like Ernst Bloch's *The Spirit of Utopia* suggests that Scripture had suddenly acquired an entirely unforeseen resonance and intensity across the political spectrum. If we are to understand Schmitt's relationship to theology, it is important for us to realize that there was no comparable ferment in German Catholicism, which during this whole period remained either neoscholastic or Romantic.

Schmitt's adoption of a highly idiosyncratic Catholic political stance cannot be explained in terms of some renewed faith in the tenets of the Church. Not only was he too much of a modern intellectual to be a believer in the conventional sense; he had an only partly concealed hostility to Catholic theologians and mainstream theology.[2] His relationship to the Catholic Church and to its theological traditions was deeply politically mediated, as is evident even in the titles of the two works which he claimed to have completed during his brief stay in Greifswald: *Politische Theologie* ('Political Theology') and *Römischer Katholizismus und politische Form* ('Roman Catholicism and Political Form').[3] In Schmitt's view, in the early 1920s modern mass politics seemed to be veering towards permanent revolution; in these texts he looked to certain strands of Catholicism for a perspective on the present which could inform a radical counter-offensive, an alternative to a fatalistic acceptance of the decline of European political civilization.[4]

His first response was to explore the possibility of total opposition to the rise of the masses by exhuming the counter-revolutionary tradition

in nineteenth-century Catholic political thought. But this counter-
revolutionary interpretation of history was presented only as the conclusion of a work which addressed the more modest problem of the
constitutional limits to the scope of emergency powers which the Reich
government could exercise during a 'state of emergency'. The crosscutting theme of *Politische Theologie* is the 'state of emergency', considered from a number of perspectives. The term 'state of emergency'
was in wide circulation in the early 1920s. A knowledge of the context
of contemporary controversies in politics is necessary if we are to
understand the link Schmitt was attempting to make between its
significance as a constitutional problem and its significance in his
theologically conceived, counter-revolutionary philosophy of history.

What was 'the state of emergency' or 'the state of exception' in legal
terms? By describing it as a 'state' one might – mistakenly – be inclined
to think that in the early 1920s it was an objectively identifiable
condition, a period of time during which extraordinary measures could
be adopted by the government in a manner spelled out in Article 48.
In actual fact, the practice of government revealed that the reality was
the inverse: anything the government decided to do on the basis of
Article 48 fell in its view into this 'state of emergency', and just about
anything the government normally did could now be pursued in an
'emergency' fashion, and thus without any of the normal restraints.[5]

This practice unleashed theoretical controversy in legal circles over
which limits such emergency measures could not overstep without
falling into contradiction with other provisions of the Constitution. It
was a widely held view that the Constitution gave considerable latitude
to the President, but that only those protections which were specifically
referred to in Article 48 could be suspended.

Schmitt held the extreme view in this controversy. In 1924, after the
storm had passed, he maintained at a conference of legal scholars in
Jena that everything in the Constitution could be suspended except the
identity of the institutions which, according to Article 48, were the
agents of this suspension: the Reich President, the Reich government,
and the Reichstag, comprising together an 'institutional minimum'
which was not subject to suspension.[6] This position was alarming to
many of his colleagues, who pointed out how far it stood from the
conception of the state of siege in the *Rechtsstaat* tradition.

Indeed, Schmitt's position pointed to, and anticipated, ongoing and
far-reaching departures from this tradition. In interwar Europe, emergency measures issued by the executive were becoming a form of
accelerated legislation – not just in Germany, but throughout the
Continent. Schmitt thought that this had profound implications for the
role which formal legality itself plays in the exercise of legitimate
domination.[7] Schmitt reframed one of the original problems of politico-

legal philosophy in a modern setting: what is the 'rule of law', what makes it more legitimate than rule untrammelled by law, and how do they coexist in the real historical time of political systems?

Schmitt's vision of the changing relationship between legality and legitimacy forms a striking contrast to the views of Max Weber. Here is Weber's ideal-typical sketch of legal positivism:

> Present day legal science, at least in the forms which have achieved the highest measure of methodological and logical rationality, i.e. those which have been produced through the legal science of the Pandectist's Civil Law, proceeds from the following five postulates: viz. first, that every concrete legal decision be the 'application' of an abstract legal proposition to a concrete 'fact situation'; second, that it must be possible in every concrete case to derive the decision from abstract legal propositions by means of legal logic; third, that the law must actually or virtually constitute a 'gapless' system of legal propositions or must at least be treated as if it were such a gapless system; fourth, that whatever cannot be 'construed' rationally in legal terms is also legally irrelevant; and fifth, that every social action of human beings must also be visualized either as an 'application' or 'execution' of legal propositions or as an infringement thereof, since the 'gaplessness' of the legal system must result in a gapless legal ordering of all social action.[8]

Weber's theory of the formal rationality of Western law was based on the assumption that modern capitalism and bureaucracy required technically precise legal rules. Although Schmitt was deeply impressed by Weber's writings on legal sociology, he argued that the growing interpenetration of state and society was undermining the systematic and formally rational qualities of the legal process. He believed that it was no longer possible to insulate the legal system completely from the dynamics of conflict over substantive political questions.

Politische Theologie attempts to redefine the concept of sovereignty in terms of the role which largely undefined emergency powers play in the interpretative 'gaps' of a constitutional order.[9] It consists of four very short chapters, each exploring different aspects of the problem which the extreme – or emergency – situation poses for legal and political theory.

The first chapter begins with a striking formulation: 'Sovereign is he who decides on the emergency situation'.[10] Schmitt claimed that sovereignty is a 'limit concept' which can be correctly understood only in the light of an emergency situation, when the very existence of the political community is at stake. A 'sovereign' decision determines what constitutes a threat to public safety in situations where the meaning of public safety has become an indeterminable object of contention.[11] Emergency situations are like X-ray flashes which suddenly reveal the antinomies of legal reason. At such moments, it becomes clearer that the state is more than a set of legal rules which define jurisdictions. In the rule-warping context of an emergency, an extra-legal surplus of discretionary power accrues to a 'sovereign' agent; in legal language, terms like 'threat', 'danger' and 'enemy' are the vectors of an anticipated transgression of legality.

Schmitt thought that even short of an extreme emergency in which all legal protections and jurisdictional boundaries are suddenly suspended, the problem of the exception, of 'gaps' in the legal order, was unavoidable. A gap is a grey area in the Constitution, a point at which the Constitution avoids specifying how a particular conflict should be resolved, and leaves it open to interpretation, which in the absence of a norm invariably becomes political.[12]

Modern positivism seeks to eliminate sovereignty, as an ungrounded political decision, from the legal process. But the possibility of eliminating this transgressive moment of sovereignty depended upon dubious assumptions about the course of history; as long as states are periodically confronted with threats to what they perceive as their essential interests, the legal order has to remain open to the possibility of its own suspension. It could be said that Schmitt agreed with Lenin that even the most liberal government, in the event of a sufficiently grave threat, had to be able to become a dictatorship 'untrammelled by law'.

The concept of sovereignty sheds light on the gaps and weak links in a legal system, points at which legal interpretation depends upon a political decision. Schmitt claimed that looking at the legal system from the vantage point of the emergency situation was 'more interesting'[13] because it was only from this perspective that one could understand the nature of the relationship between the norms of a legal system and the facts of political power. One of the central themes of Schmitt's legal theory is that this relationship is mediated by the nebulous factor of 'legitimacy'. Too often, in Schmitt's opinion, disciplinary preoccupations lead to a focus either on pure power relations or on legal rules, while the relationship between the two is left unexplored.[14] This passage from Weber's *Economy and Society* is a precise illustration of this tendency: 'It should be self-evident that the sociologist is guided exclusively by the factual existence of such a power to command, in contrast to the lawyer's interest in the theoretical content of a legal norm.'[15] According to Schmitt, the result of this perspectival duality was an inability to bring the nature and role of political legitimacy in legal systems into sharp conceptual focus. In his view, the legal theorist Hans Kelsen was the most extreme representative of this tendency. According to Kelsen, since the 'will' of the legislator was an extra-legal political or psychological fact, it could not be a point of reference for legal reasoning. The theoretical object of legal science was the state conceived as a unified system of legal rules: the general rules of enacting and concretizing general rules through procedurally correct decisions – and nothing else.

Schmitt considered Kelsen's 'pure theory of law' a true camera obscura. It was not at all clear to him whether this seamless system of legal norms was supposed to be an objective order, or the subjective result of a retrospective conceptual synthesis by the jurist. Kelsen had extended the positivist premisse to the point of manifest absurdity, utterly succumbing to the illusion that the legal order was a self-enclosed, seamless system in which norms somehow interpreted and concretized themselves without having to be interpreted and concretized in contexts of contestable authority.[16] Schmitt argued that statehood could never take the form of a fully depersonalized, neutral and disenchanted system of norms, because it involved an irreducibly political relationship of authority between concrete persons. He suspected that the attempt to depoliticize legal interpretation completely stemmed from the utopian desire to replace the government of men with the administration of things. This would be a world in which the whole field of political contention, and the problem of legitimate authority to which it gives rise, would have withered away.

While Max Weber had been dissatisfied with purely technical approaches to law, he reduced the problem of legitimacy to the psychological probability of obedience to commands. Very much in the spirit of late-nineteenth-century National Liberalism, Weber thought that in the modern world legitimate authority had to be exercised in the form of general legal rules, and that whatever legitimation deficit arose could be filled by charismatic leaders. Similarly, many of Schmitt's works pose a discomfiting question: if natural law is no longer plausible, is it even possible to account for legitimate authority without falling into irrationalism – that is, the view that legitimacy is ultimately based on a political will which defies rational justification? The last two chapters of *Politische Theologie* reveal a tendency on Schmitt's part to overcome theoretical problems through a flight forward into myth.

In Chapter 3 of this work, he explained what he meant by 'political theology': the claim that all significant political concepts are secularized theological ones.[17] This claim, however striking, taken literally, seems manifestly implausible, and Schmitt did not even attempt to prove that it applied to other core concepts of political theory, like 'state' and 'constitution'. In fact, the only concept he discussed in these terms was the concept of sovereignty. He claimed that the early modern idea of sovereignty developed out of analogies to already existing theological conceptions of the relationship between an omnipotent God and his laws – that is to say, the problem of whether a supreme legislator could break his own laws. The state of emergency was a secularization of a theological conception of the miracle as a temporary suspension of the divinely created order of nature.

But again, it is hard to accept this at face value: did not the Romans – to mention only one example – have to deal with the problem of an emergency suspension of the laws, without any comparable theological analogy to conceive of or justify it? Schmitt did not spell out why exactly the theological analogy is important for understanding the concept of sovereignty, but he implied that only in an eschatological light is it possible to conceive of the most extreme state of emergency.

Schmitt believed that the contemporary legitimation crisis of the secular state made it both possible and politically imperative to uncover the theological thought forms once used to imagine, build and defend the European state. These were difficult to bring to light because the liberal project of neutralizing deep conflicts in a legalistic spirit had effectively suppressed a theologically conceived moment of transgression involved in the idea of sovereignty. But for Schmitt, there were limits to how far inherently political questions of the legitimacy of the European state could be transformed into less politically charged questions of legality, and contemporary Germany was now experiencing these limits.

Schmitt suggested that this legal neutralization had left the state powerless in the face of the menacing spectres of social revolution. In the final chapter, he presented the potential antidote to this neutralization in a nineteenth-century French and Spanish counter-revolutionary tradition. The principal figures in this tradition were De Maistre, Bonald and Cortes. All three had sought to trace the mystery of revolutionary evil back to its origins in order to annihilate it, root and branch. It should be pointed out that this current of political thought, in its radicalism, often had an uneasy relationship to traditional conservatism. De Maistre's polemical negation of all liberal values – peace, security, reason, freedom and equality – eventually resulted in a deeply ambivalent relationship to Christianity itself as the original instigator of these contaminated values.[18] According to Ernst Nolte, counter-revolutionary theorists initially found it difficult to explain the very existence of revolutionary violence, and sought to portray it as inherently self-undermining.[19] De Maistre, who did not live to see 1848, was confident not only that an absolute monarchy could be restored, but also that it was the only viable regime. In 1848 it became clear that the *ancien régime* could no longer bank on this, and the radicalism of the Spaniard Donoso Cortes expressed a mood of almost apocalyptic panic that the foundations of the social order were dissolving, never to be restored. Cortes exemplified the intensification of counter-revolutionary thought during the Europe-wide civil wars of 1848. Nolte explains the difference between the first and subsequent generation of counter-revolutionary thought by pointing out that while De Maistre had only been acquainted with the rabble, Cortes witnessed the birth of modern proletarian radicalism in the form of anarchism and socialism. The terrifying novelty of these ideas can be discerned from the opening line of *The Communist Manifesto*, where Marx mockingly refers to a spectre haunting Europe.

Although Schmitt had exhumed what, for a German public, would have been an exotic figure, he did not elaborate here on Cortes's life and ideas.[20] The Marquis de Valdegamas Donoso Cortes was born in 1809 in Extremadura into a world of grandees, who occasionally toyed with liberal ideas. Spain was the weak link among the restored monarchies of Europe, divided between liberals and Absolutists and, throughout much of the nineteenth century, always in or on the brink of civil war. Cortes was renowned for having argued in 1849, in a famous speech to the Spanish parliament, that legitimate monarchy was dead, because no king now dared to assert his right to the throne against the wishes of his people. According to Schmitt, this intransigent view that there was no middle ground, that sovereign power had to lie with either the king or the people, revealed a deep insight into the irreducibly political foundations of a constitution, and exposed the evasiveness of nineteenth-century German jurisprudence, which held that neither the king nor the people was sovereign but rather, in the spirit of compromise, the state itself.

Cortes's speech captured a large European audience; Metternich, Count Montalembert, Ranke and Friedrich Wilhelm IV all read it, and for a short time Cortes was a figure of European significance. Cortes put forward a grim vision of the darkening of the world and the alternatives facing Europe:

> Mark it well; there is no longer any moral or material resistance.... It is a question of choosing between the dictatorship from below and dictatorship from above. I choose the one from above because it comes from regions which are pure and more serene. In the last resort it is a question of choosing between the dictatorship of the dagger and that of the sabre: I choose that of the sabre because it is nobler.[21]

Such passages provided the elements of a concept of sovereignty which would be the negation of popular sovereignty: so-called 'sovereign dictatorship' as defined in *Die Diktatur*. The modest figure of the classical, 'commissarial' dictator to whom Schmitt had given the task of saving society in *Die Diktatur* was transformed in *Politische Theologie* into a punitive, dictatorial regime whose 'sovereign' acts would take on an eschatological significance after the age of legitimate monarchy. It was as if the commissarial dictatorship of a General Cavaignac was no longer enough to overcome the historical emergency as Schmitt now conceived it. According to Cortes, the catastrophic crisis which Europe was experiencing would continue until some future, final battle in which the rebelling, atheist proletariat would be definitively crushed. Until then, the task of holding the fort fell to various and sundry reactionary adventurers heading regimes no longer sanctioned by tradition. This was how Cortes saw the *coup d'état* of the 18th Brumaire.

How Catholic was this 'political theology'? The claim – common to the whole counter-revolutionary tradition – that man is utterly corrupt has an ambivalent relationship to Catholic doctrine, which has always qualified this harsh judgement by emphasizing the redeemability of humanity. Even in the 1850s Cortes's pessimism had been attacked by those who thought it incompatible with Church teaching. Indeed, the historical vision of Donoso Cortes was so bleak that it was inclined to accept the nihilism which he attributed to the enemy:

> After the deist, and after the pantheist, the atheist appears and declares: God neither rules nor governs, neither one individual nor the mass is God; there is no God whatsoever. And then Proudhon appears and explains: there is no government whatsoever. Thus one negation causes another, like one abyss bringing forth another. And beyond this last negation is the abyss itself, in which there is nothing, nothing but darkness, deep darkness.[22]

No one can doubt that Cortes had sincerely wanted to be a pious Catholic, so he must have been totally unaware of the implicit atheism of such formulations. Can the same be said of Schmitt? Despite the eschatological current running through some of his writings, and his conception of himself as in some way a Catholic thinker, it is clear that even in the much less ambiguous case of Cortes, political theology was not Catholic in any conventionally understood sense. Although Carl Schmitt is often thought of as a Catholic political theorist, his brief turn in the early 1920s towards a highly idiosyncratic political theology cannot – as we have said – be explained in terms of renewed faith or respect for Catholic theologians and mainstream theology: the Catholics whose views he found most compelling were often on the fringes of respectability.

But even from a secular political perspective, the prognosis which Cortes had to offer was not comforting, and even upon completing this essay Schmitt perhaps sensed the futility of its openly anti-democratic stance in an age of mass politics. Cortes had written:

> The world hurries with great strides towards the establishment of a despotism more violent and destructive than men have ever experienced. . . . I hold it for proven and evident that until the very end, evil triumphs over good and

that the triumph over evil is, so to speak, personally reserved to the Lord God. There is therefore no historical period which does not end in a catastrophe.[23]

Schmitt later acknowledged that opposition to 'the rise of the masses' in the name of a counter-revolutionary eschatology led down a historical cul-de-sac. The attempt to negate popular sovereignty theoretically through an ingenious, theologically conceived counter-definition could only be anachronistic in the twentieth-century political world.[24] Although Schmitt would remain residually sympathetic to this tradition, he came to the conclusion that there could no future for a purely reactionary politics, however radical-sounding. Just as significant was the realization that eschatological political visions were not easily compatible with the political rationality which he saw embodied in the classical European state form. Suggestive of this incompatibility was Cortes's hatred of Prussia and the spirit of Hegelianism which permeated its capital, Berlin.[25] Initially this anti-Prussian streak might have held an oppositional attraction for this Rhinelander in his Greifswald misery, but its reactionary incomprehension of the modern state would always be more troubling for him thereafter. After this work, one could say that the two diametrically opposed meanings which Schmitt had attached to the term 'sovereignty' (democratic, as in the 'sovereign dictatorship' of French Revolutionary origin; and ultra-authoritarian, culminating in this counter-revolutionary political theology) cancelled each other out, and after *Politische Theologie* his use of the term was almost exclusively confined to the more conventional context of international relations.

Shortly after Schmitt had completed *Politische Theologie*, he finished another work in which he presented a wholly different conception of the role of Catholicism in modern politics. In *Römischer Katholizismus und politische Form* ('Roman Catholicism and Political Form')[26] the Church is presented as an institution which provides a mediating centre and balance to a Europe divided into hostile nations and classes. This Catholic legacy offered the basis for a European, cosmopolitan and moderate politics which avoided the Manichaean and extremist logic of decisionism.

As we shall see, the contrast between *Politische Theologie* and *Römischer Katholizismus und politische Form* is so striking that it is hard to believe that the author had written one book right after the other. The Church's capacity to arbitrate, which was portrayed here as the office of a great 'representative' institution, was based on a conception of politics almost diametrically opposed to the 'political theology' of a Cortes, with its eschatological image of a counter-revolutionary civil war. Although *Römischer Katholizismus und politische Form* was published two years later, and probably after many revisions, its diametrical opposition to *Politische Theologie* on this point is symptomatic. An eschatological vision of catastrophe and renewal at one pole, and a more sober vision of a mediating classical political civilization at the other, formed the antipodes between which Schmitt's thinking would continue to move.

4

Catholicism and Nationalism
in Modern Politics

By the beginning of 1922 Schmitt had finally managed to escape from Greifswald and find a position in the culturally more congenial atmosphere of Bonn. Its well-respected – if not highly ranked – university loomed large in this quaint, largely Catholic, small city of 50,000 inhabitants. This was a region where Catholics, who made up less than a third of the nation at large, constituted over 60 per cent of the population. The university was located near the Rhine, in a landscape with which Schmitt had been acquainted since childhood. Adding to its attractions, Bonn was one of the centres of Germany's Catholic Renouvelle, and on the basis of his Greifswald writings Schmitt quickly became a highly respected figure within these literary and political circles.[1]

During his early years in Bonn, Schmitt professed to see in Catholicism the profile of a European political and intellectual order within which the narrow nationalisms of the prewar era could be surmounted. At Greifswald he had nearly completed *Römischer Katholizismus und politische Form*, in which he had argued that the Church provided a model for societies struggling to reconcile deep conflicts of interest and ideology. The Church was an institutional embodiment of the underlying unity of European political civilization, a 'political form' which relativized the significance of national and class oppositions: Complexio Oppositorum, a complex of opposites.[2]

At the time Schmitt felt that the Catholic Centre Party represented some of these virtues in the realm of practical politics. On a more mundane level the Centre was a complex of opposites in that it could claim to be the one major party which was not based on a divisive class appeal.[3] Before the war the Centre had frequently been attacked for separating itself from the dominant dispensation around issues of education and foreign policy. For this reason, Catholics were often seen as a not entirely trustworthy element by the main pillars of Wilhelmine state and society. From the very beginning of the Weimar Republic, by contrast, the Centre was a government party *par excellence* and, because of its active collaboration in shaping the new order, previously formidable – if subtle – obstacles to Catholic advancement in politics soon disappeared. Representing a solid 12–13 per cent of the electorate, the party possessed unsurpassed leverage because it literally held the centre of a fragile political consensus linking the Social Democrats to bourgeois parties which were – with the exception of the Democratic Party – either unenthusiastic about the Republic or downright hostile to it.[4] Since it occupied this strategic mediating position, no coalition government could be formed without its participation; indeed, the Chancellorship fell to it eight out of fourteen times.

Despite – or perhaps because of – the fact that this new kingmaker position had helped to break down the walls separating Germany's Catholic minority from the rest of society, the party's previously solid constituency began to fray around the edges. Whereas before the war Catholic support for the Centre was in the order of 80 per cent, by the mid 1920s it had fallen to 60 per cent.[5] In addition to the slow, steady heamorrhaging away of Catholic workers to the Left, its base of support in the 'test-taking classes' was diminished by the tendency in this group to put the nation more assertively before confessional identity. The postwar Centre was no longer a party led by Catholic noblemen who could command and expect deference from their constituents. A new type of functionary now dominated the party, one who was likely to come from a background of little social distinction. Schmitt's own family history would have made him typical, had the course of his own life not taken him into the much more socially elite world of the university, where any too close association with the Centre might still be seen as compromising. Although he was known to be sympathetic to the right wing of the party, Schmitt was not one of those who had left the Centre for parties further to the right. This was an option exercised by an elite element in Catholic society which had strongly identified with the old monarchy, and considered the new Republic a national and social scandal. The history professor and German Nationalist Party delegate Martin Spahn was the spokesman for such Catholics, and it is useful to consider such cases when we are attempting to plot Schmitt's position on the political map. Whatever his misgivings about the Republic at this time, he had reservations about the old Right and its schemes to restore the privileges of castes to which he did not belong.

During the period of relative stabilization which set in after 1923, Schmitt's allegiance to the Centre, like his support for the Republic, was based on the absence of what he considered any realistic alternative to the unprincipled but functional compromises underlying the new Constitution. In these early years at Bonn, Schmitt's relationship to the Centre was so cordial that it was thought he might be persuaded to represent the party in the Prussian Landtag. His candidacy was locally supported by the Republican Centre Students[6], among others, and this suggests that although he was thought to identify with the party's right wing, he was not considered hostile to the Republic.[7] But even at this time he did not become a party member, arguably because he could not get over a deep intellectual dissatisfaction with the whole system of political parties.

Despite these reservations about the Centre, Schmitt was well established in Bonn's flourishing lay Catholic civil society. Much of the impetus to the so-called Catholic Renouvelle was based on a mild disaffection with the philistinism of party-approved literature and art. In the 1920s this cultural movement adopted a politics associated with the idea of a restored Great German Reich, conceived in the image of the medieval Holy Roman Empire, as the divinely ordained leading power of Europe. This conception of a Catholic 'Abendland', 'the West' apocalyptically rescued from Spenglerian decline, was avidly discussed and promoted in certain circles of the local Catholic literati.[8] Although in his first few years at Bonn he was held in high esteem in this milieu, Schmitt was intellectually very distant from its vaporous, Romantic medievalism.

While he had nearly finished *Römischer Katholizismus und politische Form* in Greifswald, he had it published a year later, after he had settled in Bonn. It is conceivable that it might therefore have undergone considerable revision in anticipation of the episcopal imprimatur which was forthcoming in a subsequent edition. Whatever the case may be, the work as published reveals Schmitt's own distinctive conception of the Church as first and foremost a political institution, and does not appear to be influenced by any intellectual current within contemporary German Catholicism, whether from the seminary or from the local literary *demi-monde*.[9]

Although Schmitt was the only legal academic in the country to cultivate a Catholic identity,[10] his ideas owed very little to the theological traditions of the Church. Hostile to the identification of Catholic with Romantic, he also objected to the association of Catholicism with the undeniably orthodox, Thomistic natural-law tradition. In *Römischer Katholizismus und politische Form*, names like Augustine and Aquinas are nowhere to be found. His portrayal of the political identity of the Church was a cocktail of themes from Dostoevsky, Léon Bloy, Georges Sorel and Charles Maurras.

Of all of these conspicuously un-German figures, only the last invites a direct comparison. Waldemar Gurian, a Russian-born Jew raised as a Catholic in Germany, was a student of Schmitt's and an expert on French integral nationalism. In his opinion, Maurras was an unacknowledged, subterranean influence on Schmitt.[11] 'Influence' is perhaps too crude a word to describe the pattern of negation and selective appropriation which characterized Schmitt's relationship to this figure, as to so many others. But a profile of this notorious Frenchman can reveal, even through sharp contrasts, the equally unusual political affinities of a comparable figure operating in a very different national context.

As the editor of the widely read journal *Action Française*, Charles Maurras had for years tirelessly advocated a military *coup d'état*, with the backing of the Church, to overthrow the Third Republic.[12] Maurras was a pioneer in modern counter-revolutionary thought – arguably the first in this largely French tradition to conceive of the ideal political order in explicitly national terms. For Maurras, the nation had nothing to do with popular sovereignty.[13] The France of his imagination was a perfect royal polity consisting of the Church, the army, and the Académie Française.[14]

Although Schmitt admired the cultivated intransigence of the journal, he did not subscribe to the Catholic integral nationalism of Maurras and his allies. In France, Catholicism could intensify nationalism, giving it a fanatical coherence. For obvious historical reasons this was not as promising a combination in Germany, where Catholic and national often pulled in different directions. A sentence from *Römischer Katholizismus und politische Form* conveys a sense of the distance separating the Schmitt of the early 1920s from the right-wing nationalisms of his time: 'The possession of the earth's oil wells can perhaps decide the struggle for world domination, but in this struggle the Regent of Christ on earth will not be involved.'[15] Maurras was of the opposite opinion, ardently believing that the Vatican was the natural ally of France in any European contest for power.

If in this respect Schmitt was 'less' nationalist than Maurras, in another respect he was becoming more attuned to the demotic, plebiscitary side of nationalism – that is, more open to mass politics, 'politics from below', than Maurras would ever be. In *Römischer Katholizismus und politische Form*, Schmitt's stance towards the new realities of mass politics was one of resigned but critical toleration, in contrast to his much more hostile stance in *Politische Theologie*. Unlike T.S. Eliot, whose admiration for Maurras was based on his enthusiasm for the cause of Catholic royalism, Schmitt considered the politics of monarchical restoration totally anachronistic in postwar republican Germany. One of the main arguments of *Römischer Katholizismus und politische Form* was that the Church was not based on the persistence of the *ancien régime*, and could therefore be reconciled to a democratic republic.

Finally, 'political theology' separated Schmitt from Maurras. Maurras was heavily influenced by Renan's portrayal of early Christianity as a primitive socialism inflamed with the Semitic spirit of Messianic enthusiasm, essentially a slave revolt against aristocratic and heathen Rome.

The crucified figure of Christ awoke in Maurras intense feelings of antipathy, and his idea of the Church as an institutionally enclosed order excluded any eschatological promise of a Redeemer.[16] It was not because this view entailed atheism that Schmitt rejected it – as we have seen, he was not a believer in any conventional sense, even when he might have wanted to be. Although, like Hobbes, he thought that millennial expectations needed to be restrained and disciplined, he also believed that an eschatological horizon was essential for a politics of radical renewal: a world which did not live in expectation of redemption would shirk all political problems, and sink into philistine security and pleasure-seeking. This was also what separated him from Maurras: Maurras – who had 'reliable' institutions under his feet, or at least in his mind – equated eschatological expectations with the Revolution; Schmitt, who did not, intermittently associated this state of mind with the promise of a counter-revolutionary deliverance. This theological dimension remained the one level of his thought which was now more German than Latin European in orientation. It was mainly in interwar Germany that eschatological themes came back into educated political discourse – a development that was not confined to the Right.[17]

The label 'Catholic' suggests different things in different national contexts. The same Maurras who held that the Church was the bedrock of an older and greater France was actually a professed atheist. Even if this 'catholique, mais athée' stance never appealed to Schmitt,[18] he, too, had a deeply ambivalent relationship to the traditions of the Church, always preferring his own intellectual picture to actually existing Catholicism. While Catholicism played a decisive role in the formation of Schmitt's intellectual habitus, the idiosyncratic and political nature of this filtered inheritance was evident to many who knew him well. Waldemar Gurian, whose relationship with Schmitt took a turn for the worse in the late 1920s, compared him with Maurras, claiming that the Frenchman was the more honourable of the two, because at least he did not outwardly pretend to be a believer.[19] According to Gurian, the two men had none the less had something in common: 'the same fear of theologians as external authorities', 'the same moodiness', 'the same mixture of ... diligence and *bohème*, leaving behind the same impression: uncanny'.[20]

Römischer Katholizismus und politische Form begins with the pronouncement: 'There is an anti-Roman affect.'[21] The pretension of a 'celibate bureaucracy' to represent the dominion of Christ in political form has been rejected as un-Christian by a wide range of adversaries: Protestant sectarians, liberals and a Russian Orthodoxy, which – as Dostoevsky's portrait of the Grand Inquisitor demonstrated – was a culture infused with a deep hostility to Catholic legal and political traditions. Schmitt believed that he was attacking the nerve centre of this 'anti-Roman affect' by arguing that in fact it was one of the great historical accomplishments of the Roman Church to have subdued the wild, unearthly utopianism of early Christian communities by insisting that Christendom was a jurisdiction.[22]

Since the Reformation, hostile commentators have portrayed the political opportunism of the Church in notorious, Machiavellian colours. Schmitt, no doubt, had fresh memories of such accusations from the war, when high prelates of the Church blessed the canons of all the belligerent powers. Countering this charge, he claimed that the Church's ability to accommodate itself to the opposing sides of political conflicts did not stem from any lack of principle; on the contrary, it was the legacy of a universalism which looked upon such conflicts from a higher political perspective. The Church could see through the borders which divided nations because it was the inheritor of the Roman imperium, the living embodiment of the classical political civilization which all Western European peoples shared. Every world empire, he claimed, contains within itself great local variations which it tolerates in the interests of preserving the whole, and in this respect the 'Roman and English world empires exhibit enough similarities'.[23]

Despite this political universalism, Schmitt claimed that the Church had also been responsible for the historical evolution of Europe into a mosaic of distinct national cultures.[24] He shared this conception of a European culture as a unity expressed in diverse national forms with his colleague at Bonn, Ernst Robertus Curtius. He would later grapple with the problems of determining the boundaries and identity of Europe in his articles on international law. Here this determination of European identity occurred through a double negation: on the one side, of American capitalism as a dim and distant threat; on the other, of Russian radicalism as a clear and present danger. Nearly a decade later, Curtius would portray Bolshevism as a nihilistic world power, armed to the teeth.[25] Curtius's emphasis was on Bolshevism's threat to the European literary and cultural tradition. Although Schmitt saw this threat in more explicitly political terms, he used both Dostoevsky and the anarchist Bakunin to represent the spirit of Russian radicalism, lurking on the boundary of Europe.

Not only was the Church presented as an arbitrator of national and civilizational divisions; the nineteenth-century conflict between liberalism and the *ancien régime* could also be reconciled in its bosom. Although the Church was historically allied with Divine Right monarchy, Schmitt claimed that, as a complex of opposites, it could work in tandem with all old and new regimes within the Western European tradition. But this capacity to arbitrate between opposites entailed a politics quite different from the counter-revolutionary political theology of a Donoso

Cortes.[26] Schmitt acknowledged that Catholic trinitarian dogma was incompatible with the idea that man is an inherently evil being.[27] This idea had been the deep theological assumption of the whole counter-revolutionary tradition, and Schmitt explicitly rejected its Manichaean vision of the political world. In fact, he expanded this criticism of the either/or logic of decisionism by arguing that it was the expression of a dualism inherent in modern societies, locked into a ceaseless struggle to dominate and transform nature.[28]

The constant transformation in human affairs which an unbridled modernity brings in its wake destroys the 'representative' aura surrounding the institutions of public authority. 'Representation' in this sense presupposes a sharp separation between those on a sacral public stage and those who are spectators, and a symbolic order in which it is possible for the former to stand unproblematically for the latter. But the necessity of a majestic public power, perched above the realm of socioeconomic relations, becomes increasingly difficult to justify in the modern world. The classical institutional forms – even the rhetorical traditions – which delineate the world of high politics from the subaltern world of modern party politics come to be perceived as irrational and wasteful 'superstructures'. According to Schmitt, the pathos of distance between representative and represented is radically alien to the sensibilities of the principal classes of modern society.[29]

The *esprit de corps* of a great political order stems from a legitimating myth. The myth of the Catholic Church is that it represents the dominion of Christ until his triumphant return on the Day of Judgement. The Church represents 'the reigning, ruling, conquering Christ'.[30] By contrast, Schmitt claimed that there was a void, an absence of myth, at the centre of the modern bureaucratic state. Social movements across the political spectrum were beginning to generate their own highly partisan myths, which were less likely to establish an enduring political civilization. Schmitt's use of the term 'myth' was indebted to the French syndicalist theorist Georges Sorel, who had claimed that the modern parliamentary bourgeoisie was agnostic and decadent, lacking the spirit of discipline and sacrifice which belongs to groups held together by an epic myth. In *Reflections on Violence* Sorel had claimed that the General Strike was an apocalyptic narrative of the modern working class: 'the myth in which Socialism is wholly comprised, i.e. a body of images capable of evoking instinctively all the sentiments which correspond to the different manifestations of the war undertaken by Socialism against modern society'.[31]

Schmitt was rather sceptical of this claim that the European proletariat could ever play the role of an epic hero.[32] As he saw it, class conflict within Western Europe could be contained only by political institutions with the authority to stand above the contending classes, and arbitrate. In the face of such conflicts, even a secular republic had to assume a more majestic political form in order to govern with authority, and Schmitt thought there was much that postwar Germany could learn from the Roman Church in this respect: 'An alliance of the Catholic Church with the contemporary form of capitalist industrialism is not possible. The Alliance of Throne and Altar will not be followed by Office and Altar, nor by Factory and Altar.'[33] The Church was a fragment of an old European political civilization, standing out sharply against a grey, modern landscape of offices and factories. 'Representation' through the arcana of mythic personification was the antithesis of the economistic ideal of social transparency. In the coded language of this short book, Schmitt was making the claim that the Weimar Republic – and, more broadly, the modern European state – could not last if it was based merely on drab, corporatist compromises between social classes. This was because, as he put it, '[no] great social antagonism allows for an economic solution'.[34]

Unlike the formless proletarian masses, the bourgeoisie had a massive stake in the inherited legal forms of private property: 'To the economic sphere belong juristic concepts like property or contract.'[35] But the problem was that an unbridled capitalism, breaking out of familiar nineteenth-century bourgeois forms, was threatening to pull away, in proper dialectical fashion, the juristic foundations of private property itself:

> It is a matter of the moral and legal responsibility of who the actual producer, creator and in consequence the master of modern wealth is. As soon as production becomes restlessly anonymous, and a veil of joint-stock companies and other 'juristic' persons makes the attribution of responsibility to concrete men impossible, the private property of the capitalist, who is nothing but [the embodiment of] capital, will be cast away like an inexplicable decoration.[36]

Many of these 'inexplicable decorations' now needed to be salvaged in the face of a revolutionary onslaught, but a rigidly reactionary, antiquarian posture was doomed. The antithesis of Europe's classical political civilization was not liberalism but a Bolshevism which saw conservative and liberal, Catholic and nationalist, monarchist and republican as the interchangeable faces of the same class enemy. All of old Europe needed to realize that this was how they looked in the eyes of the enemy, and that the time had now come to leave the internecine quarrels of the last century behind.

It was in this context that Schmitt portrayed that old enemy of the Church, Freemasonry, rather positively, providing a clear demonstration of his distance from conventional confessional prejudices. In his view, the great representatives of the bourgeoisie in the age of its revolutionary ascendancy were to be found in these elite secret societies dedicated to the Enlightenment myth of Humanity, a humanity conceived in militantly anticlerical terms.[37] The role he attributed to Freemasonry in the Enlightenment, while it was certainly exaggerated, was presented as an example of a politics with European horizons. Like its enemy, the Church, Freemasonry was both cosmopolitan and national. In the nineteenth century its legacy lived on in the liberal nationalism of the Italian Freemason Mazzini. In Schmitt's view, Mazzini embodied the spirit of this liberal nationalism which, while anticlerical, none the less belonged to a common Catholic – and by this Schmitt meant Western European – civilization.[38] It was now time for a historic compromise against a common enemy.

Schmitt saw emerging from the nineteenth century two great political forces which threatened Western European civilization: from within, a class-conscious proletariat; from beyond, a radicalized Russian intelligentsia filled with an implacable, demonic hatred of the Western bourgeoisie. The initial distance separating the agendas of this radical Russian intelligentsia from Western European socialism comes across clearly in a tirade by Bakunin against Marx and Engels, which Schmitt quoted: 'By flower of the proletariat, I mean that grand mass of the uncivilized, the disinherited, the immiserated, and the illiterate which Messrs Marx and Engels would presume to subject to a paternal regime of a very strong government.'[39] But the Russian Revolution had fused the agendas of a radical Russian intelligentsia fighting for the utterly disinherited, lumpenproletarian 'wretched of the earth' and a Marxist socialism fighting for an industrial proletariat, the alleged inheritor of the progressive traditions of the Western European bourgeoisie. This fusion represented a historically unprecedented threat. The Revolution headquartered in Russia had become a force transgressing all national boundaries, and it was imperative that old Europe respond on a 'Catholic' – that is, a Western Europe-wide – basis: 'And here I believe, in that preliminary battle with Bakunin, the Catholic Church and the Catholic concept of humanity was on the side of . . . West European civilization, next to Mazzini, not next to the atheist socialism of the anarchist Russian.'[40]

The depiction of Mazzini as a liberal nationalist creates a certain ambiguity in interpreting the political allegiances of the text. Although he was in his own way a liberal, by 1922 this nineteenth-century partisan of Italian unification could be seen very differently in the light of Mussolini's March on Rome. Although there were those who saw Fascism as the negation of the political traditions of the Risorgimento, both Mussolini and Gentile preferred to interpret it as the twentieth-century culmination of its unfinished business. One reason for Schmitt's great admiration for Italian Fascism was that it seemed poised to creatively overcome the divisive legacy of the Risorgimento, the bitter feud between the modern nation-state and the Church. He was deeply moved by the recent spectacle of the Church standing on the nationalist side against the socialist, Russian enemies of civilization. A clear strategic image of Catholic Europe as an alliance of authority, nationality and liberty had taken shape in his mind.

But shortly after the publication of *Römischer Katholizismus und politische Form*, this complex of opposites began to unravel in his mind. In Italy the Fascist *rapprochement* with the Church had been sealed at the expense of the Italian counterparts of the German Centre Party, the Popolari. In Germany the Church seemed committed to exercising its influence through the Centre Party. Although at the time Schmitt was closer to the Centre than to any other party, not too long after the book was published he began to see it more critically as one of the forces contributing to the state's 'pluralistic' break-up into party fiefdoms.

Misgivings about political Catholicism in Germany were afterthoughts in Schmitt's mind, until he found himself in conflict with the Church over a rather more personal matter. As we have seen, in wartime Munich he had married, in a moment of passion, a somewhat disreputable woman. As late as 1921 he attached to his own very ordinary name her rather exotic-sounding one; thus the author of *Die Diktatur* appeared as Schmitt-Dorotic. Very shortly thereafter all contact must have been broken off, and he began the long process of attempting to have the marriage annulled. While he was preparing his case he employed the services of another Serbian woman, *née* Todorovic, whom he shortly thereafter sought to marry. His first marriage was annulled by civil authority on 18 January 1924. In 1926, after two attempts to have his marriage annulled by the Church had been rejected, he went ahead with a civil marriage.

For the second of these two acts, this esteemed Catholic professor was immediately excommunicated and remained so until 1950, when his second wife died. Today it is probably difficult to imagine the trauma of such an experience, and it is inconceivable that it did not have a dramatic effect on his perception of the Church. The small Catholic city of Bonn, which a few years before he had found so congenial, now seemed thick with belittling gossip. His previously cordial relationship with the local Centre Party had also taken a turn for the worse, and any chance that he might have been nominated as a delegate in Berlin, if he had ever wanted it, had now obviously passed. Understandably, this whole experience confirmed his already deep misgivings about the clergy: 'As I noted the impact of this essay from 1923 . . . this saying came to me: "ubi nihil vales, ibi nihil velis", because a layman has nothing to say in this celibate bureaucracy.'[41]

Schmitt never openly attacked the Church, and maintained an outwardly respectful attitude. Here his disillusionment with the Church was much more subdued than Heidegger's bitter rejection of Catholicism. He continued to write for Catholic publications, including those closest to the Centre Party. He even continued to see his own political ideas as in some paradoxical way Catholic, even when he later concluded that the Church's historic attitude towards the state was part of the problem, and could not be part of the solution.

The open break would not come until later, but even before this happened Schmitt would already have rejected two of the central ideas put forward in *Römischer Katholizismus und politische Form*. The first was the idea that the secular state and the Church should be joined in a partnership in which the former had direct power and the latter indirect authority. He claimed that the aim of the Church was to have a special relationship with the secular state, sealed in a Concordat 'in which the two representatives face each other as partners'.[42] But there was an indissoluble connection between Catholic doctrine on Church–state relations and Catholic doctrine on state–society relations. The following passage suggests how the terms of these oppositions were linked in Schmitt's mind, and why questioning the boundary separating state and society might have led him to change his understanding of the inherited scheme of Church–state relations.

> [N]ear the state and certainly independent of it stands the Church as a free, self-sufficient *societas perfecta*, which in its domains – namely, in the divine things entrusted to it – does not tolerate the interference of the state, just as conversely, it is not supposed to interfere in the worldly affairs of the state. . . . It follows from this that according to Catholic doctrine a state absolutism, in the sense of a limitless, all-powerful executive freely determining its own jurisdiction, is just as impermissible as the heathen state of antiquity, which encompassed the entirety of man, and did not even know of private life. The Syllabus of 1864 prop. 39 explicitly condemned this doctrine of the omnipotence of the state as un-Christian.'God must be obeyed more than men.'[43]

This ideal of an 'indirect authority' attenuating the sovereignty of the state would later be rejected in the name of an enclosed political totality, a state in which – to use the words Rousseau chose to characterize the Hobbesian ideal – 'the two heads of the eagle' would be fused in a 'complete political unity'. Schmitt certainly never became an opponent of the Church, and always saw himself as representing an authentically Catholic perspective. But even without the personal reasons he would soon have for feeling less warmly about the Church, his hostility to pluralist theories of the state would force him to confront their all-too-plausible claim that the Church, in securing its independence from the state, had opened the space for the later emergence of independent associations, now consisting mainly of trade unions and political parties.

The second idea which Schmitt would come to reject was the idea of an authority claiming universal jurisdiction. Did he really believe when he wrote this work that modern Europe would accept the Church as an interstate arbitrator? Although this seems almost absurdly utopian, it was, to some degree, based on a real political tendency. The Vatican – which had been effectively shut out of European politics after the Risorgimento, the *Kulturkampf* and the disestablishment of the Church in France – had made a modest comeback as the belligerents of the world war attempted to cultivate contacts with Rome for propagandistic advantage. These efforts of governments during and after the conflict to be in good standing with Rome briefly gave Papal diplomacy a stature which it had not enjoyed for a long while, and seemed to signal a new era of Church–state relations.

In *Römischer Katholizismus und politische Form*, Schmitt was explicit about the role which the Church could play as the inheritor of the Roman imperium: 'The Church will bring, like any other world-encompassing imperialism, peace to the world when it achieves its goal, and an anxiety, hostile to form sees in that the victory of the Devil.'[44] This formulation should be kept in mind, if only because it is so completely different – even opposed – to everything Schmitt would soon come to believe in. In *Leviathan* Hobbes had described the Church not as the inheritor of the Roman imperium but as its ghost, making fantastic claims to an indirect, universal authority. Schmitt also came to believe that such claims were part of the arsenal of 'world empires' claiming international jurisdiction over sovereign states – those weak, defamed states which had no say in deciding when international law applied and when it did not. In much later work he did not hesitate to cite Hobbes to make his case against the verdicts of the 'international community': 'When a Pope excommunicates a whole Nation, methinks he rather excommunicates himself than them.'

It was Schmitt's position as a Catholic outsider which had in part shaped his previously rather diffident attitude towards the great-power chauvinism of National Liberals like Max Weber, who once proudly announced that his lodestar was Germany's destiny as a world power. Before the war Schmitt had found it difficult to identify wholeheartedly with the Protestant and Prussian-centred nature of official nationalism. Revealingly, not even the victors' justice at Versailles had been enough to jolt him out this curious indifference: Germany's status as a defeated nation was not mentioned in any of his writings before 1923, all of which were preoccupied exclusively with internal affairs. Seen in his own context, not our own, he was never first and foremost a 'nationalist'. Later, in 1936, Franz Blei could still recollect the cosmopolitan

Schmitt of these Weimar years: 'As a Rhinelander Carl Schmitt had never been what one in Austria calls a "nationally accented" German, not to mention a German Nationalist.'[45] Even as the nation became an increasingly central category in his writings, he did not abandon the idea that European political unity was desirable, and ultimately the only alternative to fratricidal European wars.[46]

This tension between national and European frames of reference is the most distinctively and enduringly Catholic element of Schmitt's thought. Indeed, he was instinctually prone to see the crisis of his own state in a larger *Western* European context. Spread across his work is a distinctive vision of the history of Europe culminating in the catastrophic crises of the interwar era. Europe as he imagined it was structured in concentric zones: a divided Franco–German core, an Italo–Hispanic semi-periphery, an uncanny Russian periphery, and an anomalous, often mythically conceived Britain. Catholicism played a decisive role in the formation of his understanding of Europe as both a landscape and an era in history. Although in *Römischer Katholizismus* he praised the institution of the Church, 'Roman Catholic' meant more to him than a mere ecclesiastical polity or a particular theological tradition. He had an ultimately critical relationship to both. Rather, it was an image of an endangered, 'classical' civilization, and the placeholder for future, Europe-wide political agendas.

5

The Legitimation Crisis of Parliament

In 1923, after a brief respite, the Weimar Republic once again seemed to be on the verge of collapse. The 'Left Course' of the German Communist Party was unfolding, resulting in gigantic strikes and demonstrations by workers in Hamburg, Saxony and Thuringia. In order to stabilize the fiscal situation, the government attempted to liquidate its domestic debts by effectively expropriating middle-class *rentiers* through hyperinflation. In the midst of an ongoing civil war, enormous speculative fortunes for those with money to move, and bankruptcy for those on fixed incomes, created an atmosphere conducive to a feverish, right-wing radicalism.

The threat of insurgency and paramilitarism was massively amplified by the international weakness of the German state. Germany's failure to pay scheduled reparations had resulted in the occupation of the Rhineland by French and Belgian troops. After encouraging a campaign of passive resistance, the government was forced into a humiliating retreat, immediately galvanizing the Right for a campaign which promised a thorough springclean. Since the suppression of the local revolutionary Left, Bavaria had become a breeding-ground for right-wing extremism of the Pan-German as well as the Bavarian separatist variety, and thus an ideal launching pad for a paramilitary putsch directed at Berlin. Mussolini's paramilitary pseudo-insurrection against a weak parliamentary government, the so-called March on Rome of November 1922, was a not too distant beacon on the horizon, and Schmitt, like many on the Right, looked south to Italy for orientation, just as many on the Left were looking east, to Russia. Schmitt had imbibed the atmosphere of this moment while writing *Die geistesgeschichtliche Lage des heutigen Parlamentarismus*[1] ('The Crisis of Parliamentary Democracy'[2]). It was completed in the summer of 1923, just months before Ludendorf's and Hitler's attempt to follow Mussolini's road to power; as a result, the author was deprived until much later of the opportunity to reflect seriously upon the unsettling presence of a local version of the Italian original.

Where does this work stand in the evolution of Schmitt's political views? Ambivalence towards the idea of popular sovereignty generated nearly all the intellectual energy running through the works considered so far. In *Die Diktatur* and *Politische Theologie*, popular sovereignty was portrayed as a power which had to be brought to heel. In *Politische Theologie*, Schmitt had gone so far as to quote approvingly Cortes's depiction of the masses as a vile and ungodly multitude. Even in *Römischer Katholizismus und politische Form*, the proletariat was portrayed as a formless mass, in need of government from above.

The outlook of *Die geistesgeschichtliche Lage des heutigen Parlamentarismus*, published a year later, seems almost entirely the opposite: instead of a political theology in which an unruly, insurgent multitude is cast in the role of the villain, Schmitt now admiringly appraised the heroic spirit of mass mobilizations and, drawing on the work of the French syndicalist Georges Sorel, identified the motive force behind them in great political myths. This shift from 'political theology' to 'political mythology' signified an increasing openness to the possibilities of modern mass politics, and a marked departure from the note of hostility running through *Die Diktatur*, *Politische Theologie* and, to a lesser extent, *Römischer Katholizismus und politische Form*.[3]

Die geistesgeschichtliche Lage des heutigen Parlamentarismus belongs to a wider literature in which the marginalization of classical liberal projects in the arena of mass politics is the main theme. It begins with the argument that the classical liberal defence of parliament had been based on a belief that the best laws were the product of rational discourse.[4] Put in Kantian terms, this was the view that just legislation must always conform to the principle of publicity. The forensic competition of opposing perspectives within the chamber was supposed to concentrate the more diffuse discourses of public opinion, which received daily enlightenment from a free press which reported and editorialized on the world as represented in parliamentary debate. Guizot, the foremost representative of early-nineteenth-century French liberalism, clearly articulated this relationship between parliament and public opinion:

> It is moreover, the character of [the parliamentary] system, which nowhere admits the legitimacy of absolute power, to compel the whole body of citizens incessantly and on every occasion, to seek after reason, justice and the truth, which should ever regulate actual power. The representative system does this, 1) by discussion which compels existing powers to seek after the truth in common; 2) by publicity, which places these powers when occupied in this search, under the eyes of the citizens; and 3) by the liberty of the press, which stimulates the citizens themselves to seek after truth, and to tell it to power.[5]

Although the franchise might be restricted to the educated and propertied, parliamentary government was based on a concept of representation very different from the narrow corporatism of the *ancien régime* estate. Those elected were not deputies tied to their constituencies by written instruction but became representatives of the nation, in theory bound by their conscience to vote for the side with the best arguments. Even if the reality was always very far from this ideal, the main arguments for parliament of Constant, Guizot, and Mill presupposed this model of discursive rationality. By contrast, the idea that parliament is a site where the contending interests of a pluralistic society reach a working consensus through clever compromises plays a much smaller, if any, role in this older tradition of parliamentary thought.[6]

It could be argued that theories from a distant nineteenth-century world do not have much bearing on the reason why an institution like parliament works today. Even in times of trouble, it could function passably, and under conditions very remote from the bygone era of Constant, Guizot and Mill. But in Schmitt's view, the idea that the ideal of government by discussion as the centre of an educated public sphere could be obliterated without affecting the historical viability of the parliamentary government was absurd.[7] The alternative view – that parliament is merely a site where compromises between interest groups are hammered out – provided no justification for parliament as an institution, as opposed to any number of other institutions which could serve this function equally well. Without a belief in the power of debate in public chambers to generate rational laws, there is nothing to distinguish parliamentary procedure from collective bargaining, in which representatives of interest groups work out the details of the distribution of public funds and the tax burden. Even if such a body were called a parliament, it would no longer be one in the meaningful historical sense of the word.

According to Schmitt, it was precisely this belief in institutionalized discursive rationality which was evaporating in contemporary Europe. Extra-parliamentary zones of conflict and negotiation between parties representing social groups with antagonistic interests had suddenly emerged, tenuously institutionalized in an uncoordinated corporatism. It should be said that classical liberalism was almost never the target of Schmitt's specifically polemical formulations; it was, rather, this post-liberal, multiparty corporatism.[8]

After the early idealistic phase of European liberalism, parliamentary government came increasingly to be seen as a purely formal, procedural principle. Schmitt believed that exclusively emphasizing the rules of a multiparty electoralism foreclosed discussion on deeper problems of the social preconditions of government by discussion. By contrast, the great minds of early European liberalism had been acutely aware of the class milieus and forms of life which made parliament the centre of an ongoing mobilization of public opinion, directed at a reactionary bloc of *ancien régime* ministers, courts and armies. The classic liberal justification of parliament was embedded in the political oppositions of a bygone era. What were the long-term prospects for the institution of parliament in the absence of any comparable belief in the political efficacy of discursive rationality? Schmitt believed that it was no longer possible to foreclose debate on the legitimacy of government by discussion, as a value-laden political project.

But for all his insights into the role of theoretical justification in politics, Schmitt tended to see historical trends through the spectacles of his own theoretical ideal-types. Although these lenses were often penetrating, they led him – misleadingly – to assimilate Germany into a general history of Western European parliamentarianism. If Imperial Germany was simply a variant of European parliamentarianism, the chaos of Weimar could be presented as the crisis of an idea, and an institution, which world history was everywhere leaving behind. Although it is possible to exaggerate the German *Sonderweg*, Schmitt's analysis is occasionally marred by the equally implausible assumption that the Reichstag in the age of Wilhelm II possessed the same power and prestige as parliamentary chambers in London and Paris. In Imperial Germany, governments were responsible not to parliament but to the monarch, and it was the monarch who summoned parliament. The strongest weapon which parliament wielded was the Budget Law, which mandated parliamentary oversight of the government's budget assessment. Laws which affected the personal freedom or property of subjects had to have the consent of parliament, but in all other domains the monarch was the primary legislator, even though the association of law with parliamentary approval meant that such laws nominally had the status of executive decrees.[9] Schmitt's conception of parliament in the nineteenth century seems to be formed from a cross between the classic liberal, Western European ideal and the more authoritarian realities of the German 'constitutional monarchy'. Whatever is valid in his analysis can therefore be better understood as a critique of a plausible parliamentary ideal-type.

The objective Schmitt set for himself in this work was to identify alternative visions of political legitimacy emerging out of the force fields of modern mass politics. We are accustomed to thinking of liberal democracy as a distinct form of government. One objective of Schmitt's book was to argue that far from forming a harmonious pair, liberalism and democracy were antagonistic programmes. *Die geistesgeschichtliche Lage des heutigen Parlamentarismus* belonged to a wider literature which addressed the significance of the Weimar Republic in terms of the history of the troubled relationship between liberalism and democracy. Retrospection on the events of 1848 loomed large in this literature: in that year the constituencies of middle-class liberalism, terrified by inchoate demands for a social revolution, had bolted back into the protective custody of the *ancien régime*, abandoning not only more radical, democratic allies but also many of their own ideals. These events had left a legacy of deep mistrust between a subsequently much more conservative liberalism, which tended to equate liberty with the legal protection of private property, and a democracy, subsequently a social democracy, which tended to look upon such liberties as anti-democratic privileges. Although in 1919 the recently established German Republic seemed for a moment to have brought an end to seventy years of conflict between German liberalism and democracy, only four years later little enthusiasm was left for this too belated, too cheaply won, historic compromise.

Schmitt's critique stood out in this wider literature on parliamentary government for two reasons: he claimed that this conflict had been based on antithetical principles, not just on the accidents and misunderstandings of the past century; more distinctively, he predicted that the now victorious democratic principle would assume political forms shockingly disappointing to its traditional left-wing representatives. Compared to figures like Max Weber and Friedrich Meinecke, Carl Schmitt was far more attuned to a cultural atmosphere in which nineteenth-century ideals were suffering limitless humiliations.

According to Schmitt, the principal objective of the nineteenth-century liberal movement had been to protect an individualistic civil society from the encroachments of the state. The ideal of general – and thus impartial – laws passed by parliamentary majorities offered a compelling solution to this problem. The principal objective of modern democratic movements, in contrast, had been to establish a relationship of 'identity' between a collectively conceived people and 'its' state.[10] Even if any absolute antithesis between liberalism and democracy is now bound to seem implausible, we should not forget that at one time the conflict between the two was the subject of a vast literature; the sceptical Anglo-American should be reminded that compared to Schmitt on this point, Lord Acton was the more extreme dichotomizer.

Schmitt acknowledged that so long as democracy was a movement directed at the *ancien régime*, it could opportunistically combine with other currents like liberalism and, later, socialism. But democracy was, in his view, unlike these other political ideas, in that it occupies no necessary position on the political spectrum, being based entirely on the open-ended idea that government is legitimate to the degree that its actions reflect the will of the people.[11] Democracy raises the problem of the identity of the demos, its borders, its homogeneity. This was the very point that Lord Acton made about the 'nationality principle'; in the aftermath of the Risorgimento, Acton argued that nationalism was the extreme logical extension of democracy, and was heading towards self-destruction because of the violent exclusions which would be necessary to reach the always elusive – because ultimately spectral – goal of homogeneity. Schmitt predicted a more promising future for democracy, but he, too, thought that it was essentially a nationalist phenomenon.

The argument that democracy requires the homogeneity of a demos seems ominous. In this sense plebiscitary dictatorships, albeit anti-liberal, could plausibly be described as true democracies. Schmitt also claimed that in a crisis, the homogeneity of the demos often had to be secured by exclusion of the 'heterogeneous'. In the light of retrospection, homogeneity might seem to be attribute of an ethnically or racially defined people, as it was for Acton. But Schmitt was explicit in rejecting this view, arguing that homogeneity could not be permanently defined along any one dimension because it was impossible in a democracy to stabilize the essentially polemical-political meaning of the term 'the people'. In passages from a later work, *Verfassungslehre*, more than reminiscent of Renan and Weber, his distance from the *völkisch* idiom is clear:

> 'Nation' and 'Volk' are often treated as synonymous concepts, but the word 'nation' is terser, and less subject to misunderstanding. It designates, that is, the 'Volk' as a unit of political action, while the Volk that does not exist as a Nation is only some kind of ethnic or cultural group, not, however, a real political bond among human beings.[12]

> Diverse elements can contribute to the unity of the nation, and to the consciousness of this unity: common speech, common historical fates, traditions and memories, common political goals and hopes. Language, while it is an important factor, is not in itself decisive. . . . Authentic revolutions and victorious wars can overcome linguistic oppositions and establish the feeling of national belonging, even when the same language is not spoken.[13]

The cultural identity of the demos was politically significant only as the basis of the 'General Will', whose existence had to be presumed if laws were to be legitimate in a democracy. On this point Schmitt was essentially in agreement with Rousseau in claiming that the people has to be a sufficiently concentrated, homogeneous group for the will of a majority to generate legitimate outcomes. In the Weimar Republic political homogeneity remained elusive, partly because its Constitution had failed to discover any new framework for collective will formation, and fell back half-heartedly on an anachronistic ideal of government by discussion.

There was probably no purely organizational solution to this problem under Weimar conditions. Indeed, Schmitt implicitly acknowledged that 'homogeneity' was always a provisional state of affairs, because there could never be an objective reconciliation of the conflicting

interests within a political community. But he also felt that the twentieth-
century *Zeitgeist* was increasingly becoming receptive to philosophies
of history which ultimately rested upon irrational foundations, and
'myth' provided a tempting solution to this problem of deeply rooted
conflict and irreducible heterogeneity. Although he never gave a precise
definition of what he understood by myth, the following passage by
Terry Eagleton provides an indication of the role it played in Schmitt's
thought:

> The steady draining of immanent meaning from objects clears the way for
> some marvellous new totalization, so that in a world depleted of significance
> and subjectivity, myth can furnish just those ordering, reductive schemas
> necessary to elicit unity from chaos. It thus takes over something of the role
> of historical explanation at a point where historical forms of thought are
> now themselves increasingly part of the symbolic rubble, progressively hollow
> and discredited in the aftermath of imperialist world war.[14]

In this context, revolution, counter-revolution and world war could be
reinterpreted in a glamorous, mythical light. Continuing a pattern
established in his earlier works – of drawing on figures, usually Latin
Europeans, from outside the mainstream of German intellectual life –
Schmitt was one of the first in Germany to read Sorel's *Reflections on
Violence* seriously. But his affinities for Sorel cannot be explained simply
in terms of a taste for the intellectually exotic. Sorel's reflections on
the role played by mythic battle images in upsurges of collective action
were, in the words of Wyndham Lewis, 'the key to all contemporary
political thought' – an assessment which Schmitt cited approvingly.

> He is the arch exponent of extreme action and revolutionary violence *à
> l'outrance*, but he expounds this sanguinary doctrine in manuals that often,
> by changing a few words, would equally serve the forces of traditional
> authority, and provide them with a twin evangel of demented and intolerant
> class war.[15]

Although the insurgent proletariat was cast in the role of an epic
hero in *Reflections on Violence*, its true enemy in Sorel's mind was not
the capitalist captain of industry, a figure of equally epic proportions,
but the decadent, besuited, apéritif-sipping parliamentary bourgeoisie
of the Third Republic. Even when he considered himself a socialist,
Sorel was unduly troubled by the thought that the contemporary ruling
classes were no longer hard and cruel enough to inspire a heroic
proletarian opposition:

> When the governing classes no longer dare to govern, are ashamed of their
> privileged situation, are eager to make advances to their enemies, and
> proclaim their horror of all cleavages in society, it becomes more difficult to
> maintain in the minds of the proletariat this idea of cleavage without which
> Socialism cannot fulfil its historic role.[16]

Despite its pretensions to being a science, Schmitt considered the new revolutionary Marxism to be one such mythic philosophy of history. It is probable that Lukács's *History and Class Consciousness* had made a strong impression on him, as on so many of his contemporaries, giving him a newfound respect for Marxist theory.* While classical Marxism had often downplayed the role of force in history, this exuberantly Hegelian construction captured the uninhibited voluntarism of the Russian Revolution – in Gramsci's words, the revolution 'against *Capital*': 'The dialectical conception of immanent development seems to undermine the necessity of dictatorial force, but the systematic concentration of all class struggles into a single last battle of human history, [achieves] a dialectical highpoint of tension: bourgeoisie and proletariat.'[17] The political voluntarism that this philosophy of history promoted stemmed from the belief that when 'an epoch of history is grasped in human consciousness, this provides proof ... that the theorized epoch is finished'.[18] Schmitt read this work against the grain, detecting the mythic dimensions in this dialectic. In his view, 'the proletariat' was not simply an economic class, but a political myth which promises, to those who have nothing to lose but their chains, that they are the 'negation' of the existing bourgeois world of obsolete privileges. He could read it in this way, perhaps, because he noticed certain affinities to Sorel's *Reflections on Violence*. In any event, he credited Sorel with the insight that 'scientific socialism' was ultimately a proletarian battle myth.[19] It was not Schmitt's intention to cut 'the proletariat' down to size by pointing out that it was only a myth: if it was no longer the only spectre haunting Europe, it was none the less a disturbing manifestation of the far-reaching legitimation crisis eating away at bourgeois society:

---

* Schmitt's citation of *History and Class Consciousness* in this work reveals a more than cursory familiarity with its contents. This was not the last point of contact between these two figures: there are numerous indications that each perceived, in the ideas of the other, the deepest expression of the legitimacy claims of the enemy. In Schmitt's postwar notebooks (*Aufzeichnungen der Jahre 1947–1950* [Duncker & Humblot; Berlin 1991], p. 50) he offered an unforgettable assessment of the significance of Lukács, in a passage which captures the essence of his own relationship to Marxism:

> Lukács also came to the antithesis legality/legitimacy. The revolutionary struggle of the proletariat is 'legitimate'. In the conclusion it literally states:
>
> > The proletariat of central and western Europe still has a hard path before it. In order to come to a consciousness of its historic calling, to decide for the legitimacy of its rule, it must first learn to understand the merely tactical character of legality and illegality, as well as put away legal cretinism and the romanticism of legality.
>
> One cannot doubt the actuality of this distinction between legality and legitimacy. ... There is also no doubt that those who were so dialectically clear about legality and illegality on this point – namely, in the face of illegality practised against them – didn't get the joke.

That everything which concerns the proletariat can only be negatively
determined is a systematic necessity. Only after that was forgotten could one
attempt to characterize the proletariat positively. One can rightfully say of a
future society that there will no longer be any class antagonisms, and of the
proletariat that it is that social class which does not share in the surplus-
value, does not know family or country, etc. The proletariat is the social
nothing.[20]

Sorel's conception of myth seemed to offer a promising solution to
problems of political theory in the irrational atmosphere of modern
mass politics, where few believed that problems of the distribution of
wealth and power could be solved through rational discussion. Schmitt
liked this idea that it was only through a shared myth that the people
become a politically unitary subject. Gramsci, at the other end of the
political spectrum, saw the Sorelian myth in a similar light, defining it
as: 'a political ideology expressed neither in the form of a cold utopia
nor as learned theorizing, but rather . . . a creation of concrete phan-
tasy which acts on a dispersed and shattered people to arouse and
organize its collective will'.[21] The decisive issue of European politics
had become which myth would politically integrate the masses, and
who would be the integrators.

From this vantage point Schmitt compared the significance of two
great contemporary events: the Russian Revolution and the Fascist
March on Rome. Sorel had claimed that Bolshevism was able to seize
state power in a vast empire on the periphery of the European world
because its class-struggle ideology fused in the popular imagination
with powerful Messianic images of a world redeemed by Russia. Schmitt
offered this as an illustration of the superiority of the national myth
over the class myth. But in his eyes the victory of Fascism over the
Italian Left was even more demonstrative, because in Italy the national
myth had defeated the class myth not through co-optation but in an
open battle, demonstrating that in the classical heartland of Western
Europe, socialism would remain – in Mussolini's words – 'an inferior
mythology'. It had shown itself incapable of extinguishing or even
fusing with a force historically at the disposal of the class enemy.

Over the course of the nineteenth century, an originally Bohemian
literary demonization of the bourgeoisie had metamorphosed into a
political image of an absolute class enemy, and this was further radicalized as Marxism fused with the native traditions of the Russian intelligentsia. In Schmitt's view, Fascism was the first political movement to
strike back against this demonization with an even more fearsome
image of the Bolshevik enemy as a Mongolian barbarian. In Western
Europe, Mussolini, not Lenin, was the true disciple of Sorel's theory.

This last claim is certainly true, although ironically Sorel, near the
end of his life, felt closer to Lenin than to Mussolini. Despite Sorel's

reservations, Mussolini had absorbed many of Sorel's key ideas and, in his violent, pseudo-insurrectionary rise to power, undeniably came to embody many of them. Schmitt admiringly quoted a speech delivered by Mussolini on 22 October 1922, before the March on Rome: 'We have created a myth; myth is a belief, a noble enthusiasm; it does not have to be a reality; it is an impulse and a hope, belief and courage; our myth is the Nation, the Great Nation, which we want to make into a concrete reality.'[22] Compare the tone of this speech to the one Donoso Cortes delivered in 1849: a sudden sea change had revealed the presence of a more vigorous and confident – if also more improbable – paladin of God, country and religion. From early on Schmitt was an ardent enthusiast for Mussolini, the man who had overwhelmed the menacing spectres of the social revolution in open battle.

Mussolini's March on Rome (23 October 1922) provided a powerful pole of attraction for intellectuals who were deeply dissatisfied with the nineteenth-century liberal–conservative political spectrum, yet temperamentally hostile to the Left. The Fascist movement captured Schmitt's political imagination. Not only had it saved bourgeois society, but in its violent counter-offensive it had given the state a boldly improvised, alternative configuration. For Schmitt, this electrifying show of force had generated a powerful afterimage of national liberation, a modern legitimating myth sorely lacking in the counter-revolutionary eschatology of Cortes. The whole spirit of early Fascism, with its experimental fusion of avant-garde and classical styles, made a lasting impression on him.

But Schmitt's enthusiasm for Fascism did not prevent him from expressing certain reservations about the consequences of conceiving of politics exclusively in terms of battle myths. First, he was never really enthusiastic about insurgent violence, always preferring the security provided by the state's territorial monopoly of it. Secondly, it seemed unlikely that radical nationalisms on their own could re-create a viable European interstate order. While Schmitt had decided to flirt with irrationalist solutions to the theoretical problems he had raised, he concluded the book by acknowledging the dangers of this path: 'Certainly the danger of this kind of irrationality is great ... as the remaining bases of co-operation might be destroyed in a pluralism of an unforeseeable number of myths.'[23]

What were Schmitt's politics when this book was written? Although he came from a background in which the Centre Party defined one's whole political outlook, his writings from this period reveal a deep desire for a more inspiring kind of politics. In 1925, almost two years after it was first published, Richard Thoma, a prominent legal scholar, wrote a review of *Die geistesgeschichtliche Lage des heutigen Parlamentarismus* in which he claimed that Schmitt's criticisms of liberalism barely concealed a political preference for a military dictatorship aligned with the Catholic Church.[24] Schmitt vehemently protested the charge, but since he had written so sympathetically on dictatorship, counter-revolution, the Church and Fascism, it was hardly surprising that someone could conclude that he shared many of the views of Charles Maurras, leader of Action Française, and very open advocate of a military government backed by the Church. Although Thoma's comments tersely condensed the cumulative impression which his writings might have generated, Schmitt felt that the imputation of this political identity and programme was utterly unfair.[25] Perhaps this was only because by 1926 the Republic had stabilized, while in 1923 it had seemed as if its days might be numbered. But even putting this aside, there were far too many shifts of political perspective in the writings so far surveyed for any label to capture its drift, and in this sense Thoma's summary encapsulation did not do justice to the protean quality of Schmitt's political imagination. Certainly the monarchism of Action Française held no attractions for him, and the idea that a military dictatorship allied with the Catholic Church could last a day in power in Germany was simply absurd; as a matter of simple fact, he could legitimately reject Thoma's identification of his politics with those of Maurras. Despite his open sympathy for Mussolini, he did not believe it was possible for an Italian-style Fascism to come to power in an industrially developed country like Germany. At the time, Schmitt would have considered the idea of abolishing – as opposed to simply curtailing – parliament out of the realm of possibility; Mussolini himself took this step only in 1926, after a severe challenge to his authority. And while the menacing political vision of the Spanish Marquis held certain attractions for him, he was beginning to sense that it was now a historical anachronism. Carl Schmitt was drawing strands from the diverse historic programmes of the European far Right: Donoso Cortes, Charles Maurras, Benito Mussolini. In a sense, he was a *bricoleur* weaving a political programme of his own, without any fixed image of its final shape, or of its immediate application to contemporary German realities. His analysis of the crisis of parliamentary government was part of an agenda *in statu nascendi*.

But one does not have to subscribe to that agenda to recognize the plausibility of the fundamental argument of Schmitt's analysis of parliamentary government: that its viability ultimately depends upon a strong belief in the power of rational discourse. Instead of denying this, real liberals should accept it as a challenge to reinvent a public sphere in which informed discussion about the legitimacy of the distribution of power and property becomes the focal point of political life. The alternative is myth, or venality, or both.

6

Status Quo and Peace

In the preceding chapters I have laid out Schmitt's criticisms of mainstream intellectual traditions inherited from the nineteenth century, his analysis of the political nature of legal interpretation, the difficulties of institutionalizing political legitimacy in an age of mass politics, and the provisional, often conflicting, solutions he proposed to these problems. In these writings he focused primarily on the domestic front, even as he implicitly framed his themes in a comparative European context. In this chapter, I will survey a series of articles in which he analysed how these domestic problems were intertwined with the postwar crisis of the European interstate order.

A number of developments conspired to bring about the brief Indian summer of 'relative stabilization' for the Weimar Republic which began in 1924 and continued until 1928. The economic situation improved considerably as the provision of American credits through the Dawes Plan not only stabilized state finances and kept the economy turning over, but also set into motion a private-sector investment boom. Economic expansion in turn generated a rationalization of the capital stock within an emerging corporatist framework of industry-wide agreements with trade unions. This was also the period during which the international standing of the German state, after the brutal humiliations of 1923, modestly improved. In early October 1925, representatives of England, France, Germany, Italy, Belgium, Poland and Czechoslovakia met at Locarno, an event which seemed to augur a relaxation of international tensions.

The year 1925 marked a watershed in the history of the Weimar Republic. Although the Social Democrats were firmly in control of Prussia through an alliance with the Centre and Democrats, no Chancellor had come from the party since 1920, and the 1924 electoral triumph of the ultra-conservative DNVP effectively shut it out of the governing coalitions of the Reich until 1928. In 1925 the first President of the Republic, the Social Democrat Friedrich Ebert, died a year before his seven-year term was due to end. Although he was ranked among 'the November criminals' by right-wing opponents of the Republic, few could really deny that he had repeatedly been willing to hit the Left very hard to achieve stability. In an article for the *Kölnische Volkszeitung*, Schmitt praised the even-handed, mediating role Ebert had played in the years of dire crisis as he cautioned readers to vote for a candidate who would exercise the potentially immense powers of this office with an equal degree of prudence.[1] This was a far cry from the inflammatory language used by the right-wing enemies of the Republic.

While the Social Democrats were criticized for the way they had made the election a matter of 'party prestige', and the message to the reader was obviously to support the candidacy of the Centre Party leader Marx, the warning was directed to those on the right wing of the Centre who might be inclined to vote for the ultra-conservative DNVP candidate Jarres.[2] When, in the second round of voting, the choice was between the hero of old Prussia, General Hindenburg, now standing as the united candidate of the Right, and Marx, representing all those who, in one way or another, identified with the Republic, Schmitt might have stuck with the latter, if only out of habit.

As it turned out, the victorious Hindenburg did not immediately use his powers to undermine the Constitution, as many had feared; while the very fact that 'their man' was now President acted to reconcile the old Right temporarily to the Republic. An early sign that Schmitt's future would become fatefully intertwined with the Hindenburg presidency was the release in 1926 of a communiqué prepared by Otto Meissner, a state secretary in the Reich Interior Ministry and member of the President's inner circle, arguing against a bill before the Reichstag which would place limits on the use of emergency powers available under Article 48.2. This communiqué, without acknowledging Schmitt, essentially plagiarized his arguments from two years earlier.[3]

During the early years of Hindenburg's tenure, the domestic stabilization of the Republic was accompanied by a moderate improvement in its international standing. The policies associated with the DVP (National Liberal) leader and Foreign Minister Stresemann were based on the assumption that Germany needed to work within the framework of the Versailles Treaty in order eventually to receive better terms. The admission of Germany into the League of Nations, American loans, and separating the more accommodating British from the French, but with the eventual objective of a *rapprochement* with the latter – these were the key elements of Stresemann's foreign policy. The alternative preferred by the army was a more risky clandestine strategy of rearmament through co-operation with the Soviet Union, the other power held down by the Versailles system.

During these years Schmitt's relationship with the secular state became less mediated by any residual allegiances to the Church. From this point on, all his writings were quite explicit attempts to conceptualize the intertwined crisis of the German state and the European state system.[4] But while he explored both the domestic and interstate dimensions of this crisis, during this phase of so-called 'relative stability' his strongest misgivings about the status quo concerned the extremely exposed and precarious position of Germany as a sovereign state. By contrast, the business-friendly corporatist consolidation of the mid-1920s seemed to provide a functional – if, for Schmitt not entirely inspiring – framework of crisis management.

Both Schmitt's foreign and domestic policy concerns were expressed in his review of an intellectual history by Friedrich Meinecke entitled 'Zu Friedrich Meineckes *Idee der Staatsräson*' ('On Friedrich Meinecke's *The Concept of Raison d'État*'). Meinecke had traced the emergence of this doctrine from its early modern origins to the present, and – revealing the deep influence of his teacher, Ranke – equated it with the Machiavellianism of the Great Powers – that is to say, he considered it in terms of the relationship between power and morality in international relations. But in the conclusion to his book, Meinecke indicated that he no longer accepted the traditional Rankeian assumption of a pre-established harmony between might and right. Although Schmitt was full of praise for the book, he rejected the author's claim that the opposition between power and morality was the central theme in the classical texts of early modern political theory:

> Many modern historians come very close once again to justifying the perspective of the German philosophy of identity with respect to the primitive oppositions of Machiavellianism and anti-Machiavellianism, power politics and morality . . . and so affect a kind of superiority out of a constant change of standpoint, an eternal back and forth.[5]

In his view, the critical issue in the classical literature on 'raison d'état' was not the crypto-Hegelian 'tragedy' of the irreconcilability of morality and power but, rather, 'quis judicabit?' – that is, who decides when, as is always the case, all parties claim to have morality on their side, yet all parties, in so far as they can, none the less pursue power politics? He argued that abstract talk about morality in international relations had become especially problematic, because certain states now claimed for themselves the exclusive right to decide not only what was moral but, on this basis, what was legal.

The increasing difficulty of identifying clear and distinct centres of sovereign authority in the sphere of interstate relations was not simply the consequence of the victors' justice at Versailles; Schmitt saw the postwar breakdown of Westphalian interstate conventions of war and peace based on the principle of sovereignty as intertwined with the breakdown of a domestic political order in which the state had been more clearly distinguished from society. Arguing against Meinecke's generalization of the theme to include the power politics of all ages, he argued that 'Staatsräson' was the governmental metaphysics of the early modern sovereign state. The sovereign was the apex of a war and tax collection machine which had so effectively levelled even its mightiest subjects that it soon came to be conceived of as *the* all-encompassing 'status' of a political community, whence came the concept of the 'state'. The concept of the state was historically based on the existence of a public realm both distinct from and higher than the realm of private interests. According to Schmitt, the interpenetration of state and society was undermining this status of uniform compulsory subjection by promoting the development of powerful, partial societies, straddling the faltering boundary line between public and private. A dynamic and decentred political field, in which the manipulation of a spectral 'public opinion' increasingly becomes the decisive source of power, was emerging from the break-up of the remaining outposts of this classical sovereign state.

In Schmitt's opinion, this was all leading inexorably to an ever more complete fragmentation of the political world into unintegrated systems. This was a world in which the unity of the political community could be only mythically conceived, as it had lost all those qualities which had once made it – in Hegelian terms – an artifact of objective reason. The main contemporary danger was that these remnants of the state, of the rational political status, would be sucked into the vortex of party and interest politics, with catastrophic consequences. He believed that contemporary pluralist theory expressed this ongoing decentring of the state, with the facile expectation that the resulting dynamic 'self-organization of society' could go on indefinitely without erupting into civil war.

But in the midst of prosperity and domestic stabilization, civil war seemed an unlikely scenario. The uncertainty of Germany's status as a sovereign state, on the other hand, was a more intractable problem for the Weimar Constitution, as it explicitly recognized the validity of the Versailles Treaty, and thus a debilitating attenuation of the Reich's jurisdiction over its own budget and national security. Before 1923, Schmitt had not written anything about the postwar international scene, preoccupied as he was with security on the domestic front. The 1923 occupation of the Ruhr valley by French and Belgian troops was a deep shock and a formative political experience: he felt the precarious status of the Rhineland as a territory on a personal level. Whereas previously this regional identification had been the source of a mild hostility towards a Prussian-centred conception of Germany, foreign occupation gave him and many others a lesson in the concrete meaning of national sovereignty. He concluded that the punitive measures of the Versailles Treaty threatened to bring about the breakdown of traditional conventions of interstate relations by establishing a 'peace' which was increasingly difficult to separate from the state of war. This in-between condition of nameless, ongoing, low-level warfare created an exceptionally tense and dangerous international environment in which hostilities, no longer channelled into cut-and-dried instruments of settlement, were indefinitely perpetuated through international sanctions and propaganda directed at defeated, second-class states.

The Paris Peace Settlement was indeed vindictively harsh, an almost perfect example of the politics of imperialism, which Lenin had described in a work by that name. In the peace, Germany had lost 75% of its iron ore reserves, 26 per cent of its coal, 44 per cent of its pig iron and 38 per cent of its steel. Although the French were not permitted to annex the Saar valley openly, they effectively seized its mines under a League of Nations mandate. In comparison to his constitutional writings from this period, Schmitt's writings on international relations more deeply called into question the whole framework of the status quo.

At a very patriotic gathering celebrating one thousand years of Rhenish history, Schmitt gave a speech, later published as an essay entitled 'Das Rheinland als Objekt internationaler Politik' (1928),[6] in which a 'demilitarized' Rhineland was portrayed as the most striking example of the nebulous status of the sovereign state in the postwar international order. The punitive occupation of his native Rhineland triggered an authentic nationalist reaction from Schmitt, and his writings on this subject are filled with an uncharacteristic note of moral outrage. It is important to bear in mind, though, that Schmitt did not argue that the occupation was in itself morally unpardonable; the history of Franco–German conflict was too obviously a history in which military force prevailed over ethnic considerations in determining the location of the border for him to have argued along these lines with a straight face. But the attempt to legalize the postwar European status quo, criminalizing Germany's attempts to restore its status as fully sovereign state – this was an ominous novelty. Whereas in the traditional European law of war, occupation meant subjecting territories to foreign administration with the option of either annexing them or restoring them to the occupied power, the Rhineland had become a grey area, in which nominal German sovereignty was qualified by a system of indirect controls which made it difficult to determine who ultimately decided what was illegal. He argued that since outright annexation of territories inhabited by foreigners was more difficult in a modern nation-state system, it was all the more tempting for powerful states to impose extraterritorial claims on weaker states, thus avoiding the responsibilities and costs of having to govern directly what they sought to control.

The growing scope of extraterritoriality made it increasingly difficult to distinguish war from peace, because what a controlled state could perceive as the normal exercise of its sovereign power over its own territory could be interpreted by the controlling power as a violation of international treaties whose integrity had to be restored – not by war, but by 'police measures'. Schmitt offered examples which have many contemporary parallels: he pointed out that German soldiers could not enter the Rhine to suppress domestic disturbances, nor was it even possible for the government to invest in a railway line without this being considered a potential preparation for illegal hostilities. The imposition of demilitarized zones on the domestic territory of a state results in the degradation of its statehood, and the attempt to legalize a 'status quo' based on the pigeonholed sovereignty of the recently defeated did not preserve peace, but opened up new spheres of intense political conflict.

Weak states were often created and held together by the fragile international compromises of foreign powers.[7] Without any internal centre of gravity, they become geopolitical shells. The most clear-cut example of this in postwar Europe was the artificial construction of Austria, the ethnic German rump of the Habsburg Empire, forbidden under the terms of the Versailles Treaty to unify with Germany. Schmitt maintained that Germany was simply too great a concentration of power for it to be similarly deactivated by international arrangements without threatening its very existence as a state. The question was 'whether and for how long it will belong to the [ranks] of the politically existing states or whether it should degenerate into an exclusively international, "valid" complex of legal norms'.[8]

Under the terms of the peace treaty, management of German railways was taken out of the hands of the state and subjected to international supervision. The central zones of the national banking system were also taken out of the jurisdiction of the German state and given a quasi-autonomous status so that they could handle international reparations without domestic interference. In his capacity as American reparations agent, Parker Gilbert could directly influence the fiscal and monetary policies of the German state. The problem was not just that strong states wished to make the existence of weak states dependent on these arrangements but, more seriously, that a defeated people might be willing to renounce full sovereign statehood in the expectation that international law would eventually be made binding on all states.

Schmitt argued that the League of Nations was not an authentic federation of states because none of the few fully sovereign Great Powers within it would ever subject themselves fully to its authority – that is, they would never subject themselves to it to a degree equal to that expected of weaker states. His working assumption was that if law presupposed equality of legal subjects, then international law had little meaning if the political communities which were supposedly subjects of international law were in fact subject to its jurisdiction to widely varying degrees. In the realm of geopolitics, great white sharks swam alongside minnows, and in Schmitt's opinion this fundamental problem of international law could not be solved by attributing a nominal sovereignty to political communities which did not possess the real substance of sovereignty: to the minnows.

The existence of a state could never be eternally guaranteed by international convention. This made it a matter of urgency not to be one of those states sinking into a murky semi-statehood. It was important to recognize that the evolution of modern technology in warfare, communications and transportation was hollowing out the sovereignty of all but the greatest powers. As the world grew smaller, states would have to become 'bigger', more concentrated, in order to survive; peoples who sought to shirk the costs and dangers of the competition were doomed to sink into the shadows and be drawn into the orbit of one of the remaining Great Powers. In an article from 1925 entitled 'Status Quo and Peace',[9] Schmitt pointed out that France was seeking to avoid this fate by insisting on the unconditional observation of Versailles Treaty provisions. The question for him was whether Germany could secure peace by permanently retiring from the ranks of Great Powers. The policy of successive Weimar governments had been to try to ward off any further deterioration of German statehood, but also to compensate for this deterioration by promoting economic growth. Schmitt held that this risk-averse strategy ignored the fact that as a nation of sixty million in the middle of Europe, Germany was too large to be unthreatening, even if it was now too weak to be a full state, and was thus fatefully trapped in an unenviable, intermediate position.

It was a clear indication of how deep an impression the crisis in the Rhineland had made on Schmitt that by the mid-1920s he was claiming that an alliance of nationalists and Communists had to be considered as an option in the struggle against the Versailles system. Precisely such an alliance had been offered to right-wing nationalists by the Communist Radek in a speech extolling the recently executed saboteur Schlageter. Schmitt, who had hitherto depicted the 'Russians' as the main enemy of Western European civilization, was now willing to see them in an entirely different light, and his attitude towards the 'revolutionary East' would henceforth be more ambivalent than straightforwardly hostile.

Although Schmitt looked at the international scene from a German perspective, a nationalism which saw the main enemy across the Rhine was, in his view, a nineteenth-century anachronism which would condemn Europe to decline. In an essay on the League of Nations written in 1928, he grappled with the problem of how a Europe divided by nationality could be defined as a politically relevant unit, something more than a geographical entity: 'It is already difficult to identify, in the distinct projects and concepts of Europe, a convincing geographical delineation.'[10] Before posing the question of what Europe was and who belonged to it, it was first necessary to ask which power represented the main threat and obstacle to European unity. In his view this question was directly connected to the historic status of the German state, because in the absence of an overarching European order there would be no way to handle such a massive concentration of political power in the centre of Europe.

The League of Nations had a deeper significance for Schmitt as an institutional expression of the world-historical decentring of Europe, a painful relativization of its claim to be the unique stage of world history. Although he probably saw German entry into the League as a tactically sound measure, he claimed that in its existing form the League was a potentially dangerous framework not just for Germany but for Europe as a whole. The idea that by joining the League, Germany would be in a stronger position to work in concert with other European powers was simply wishful thinking. The postwar status quo was based on the fragmentation and impotence of Europe, and there were now many forces which had acquired a stake in the indefinite perpetuation of this state of affairs:

> Even in contrast to this [improbable nineteenth-century] unification of Germany, the unification of Europe would be a true miracle. If this Europe were not merely a harmless decoration, but rather a political unity, and that means a strong unity capable of action, and independent of shifting economic interests and conjunctures, it would be nothing less than a new world power.[11]

While European unity in some form would be the solution to many contemporary problems, Schmitt argued that it could not be achieved in the framework of the League of Nations, dominated as it was by the USA, a non-member, exercising massive indirect influence through a bloc of Latin American proxy states.[12]

In *Römischer Katholizismus und politische Form*, American economic power was overshadowed by Bolshevism as the existential negation of European political identity. From the mid-1920s Schmitt began to see the dawning of the American century as the most serious challenge to a divided and weakened Europe. The USA had come to occupy strategic positions within the European state system, largely because postwar Europe had become dependent on gigantic loans from American banks. While the massive influx of American loans enabled Germany to make its reparations payments, this circuit of influx and outflow created an increasingly irrational circulation of money in the world economy. These transfers also stabilized a politically untenable status quo, and created in Germany the dangerous illusion that as long as the economy was growing, radical steps to counteract the deterioration of Germany's geopolitical status would not have to be taken. Reparations and American loans locked Germany into an embryonic and highly unstable Atlantic order, which precluded overt attempts to change the domestic German status quo.[13] The contemporary denigration of politics as a sphere of coercion and conflict struck Schmitt as a particularly perverse concession to the new financial controllers. In his view, a world ruled by the invisible hand was a world of pervasive, anonymous coercion.

As a system of indirect economic control, US financial hegemony was only the most modern form of imperialism. Schmitt felt a strong aversion to what he saw as the euphemisms which concealed the power politics of a system based on the economic control of creditors over debtors. He pointed to the nominally sovereign 'banana republics' lying in the American sphere of influence, occupying a level of the world power order to which Germany, the sick man of Europe, could eventually descend. The Dawes Plan represented the declining powers of the European state in an American-dominated world market: Dawes was a private American citizen, not even an official representative of his own government, yet in order to secure an American loan he was given voting rights on the reparations commission.

Schmitt rejected what would later be called 'Atlanticism': the idea that the USA and Western Europe belonged to a common civilization, and thus shared political interests. In his view, the massive leverage which the USA had in European affairs raised a disturbing question: why were major European states willing to accept American arbitration as an inevitable and natural solution to the historical crisis of the European interstate system? As he saw it, an internal 'federal' solution to this problem contained the danger that one European state would 'federate' Europe on its own terms. While the USA was portrayed in these Weimar essays on international relations as the principal obstacle to European self-determination, Schmitt was unsure whether Britain, with its vast overseas empire, was politically a part of Europe. Only later would he come to the conclusion not only that the British Empire was definitively outside Europe, but that its destruction was the *sine qua non* of European 'self-determination'.

It would be wrong to think that Schmitt completely opposed the moderate diplomatic line of Weimar governments in this period, including the eventually successful bid for German membership of the League of Nations. One could say on his behalf that he was concerned that harsh necessity should not be deceptively presented as a great victory. Schmitt's criticisms of the postwar international legal regime did not stem from any rigid belief in the impossibility or intrinsic undesirability of a federation of European states. His claim was that any such federation had to be based on shared historical conventions of statehood which would allow member states to pool sovereignty without fear of losing the benefits of sovereign liberty.

In his various writings on the subject of international law, Schmitt sought to draw attention to how the essential interests of the Great Powers nested in the gaps, qualifications and silences of international treaties and the lofty resolutions of the League of Nations. In his assessment, the very existence of whole political communities, Germany first and foremost, depended on the ability to see through the soothing language of international conferences and read the hard political subtext. The belief that these agreements, resolutions and treaties were the fragments of a yet-to-be-realized complete international law was a utopian illusion fostered by a legal positivism which dangerously dulled the political awareness of those nations which had the most to lose.

After the end of the First World War, the concept of sovereignty became the focal point of a many-sided intellectual combat. Schmitt's writings articulated the case which was being made by German diplomats: that Germany's compliance with the international obligations imposed upon it after the war was conditional upon its rapid restoration to the status of a viable sovereign state. But his arguments were not simply rationalizations of his own government's position. They were an extension and further development of his criticisms of legal positivism. Concepts like 'state', 'sovereignty' and 'constitution' had served as points of orientation, co-ordinates of thought in the political struggles of the past four centuries. The residues of these older political meanings were in danger of being neutralized by legal positivism. Schmitt declared that these concepts needed to be re-examined and reinvented from a contemporary political perspective – that is to say, made battle-ready.

7

Rechtsstaat and Democracy

The German revolution of 1918–19 and its aftermath had placed an evasive and incomplete constitutional settlement at the centre of political life, raising issues which bypassed prewar schemes of legal interpretation. Political questions concerning the ultimate identity of the state had become unavoidable, yet answering them seemed extraordinarily difficult: the old dynastic framework centred on Hohenzollern Prussia had fallen away, yet the federalist legacy of the old regime was maintained; the Republic had emerged out of a period of worker and soldier insurgency, but assumed a more definite shape with the counter-revolutionary suppression of the revolutionary Left; in short, while the Republic was a new constitution, in many respects it was the same old state. In this context even technical issues of legal interpretation often raised highly theoretical, politically charged problems.

In 1928 Schmitt completed the longest work he would ever write: an erudite, synoptic overview of the common problems of constitutional jurisprudence and political philosophy. His was one of several works on constitutional law published in the mid 1920s, after the return to stability and before the terminal crisis of the Republic. The work of Heinrich Triepel, Gerhard Leibholz, Rudolf Smend and Hermann Heller formed a cluster of politically diverse post-positivist treatises on the Weimar Constitution which sought to adapt the legacy of the *Rechtsstaat* to novel postwar conditions.[1]

In many respects this new post-positivism represented a return to an older pre-positivist German tradition of *Staatslehre*, a comparative and empirical study of constitutions, addressing the problem of the relationship between state and society. The wide-ranging concerns of the major figures in this mid-nineteenth-century tradition – Robert von Mohl, Lorenz von Stein, and J.K. Bluntschi – had been eclipsed in the 1870s by new positivism, which was thought to have elevated the study of public law to the status of a proper academic discipline by eliminating now discomfiting political problems from the field. The impulse to evasion was encouraged by the lack of clarity on the most basic matter of principle: the ultimate locus of sovereignty. On the one hand the Germany of Wilhelm II was a national state deriving its legitimacy from the people; on the other it was a federation of dynasties led by the Prussian king. The prewar hegemony of legal positivism was based, in Schmitt's view, on an unwillingness to explore the consequences of this theoretically inchoate construction.

Even before the war, the hegemony of legal positivism was beginning to fray around the edges. The grand isolation of academic jurisprudence was increasingly criticized as untenable in the face of new sociological perspectives on the relationship between law and society. Georg Jellinek's *Allgemeine Staatslehre* had attempted to take cognizance of these neglected dimensions by advocating a dualistic approach: the state was simultaneously a system of legal norms and a factual social order, joined at the point of legislation, but separate for purposes of analysis. Both the major positivist and post-positivist legal theorists of the Weimar period rejected this attempt at disciplinary diplomacy, and pulled further away from each other by developing either more austerely normative or more straightforwardly political-sociological approaches.

While the founders of modern legal positivism, Laband and Gerber, had been, under the monarchy, Conservative and National Liberal in outlook, the principal representatives of legal positivism during the Weimar Republic – Gerhard Anschütz, Richard Thoma, and Hans Kelsen – were supporters of the Republic, with positions on the political spectrum from centre to the left of centre. This shift illustrates the deep affinities between legal positivism and the status quo, resulting from a tendency to foreclose discussion on the origins and legitimacy of the entire political–legal system as a non-juristic problem. But while the Constitution of the old monarchy had been overwhelmingly taken for granted in the legal community as the fixed frame of political life, a large majority of that community viewed the new Republic with hostility and suspicion. The few who embraced it sought to defend its legitimacy. This was the context in which a post-positivist literature flourished, exploring political and sociological dimensions of the Weimar Constitution, critically evaluating it as an institutional framework dependent upon ongoing political decisions, compromises and interpretations.

This post-positivist literature was politically diverse: the focus on legitimacy could have a pro- or anti-Republican slant. The common assumption was that the Constitution could not be seen as an insulated system of legal norms, because it was a framework open at nodal points to the conflicts and compromises within an always problematic, but ever present, national community. Rudolf Smend argued that the key to constitutional interpretation was the process of 'nation formation' – that is, conservative integration around shared values. Hermann Heller, one of a handful of left-wing professors in Germany, put forward a more explicitly democratic conception of the Constitution, arguing that legal reasoning had to follow the grain of political–institutional power relations sanctioned by the victory of the principle of popular sovereignty. Although they were perhaps not as brilliant or erudite as Schmitt's, Heller's criticisms of the conservative biases lurking in supposedly neutral legal language were often more far-reaching.

One of the central terminological inheritances of nineteenth-century legal thought was the distinction between material laws, which contained a binding general norm, and so-called formal laws, which were all other acts of the legislature – including those which supposedly contained no such norm, like the annual parliamentary budget assessment. Laband had used this distinction in the aftermath of Bismarck's successful confrontation with the Prussian parliament to argue that executive violation of the parliamentary budget allocation did not contravene a material law, and was therefore not, strictly speaking, a legal matter. An older pre-positivist tradition of jurisprudence had justified this distinction by attributing to material laws the substantive characteristics of impartial generality and duration, to distinguish them from particular and provisional, formal laws, which were measures supposedly containing no legal rule. Although Laband and most positivists after him discarded these substantive criteria, they continued, with the exception of Kelsen, to fall back on the distinction between material and merely formal laws. While Schmitt criticized what he considered Laband's sophistic attempt to have his cake and eat it too, he also sought to maintain the distinction, and the limitations on legislative power which it entailed, by returning to the pre-positivist substantive justification.

Heller rejected the distinction between material and formal laws altogether as the anachronistic legacy of the prewar, semi-parliamentary monarchy in which parliament's legislative prerogative was tightly confined to the protection of persons and property against the arbitrary encroachments of the state. In Heller's view, all legal acts, statutes, ordinances and contracts had a normative content in that they were ultimately authorized or concretized by the legislative power.[2] The explicitly parliamentary-democratic nature of the Weimar Constitution merely made it more obvious that there was no logical distinction between material and formal laws – that is to say, unless the Constitution explicitly forbade it, all legislative statutes generated binding norms. Ingeborg Mauss succinctly identifies the procedural nature of this parliamentary-democratic conception of law with a formulation which makes it easier to grasp the anti-parliamentary thrust of Schmitt's attempt to distinguish laws from measures on the basis of the substantive criteria of generality and duration: 'Positive law is therefore legitimate not because it corresponds to substantive principles of justice but, rather, because it is enacted in a procedure, which according to its structure is just, that is democratic.'[3]

Schmitt held that such a purely procedural conception of democracy could provide no limits to what could be done in the name of the people. He pointed out that Rousseau himself had recognized that financial matters could play no role in a true democracy which, by necessity, concerned itself only with general laws affecting the community 'equally', thereby disqualifying uncompensated expropriation, or even perhaps measures distinguishing different classes of citizens for the purpose of determining fiscal burdens. The limits of popular sovereignty implied by Rousseau and made explicit by later parliamentary theory were those entailed by a natural law, later a liberal conception of property rights. *Juste-milieu* parliamentary liberalism had been based on the assumption that representation came with paying property taxes. The fact that the majority of people who owned no property were now in a position to impose burdens on the minority who did was the central problem of modern democracy. The solution, according to Schmitt, was to reconstruct limits to popular sovereignty when liberal institutions based on an older conception of the limits of government were being undermined by the State's growing involvement in the national economy.

The problematic relationship between democracy and the *Rechtsstaat* was the focus of Schmitt's work on constitutional law. *Verfassungslehre* is the synthesis of his reflections on the fate of the European *Rechtsstaat*, now in its autumnal moment:

> The realization of the liberal programme, if it had been won in 1848, would have been a brilliant victory; in 1919, as it fell without a struggle into our lap as the harvest of collapse, it had come too late. That is a further reason for that feeling of emptiness, that lack of enthusiasm, which one feels towards the Constitution today.[4]

All along the political spectrum, the legacy of national defeat and civil war diminished the lustre of the new republican Constitution. But its fate was not determined only by these extraordinarily adverse external circumstances: those who drafted the Constitution left many fundamental issues undecided because of the urgency of constituting a standing government. As a result, instead of a strong and recognizable political vision, large parts of the Constitution seemed to reflect interparty compromises hammered out in order to achieve some minimum political consensus. Schmitt sought to distil a more politically determinate, internally consistent constitution out of this ramshackle charter by playing certain points off against others.

The materials assembled in *Verfassungslehre* were drawn in large part from lectures, without a transparent organizational principle. In trying to bring its sprawling mass into focus, it is necessary to pose more sharply the questions which the various sections of the book are addressing. All the fundamental questions at the beginning concern the essential nature of a constitution. What is a constitution? How does it express and regulate the structural relationship between state and society? To what degree and from what perspective can it be conceptualized as a closed system? Schmitt believed that the very different answers given to these questions reflect deep, partially incommensurable, assumptions about the nature of law.

He began by identifying an 'absolute' conception of the constitution. Absolute conceptions of a constitution are those in which the political community is completely identified with a particular constitution, which cannot be significantly altered without dissolving that political community. The realist version of this 'absolute' conception is captured by a famous passage from Aristotle's *Politics*, where he poses the question of how we are to know whether a polis is still the same polis or has become a different one. Aristotle answers by identifying a people with its constitution, arguing that it is the constitution which defines the identity of the people – that is to say, the people has no politically relevant existence outside the constitution which defines who is a citizen: 'Since the polis is an association of citizens in a constitution, when the constitution of the citizens changes and becomes different in kind, the state also does. ... If this is right, it would seem that the criterion of continuity or continued identity ought to be the constitution rather than the race [people].'[5] In this sense of the term, a constitution is not a written charter. Even the 'fundamental laws' of medieval and early modern Europe, like the Magna Carta, presupposed an already existing legitimate political power and an already existing distribution of proprietary rights, while attempting to regulate and limit specific aspects of the relationship between the two. Dieter Grimm argues that even early modern and Enlightenment social contract theorists used the word 'constitution' in this older sense, and conceived of the social contract as a standard of legitimation for an already existing political community, not as the foundational law of a new one. By contrast, the idea that a written constitution is the legitimating foundation of state power, the comprehensive script specifying the origin, mode of operation and limits of a state power to which all citizens are uniformly subject, is a more modern idea of bourgeois revolutionary origins.[6]

Schmitt believed that Kelsen's pure theory of law highlighted one of the disturbing consequences which flowed from this modern, purely normative conception of the constitution: the distinction between private and public law loses its justification, because terms like 'state' and 'property' cease to refer to any legally relevant realities prior to or outside the system of generating derivative legal norms from basic norms. Substantive limits to what the legislative power can legally create or abolish then become exceedingly difficult to establish. In Schmitt's view, Kelsen was the last in the line of the epigones of a once great tradition of bourgeois legal and political thought, which now openly acknowledged the arbitrary and purely formal nature of its own criteria of validity:

> In its epoch of greatness, the seventeenth and eighteenth centuries, the bourgeoisie had the energy to establish real systems, namely the laws of reason and nature. It formed out of concepts like private property and personal freedom, norms which were self-validating, which were valid before and above any political entity, because they were right and rational and contained, without regard to the existing, positive-legal reality, an authentic ideal. That was consequential normativity; here one could speak of system, order and unity. With Kelsen, by contrast, only positive norms are valid, that is, only those which really exist; they are valid not because they should rightfully be valid but, rather, without regard to qualities like rationality and justice, simply because they are positive. At this point ideality and normativity break off, and in their place appears the raw tautology of facticity; something validates when it is valid because it is valid. That is positivism.[7]

Jurisprudence is, by any definition, the interpretation of legal norms and the relationships between them. This is not what separated Kelsen from Schmitt. The issue is what is involved in interpretation. Schmitt argued that the hardest cases of legal interpretation involve the problem of the legitimacy of a law, and sometimes even the authority of those who enact and administer it. In such situations, simply referring to what the law says will not suffice, because the most difficult problems of justification cannot be addressed within the language of legal rules. Even if it is true that the dull force of habit largely suffices during periods of normality to secure subjects' obedience to state power, he was not living in such a period:

> There are two critical points in the life of power when habit does not suffice. The first is at its birth, when habits of obedience have not formed. The other comes when the customary ways and limits of power are altered, when subjects are presented with new and disturbing uses of power, and are asked to assume new burdens and accept new claims. At these two points . . . theory must be called in to buttress and justify obedience.[8]

The recurrence of the problem of legitimacy prevents the rules of the legal system from ever becoming a fully self-enclosed game. Because Kelsen's theory was concerned exclusively with the technical validity of legal judgements, it could not adequately address the problem of the political conditions behind the obligation to obey legal commands, and how these conditions are present as background assumptions in the entire legal process. Interpretations of fundamental provisions of a constitution involve assumptions about the relationship between political authority and subjects' rights and, as such, are irreducibly political. Schmitt thought that a 'pure theory of law' which claimed to eliminate politics from the interpretation of the constitution in fact simply eliminated all consideration of the essentially political, interpretative mediations which are always involved in conceiving of a constitution as the legal–institutional map of a concrete state.

For Schmitt, the implausibility of Kelsen's construction was particularly evident when he addressed the problem of how one could account for the origins of a constitution without referring to an extra-legal political agent, the constituent power behind the constitution. Kelsen offered an ingenious solution to this problem by transmuting even this legally ungrounded constitution-founding act into the form of a legal norm. According to Kelsen, this ultimate norm, which he called the Basic Law, defines the highest source of legislation, the starting point in the generation of norms:

> This presupposition for law, this starting point, this originary norm, which I also term constitution in the juridico-logical sense, since it sets in place the 'highest' organs of the state, the highest sources of law, has the function throughout of a fundamental hypothesis. When it was maintained above that the whole legal order is 'derived' from it, this naturally cannot be so understood as though all positive statements of law were presupposed to be a priori already determined in content. The hypothetical originary norm is only the highest rule of production.[9]

Kelsen conceded that because the generation of the Basic Law, the *non plus ultra* of the legal system, could not itself have been authorized by a norm, strictly speaking it was not really a positive law at all, but a 'hypothetical' or 'presupposed' norm. Although no positive law authorized this original legislative agency, for Kelsen the legitimacy of this foundational 'enabling' act concerned problems outside the field of jurisprudence altogether.[10] He thus all but acknowledged that the underlying premiss of his whole construction was a useful theoretical fiction.

Schmitt found it impossible to accept the idea that a hypothetical norm 'generates' a constitution. He held that it was a simple matter of logic to realize that a norm was not an agent. A constitution has to have a foundation in a political will which has to pre-exist it: this presumption of anteriority is made in order to justify the establishment, interpretation and alteration of the constitution. The problem involved in his rejection of the purely normative approach can be better understood from H.L.A. Hart's discussion of the Basic Law as an ultimate rule of recognition:

> Even if it were enacted by statute, this would not reduce it to the level of a statute; for the legal status of such an enactment would depend on the fact that the rule existed antecedently and independently of the enactment. . . . This aspect of things extracts from some a cry of despair: how can we show that the fundamental provisions of a constitution which are really called law are really law? Others reply with the insistence that at the base of the legal system is something which is 'not law', which is 'pre-legal', 'meta-legal' or is just 'political fact'. The uneasiness is a sure sign that the categories used for the description of this most important feature in any system of law are too crude.[11]

Schmitt claimed that it was deeply misleading to attribute the process by which the constitution was established to a legal norm. Examined closely, this process reveals 'meta-legal' dimensions of a legal system, posing problems of political legitimacy, not simply formal legality.

According to Schmitt, these meta-legal dimensions become relevant in determining what in a constitution could be changed, even by legally specified channels, without undermining its coherence. If there is no limit to what the legislative power within the constitution can change, then it follows that every provision of the constitution could be altered by the very procedure the constitution specifies. At a certain point this would not be the 'same' constitution, unless a constitution is nothing but that provision which specifies how the laws can be changed in any way a qualified majority of the legislature wishes. Article 76 of the Weimar Constitution specified the ways in which it could be changed. Schmitt argued that 'change' could not mean 'replace'.

Legal positivism, he argued, provides no answer to one of the fundamental questions of constitutional jurisprudence: how open can a constitution be to legislative alteration, given that this legislative power is authorized by the constitution itself? Kelsen's presupposed Basic Law is simply too indeterminate to provide any solution to this problem, and simply displaces the question of who decides.

Schmitt argued that if a distinction was not made between an 'institutional minimum' – that is, the non-transformable core – and more secondary provisions in the constitution, then every statement in the constitution would carry the same weight – for example, 'the German Reich is a Republic' has just as much, or just as little, value as a provision protecting the pay level of state officials. The most important problem in the basic rights section of the Weimar Constitution was the potential incompatibility of provisions guaranteeing private property with those promising to socialize the means of production in some unspecified future. The written script of the Constitution did not make it clear whether the state was a *Rechtsstaat* or some kind of *Sozialstaat*, and this could not be answered by simply examining isolated, individual provisions.

The question then is whose interpretation of a constitution is authoritative in a political system in which the people are supposedly sovereign. Schmitt believed that the 'unlimited' power of the sovereign people can never be fully identified with the limited legislative power of those bodies within the constitution authorized to represent the people. He was insistent that the constitution could not be altered by the legislative power which the constitution itself establishes. While 'the people', as the ultimate sovereign power, cannot be bound to any form of government, and is free to decide which it will have, 'the people' as *represented* by the legislative power is bound to the constitution-founding manifestation of its sovereign will. Although Schmitt did not say so, this is the real meaning of Rousseau's otherwise enigmatic claim that the General Will cannot be represented. Only the people as a 'whole' – that is, the General Will – can change the constitutional law.

But how has any progress over the 'relativist' position been made, if all modern constitutions are taken to be artifacts of the essentially arbitrary will of the people? The implication is that since political revolutions are rare, these founding collective decisions for a particular constitutional form provide something like a 'relatively' absolute frame of interpretation, since in this view the people are bound to a constitution until they collectively decide to replace it.

If a purely 'relative' conception of a constitution was then incompatible with the very idea of a constitution, in Schmitt's opinion an 'absolute' conception of the constitution as a seamless system of norms failed to represent the role a constitution plays in a modern democracy: 'With the belief in codification and systematic unity, so too the purely normative conception of the constitution falls away, as it is conceived in the liberal idea of an absolute *Rechtsstaat*.'[12] Rousseau's theory of the General Will expresses a fundamental truth about the nature of political legitimacy in a modern democracy: the will of the people is anterior to any constitution; therefore no constitution can be considered the definitive form of this popular will. This is because the existence and intrinsic legitimating authority of the people is partially outside any written scheme of constitutional norms. It is instructive to ponder on Schmitt's image of the role of the people, as the imputed constituent power of a modern democracy:

> In many remarks by Sieyès, the '*pouvoir constituant*' appears in its relation to the '*pouvoir constitué*' in the form of a metaphysical analogy to the '*natura naturans*' in its relation to the '*natura naturata*' in Spinoza's theory: an inexhaustible, primordial source of all forms, itself never identical to any one form, eternally producing new forms out of itself, formless generator of all forms.[13]

The meaning of this passage is very similar to De Tocqueville's description of the fundamental idiom of American political life: 'The people reign over the American political world like God over the universe. It is the beginning and end of everything, everything springs from it and everything leads back to it.'[14]

Schmitt thought that without a clear elaboration of the consequences of popular sovereignty – how it is expressed in any given written constitution, and which branch of government can make the best claim to be acting in its name, and thus claim the right to interpret it – a constitution would provide little indication of how it should be interpreted. If this irreducibly political dimension of constitutional interpretation is always ignored, it will eventually become impossible for a constitution to function as the deep script of government, because the improvisational activity of state institutions would continually place the relevance of the constitution in question. In a modern work on problems of German constitutional law, Dieter Grimm argues that this is a problem which has not gone away:

> Once the Constitution no longer succeeds in bringing all public authorities into its regulatory framework, one must also expect that it will no longer cover every state action. Whether a different understanding of the Constitution can absorb this loss of validity, or whether the Constitution will atrophy into a partial system, remains an open question at this point.[15]

Schmitt argued in *Verfassungslehre* that there was a different understanding of the constitution which was in the best position to address this problem. He called his alternative to both 'absolutism' and 'relativism' the 'positive' concept of the constitution. He called it 'positive' not because it was positivist, but because it was the opposite of 'natural', or 'unwritten': not only did a modern constitution need to be written (even if the written words could not fully express the political meaning of the constitution in all circumstances) but it was also the product of human will, not based on natural law. He described a modern constitution as something which arises out of a 'collective decision over the nature and form of a political community'; the active – or at least imputed – subject of a modern constitution is always the people: 'The constitution is to this extent nothing absolute, as it does not emerge out of itself. It is valid not by virtue of its systematic closure. It does not "give" itself, but is "given" by a concrete political entity.'[16]

While the whole people obviously does not literally 'collectively decide' to reject an old constitution and adopt a new one, it is an established convention in the modern world that a provisional constitutional assembly can legitimately claim to be acting in the name of the people. This was not true prior to the French Revolution. While he was opposed to a completely 'relativist' conception of the constitution in which qualified legislative majorities could change anything, on the same grounds Schmitt was also opposed to those who claimed that a constitution could not be replaced, except by its own legal channels. In his opinion, this was precisely how a constitution should *not* change.

A problem which constitutional theory had to confront during the Weimar Republic was how to conceptualize the constitution as a totality, without making such revolutionary transitions seem as if they were taking place in a void between two self-enclosed totalities. Without some conception of the continuity provided by a transitional constituent power, any change of government could create the dangerous impression of a constitutional *tabula rasa*. The problem was the legal status of a social order based on private property: had the matrix of private property rights been established 'out of nothing' by the new constitutional legislator, or was it an irrevocable limit on the legislator? Was it possible even to allude to rights anterior to positive law without invoking the spectre of natural law?

According to Schmitt, the Weimar Constitution contained many interpretative ambiguities, because the coalition of parties which framed the document sought to avoid clear decisions on divisive points. But it did not entirely lack in principle: on the fundamental point, the alternative between socialism and a bourgeois *Rechtsstaat*, he argued that the constitutional settlement of 1919 was clearly for the latter:

> The decision had to fall for the previous social status quo, that is, for the preservation of the bourgeois social order . . . because the other decision, a social revolution carried to its final consequences in the manner of the Soviet revolution, was explicitly rejected even by the Majority Social Democrats.[17]

Schmitt wanted to capture in freeze-frame this moment of decision, when something like a collective will made a brief shimmering appearance: the suggestion was that in thinking about issues involving the relationship between democracy and the *Rechtsstaat* in the Weimar Constitution, a jurist should keep this picture in mind. Indeed, the tension running through Schmitt's constitutional theory emerges from a never fully accomplished reconciliation of these two antithetical principles: unattenuated popular sovereignty and an inviolable bourgeois social order.

Schmitt claimed that if the constitution was to be coherently interpreted, it had to be interpreted as the organizational script of a bourgeois *Rechtsstaat*. Because the term *Rechtsstaat* indicated only the way in which power over free, private subjects was exercised – through laws – and not who exercised it, it was compatible with diverse forms of government, not just purely parliamentary systems. The *Rechtsstaat* was the part of the constitution that protected the basic rights of individuals, and was thus always connected to a second part which regulated the organization of public power. But the problem was that in a democratic age it was entirely possible that a legislature based on universal suffrage could chip away at the rules of property and contract which regulate the intercourse of bourgeois society.

The background presence of this social order was no longer transparent through the words of the constitutional text: unlike older bourgeois constitutions, its first part did not just place under its protection the basic individual freedoms of property, contract, movement, domicile, press and assembly; it added to these a heterogeneous assortment of provisions protecting a whole new class of rights. Reflecting interparty compromises among Socialists, Catholics and the conservative Nationalists, this assortment included provisions which protected the interests of organized labour, the major churches, and the tenure of public officials. Schmitt felt that this re-emergence of collective or corporate rights within the state was one of the most disturbing developments in modern politics. Unlike Friedrich von Hayek, however, he did not believe that it was possible to return to the age of the night watchman state. The boundary between the political and the economic could no longer be determined by the norms of nineteenth-century liberalism, and Schmitt was becoming more comfortable with the idea that the state had to take a strong directive role in supplementing and correcting the invisible hand.

Schmitt was not attached to the inner principles of the bourgeois social order for purely bourgeois reasons. A follower of Hobbes in this respect, he was not principally concerned with the protection of individual titles to property: 'Private property can certainly be considered as something prior to the state, a natural right before any social order, but also as merely a legal establishment.'[18] His criticisms of the Weimar Constitution therefore came from two different directions: he wanted to limit parliament to passing general laws in conformity with the inner principles of a bourgeois social order, but the problem was that the part of the Constitution which did place limits on parliament, apart from articulating these principles, also ensconced the privileges of 'corporate interest groups' which could, on this basis, defend their privileges as guaranteed rights. Trade unions were recognized by Articles 159 and 165 of the Constitution, legally protecting their entrenched position on social insurance boards, arbitration boards, the National Economic Council, and so on. Article 165 guaranteed collective bargaining rights and established guidelines for the 'socialization' of industry; Article 152 guaranteed social insurance. And all these constitutional protections were uniquely exempt from being suspended during an emergency.[19]

Schmitt argued that the modern state, as opposed to pre-modern political communities consisting of status groups with irrevocable privi-

leges, brings about the destruction or subordination of these intermediate institutions, and thus a much more direct relationship to the
individual, who then becomes subject to a more uniform state-made
law. Recognizing this indissoluble link between the state's monopoly of
legal violence and the individual as a subject of uniform law, he was
consistently hostile to both left- and right-wing corporatism, pluralism
and 'association theory'. This does not mean that he embraced the
liberal ideal of *laissez-faire*; he valued the private individual not as
the opposite of state power, but as its necessary complement:

> The true basic right presupposes the individual with his, in principle,
> unlimited sphere of freedom. An institution cannot be presupposed as given
> in such a way. The modern state is a closed political unit and, by its nature,
> *the status*, that is, a total status relativizing within itself all other statuses.[20]

The two parts of a bourgeois *Rechtsstaat* – the part which organized
state power and the part which placed limits upon state power – were
coming unhinged in modern democracies, and soon after *Verfassungslehre* was published, Schmitt would start slowly moving to the conclusion
that the solution could not be found in the traditions of the *Rechtsstaat*.
But in this work he limited himself to criticizing the proposed solutions
of an earlier generation of German National Liberals, for whom far-
reaching reforms were needed to reconcile the 'people' to a nation-
state governed by bourgeois notables. But Schmitt's definition of the
'people' was indicative of how much more severe he perceived the
problem of integration to be:

> The 'people' in the special meaning of the word includes all those who are
> not distinguished and different, all the unprivileged, all those who do not
> stand out through property, social position, or education (thus Schopen-
> hauer says: 'Whoever does not understand Latin belongs to the people'). In
> the French Revolution of the year 1789, the bourgeoisie, as the Third Estate,
> could identify itself with the Nation; thus the bourgeoisie was the people,
> because it stood in opposition to the aristocracy and the privileged. Sieyès
> posed the famous question 'What is the Third Estate?', and gave the answer
> that it was the Nation; the Third Estate was nothing and shall become
> everything. But as soon as the bourgeoisie itself appears as a class dominating
> the state, distinguished by property and education, the negation wanders
> away. Now the proletariat becomes the people, because it is the bearer of
> this negativity. It is the part of the population which does not own, which
> does not have a share in the produced surplus-value, and finds no place in
> the existing order. . . . Democracy turns into proletarian democracy, and
> replaces the liberalism of the propertied and educated bourgeoisie.[21]

Liberals like Max Weber, Friedrich Neumann and Hugo Preuss had
thought that the social question would lose its revolutionary significance as soon as the working classes were allowed to defend their

collective interests as fully enfranchised citizens. Weber advocated parliamentary rule in the last year of the monarchy by arguing that it was simply a technical procedure from which a higher calibre of political leaders could emerge to mobilize the masses. In Schmitt's opinion, none of these liberals fully realized the degree to which the parliamentary ideal depended on the existence of an educated, rather genteel, public sphere:

> Only much later in the twentieth century, as one forgot the actual struggle, could one say in Germany, of parliament, that it was a matter of a practical rule in the game. For the French and German bourgeoisie of the period from 1815 to 1870, it involved something other than a rule in a game, or other consciously relativistic methods. . . . Among the later German liberals, who are also indiscriminately characterized as democrats – Friedrich Neumann, Max Weber and Hugo Preuss – the idea that the working class must be incorporated into the state is in part decisive; here the specific liberal bourgeois integration method, parliament, is transferred on to a new class without understanding the ideal structure of parliament, which is essentially determined from the characteristics of education and property.[22]

Although it struck him as a flawed solution to a real problem, Schmitt offered no alternative to parliamentary government here.[23] But the moderation was proportionate to the perceived danger. The threat to the *Rechtsstaat* posed by democracy, while it was substantial enough to occasion troubled afterthoughts, seems less serious here than it did in *Die geistesgeschichtliche Lage des heutigen Parlamentarismus*. In *Verfassungslehre* 'the people' were no longer the threatening insurgent mass which Lukács and Sorel had made them out to be; in fact, on the eve of the terminal crisis of the Weimar Republic, 'the people' seemed to be losing some of that theological and mythical stature they had possessed in earlier works. Although support for the Weimar Republic was thin and uneven, by the mid 1920s some of the worst problems of integration seemed to be over. Popular sovereignty seemed to be becoming what it should be in a stabilized constitutional democracy: an all-pervasive idiom of political life, a formless source of legitimating acclamation. A sovereign people, leaving the social–property relations of old Europe unmolested; this was Schmitt's idea of democracy.

8

The Crisis of Political Reason

Although the mid 1920s constituted a period of impressive intellectual achievement for Schmitt, he was finding the atmosphere in sleepy Bonn less than bracing. Adding to his dissatisfaction were the rumours surrounding the humiliating matter of his failed annulment and excommunication, which in a small city were difficult to ignore. From 1925 he branched out of Bonn and began to enter an intellectual network whose centre was in Berlin.

The material which went into the first 1927 edition of *Der Begriff des Politischen* ('The Concept of the Political') was based on ideas developed in 1925–26 for seminars in the new field of political science. Although one could attend a seminar on the subject in Berlin, elsewhere in Germany they were rare, and in Bonn, Schmitt was the only one to offer them. Indeed, few professors of law in Germany had such wide interdisciplinary interests in the social sciences. In 1923 excerpts from *Politische Theologie* had been published in a volume dedicated to the memory of Max Weber and his work, and this was no incidental publishing encounter. Earlier, while he was in Munich, Schmitt had attended Weber's seminars, and his ongoing engagement with Weber's views on capitalism, bureaucracy, law and world religion subsequently drew him deeper into the emerging network of German academic sociology.[1] From at least 1926 he was in contact with the Berlin Hochschule für Politik, one of the many academic institutions outside of established university system, where he was encouraged to expand on ideas far beyond the horizons of mainstream jurisprudence. As a broadly pro-Republican institution, the Hochschule was unique in the world of German higher education. Throughout the Weimar Years, the academic establishment and student body was overwhelmingly hostile to the Republic from the Right. It is revealing that Schmitt had no direct contacts with the Hochschule für Politik's right-wing counterpart – also in Berlin – the Politisches Kolleg, an institute then subsidized by the media tycoon and DNVP kingpin Alfred Hugenberg.[2] It was at a conference held at the Hochschule in May 1927 that Schmitt gave a series of lectures, the texts of which were published later that year by the *Journal for Social Research* as *Der Begriff des Politischen*. It is indicative of his unusual position on the map of Weimar intellectual life that Schmitt, although clearly a man of the Right, published in a journal in which liberals and even Marxists set the agenda.[3] In a country and at a time in which intellectuals of Left or Right almost never followed intellectual developments at the other end of the spectrum, Schmitt was conspicuously different.[4] This intellectual networking culminated in his membership from 1928 of the German Sociological Association, through which he came into contact with Karl Mannheim. Despite his political distance from it, it is even possible that he became acquainted with some of the projects of the so-called Frankfurt School.[5] His most gifted student at Bonn, Otto Kirchheimer, later became attached to this School, and even in exile was considered one of its peripheral members. The young Walter Benjamin sent Schmitt a copy of the manuscript of *The Origins of German Tragic Drama* in 1930, with a note acknowledging his intellectual debt:

> You will quickly notice how much the book in its presentation of the seventeenth-century doctrine of sovereignty owes to you. Perhaps I could say in passing that I have also inferred from your later [sic] work, above all *Die Diktatur*, a confirmation of the research approach of my philosophy of art through your philosophy of state.[6]

The attempted synthesis towards which Schmitt thought he might have been moving in the research which went into *Verfassungslehre* never came off. The relative stability of the period was perhaps too fragile to encourage any push towards theoretical closure. Polemical intensity on the subject of Germany's status as a sovereign state jostled with a tacit, moderating acknowledgement of the tenuous stabilization of the state on the domestic front. But these semi-compartmentalized perspectives began to enter into a more dynamic relationship as Schmitt wrote *Der Begriff des Politischen*.[7] Over the next five years he became increasingly convinced that the interpenetration of interstate and domestic arenas of conflict taking place in contemporary Europe was creating a new, decentred political system whose emerging boundaries and rules could not be grasped by classical state-centred political theories. He was coming to the conclusion that in such a field all attempts to delineate some ultimate subject of politics would be confounded. This shifting away from a more state-centred perspective can be detected in the alterations which were introduced with successive new editions. In the first edition (1927), Schmitt implied that authentic, 'high politics' was something which took place only between states, not within them; in subsequent editions, however, traces of this implication were progressively erased.[8]

The first line of the book is a curious and provocative formulation: 'The concept of the state presupposes the concept of the political.'[9]

What did Schmitt mean by 'presuppose'? The argument he seems to have been making is that conflict is a primordial condition which gives meaning to the word 'political', and that order, the state, is secondary – perhaps because order arises out of this primordial condition of conflict without ever fully suppressing it. This formulation was challenged on etymological grounds by Leo Strauss, who pointed out that the Greek word closest in meaning to 'state' is 'polis', and it is from 'polis' that the term 'political' has come to us:[10] in this respect, 'the concept of the political' does not seem to be distinguishable enough from 'the concept of the state' to be its presupposition.

But in Schmitt's lexicon the word 'state' was not a generic term for political community, and certainly not equivalent to 'polis'. Although in this work he often used the term 'state' interchangeably with other terms for political community, it is important to bear in mind when we are interpreting that enigmatic first line that 'state' originally meant a specific 'status' of political relations – a condition approaching a territorial monopoly of legitimate violence. The claim that the concept of the state presupposes the concept of the political cryptically expressed a point which had already been made on other occasions: the classical European state of early modern origin was losing this monopoly of legitimate violence, and thus could no longer be the unproblematic, natural centre of the political universe.

To accommodate these new realities, Schmitt defined the state more loosely in this work, as a territorially enclosed community, membership within which is overriding in all critical situations of conflict. But Schmitt's objective was to define not the state but 'the political'. He argued that in contrast with the availability of a number of suitable definitions of the state, there has never been a clear, non-circular definition of the political: while the state is defined as a particular type of political organization, the political is usually defined as action seeking to influence the state. The problem with this definitional circularity was that it falsely implied that 'social' action is apolitical. He argued that the equation of the political with state-related affairs becomes more evidently incorrect when the advent of mass democracy results in the interpenetration of state and society. Under these conditions the definition of the political becomes more problematic, because the boundaries of the political become far more elastic. An untrammelled, unruly democracy had recently arrived, and all those affairs which nineteenth-century liberalism had confined to the sphere of civil society were now becoming sites of intense political conflict:

> The equation the state = the political becomes to the same degree incorrect and deceptive where state and society interpenetrate one another, where all previously state affairs become social, and where all 'purely' social issues

involve the state, as necessarily occurs in a democratically organized common-wealth. Then previously 'neutral' domains – religion, culture, education, economy – cease to be neutral in the sense of being non-state-related and non-political. As a polemical counter-concept to such neutralizations and depoliticizations of important domains there appears the total state, no longer disinterested in any affair, potentially encompassing all domains, based on the identity of state and society.[11]

Schmitt's reference to the 'total state' in the 1932 edition carried unmistakably negative connotations attached to the embryonic Euro-pean welfare state. But his attitude to the welfare state comes across in an earlier quotation from Jacob Burckhardt:

[Democracy] blurs the boundary between state and society, and expects from the state everything which society probably will not do, but wanting to keep everything up for discussion and in a state of mobility, finally vindicates for particular castes a special right to work and subsistence.[12]

But the reasons for Schmitt's hostility to the welfare state were different from Burckhardt's. He did not subscribe to the conservative–liberal view that the state should confine itself to protecting property and culture. In fact, until very much later in his life, there is no evidence to suggest that he was plagued by reactionary fears of 'levelling'. In Schmitt's view the polycratic, corporatist, welfare state threatened the existence of the state as a higher power standing above society, or even as a neutral power standing impartially between the major social classes. The German state in particular was progressively losing its statehood, as political parties and organized groups divided it up among them-selves in ongoing, precarious settlements. It could be said, then, that for Schmitt, the welfare state was the negation, not of the market, but of the state itself.

While in earlier works the Revolution appeared as the main problem of modern European politics, from the mid 1920s to the end of the Weimar Republic, Schmitt increasingly came to see the bigger problem in the less catastrophic but equally disturbing prospect of an endless, unprincipled, social war of position. The corporatist politics of interest groups naturally gravitated towards risk-averse, unprincipled compro-mises. The attempt to avoid difficult decisions which might disrupt the pluralist, polycratic system of compromises required that the power to govern effectively be kept at a minimum, precisely so that it could not be used to disrupt a delicate status quo. This was the real meaning of 'pluralism': a political system without a centre, drifting towards cata-strophe. Schmitt thought that it was a cruel irony of the times that this system of evading hard decisions gave rise to the dangerous illusion – among those who were not willing to confront the risks and uncertainties of breaking with the status quo – that politics could be rendered superfluous.

It could be said, then, that there are two lines of attack running through *Der Begriff des Politischen*: against the hyperpoliticization which was undermining the centrality of the state by making 'everything' potentially political; and against the resulting drop in the level of political life which stemmed from the very same cause and had thoroughly adulterated politics with the language of moral platitudes, electoral campaigning and litigation. As a polemical contrast to the mundane and mendacious politics of the status quo, Schmitt defined 'high politics' as politics stripped of deceptive, rationalizing ideology, where the fundamental battle lines of an age stood exposed, and people divided accordingly: 'The heights of great politics are at the same time the moments in which the enemy is seen in concrete clarity as an enemy.'[13] Schmitt wrote *Der Begriff des Politischen* because he believed that the twentieth-century crisis of the state might be clearing the way for the reinvention of classical political virtues.

Schmitt's conception of 'high politics' captures certain aspects of his relationship to Machiavelli, who is mentioned only occasionally in this book, but whose spirit pervades it. To avoid misunderstanding, it should be said that it was not Machiavelli's specific recommendations which appealed to him but, rather, a distinctive style of writing on political subjects. The following passage on *The Prince* from an essay on Machiavelli is probably one of the most profound things ever said about the book and its author:

> But this short essay, the actual cause of his fame, has little that is spectacular. It has little of that which has made other thinkers famous: neither the depth and nobility of the Platonic dialogues, nor the systematic erudition of Aristotle's books. It is not a great document of the political transformation of the religious spirit, like the *Civitas Dei* of Saint Augustine. It has nothing sensational or brilliant, also nothing pedantically profound, no new political theory and no new philosophy of history. It is condemned as especially immoral because of some lines on the political necessity of breaking treaties and pretending to be pious. But even this 'immorality' does not flaunt itself and does not make itself morally significant. It remains modest and objective, having nothing enthusiastic or prophetic like the immoralism of Nietzsche. . . . The literary naturalness is only an expression of an unconcealed interest in the subject with which this man sees political things politically without moralistic but also without immoralistic pathos.[14]

Schmitt thought that in order to strip away the veil of ideology from political conflict in this 'Machiavellian' spirit, it was first necessary to determine 'a criterion' specific to the political. To this end he proposed that each *sphere* of human judgement and action has an opposition specific to it: good and evil in morality; beautiful and ugly in aesthetics;

profit and loss in economics. Again, he put forward another provocative formulation, easily misinterpreted: the criterial opposition which defines the political is the opposition between friend and enemy.[15] He stressed repeatedly that the political 'friend and enemy' were not private adversaries, but political communities whose very existence posed a potential threat to other political communities. He was not the originator of this conception of politics. In Book One of Plato's *The Laws*, a similar view is expressed in a far more extreme form in the speech delivered by Clinias, the Cretan oligarch, who explains why the original Cretan legislator had sought to make his city such a harsh and warlike polity:

> Clinias: He meant, I believe, to reprove the folly of mankind who refuse to understand that they are all engaged in a continuous, lifelong warfare against all cities whatsoever. . . . In fact the peace of which most men talk – so he held – is no more than a name; in real fact the normal attitude of a city to all other cities is one of undeclared warfare.[16]

The very un-Platonic idea that moral and aesthetic judgements cannot help us to distinguish correctly between political friend and enemy seems to be one of the main ideas in *Der Begriff des Politischen*. Perhaps Schmitt believed that a *differentia specifica* could also delimit the boundaries of the disciplinary field of a new political science. Anyhow, it was in the context of attempting to establish the 'autonomy' of this new discipline that Schmitt developed a criterion by which the political could be distinguished from other spheres of 'cultural life'. But subsequent editions of the book suggest that he was ambivalent about this supposedly central idea of the 'autonomy' of the political. In the first edition he claimed that the introduction of criteria from the aesthetic and moral spheres into the political infringed on the autonomy of the political, and clouded the purity of a purely political perspective on 'friend and enemy'.[17] In later editions he tended to argue that any conflict can become political if it reaches the point of intensity at which individuals are grouped into friends and enemies. The political was not so much an autonomous *sphere* of action and judgement as a *process* of intensification moving towards an extreme case of conflict.[18]

The implications of this claim are theoretically significant. Schmitt held that political conflicts over interests transform the very content of these interests, as they are polemically formulated and reformulated in struggle with an enemy whose own interests come to be seen as the negation of one's own. Collective interests are forged and have a mobilizing power only in a particular context of opposition. Political identities like 'proletariat' and 'bourgeoisie' are not simply roles in an economic system based on wage labour, but opposing solidarities forged in a series of historic battles. The escalation of a conflict beyond a certain level of intensity generates new clusters of claims and counter-claims which acquire an increasingly complex, sometimes even tenu-ous, relationship to the pre-escalation interests of the contending parties. Experiences of life-and-death struggles, even when they are vicarious and imagined, crystallize into stereotyped, opposed and dis-tinct 'ways of life', generating zones of contention which cease to be explicable in terms of a simple conflict of interests. This does not mean that the clash of interests has ceased to be the focal point of such contentions, only that in such contexts, interest itself becomes a more plastic and multidimensional reality which is grasped by the contending forces through the 'existential' categories of friend and enemy. Schmitt believed that such dialectical transformations of perspective and cat-egory were not specific to class conflicts, but occurred in any conflict as it approached this point of total opposition. However remote this extreme point of life-and-death struggle is from the actual conduct of politics, it is what gives a struggle its urgency, mobilizing power and pathos of commitment.

Of course, many who wrote before Schmitt had seen politics as a spiralling process of ever more intense enmity between friend and enemy. Without theoretically foregrounding it, Thucydides' account of the Peloponnesian War is a dramatic representation of a similar vision of politics:

> Thucydides' conception of *Staatsräson* entails an autocatalytic process in which the foundations of power will be used up and destroyed through its defence, the reason for having power more or less turning against itself. . . . Regardless, moralizing objections against power and its use concern, at most, the intentions of actors, not the intention-diverting-and-reversing course of events. And Thucydides' account is directed precisely at this reversal of intentions in the course of their realization.[19]

Schmitt saw politics in a similar light: as a process of intensification which often spills over into a danger zone where the security of the status quo is abandoned in pursuit of the highest stakes. But because there really were things worth pursuing to the end, he thought that this process had to be evaluated on its own terms, and should not be subject to moralizing objections. It was not that morality was irrelevant in politics, but since there had probably never been a conflict in which the belligerents did not believe that right was on their side, he argued that the attempt to justify killing people in the name of 'humanity', or other universal moral norms, generated a murderous self-righteousness. He claimed that, by contrast, there was an ethic to 'high politics', politics stripped of self-righteous moralizing, in which the enemy was treated not as a criminal to be punished, but simply as an enemy to be overcome.

This was indeed a minimal ethic: not love your neighbour, but respect your enemy.

The only thing which confers the right to dispose over the lives of other men is a threat to one's own existence; this is what Schmitt meant when he said that the 'decision' which distinguishes between friend and enemy is existential, and cannot be determined by moral or even utilitarian criteria: 'No programme, no ideal, no norm and no expediency confers a right to dispose over the physical life of other men.'[20] The enemy is the other, the stranger, with whom there is the real possibility of a violent struggle to the death. There is no particular difference in kind which gives rise to this existential threat. In fact, from a non-partisan perspective, the differences which distinguish the bitterest enemies can often seem inconsequential. But what constitutes an existential danger to one's own form of life can be judged only by the participants in a potential conflict, because it is they who have experienced the challenge of the enemy. The specifically political perspective which informs this judgement emerges out of a first-hand encounter with the enemy. Schmitt was not arguing here that those who had not been in the trenches had no business talking about war, because they had not 'experienced' close-quarters combat. The political moment in this scenario is not even the military side of this conflict, but the potentially groundless, high-stakes decision as to whether a particular group of men are to be considered friends or enemies.

Schmitt claimed that the logic of these decisions cannot be grasped from a non-partisan perspective. The point he was making was directed at those who, failing to understand the irreducibly partisan, emergent dynamics of such scenarios, see the causes of major political events in the small tricks and mistakes of individuals. Lenin, he said, understood that such people must be decisively refuted. In retrospect it often seems that wars and revolutions were avoidable, but this is only because the parallelogram of forces, in which the battle lines of an age took shape, has been deactivated. The projects of contending political groups then come to be seen as 'irrational'. Schmitt would say that such judgements, even if they are not always false, fail to take into account the fact that the partisan perspective structures the entire field of vision in complex systems of strategic action, and this is a perspective which is often lost to the impartial, or retrospective, observer.

Despite all that is compelling in this analysis, its seemingly lucid form concealed deep conceptual antinomies. Schmitt conceded that if the enemy represents a threat to one's own form of life, he will probably also be portrayed as evil and ugly, because this intensifies the opposition. But if the political is this very process of intensification, then the introduction of the moral and the aesthetic must be seen not as an adulteration of the political – that is, as an infringement on its 'autonomy' – but as an inevitable moment. He wanted to avoid this conclusion, as it seemed to compromise the autonomy, and the ethic, of 'high politics'. But to avoid defining the political as just any process of intensification heading towards a violent settling of accounts, he had to change course and introduce a limit to this process.[21] This limit was then presented as part of the definition of the political. In the 1932 edition of the book he argued that to portray the enemy as morally evil, as the so-called just war doctrine does, intensifies the impulse to annihilate him, and that precisely this limitless intensification takes the struggle out of the realm of the political altogether. This happens because the enemy, by being totally morally disqualified, is no longer recognized as a legitimate form of life.

Schmitt was responding to what he considered the most irritating of the criticisms which followed the initial publication of *Der Begriff des Politischen*: that he had advocated annihilating one's political enemies. He had been accused of holding this view by a former friend and now bitter enemy, the legal theorist Hermann Heller. In response, he made it clear that analysing and advocating are two different things:

> Whoever struggles against an absolute enemy – whether this is a class, or a race, or some timeless, eternal enemy – is not anyhow interested in our concern for the criteria of the political; on the contrary, he sees therein a danger to his immediate fighting power, a weakening through reflection, and a suspicious relativization.[22]

In a much later work, he claimed that the virtue of this concept of the enemy lay precisely in its formal nature: 'In this reciprocal recognition of recognition lies the greatness of the concept. It is little suited for a mass age of pseudo-theological enemy myths. The theologians are inclined to define the enemy that must be annihilated. I, however, am a jurist, not a theologian.'[23] Thus the political was no longer identified with the sheer intensification of the struggle against an enemy, but with the limit which keeps this intensification within bounds, a reciprocity in which the enemy is recognized as legitimate, and respected as an enemy – that is to say, not just in his harmless, non-political status as a fellow human being. But through this qualification Schmitt ended up describing the process of intensification of conflict both as a flight into the realm of the political towards the extremes of the friend–enemy opposition, *and* as a flight forward *out of the political* moving along the very same path of intensification.

It is also not clear whether Schmitt thought that the political was inherently part of the human condition. If it was, then it is not clear why he thought that he had to affirm its value against the current of contemporary prejudice. It should now be obvious that what was in danger was not politics in the mundane sense of the word, but 'high politics', politics without illusions and fear of the unknown – Schmitt felt that in the absence of life-and-death struggles, and the challenge of an enemy to one's own form of existence, life would come to revolve around empty diversions and entertainments. Many of these real and apparent inconsistencies in Schmitt's argument stem from the fact that his conception of the political could not clearly distinguish between different levels of the political – most fundamentally, high and low – because in the process of intensification they all lay on a continuum.

But if there are different gradations of politics, and the only politics which deserves affirmation is 'high politics', what sort of friend–enemy oppositions can form at this highest level, and what sort cannot? Although Schmitt began *Der Begriff des Politischen* by claiming that the concept of the political must be defined apart from a definition of the state, he often surreptitiously reintroduced the state as the natural subject of political life. He suggested that only secondary political oppositions can emerge *within* states – that is, by implication, between classes and political parties. In fact, much of what is conventionally thought of as politics is not political at all in Schmitt's conception but pantomimes of real political struggles – intrigues, schemes, and competitions involving no serious stakes.

Although the formal nature of the concept of the political did not allow for domestic conflicts to be analytically disqualified as a site of potential friend–enemy oppositions, Schmitt, in a rather revealing footnote, mentioned Plato's claim that war is something which takes place only between natural enemies, Hellenes and barbarians; while civil war is chaos and corruption. In a later edition of *Der Begriff des Politischen*, published in 1933, Schmitt articulated the problem more explicitly: '[It] remains open whether in such [domestic] oppositions a merely 'agonal' competition that affirms the common unity is present, or whether the beginnings of a genuine friend–enemy opposition that negates the political unity – that is, a latent civil war – is already at hand.'[24] Schmitt believed – but did not say – that the friend–enemy opposition of class-struggle politics had opened up a division that was antithetical to a more natural, 'classical' schema in which human beings were divided into separate, hierarchically organized political communities.

There were two, equally compelling modern conceptions of the fundamental axis of political division: one which saw history as the history of class struggles; and another which saw nation-states as the subjects of all world-historical conflict. Although Schmitt was closer to the latter conception, he never dismissed the plausibility of the former, and much of the intellectual power of this book emerges from the movement between these two visions of friend and enemy. In his view, the question of which of these two conceptions was the politically decisive one could be determined only historically. Referring ironically to the predictions of prewar syndicalism, Schmitt suggested that the workers' movement had had a tougher time dealing with the state than it anticipated:

> As one realized the great political significance of the economic associations and noticed in particular the growth of the unions, against whose economic means of power, the strike, the laws of the state were seemingly powerless, it was claimed, somewhat prematurely, that the state was dead.[25]

Although the jury was still out, he believed that there were signs that the verdict would be against the class-struggle theory of history. If the international socialist movement had been strong enough to prevent a war detrimental to its interests, then class membership would have proved decisive, and membership in states secondary. In 1914, with the outbreak of the First World War, this is, of course, precisely what did not happen. It is understandable, then, that Ernst Niekisch could describe *Der Begriff des Politischen* as 'the bourgeois answer to the Marxist theory of class struggle'.[26]

This opposition of class and nation provides the context for understanding Schmitt's claim that all great political theories presuppose that man is evil. In *Politische Theologie* he had argued that this was the presupposition of a nineteenth-century counter-revolutionary tradition in which the masses were thought to embody the evil – that is to say, revolutionary – impulses of a corrupt species. In *Der Begriff des Politischen* the meaning of this claim takes on a whole new significance as a theologically conceived, revolutionary evil was replaced by what he called an anthropological conception of evil, in which man is a dangerous and dynamic being. In striking contrast to the earlier work, Schmitt's sympathies now clearly lay with 'evil' in this morally neutral, anthropological sense. In fact, Schmitt was explicit in criticizing his earlier heroes:

> The relationship of political theories to theological dogmas of sin, which is conspicuous in Bossuet, De Maistre, Bonald, Donoso Cortes and F.J. Stahl . . . can be explained by the relationship of necessary conceptual preconditions. . . . But the theological support often confuses the political concepts because it usually pushes the distinction into moral theology . . . frequently dulling the awareness of existential oppositions.[27]

The classical representative of political evil in the anthropological sense, was, of course, Machiavelli, and Schmitt compared his realism favourably to the theological speculations of the counter-revolutionary masters. In a footnote he quoted a passage from Dilthey which explores the qualified sense in which Machiavelli saw politics as the by-product of human evil:

According to Machiavelli, man is not naturally evil. Many lines seem to say
this . . . but what he wants above all to say is that man has an irresistible
inclination to slide over from the passions into evil, if nothing holds him
back: animality, drives, affects, above all fear and love, are the core of human
nature. He is exhaustive in his psychological observations on the play of
affects. . . . Out of this basic trait of our human nature, he derives the
fundamental law of all political life.[28]

In correspondence with Schmitt, Leo Strauss recognized the political
consequences of this shift in the meaning of 'evil': while the opposite
of 'evil' in *Politische Theologie* was 'authority', its opposite in this work
was something like 'pacifism', or 'humanitarianism'.[29] Again, Schmitt's
sympathies were now clearly with 'evil' in this latter sense. Machiavelli
had a contemporary significance for Schmitt, then, because his wicked
amorality could be a powerful elixir for a weakened and demoralized
nation:

In reality Machiavelli was on the defensive, as was his fatherland Italy, which
was exposed to invasions in the sixteenth century from the Germans, the
French, the Spanish and the Turks. The situation of the ideological defence
repeated itself at the beginning of the nineteenth century during the
Revolutionary and Napoleonic invasions of the French. At that time Fichte
and Hegel restored Machiavelli's honour, as it was then a matter of the
German people defending itself against an expansionist enemy with a
humanitarian ideology.[30]

There was a final ambivalence, which indicated the author's own
political disorientation in the face of so many intersecting and diverging sites of conflict, expressed in the very formula of the political as
the opposition between friend and enemy. Many of the political
dynamics pitting friend against enemy resemble the dialectic of self
and other as a struggle for recognition ending in lordship and servi-
tude. Despite this resemblance, Schmitt's concept of the political subtly
reworks the terms of the Hegelian struggle for recognition. For Hegel,
this dialectic arises out of two colliding perspectives – the self and the
other. But the opposition between friend and enemy cannot fully
overlap with the latter, for the obvious reason that even if the other
can be the enemy, one cannot sensibly refer to oneself as a 'friend'.
But if the friend is not the 'I', who is the 'I' – that is to say, from whose
perspective are there friends and enemies, and what is their relationship to me, if 'I' am neither? Only once, in a private notebook after
the war, did Schmitt make this distinction clear:

Germans were in general previously only able to distinguish between 'I' and
'not-I', not, however, between friend and enemy; the consequence of this
was that they confused every 'not-I' with the enemy, and then, as they
recognized the madness of this, believed that with an embrace of the entire

world everything was brought back to order. . . . But the 'I' is not the friend, nor is the 'not-I' the enemy. It is not a matter of phenomenology; it is a matter of accumulations of power in which one must assert oneself.[31]

But just as there are no 'natural' political agents for this theory, there is, for this very reason, no fixed perspective from which friends are to be distinguished from enemies. The determination of friend and enemy can be made only from the perspective of a *third* figure whose identity and orientation are never specified. One potential implication of Schmitt's own definition is that the most penetrating perspective on political conflict would be that of the one who sees both friends and enemies from a certain distance. According to Derrida, what ultimately lay behind Schmitt's fascination with the political was a fear of the political, a fear of concealed enemies:

> Where the principal enemy, the 'structuring' enemy, seems nowhere to be found, where it ceases to be identifiable and thus reliable – that is, where the same phobia projects a mobile multiplicity of potential, interchangeable, metonymic enemies, in secret alliance with one another: conjuration.[32]

The sense that this was a problem which could be mastered only in a world of transparent concepts and political forms emerges in a passage from Schmitt's postwar notebooks:

> Franz Kafka could have written a novel: the Enemy. Then it would have become clear that the indeterminacy of the enemy evokes anxiety (there is no other kind of anxiety, and it is the essence of angst to sense an indeterminate enemy; by contrast, it is a matter of reason (and in this sense of high politics) to determine who is the enemy (which is always the same as self-determination), and with this determination, the anxiety stops and at most fear remains.[33]

These oscillations and ambivalences are not simply logical inconsistencies: they express the breakdown of the familiar co-ordinates of political action and identification of a state-centred political world. Unable to integrate his disconnected insights and judgements into a unified theoretical framework, Schmitt opted for a jagged and fragmentary clarity over a smooth and featureless system. Many years later he reflected on why a contemporary attempt to define a 'concept of the political' could not assume the systematic form of a classical political treatise:

> The age of systems is past. As the epoch of European statehood began its great ascendancy three hundred years ago, majestic conceptual systems arose. Today it is not possible to build like that. . . . [The] other, alternative possibility would be the leap into aphorism. As a jurist, this is impossible for me. In the dilemma between system and aphorism there remains only one way out: to keep the phenomenon in view and to probe the criteria of what

are always novel questions thrown up by what are always novel, volatile situations.[34]

The political field which Schmitt was trying to conceptualize was the product of the cracking open of the European state system in which friend–enemy oppositions could, by and large, be contained in the sphere of interstate relations, and regulated there through diplomatic and military convention. The League of Nations and the Versailles Treaty were attempts to institutionalize the increasingly nebulous status of the sovereign state in international affairs. For Schmitt, the existence of the state, as a particular form of political organization, was dependent on its independence which, in concrete terms, meant its right to decide on matters of war and peace in its relations with other states. But this *jus belli* as the criterion of full statehood was moving out of the reach of many states, and Schmitt was determined that Germany should not sink permanently below this level: 'Each of the innumerable changes and transformations of human history ... has brought forth new forms and dimensions of political association, annihilating earlier political structures, calling forth foreign and civil wars, suddenly increasing or decreasing the number of organized political units.'[35]

Although Schmitt sensed that Europe was now experiencing an epochal transformation, a weeding out of historical anachronisms, he believed that the essential legacy of the classic European state needed to be reinvented in an age of modern warfare and economics, even if there would be far fewer full states to inherit this legacy. At the very moment when what was needed was a stronger and more concentrated form of state power, German defeat and postwar deadlock had generated the complacent expectation that as long as the economy performed well, no bold and disruptive courses of action were necessary. The diminishing power of the state over increasingly independent domestic centres of power was intertwined with the diminishing power of the state within a world economy whose centre was shifting across the Atlantic. This emerging American-centred world economy increasingly bypassed the German state, establishing a complex system of indirect controls over an economy honeycombed with extraterritorial jurisdictions. In Schmitt's view, this system of controls was all the more dangerous for being indirect and seemingly devoid of any coherent programme to charge directly. The slow, paralysing extension of the power of an American-dominated world economy was changing the very language of European politics: as the state lost its monopoly of political decision, 'domination and power became at the spiritual pole propaganda and mass suggestion, and at the economic pole, control'.[36] He did not believe that a world in which states were powerless in the face of the world market would be a world at peace. In his opinion,

Benjamin Constant, the grandfather of continental liberalism, had drawn the real historical lesson from Napoleon's defeat at the hands of the English which, for Constant, had represented the historical victory of commerce over military conquest: 'In earlier times, warlike people subjugated commercial people; today it is the converse.'[37]

Carl Schmitt saw awesome new concentrations of politically unorganized power taking shape in the interstices of an old Eurocentric world order based on the sovereignty of its Great Powers and a customary division between public and private spheres. The world war and its aftermath had scrambled the distribution of power between social strata, nations, and even continents. Schmitt experienced this historical moment as a transitional period in which everything he valued would collapse, fade away, or be reborn through sovereign affirmations of the political.

9

The Elites: Between Pluralism and Fascism

By 1927 Schmitt was so tired of Bonn that he was already making arrangements for a position elsewhere. Moving to another university was common enough at the time, but moving as he did to one of the newly established, less prestigious Handelshochschulen (Schools of Business Administration) – was rare indeed. The fact that he did so suggests that he was very far from being a parvenu obsessed with rank, as is often insinuated. Certainly he suffered from the scandal of a failed annulment, but it would be an exaggeration to say that he had been socially ruined. Why, then, did he leave? For some time Moritz Bonn had offered to bring Schmitt to the Handelshochschule, hoping that Berlin's intellectual life would entice him. He had spent his first two years at college in Berlin, and although he had thereafter professed to disdain its abrasive, big-city ways, this was probably little more than the resentment of a provincial awkwardly concealing his fascination. In adulthood some of this fascination remained, but intellectually sublimated as an interest in seeing the nation's political elites at close quarters, and gaining insights into power which were not always forthcoming from academic research. In spring 1928 he made the move to Berlin, bringing with him the completed manuscripts of *Der Begriff des Politischen* and *Verfassungslehre.*

In the years 1929 to 1933 Schmitt attributed some of the central problems in European domestic and interstate politics to the crisis of elites. The passive and confused retreat of older elites in the face of the dynamics of mass politics revealed a deeper cultural paralysis. Schmitt, like many of his contemporaries, was responding to a pervasive conviction that the once solid and familiar world of social distinction based on property, titles and education was melting away. Although traditional outposts of authority continued to exist, there was no longer any hegemonic project binding them together. But he considered the desire to restore the 'good old days' of the prewar Prusso–German monarchy an irritating distraction. The inability of European elites to move beyond nineteenth-century modes of political thought and organization had left political systems without any directive centre, and vulnerable to the awesome centrifugal forces of modern party politics.

In 1927, when he was still in the process of moving, Schmitt spoke in Berlin at an event in honour of the Catholic literary editor Carl Muth, before a group consisting of many people he knew from Bonn. He spoke of how the Spaniard Donoso Cortes had come to hate this citadel of Northern hubris, the seat of power of a state experiencing an inexplicable ascendancy.[1] The point he wished to convey to his audience was that Cortes was unable to fathom the Prussian capital and its political destiny because it could not be reconciled to his static, backward-looking vision of Europe. Whatever subtle barriers of background and temperament had previously kept Schmitt from fathoming it himself, these he was now determined to surmount. Much later, after the war, he would express his feeling of hostility and fascination towards Europe's most powerful city: 'For forty years a strong current repeatedly tossed me out of western Germany towards Berlin and held me there, against all my inclinations and instincts, against all plans and intentions.'[2]

A position at the Handelshochschule, however, did not give the sort of direct access to governing circles that came with a comparable position at the Friedrich Wilhelm University of Berlin, since it was separated from the university and the whole government quarter by the Spree river.[3] It is symptomatic of the relationship between state and university in the new Republic that Hugo Preuss, chief architect of the Weimar Constitution, had not been offered a position by the more prestigious university. Schmitt's new position as Hugo Preuss Professor of Constitutional Law at the Handelshochschule placed him among those whose ideas had gone into the making of the Weimar Constitution. There was no perverse irony in the choice of Schmitt to fill this position if one considers that Preuss had often been his ally in earlier controversies over the interpretation of Article 48. Although Schmitt had argued that classical liberal institutions and values were playing an ever smaller role in contemporary political life, the fact that he was offered the Preuss Chair demonstrates that he was thought to be, in his own way, a supporter of the Republic.

The Handelshochschule, directly opposite the stock exchange, was located away from the city's fortresses of political power. Those who attended seminars there were not university students, but business and civil-service types.[4] There were fifty students at Schmitt's first lecture and twenty-five in his seminar, with no enrolled university students. Although such people leaned to the Right, the Hochschule had a reputation for being an institution with many Jews, and this probably kept away the most determined opponents of the Republic. In this new environment Schmitt came into regular contact with the world of modern big business. Previously he had been somewhat distant from the contending classes of modern economic life, and whatever anxieties he had about an unruly proletariat were never before connected to any overt identification with the cause of their employers. In a memorable line from *Römischer Katholizismus und politische Form*, he had claimed that both Lenin and Rathenau shared the dream of an electrified earth. But being at the Handelshochschule transformed a budding intuitive understanding of the legal problems of post-*laissez-faire* capitalism into a more concrete, policy-orientated perspective: 'In any modern state, the relationship of the state to the economy constitutes the essential object of the directly relevant questions of domestic politics. They can no longer be answered with the old liberal principle of absolute non-intervention.'[5] Economics was now directly in his field of vision. Over the next few years he would supplement his income with fees from lectures to business organizations, on what he now considered a politically critical subject.

Schmitt was also well connected in other sectors of Berlin. Upon his arrival he could count upon the assistance of Hugo am Zehnhoff, Centre Party delegate and former Justice Minister to expedite the process of getting settled.[6] He chose an apartment in a fashionable neighbourhood just north of the exclusive Tiergarten quarter, allowing him and his Serbian wife numerous opportunities for strategic socializing.[7] But it was his association with Johannes Popitz which really brought him closer to the world of this elite society. Popitz, highly esteemed in the Reich Finance Ministry for his technical expertise, had been promoted to the highest rank of the career civil service, permanent state secretary, at a relatively early age. He was also a gifted scholar with a powerful grasp of the historical transformation taking place in the structure of state finances, a subject he could discuss on an almost philosophical level.[8] Schmitt had approached him very respectfully while he was still a lecturer at the Handelshochschule, and the two, despite the initial difference in social rank, quickly became friends. Because Popitz was also an honorary professor at Berlin University, this friendship provided an opportunity for Schmitt to extend his rapidly expanding network into this citadel. This friendship was in equal proportions an intellectual partnership and a political apprenticeship. Even much later, Schmitt expressed a sincere gratitude to this man, who seemed to him to embody an older Hegelian ideal of the philosophically trained bureaucrat as the ruling type: 'Three years later, I experienced through Johannes Popitz a further introduction into the Prussian state, Prussian administration and Prussian style, which proved essential not only for my status and vocation as a professor of public law but also for my education as a human being.'[9] Although Popitz invited Schmitt into an elite world of political clubs, and Schmitt would later act as an important insider source of information for Popitz after his 1929 resignation from the Finance Ministry,

Popitz kept Schmitt at a certain distance, never inviting him into the inner circles. Vague but real barriers of social rank and confession intervened to keep alive the feeling of being a liminal figure amid 'the elite'.

Through his contacts at the Reich Interior Ministry, Schmitt attended the proceedings of extremely exclusive gatherings, organized along the lines of English clubs, whose overlapping memberships constituted a dense strategic network of elite opinion-formation in the city.[10] He participated in discussions at the Gentlemen's Club, occasionally published in its journal, *Ring*, and generally became something of an intellectual celebrity. 'Ring' was one of a number of so-called 'conservative revolutionary' journals. Although this is a rather vague label, 'conservative revolutionary' is generally used to describe all those who sought the intellectual refurbishment of a conservatism which had become moribund after losing its prewar hegemony. This was the collective sentiment of a nebulously defined generation, and those who met at the Gentlemen's Club saw themselves as leading a 'young conservative' movement. These were people who sought to replace 'the rule of parties' with a state dominated by the constituency of the Gentlemen's Club.[11] But although they were instinctually authoritarian, they did not prioritize the old conservative programme of a Hohenzollern restoration; they expressed their intellectual distance from old conservative, Christian-national jargon by transvaluing it a little with fashionable references to Nietzsche and their recently deceased house philosopher, Moeller van den Bruck.

Another conservative revolutionary journal to which Schmitt contributed in these years was *Europäische Revue*, edited by Prince Karl Anton von Rohan, a scion of one of Austria's oldest noble families. This journal was less directly connected to Berlin's insider network, but it could claim to be more highbrow and European than *Ring*. In its pages, Bolshevism and Fascism were often discussed as responses to the postwar crisis of cultural values.[12] Essays on the theme of cultural crisis by writers like Hugo von Hofsmannsthal and Ernst Curtius gave the journal its high literary standard. Most of Rohan's editorials portrayed the major problems of European culture as stemming from a crisis of elites. In this respect, his outlook was not altogether unlike that of one of the journal's occasional contributors, José Ortega y Gasset. But while Ortega y Gasset identified liberalism with the spirit of aristocracy, Rohan saw it as more vigorously embodied in the idealistic paramilitarism which had sprouted up all over Europe, and now needed only to be purged of its violent plebeianism to come into its own.

Schmitt was also on good terms with the editors of *Deutsches Volkstum*, who shared his taste for a politics garnished with biblical references. This publication was owned by a Christian-social professional union with headquarters in Hamburg. In 1931 it bought up the offices of *Ring* after this journal had experienced a split, making it a national publishing powerhouse of the Right. True to the philosophy of its founder, Adolf Stoecker, the union did not admit Jews, women or Marxists as members, and the journal was governed in a similar spirit. Its editor, Wilhelm Stapel – once a student of Friedrich Naumann and Clemens Brentano – later distinguished himself as a class war hero in the Hamburg *Freikorps*: 'Stapel's political philosophy was a blend of Christianity, extreme nationalism, an abiding concern for social problems, and virulent anti-Semitism, which, curiously enough, was matched only by his contempt for the National Socialists.'[13]

Stapel and his colleague A.E. Günther, later a friend of Schmitt, argued for the restoration of the prewar monarchy in dramatically theological terms. This language of restoration came naturally to middle classes of the Evangelical faith, because the establishment of the Republic had destroyed the more privileged position it had enjoyed under the old regime.[14] The Christian-social Stapel was the spokesman of this authoritarian Evangelical nationalism, and regarded the prominence in the Republic of Catholics and the Centre Party with displeasure. Although Schmitt was always pleased to have his writings reviewed respectfully, and now no longer found support in mainstream German Catholicism, he could never, for both intellectual and political reasons, go in for a programme so tinged with the old 'anti-Roman affect'. While Catholics sometimes wrote for the journal, they were often people like Othmar Spann, whose neo-Thomist, German Romantic, corporatist – later Austro-Fascist – viewpoint represented many of the things Schmitt disliked most in German Catholicism.[15]

In fact, Schmitt kept his distance from all points in this constellation of new conservatism, just as he had kept his distance from the Catholic literati in 'Abendland' while he was at Bonn. He never joined the Gentlemen's Club, even though he had received a personal invitation from Prince Albrecht von Hohenzollern as early as 1926,[16] and at no point in his life did he have a good word to say about the canonized saint of this circle, Moeller van den Bruck; until 1929 he had diffidently resisted pressure from Rohan to contribute anything to the *Europäische Revue*, and was always somewhat cool towards its conception of a European cultural elite; when he was introduced to Stapel in 1932, he referred to Luther as 'a fat man who liked to drink beer and crack dirty jokes'.[17]

What were Schmitt's reservations about these so-called conservative revolutionary circles? Perhaps he could not get over the feeling that there was something unserious and make-believe in all their talk about 'spiritual renewal', 'Christian metaphysical foundations' and 'the authentically German idea of the state'. One word seemed to capture the intellectual nerve centre of this inchoate milieu: 'restoration', the leitmotiv of German Romanticism, and the always farcical agenda of reactionary Don Quixotes. As far back as *Politische Theologie* Schmitt had claimed that Cortes was a significant figure in the history of political thought mainly because he was the first counter-revolutionary theorist to abandon the project of restoration. In 1925 von Hofmannsthal had defined 'the concept of a creative restoration' as the core of the whole conservative revolutionary imagination in the following, typically extravagant terms:

> Behind the doings of the prophets of decline, and the Bacchanalians of chaos, the chauvinists and the cosmopolitans, the worshippers of the moment and the worshippers of appearance, in the great, momentous background of European affairs, I see a few individuals dispersed through the nations who count themselves connected to a great concept: the concept of a creative restoration.[18]

When Curtius – who knew Schmitt, and had taken strong exception to his earlier evaluation of Adam Müller – wrote a piece paying tribute to the recently deceased von Hofmannsthal, he did so very much with Schmitt in mind. Characterizing Hofsmannsthal as representative of a Restoration tradition of thought, he went on to claim that 'the Restoration as a common Western European development, as the sustenance of conservative thought, as a political and cultural ideology, must be separated from the phenomenon of Romanticism. Anyone who would like to dismiss it as "Romantic" does so only because they are compelled to reject it out of instinct and interest.'[19]

We have already noted that Schmitt's hostility to Romanticism bordered on open intellectual antipathy to the intellectual traditions of German conservatism. That is not to say that he was completely outside this 'conservative revolutionary' constellation. The point is that despite personal points of contact, he appraised the amorphous cultural resentments of this milieu from an often considerable distance. In a much later work he offered a historical diagnosis of this 'conservative revolution' which underscores his perception of it as a generational wave of politically unfocused resentments:

> In Germany, since 1900, since the beginning of the inner protests[20] against official Germany, numerous trends, currents, movements, groups, circles, and associations arose. They all in some way contributed to the success of the great mass movement which fell into Hitler's hands. They were all in some way incorporated. But they were too deep, or too vague, or too manifold, or too cantankerous, to have [given rise] to a coherent conceptual structure.[21]

The postwar paralysis of elites and the sudden, shocking devaluation of their inherited status traditions is the problem which runs through

many of Schmitt's writings from this period. In them, one can sense
the desire for a new type of ruling elite capable of harnessing modern
mass politics to bold courses of action on the domestic and foreign
policy fronts. In this context it is easy to see how Italian Fascism could
once again come to provide a point of orientation for Schmitt. Schmitt,
as we have seen, was a fervent admirer. After an attempt to assassinate
Mussolini in 1926, he was reported to have said that in his view no
one's life had more value for Europe than Il Duce's, and that any news
of his death would be a heavier blow to him than the death of a close
relative.[22] Hyperbole aside, admiration for Mussolini was fairly common
in Europe at the time, and according to the state of diplomatic play,
he generally got a good foreign press. No strikes, and trains running
on time, were the accomplishments most often attributed to the
regime, and this accalamation was not handed out only by conservatives
like Winston Churchill; in 1933 the erstwhile liberal H.G. Wells considered it, under the circumstances, rather a good regime for the
Italians. For most of the German Right, Mussolini's rough treatment of
the Tyrolean Germans prevented them from seeing Fascism as a model
to be emulated. But Schmitt did not see it this way either, despite his
enthusiasm: just as there were intellectuals on the Left who admired
the Soviet Union from afar, but never seriously considered it as a
domestic model, so too Schmitt's relationship to Fascism has to be seen
as essentially selective.

Not long afterwards, Italian Fascism's reputation on the German
Right started to improve as the ultra-conservative DNVP, under Hugenberg, sought to outflank the Nazis with an endorsement from Mussolini. Over the next few years Mussolini would play the contending
factions of the German Right off each other, while only barely concealing his low opinion of Hitler. This renewed interest in Mussolini was
evident in the pages of both *Europäische Revue* and *Deutsches Volkstum*, as
Rohan and Stapel discussed the Fascist project in relation to their own
concerns. Despite their sympathy, both were convinced that in
Germany there was no need for a centralized dictatorship, 'contrary to
native traditions of self-government', to implement all that made
Fascism great in Italy. Both were inclined to see this aspect of Fascism
as evidence of a tendency to plebiscitary Caesarism in the Italian
national character.[23]

Early on Schmitt had praised the Fascist policy of reconciling the
Church to the modern nation-state. Since then his attitude towards
both the Church and Catholic political parties had become more
reserved, and his tremendous enthusiasm for the 1929 Concordat of
Rome was now based not only on the Church's abandonment of
support for such a party, but also on the Papacy's claim to be a state,
stubbornly maintained since 1870. With this, Pius XI had agreed to the

abolition of the political Catholicism of the Popolaris. Perhaps Schmitt felt that it would now be easier for Catholics in Germany to reject the claims of a party which represented the obsolete legacy of the *Kulturkampf*. Very much later in his life, he could look back at the Concordat and describe it as 'an event of providential significance for millions of pious Roman Catholic Christians'.[24]

In 1929 Schmitt reviewed a book by Erwin von Beckerath entitled *Wesen und Werden des faschistischen Staates*.[25] He sympathized with the author's view that the great domestic accomplishment of the Fascist party was to have restored the classic grandeur of the state as a 'higher power' standing above society, while incorporating and mobilizing the masses. In the context of his own concerns, Fascism represented an impressive attempt to break with, and redefine the relationship between state and society inherited from nineteenth-century European constitutionalism. It had posed the question of how autonomous the state could be in a modern capitalist country:

> Is it conceivable that today a state could play the role of a higher third power in the face of economic and social antagonisms (that is the claim of the Fascist state); or is it necessarily the armed servant of one of those social classes (the well-known Marxist thesis); or is it a kind of neutral third power, a *pouvoir neutre et intermédiaire* (what is to a certain degree actually the case in Germany today, where the remains of the old bureaucratic state play the role of such a *pouvoir neutre*)?[26]

In this review Schmitt argued that the state could not play the loftier role of a power 'above' society in advanced industrialized countries like Germany. The social structures of industrially backward countries like Italy and Russia were more fluid, and thus amenable to radical changes directed from above. This formed a sharp contrast to the situation in more industrialized societies, where the principal social interest groups, classes, were tightly organized into indestructible associations, considerably reducing the manoeuvring room for autonomous state initiatives. The state in the more highly industrialized world was ceasing to be an autonomous actor and becoming little more than a neutral meeting ground for the ongoing hammering out of a social equilibrium. On this point, Schmitt referred to the conclusions of two Social Democrats, Otto Bauer and his student Otto Kirchheimer. He accepted their claim that the institutional forms of this social equilibrium were so entrenched in the structure of modern industrial relations that if either the workers or the capitalists were to try to break out of it, and impose their will unilaterally on the other group, the result could only be 'a fearsome civil war'.[27] Although Schmitt believed that Fascism could provide a valuable example to Germany in the art of post-parliamentary government, he did not embrace this strategy of confrontation. It is important to bear this in mind, because in the last years of the Weimar Republic Schmitt would find his way into the company of elites, including the leaders of heavy industry, who were gunning for a showdown with the working class and the welfare state.

Despite Schmitt's reservations, Italian Fascism appealed to him because it represented a determined rejoinder to the chorus of voices – Harold Laski in England, Édouard Berth in France and Alfred Weber in Germany – all proclaiming the death of the state as the sovereign order. Schmitt warned that these representatives of contemporary pluralism had not thought through the consequences of their prediction. Actually existing pluralism, seen through Hobbesian eyes, was one step away from a condition of civil war within which there would be no judge to determine 'mine and thine'. The state was a visible and potentially neutral force, while parties and interest groups were powers which, if unchecked, would devour the great Leviathan from the inside out: 'Where is the asylum of objective political reason in the labyrinth of interest politics?'[28]

Labyrinth is an apt metaphor for Berlin's intricately fractured, political scene. (Henry Adams: 'a far vaster universe, where all the old roads ran about in every direction, overrunning, dividing, subdividing, stopping abruptly, vanishing slowly, with side-paths that led nowhere and sequences that could not be proved'.) Schmitt relished the teeming ultra-modern energy that made Berlin world famous in those years. He and his socially agile wife were in the habit of regularly entertaining guests from many walks of life and political persuasions, and some of the city's celebrities were guests at the Schmitt residence. These included the Jüngers, the Popitzes, the Sombarts, the Serbian diplomat Ivo Andrič, later recipient of the Nobel Prize for literature, Emil Nolde, Werner Gilles, and Werner Heldt.[29] In his writings Schmitt was always hard on the fluid discourses of the parlour, but in his personal life he revelled in them, often seeking out the most exotic intellectual types – excepting those too far to the Left. These stark juxtapositions of company, set against the backdrop of an ongoing political and economic crisis, generated a constant stream of questions. Schmitt was by nature intellectually open to the most radical lines of thought, and even when no immediate practical course of action could be drawn he derived tremendous pleasure from framing things in this way. In periods of intellectual vertigo, new combinations of ideas took shape in his mind, and he could suddenly become receptive to a perspective out of step with his more moderate instincts.

This feeling of being at the height of the times is vividly conveyed in a passage, which could have been written by Schmitt, from Karl Mannheim's *Ideology and Utopia*:

In this historical moment, where all things suddenly have become transparent and history has revealed its composite elements and structures, it is a matter of scientific thought getting at the heights of the situation, since it is not out of the question that all too soon – as is often the case in history – this transparency will disappear and the world will harden into a single picture.[30]

Derrida has provided a vivid characterization of Schmitt, suggesting why he was so often able to capture, in conceptual form, emergent, indistinct and fragile features of the interwar political terrain:

[T]his thought and this work repeatedly presaged the fearsome world that was announcing itself from as early as the 1920s. As though the fear of seeing that which comes to pass take place, in effect had honed the gaze of this besieged watchman. Following our hypothesis, the scene would be thus: lucidity and fear not only drove this terrified and insomniac watcher to anticipate the storms and seismic movements that would wreak havoc with the historical field, the political space, the borders of concepts and countries, the axiomatics of European law . . . etc. Such a 'watcher' would thereby have been more attuned than so many others to the fragility and 'deconstructible' precariousness of structures, borders and axioms that he wished to protect, restore and 'conserve' at all costs.[31]

The deep disorientation of old European elites on this unfamiliar terrain was the main problem Schmitt confronted in these years. He was soon presented with an opportunity to articulate an extraordinary account of the causes of this crisis, and how it might be overcome. On numerous occasions Rohan had asked him to contribute to his journal, but to no avail.[32] Now he was particularly anxious to have Schmitt attend a conference in Barcelona sponsored by Ortega y Gasset's European Cultural Association, an event which would be attended by intellectuals from many European countries. Schmitt finally agreed to attend, and have the text of his speech published in the *Europäische Revue*. In Barcelona on 12 October 1929, Schmitt put forward what is arguably the most disturbing counter-revolutionary manifesto ever written, a modern version of Cortes's speech from 1849.

The speech was entitled 'Das Zeitalter der Neutralisierungen und Entpolitisierungen' ('The Age of Neutralizations and Depoliticizations'), and it began with a chilling statement: 'We, in Central Europe, live under the gaze of the Russians.'[33] Since the last century the Russians had seen through the great phases which decorate the institutions of modern Europe, and drawn out the most extreme consequences from this encounter: in their view there were no limits to how far society could be transformed and mobilized by political power. Modern Europe now stood under this gaze, judged by this more radical brother, and forced by him to turn to radical solutions: 'The Russians have taken the European nineteenth century at its word, have understood its core, and drawn out of its cultural premisses the final consequences.'[34] Schmitt maintained that this was the encounter which determined the problematic within which all contemporary thought moved, because it posed the question of what could be changed in the human condition by political power, and who would exercise this power. He claimed that they had recently 'created a more intensely organized state than has ever existed'.[35] In the conclusion of *Die geistesgeschichtliche Lage des heutigen Parlamentarismus*, it had seemed as if Fascism had overwhelmed Bolshevism in open combat. There is no trace of Mussolini in this speech: the focus is wholly on the Russian regime as the embodiment of the most radical potentials of modernity. While the 'Russians' were portrayed in earlier works as Asiatic allies of European socialism, in this text they make an unsettling appearance as insiders: the enemy was now the 'radical brother', a doppelgänger. The most radical revolution in human history had taken place on the historical and geographical edge of Europe, posing a challenge and a question: what is unique about the historical evolution of the occident, in what direction is it now moving, and can that direction be changed?

These were the questions Schmitt was attempting to address in his speech. He outlined a succession of intellectual-historical phases through which Europe had passed since the late Middle Ages, when the theological world picture began to break down. Each historical phase designated was defined by an intellectual centre, the problematic within which the then dominant type of intellectual posed, and attempted to resolve, the most divisive issues of the day. What was specific about the trajectory of modern European history was that it was driven by a restless attempt to neutralize the terms of these fundamental conflicts. The result of such neutralizations could never be a definitive resolution, as new, disorderly and heavily politicized spheres of contention immediately arose to occupy the centre of intellectual attention. Schmitt's argument was that this dynamic of 'neutralization and depoliticization' was now coming to its final phase – paradoxically, the point at which everything would become political again.

This was Schmitt's first attempt at constructing a philosophy of history. Although his fascination with such constructions was evident in the last two chapters of *Die geistesgeschichtliche Lage des heutigen Parlamentarismus*, he was always suspicious of the idea that world history was a unified and intelligible process. He treated philosophies of history as more or less successful attempts to illuminate aspects of a process whose dimensions were innumerable, and on which there was no – or anyway, not yet only – definitive perspective: 'All historical knowledge receives its light and intensity from the present; all historical representations and constructions are filled with naive projections and identifications; only a consciousness of our own historical situation will provide historical insight.'[36]

In a much later work, Schmitt compared De Tocqueville's dispassionately pessimistic reflections on the future of Europe favourably, to Spengler's later, cruder attempt to frame the same process in a system: 'He did not want to discover eternal laws of the world-historical process, neither three-stage laws nor cultural cycles. He did not speak about things in which he was not existentially involved.'[37] The stage theory which Schmitt put forward here never appeared again in this form, and even here it is a construction so loose that it should really be seen only as an attempt to illuminate history from the vantage point of a contemporary problem. One of the central problems he was addressing was what the role of the intellectual would be – or, indeed, whether the intellectual had any role in a world in which consensus over shared values seemed to be playing a smaller and smaller role in politics. This was a widely discussed issue in contemporary political writing. The sharpest articulation of the issues involved took place in Germany in the increasingly hostile exchanges between Curtius and Mannheim on the 'free-floating' intellectual. Earlier, in France, similar themes, in a very different national context, were at issue in Benda's polemic against Maurras's *L'Avenir d'intelligence*, in the now classic *The Treason of the Clercs*. Despite the apparently diametrical opposition, both Maurras and Benda subscribed to an essentially Comteian view of the *clercs* as a clearly defined estate, the antithesis of Mannheim's free-floating antiestate.

Schmitt drew upon this Comteian framework in his portrayal of the basic stages of European history, defined by the type of '*clerc*' which dominated the *Zeitgeist*. The basic historical stages for Comte were the theological, the metaphysical and 'the positive' – the last and highest stage, where authority and organization are based on science. The sequence of stages in Schmitt's text was very similar, with theology giving way to metaphysics in the seventeenth century; but he departed from Comte's scheme by portraying the nineteenth century as an age dominated by the spirit of political economy, while the twentieth was dominated by what he called 'the spirit of technology'.

In the nineteenth century, the 'social question' had emerged for the first time in history and the great intellectual problem of that era was how the friend–enemy opposition which this question implied could be 'neutralized' – that is to say, depoliticized – through a distribution of property along the lines recommended by political economy. In the twentieth century, conflict over the production and distribution of social wealth remained a core site of political contention, but Schmitt claimed that in contrast to public opinion in the age of Bentham and

Mill, it was now widely believed that the definitive solution to this social question lay in the progress of technology. By 'technology' he did not mean just the sum of individual inventions. He was giving a different name to that restless transformation of all fixed, fast-frozen relations, the transgression of all natural barriers and proportions – finally, those of human nature itself.

This valorization of technology was intimately bound up with a crisis of elites: while the central problematic of intellectual life had previously been a sanctum of such elites, technology was a subaltern cult of the masses, who instinctually expected from it some future deliverance from the toils of labour:

> Under the massive influence of always novel, astonishing discoveries and accomplishments, there emerged a new religion of technological progress, which held that all other problems would solve themselves through techno-logical progress. This was an obvious and self-evident faith for the great masses of the industrial countries. They leaped over all the intermediate stages, which were characteristic of the ruling elites, and [went over] from an otherworldly miraculous religion to a religion of technological miracles, without the intermediate link. From its onset the twentieth century appears not only as the age of technology but as the age of religious belief in technology.[38]

Schmitt rejected contemporary Saint-Simonian ideas of 'scientific' man-agers and engineers as a new elite; the embryonic Fordism of Weimar culture was alien to his way of thinking:

> The hope that a political ruling class would develop out of technical inventors has so far not come to fruition.... Not even the economic leadership and direction of the contemporary economy is in the hands of the technicians, and so far no one has been able to conceive of a social order led by technicians in any other way than as a leaderless and directionless society.[39]

Indeed, Schmitt's affirmations of the political, here and elsewhere, were directed against the widespread illusion that political struggle was becoming outmoded, because science and technology would eventually solve all human problems. In his opinion, there was little evidence to suggest that technology would bring about peace on earth and the emancipation of the masses, because its progress was more than ever intimately bound up with the development of instruments of mass destruction and mass manipulation. While the Gutenberg press could be depicted as an episode in the history of liberty, Schmitt wryly observed in a later work that it was somewhat less plausible to depict cinema and radio as the continuation of that story:

> the printing press was the defining technology of the liberal era. Freedom of expression, and opinion formation, was in the last century essentially press

freedom. Today, radio and cinema are at least as important, if not more important and intensive means to shape public opinion. In both cases, a similar development has occurred in all the modern states of the world, namely that no state can let these new technological instruments slip out of its hand. Each state is forced, despite very earnest proclamations of basic rights and freedoms, and the abolition of censorship, despite parity and neutrality, none the less to exercise a far-ranging control over radio and cinema.[40]

Technological utopianism was an antipolitical politics based on the belief that History, as the history of life-and-death political struggles, could come to its end at the point at which technology renders such struggles superfluous. Western thought has always sought to overcome political oppositions by finding a neutral ground, a depoliticized condition in which dialogue becomes possible once again. Schmitt claimed that technology was widely seen as the definitive neutral ground, because its progress seems to relativize the importance of religious, national and class oppositions. Leo Strauss expressed the central assumption of the 'spirit of technology' more tersely: the struggle over the domination of men continues as the result of an incomplete domination over nature.[41]

Schmitt noted that precisely because modern technology was radically neutral, the tendency of the way of life built around it, and infused with its spirit, was to dissolve the protective atmosphere of traditional morality which had shielded society from the dangers of nihilism. While the industrial masses were spontaneously drawn to utopian images of a technological society, an older generation of German mandarins experienced the advent of these changes as the end of culture itself. They clung to Romantic, organic images in order to portray what they saw as the dawning of a dead and soulless mechanical age. Here Schmitt alluded to Spengler's image of the contemporary iron age as the beginning of the 'decline of the West'; but also to Weber's similar image of a descending iron cage:

> The previous generation of Germans was gripped by a mood of cultural decline, which was already expressed before the war, and had no need to wait for the collapse of 1918 and Spengler's *Decline of the West*. With Ernst Troeltsche, Max Weber, Walter Rathenau, one can find numerous manifestations of such a mood. . . . A German generation attached itself to a European century that complained about 'la maladie du siècle' and expected the domination of Caliban, or 'After us, the savage god', and complained about a soulless age of technology, in which the soul would be helpless and powerless. . . . This fear was justified, because it emerged out of an obscure feeling for the final consequences of the process of neutralization. . . . From this came the fear of the new classes arising from the *tabula rasa* created by a restless modernization. Out of the abyss of a cultural and social Nothing were thrown up masses estranged from and even hostile to traditional culture

and tastes. But that fear was nothing but doubt of one's own power to put these awesome instruments of technology at one's disposal, although they were only waiting to be put to use.[42]

It was in this context that the Russians were considered to have grasped the essential 'meaning' of modern technology: far from making politics superfluous, human nature itself was now something which could be politically transformed. The Russians had turned a nihilistic denial of all limits into an affirmation of the political. The breakdown of old European cultural values was creating the historical moment of opportunity for a European elite which would not retreat in fear of nihilism, but would accept it as a radical challenge to transform the world along a path very different from the one the Russians had embarked upon. On the surface, postwar Europe was filled with a sluggish desire to restore a lost prewar world. Schmitt predicted that when these new elites erupted on to the political stage, this whole restorationist façade would vanish like a phantom:

> All new and great initiatives, each revolution and each reformation, each new elite, originates in asceticism and voluntary or involuntary poverty, where poverty signifies a renunciation of the security of the status quo. Early Christianity and all major reforms within Christianity – the Benedictine, the Cluniac, the Franciscan renewal, Baptism and Puritanism – but also every authentic rebirth, with its return to a simple principle of its own kind, each genuine *ritornar al principio*, each return to pure uncorrupted nature, looks like a cultural and social nothingness compared to the comfort and enjoyment of the existing status quo. It grows quietly and in the dark, and in its first beginnings a historian perceives nothing more than nothingness. The moment of glorious representation is also the moment at which that connection to the secret insignificant beginning is at risk.[43]

This portrayal of a new European political–intellectual elite *in statu nascendi* forms a striking contrast to Schmitt's earlier depiction of Cortes as a despairing reactionary, searching for some force to deliver what was left of Old Christian Europe from the masses. We have seen that soon after he had written *Politische Theologie* – and more decisively after his relations with the Church had cooled – Schmitt concluded that this position was an anachronism in an age of mass politics. The institutional pillars of conservative Europe were breaking down, and could not be the basis of a truly radical right-wing politics. In an essay written in 1927, 'Donoso Cortes in Berlin, 1849', Schmitt had stated clearly that the problem of Cortes's position was that the radical dictatorship for which he had called in 1849 was not compatible with the traditions of conservative Europe. By tradition, European elites were divided by religion and nation, and were therefore ill-equipped to deal with the increasingly international face of the Revolution.[44] But what was anachronistic about the perspective which Cortes represented was not just that he sought to radicalize and unite an *ancien régime* order which could not be radicalized or united. More decisively, it was that Cortes could not grasp any alternative to a doomed stance of frontal opposition to the rise of the masses.

For the new, post-Christian elite that Schmitt depicted in his Barcelona speech, eschatology can serve only as the remote, never-articulated premiss of its political projects, a distant light on the horizon. In an essay written shortly before his speech in Barcelona, 'Der unbekannte Donoso Cortes' ('The Unknown Donoso Cortes',) he criticized the Spanish Marquis for abusively introducing eschatological jargon, with its 'constant Fortissimo of strong words',[45] into his commentaries on contemporary political events: 'The *coup d'état* of Louis Napoleon may have been a positive development, but it was hardly an apocalyptic event ... it can only endanger the authentic, always present and necessary eschatology if one connects it with these kind of political affairs.'[46] The dividing lines of twentieth-century politics no longer had to run along the barricades of 1848, and Schmitt suggested that the radical impulse behind Cortes's position could now come to fruition in a certain form of mass politics. But turning from the politics of eschatological civil war meant rejecting the fantasy of any 'war to end all wars'.

In Schmitt's mind, the idea of Christian redemption was no longer – as it still was for Kierkegaard – a *truth* which defies human understanding, but simply the *pathos* associated with being 'open' to its possibility. The significance of this pathos is that it reveals a readiness to act decisively *in this world*, at a turning point in world history. He believed that if the Christian idea of history as a process ending in a redemptive struggle was completely extinguished from culture, the result would be a totally disenchanted world; struggle would continue, but without any of the high stakes and political tension involved in 'authentic' friend–enemy oppositions. As he put it in *Der Begriff des Politischen*, if such struggle were ever to come to an end, many of the key ideas of modern thought would still be valid – 'ideology, culture, civilization, economy, morality law, art, entertainment, etc., but neither politics nor the state'. This exact sentiment is captured in a passage from T.S. Eliot's *After Strange Gods*, where Eliot reflected on the impact of the decline of the Christian vision of sin and redemption – not so much directly on the world of political relations, but on highly mediated literary representations of it:

> ... with the disappearance of the idea of Original Sin, with the disappearance of the idea of an intense moral struggle, the human beings presented to us both in poetry and in prose fiction today. ... tend to become less and

less real . . . If you do away with this struggle, and maintain that by tolerance, benevolence, inoffensiveness and a redistribution or increase of purchasing power, combined with a devotion, on the part of an elite, to Art, the world will be as good as any could require, then you must expect human beings to become more and more vaporous.[47]

Much later Schmitt would express this same idea in the form of an ominous and disconcerting verse:

Woe to him who has no friend, for his enemy will sit in judgement upon him.
Woe to him who has no enemy, for I myself shall be his enemy on Judgement Day.[48]

A political day of judgement often seemed to be not so far away. Was there any great, new current emerging 'out of the social and cultural abyss'? In Schmitt's Barcelona manifesto, unwillingness to identify with any particular agenda can be explained, in part, by the fact that it was addressed to an audience consisting of intellectuals of the literary-philosophical type. But the essential message to them was that such *clercs* were not condemned by history to be politically inconsequential, free-floating intellectuals, and that indeed, in an age of mass politics great opportunities would open up for those who recognized the direction in which things were turning. But what force had the historical wind in its sails? While Fascism was enormously appealing to him, he did not mention it in Barcelona. In the same review from 1932 in which Leo Strauss exposed some of the inconsistencies of Schmitt's critique of liberalism in *Der Begriff des Politischen*, he referred to the text of the Barcelona speech, and homed in on exactly this question:

The polemic against liberalism can therefore only signify a concomitant or preparatory action: it is meant to clear the field for the battle of decision between 'the spirit of technology', 'the mass faith that inspires an anti-religious this-worldly activism' and the opposite spirit and faith, *which, as it seems, still has no name.*[49]

It was an extremely astute insight on Strauss's part that the alternative for which Schmitt was looking, did not yet – in 1929 or even in 1932 – have a name: not Catholic integral nationalism, not Fascism, and certainly not National Socialism.

Schmitt's relationship to the war hero and philosopher of the trenches Ernst Jünger should be seen in this light. Their friendship began in 1930, after Jünger wrote to Schmitt effusively praising *Der Begriff des Politischen*:

Today the level of a mind is determined by its relationship to armament. You have made an unusual military–technical discovery: a mine which silently explodes. As if through magic one sees the ruins crumbling; and the destruction has already occurred before it has become audible.[50]

This was the beginning of a lifelong companionship between two intellectually opposed men who could none the less see in each other's projects intersecting perspectives on the historical moment. Jünger seemed to Schmitt different from nearly all the other literary and journalistic celebrities of the Right whom he would come to know, mainly because there seemed to be something authentically radical and modern about his political vision. Jünger represented something more than just a German version of Georges Sorel: just as Popitz, for Schmitt, embodied Hegel's ideal of the Prussian civilian bureaucrat, here was the military side of this same ideal, radicalized by war and counter-revolution. Jünger's postwar writings described the inhuman regimentation of mechanized trench warfare as the antithesis of a dying bourgeois world. He rejected the view that the awesome carnage generated by world war had been meaningless, and vividly portrayed the collective baptism of a generation by poison gas, machine-gun volleys and aerial bombardment as a world-historical experience. After the war, Jünger set out to articulate the political form of this futurist aesthetic of mechanized warfare, and found it in a version of what Oswald Spengler had called 'Prussian socialism': a state which would move beyond the German war economy to an even higher level of total mobilization.[51] This spartan militarism was widespread in what could be called the 'National Revolutionary' milieu. Despite the family resemblances, such people set themselves apart from the 'conservative revolutionaries' mentioned above; at the extreme end of this spectrum were men like Niekisch, who described themselves as 'National Bolsheviks'. Schmitt kept his distance from Niekisch and his ilk, but through Jünger he became acquainted with a milieu which saw the bourgeois *Rechtsstaat* as a historical anachronism. His exposure to this subculture, mediated by numerous connections to high-ranking officers, prepared him in many respects for the departures he would make in 1933.

For Schmitt, Jünger embodied a new kind of nationalist politics whose historical nature was deeply enigmatic. Was it revolutionary or reactionary? Was it based on a flight from reality, or did its rise call into question the liberals' and leftists' claims to have interpreted reality correctly?[52] A political myth seemed to be emerging which left nineteenth-century oppositions behind. Over the course of the interwar period, a militarized image of the worker as a symbol of the revitalization of the social order had, from its Socialist origins, spread across the political spectrum and was used by nationalisms of all sorts, including very different varieties like Zionism and National Socialism. Schmitt shared Heidegger's later assessment that Jünger had captured the mythic significance of the figure of 'the worker' in an age of mass politics: the 'worker' as the masterless, but not emancipated, Hegelian slave who transforms the earth and, in so doing, transforms human nature. Through Jünger's mediation it became easier for Schmitt to disconnect the 'worker' from the framework of capitalism, and place him in the more 'profound' context of the general phenomenon of modernity. This mediation also, perhaps, allowed him to interpret more easily the previously alien phenomenon of National Socialism after it had come to power. But Schmitt never embraced Jünger's myth of a totally mobilized, worker–soldier state; this was his image of the 'radical brother': a model, but also an enemy to be overcome.

It is important to remember that Schmitt's speech in Barcelona defined a maximum programme for a political force 'which did not yet have a name'. A few months later in Berlin, he gave another speech before his colleagues at the Handelshochschule in honour of Hugo Preuss, the main architect of the Weimar Constitution.[53] Just as the uncompromising tone of the final chapter of *Politische Theologie* was followed by a language of mediation in *Römischer Katholizismus und politische Form*, a similar sequence was repeated here, and not for the last time.

As Hugo Preuss Professor of Public Law, Schmitt was in contact with jurists whose political outlook had shaped the fragile consensus around the Weimar Constitution, and were now watching it unravel. In this speech Schmitt sympathetically assessed Preuss's attempt to fashion a constitutional practice which addressed twentieth-century political problems. He described the Weimar Constitution not as a charter of evasions and compromises, but as a flawed yet commendable attempt to come to terms with the problem of democratic legitimacy in a nation-state – a problem which had been totally ignored in the Constitution of the old Reich, improvisationally assembled from blood and iron. Despite the fact that Schmitt repeatedly dismissed attempts to tread 'a third way' between bourgeois *Rechtsstaat* and socialism, the framers of the Constitution's attempt to address 'the social question' was commendable in comparison to the indifference and hostility which the old order had shown towards the aspirations of the working class.[54] Although Schmitt was always suspicious of the welfare state, it was significant for him that a large section of the working class could now identify itself with the nation-state for the first time. Despite his hostility towards an unwieldy multiparty corporatism, Schmitt claimed that the underlying basis of the Weimar Constitution was a class truce between employers and workers, and that this sort of settlement, properly organized, was the rational basis of political order in advanced industrial societies.

But he also argued that this compromise could no longer be properly safeguarded in the framework of a liberal constitution of the nineteenth-century kind. The liberal 'agnostic state' was the state reduced to a minimum, where the solution to social problems was abandoned to the competition of social forces. The classical liberal conception of an agnostic and *laissez-faire* state presupposed the existence of an enlightened public opinion. Only in the mediating and moderating ambience of intelligent discourse could liberal institutions avoid the centrifugal consequences of a truly agnostic political order.

In the nineteenth century, the emergence of high-cultural communities was an indispensable element in the awakening of a distinctive *esprit de la nation*. The *Bildungsbürgertum* exercised a profound, albeit indirect, influence on the fluid formation of opinion within the public sphere. This public sphere was the objective power behind nineteenth-century parliamentarianism. The reading public for newspapers, and the attending public of high culture, constituted the first national class in the politically divided space of German-speaking Central Europe, and their status prestige was intimately bound up with the national idea.

But in Germany, uniquely, it was the university system which imparted a uniform cultural profile to the educated, and for this reason professors, through their control over admissions and test scores, constituted an elite within this elite. There were only a few hundred full professors in the whole of Germany, and in the social register of polite society they had the same status rank as an army major.[55] Moreover, the whole of this elite was overwhelmingly Protestant, and Schmitt, as an outsider in both social and confessional terms, never overcame his ambivalence towards the status pretensions of this group. His portrayal of its marginalization in national politics, marked by an undertone of *Schadenfreude*, closely resembled Weber's: the critical intellectual energies of this group, defeated by Bismarck, began to wane rapidly after national unification as it retreated into an obtuse political conformism and narrow academic specializations. Between 1871 and 1914 the German bourgeoisie's earlier struggles to create a national parliamentary government were abandoned.[56] German academic culture, so dynamic in the first half of the nineteenth century, became, over the course of this period, 'on the one side an apolitical, technical bureaucratic education, and on the other a just as apolitical, shadowy literary education, based on private aesthetic consumption'.[57]

Despite his hostility to the mandarin traditions of German education, Schmitt expressed misgivings about the break-up of the cultural centre which had once been occupied by the *Bildungsbürgertum*. After the First World War, the vices of Philistine complacency had only been compounded by an arid partisanship which had come to dominate German politics and intellectual life. This had resulted in a ceaseless and bewildering war of fragmentary political 'world-views' without any integrating dialogue or political synthesis. It was precisely this problem which Mannheim addressed in *Ideologie und Utopie*. In this passage he captured some of the hyperpoliticized atmosphere of Weimar intellectual life:

> To the degree that science and politics combine, there emerges the danger that the crises which affect political thought will also become crises of scientific thought. Out of this problematic, we emphasize only one fact, which is characteristic of the present situation. Politics is conflict, [and] it tends to become in increasing measure a life-and-death struggle.[58]

Mannheim argued that while the claim to represent a higher, universal perspective could no longer be maintained in the face of a sceptical public, intellectuals could nevertheless perform the crucial task of mediating between hostile world-views, because they, unlike other groups in society, were not bound to one-sided, 'interested' perspectives, 'ideologies'. But while Mannheim believed that through an ongoing, 'endless conversation', intellectuals of conservative, liberal, Marxist and even Nazi persuasion might begin to abandon the dogmatism of their fixed outlooks, Schmitt's thinking leaned more often towards cutting the Gordian Knot.

In his speech in Berlin, however, this inclination to decisionism was muted, and he expressed – half-sincerely – some unease that authentic discussion was becoming increasingly difficult, undermining the possibility of more comprehensive perspectives on political problems. This might seem disingenuous, considering that only a few months before, in Barcelona, he had spoken of a completely corrupt and unstable status quo. But despite his feeling that the whole frame of the state might be giving way, he did not easily embrace an 'après le déluge' outlook. This essay, published not long after the onset of the world Depression, ends with an astute – if cryptic – intimation of the historical stakes involved in preserving the framework of compromise: 'the fate of German intellectual and cultural life will therefore remain inseparably bound up with the fate of the Weimar Constitution'.[59]

In earlier chapters we have witnessed sudden shifts of perspective, but the effortless transition charted in this chapter – from counter-revolutionary to pessimistic *Vernunftrepublikaner* – seems to border on schizophrenia. Would a serious and engaged political thinker even be capable of such metamorphoses? I would like to suggest that the protean quality of Schmitt's political habitus reflected precisely the intellectual disorientation which he attributed to the absence of any hegemonic centre of gravity in politics: the constant shifts of conceptual focus, the terminological instability, contradictory attitudes about political institutions – all linked, perhaps, by the unarticulated premises of a system which never materializes. This is both the strength and the weakness of his thought. Although certain key problems persist through the entirety of his political and intellectual career, the answers he formulated often exhibited a 'strategic' logic, indistinguishable from opportunism. To some extent this can be explained by his position as an interloper moving between the worlds of politics, academia and the salon; his mind, never firmly ensconced in any one role, moved simultaneously along diverging paths.

10

Presidential Rule and Judicial Activism

Carl Schmitt's role in the final years of the Weimar Republic continues to be explosively controversial. I will provide a much more detailed account of the political scene during the late Weimar and early Nazi years in order to chart the evolution of his political views and assess his influence on events. He was now moving in the corridors of power as an observer and adviser; as a result, his formulations became more directly synchronized to the time line of high politics. His writings from these years are interventionist texts *par excellence*, full of tactical signifiers.

In Chapter 9 we saw how Schmitt was drawn to both radical and moderate solutions to the crisis of the political system. Shifting between the path of compromise and the path leading over the Rubicon was inherent to the whole project of investing the President with ever wider powers on the basis of Article 48. In his earlier writings on Article 48 he had claimed that the government could go so far as to suspend the entire constitution except those institutions which were the agents involved in this act of suspension: the presidency, the Reich government, the Reichstag, and the Reich Court in Leipzig, which together comprised an institutional minimum. His earlier view was that the government could go this far only because all the measures adopted during this period of suspension were temporary, and thus to be strictly distinguished from material laws. Otherwise a commissarial dictatorship would be transformed into a sovereign one. Even if the distinction between laws and measures was sometimes difficult to make, he claimed that under no circumstances could the Constitution be changed in this manner. Moreover, he did not question the fact that the government which exercised these measures, authorized by the President, needed to be based on a majority in the Reichstag; nor that a majority in the Reichstag could subsequently cancel any emergency measure issued by the government.

The parameters of these assumptions would quickly change after the beginning of 1929. A year before, a national coalition government headed by the Social Democrat Müller had been formed, with the support of every party left of the ultra-conservative DNVP: the so-called

'Grand Coalition'. The electoral balance of power in the Reich as a whole had shifted to the Left after years of bourgeois coalition governments; in Prussia, a Centre–Left 'Weimar Coalition' government (SPD, Centre and Democrats), without the participation of the moderately Right, pro-business DVP, was formed under the leadership of the Social Democrat Otto Braun. The results of this election convinced many in the camarilla around Hindenburg that the interests of the wealthy and powerful could no longer be adequately served by coalition politics of parliamentary majorities, and that the presidency had to be strengthened up to and beyond the limits of the Constitution. But checking the power of a left-leaning Reichstag did not automatically entail strengthening the power of the President. The claim of an unprecedentedly activist judiciary to be the final interpreter of the Constitution had to be effectively challenged if a government ruling by presidential decree, without a Reichstag majority, was to be established.

A government showdown with the Reich Court provided the occasion for Schmitt to begin working closely with this presidential inner circle. Just before the terminal crisis of the Weimar Republic, a dispute had broken out between the Reich government and five federal states over the issue of who had the right to fill a vacated position in the administrative board of the *Reichsbahngesellschaft*. ('Federal Rail Association').[1] Despite his reservations about the courts making political decisions, as late as summer 1928 it still seemed natural to think that since there was no emergency, the matter would go to the State Court in Leipzig, a body drawn from members of the Reich Court to rule on cases dealing with the Constitution. But when the federal states sought to submit it, the Reich government boldly went ahead in December and filled the position, claiming that the matter was outside the Court's jurisdiction; surprisingly, the justices conceded, implicitly acknowledging their subordinate position. Schmitt was duly impressed by this bold strike. Earlier, in a decision on 15 October 1927, the justices had proclaimed that the State Court was the Guardian of the Constitution – that is to say, its interpretations of disputed provisions were definitive. Schmitt had objected to this claim, was now pleased to see it effectively refuted. In early 1929 he wrote an article which argued that this resolved the previously difficult constitutional question of who was the Guardian of the Constitution, and demonstrated unequivocally that it was the President.[2] The Guardian of the Constitution had to be an arbitrating '*pouvoir neutre*,'[3] and in his view a constitutional court could not play this essentially political role.

Schmitt believed that judicial activism was a false and dangerous solution to the rapidly intensifying political crisis. Since the mid 1920s the State Court had begun to develop a jurisprudence regulating the emergency decrees issued by the federal states, but had left the prerogatives of the Reich government under Article 48 largely undefined. Schmitt was determined that they should stay that way. The intensity of his hostility to the pretensions of the Weimar judiciary is noteworthy – after all, the judiciary was a bulwark of right-wing hostility to the Republic.

Many Weimar judges looked enviously at the authority of the American Supreme Court. In a confidential letter to the Minister of Justice (1925), the President of the Reich Court, Walter Simons, had claimed that the US experience showed that judicial review could be an effective check on popular sovereignty.[4] Schmitt saw nothing in the history of the American Supreme Court which contradicted his assessment of the dangers of judicial activism:

> This rightfully world-renowned court has seemingly become, among many German jurists, a kind of myth. . . . Considering the contemporary abnormal condition of Germany . . . its activity should not be judged from periods of economic prosperity and domestic stability; rather, one must look at critical and turbulent periods. Here the famous judicial precedents from the period of the Civil War – decisions which concerned politically disputed questions like slavery or the devaluation of gold – demonstrate that the authority of the Court in such cases was highly endangered, and its conception of the issue could not be implemented.[5]

These problems were compounded in Germany by the absence of a unified system of courts. The old, prewar Reich Court had evolved as a superimposed layer on top of the pre-existing judiciaries of the federal states, as the highest court of appeal in criminal and civil cases; by 1929 it consisted of about a hundred judges seated in Leipzig in eight civil senates, four communal senates and a national labour court. Decisions were issued collectively, without indicating which judge wrote the decision and without revealing any dissent. The principles behind the constant stream of decisions coming out of these various courts were hard to determine, giving their rulings *in toto* a certain incoherence.[6] Alongside the Reich Court a specially organized State Court was established by the Weimar Constitution to hear cases outside the jurisdiction of the ordinary courts. The State Court ended up being a constitutional court without clearly defined powers of judicial review.[7]

The stereotypical role of a European judge as an administrative functionary applying but not interpreting the law was put into question by the lengthy rights section of the Weimar Constitution, establishing higher norms which were, in some unspecified way, considered to be binding on the legislature. It was precisely the Right's inability to create a more solid basis of legitimacy for its politics which made it rely on an activist judiciary to get its way against unfavourable legislation; in Schmitt's opinion, this was a strategy which aggravated the polycratic disorder of the state, because instead of strong government, the result was paralysing litigation. Unlike the executive, which was held together by an administrative chain of command, the lowest court could act independently to challenge a law. Schmitt observed with trepidation how the courts were using Article 153 of the Constitution, which protected private property, to extend the traditional category of compensated expropriation beyond its older, limited applications. 'Property' was increasingly interpreted by the courts as encompassing even the monetary value of certain investments, whose 'expropriation' by the legislator – or in this case the government acting in a legislative capacity – entitled the bearer to make a claim for compensation.

Such claims could now even be brought against the foreign policy of the government when a treaty like the one signed by the German and Polish governments in October 1929 was thought to violate the rights of those estate owners who once held property in former German territories, and still held the deeds. Schmitt agreed with his former student, the Social Democratic theorist Otto Kirchheimer, that the property rights protected by the Constitution had to be interpreted in the narrowest sense, as confined to chattels: nothing else could be guaranteed when the very dynamics of a modern capitalist economy regularly resulted in the monetary equivalent of large-scale expropriations. In June 1931 the Brüning government was compelled to issue a legal decree banning all such legal claims to compensation.[8]

Schmitt elaborated on his criticisms of judicial activism in a considerably expanded version of an article he had written in 1929 entitled *Der Hüter der Verfassung* ('Guardian of the Constitution'). He began by pointing out that a call for a Guardian of the Constitution was always a sign of crisis within a political order.[9] The first, early modern attempt to establish such an institution took place immediately after Cromwell's death, in order to stave off the further disintegration of republican institutions. Indeed, the stand-off between the Protector and rump parliaments in the 1650s formed a plausible historical parallel to the present. Trying to ward off both a restoration of the old monarchy and a slide into unchecked parliamentary oligarchy, the English republican James Harrington sought to demonstrate the importance of a senate charged with keeping the legislature within the boundaries of the balance of power. Harrington maintained that institutions like the Spartan ephorate were an integral component of an 'ancient political prudence', and he drew on a number of such classical precedents to demonstrate that the specific institution occupying this role was selected to meet a challenge from a specific direction, an anticipated threat to the frame of the state.

Schmitt argued that such a figure was even more important in a modern state because, as a territorial monopoly of violence, it had

limited recourse to 'self-help'. The legitimacy of this monopoly presupposes a tremendous trust conferred upon the state that it will not
abuse it: in this sense a Guardian of the Constitution is installed within
a legal system to make the traditional, forgone, right of resistance
superfluous.

The question of who within the system of divided powers protects
the constitutional order as a whole had been studiously ignored by
legal theory in the aftermath of Bismarck's successes, as such inquiries
were unavoidably political. It was only after the war that the question
of who exercised this function arose again, with a majority of legal
opinion maintaining that it was the newly established constitutional
court, the so-called State Court.

The thesis of *Der Hüter der Verfassung* was that the contemporary
constitutional crisis could not be resolved by setting up the courts as
the final interpreters of the Constitution; constitutional conflicts could
not be overcome by a judicial ruling, because the issues at stake were
too political to be resolved by some spuriously impartial interpretation
of a norm. This was why Schmitt was opposed to even the existence of
a constitutional court. In his opinion such a court was different from a
normal court, because its rulings could not be 'justice' in the conventional sense of decisions made on the basis of a law. A court with the
right to decide what is and is not law is no longer acting within the
limits of the division of powers: it is, in effect, a legislative upper house.
Schmitt argued that laws could be subject to judicial review, but could
not be nullified by a constitutional court, because the content of a
piece of legislation was not bound to – and could not be derived
logically from – a constitution, in the way a judicial decision can and
should be derived from a law. If the court were limited to its role in
the system of divided powers, only in the case of open, flagrant
violations was it conceivable that the will of the legislator could be
voided in this way.

Hans Kelsen rejected this argument by pointing out that it was
not the content of the statute but the authority of the issuing agent –
that is, the constitutionality of its enactment – which constituted the
'facts of the case'. In this way judicial review could be understood in a
purely procedural sense. Furthermore, he pointed out that there was a
common-sense reason why it was a constitutional court which should
decide on such matters:

> Since precisely in the most important cases of constitutional violation, the
> parliament and the executive are the disputing parties, it makes sense to call
> upon a third authority that stands apart from this conflict and is not itself
> involved in any way in the exercise of power which the constitution essentially
> divides up between parliament and the executive.[10]

Most contemporary commentators assume that with these points Kelsen decisively refuted Schmitt's arguments against judicial review by a constitutional court. But whatever one might think about the political consequences of the alternatives, Kelsen's portrayal of an impartial constitutional court is less than convincing. His legal theory was not compatible with a division-of-powers system, as he himself conceded when he wrote: '[t]here exists only a quantitative and not a qualitative difference between the political character of the legislature and that of the judiciary'.[11]

Schmitt argued that the power of the President – as opposed to that of an unelected judicial body – to interpret the law in the case of a conflict of interpretation, or to impose a settlement when no parliamentary majority could be formed, was democratically legitimate. This was the kind of argument which could help justify the cause, and even define the more distant goals, of the men around Hindenburg.

Remembering an earlier occasion when Hindenburg's Chief of Staff, Otto Meissner, had drawn on his writings without acknowledgement, Schmitt probably thought it best to send his opinion directly to the President's office, where Meissner led an entourage of monocled arch-reactionaries.[12] Thus began his first direct contacts with the clique around Hindenburg, whose star players were Meissner, Erich Zweigert and Colonel – later General – Kurt von Schleicher. On 4 April Meissner replied, commending Schmitt for having captured the mediating essence of the President's role; on 6 April, Schmitt received a letter from Erich Zweigert, State Secretary in the Reich Interior Ministry, expressing enthusiastic agreement.[13] It was not long before Schmitt was in regular contact with officials in the Reich Interior Ministry. At around the same time, Erich Marcks, press secretary of the *Reichswehr* Ministry, and his friend, Major Eugen Ott, entered into discussions with Schmitt. These two men received intellectual guidance from Schmitt's writings on Article 48, and regularly passed on some of the main ideas to Von Schleicher, who headed the newly created Ministerial Office at the *Reichswehr* Ministry and was in close contact with the President. In fact, in the last years of the Republic he became the behind-the-scenes master fixer, who could make or break a government.

Soon after the Reich Court's show of deference towards the President in December 1928, Erich Zweigert, State Secretary of the Interior Ministry, saw the opportunity to create a government independent of parties, ruling by decrees authorized by the President. Initially Hindenburg and even his favourite, Schleicher, might have wanted only to return to the right-wing coalition governments of the mid 1920s,[14] but the onset of the Depression soon created unexpected problems and opportunities. Schleicher soon emerged as the leading figure in a conspiracy to send the Reichstag packing as soon as the fragile, existing coalition government came apart. In this endeavour he enlisted the support of State Secretary and aide to the President Otto Meissner, who convinced Hindenburg of the legality of the enterprise.

Schleicher's partner in these clandestine negotiations on the Reichstag side was the very conservative head of the Centre faction, Heinrich Brüning – a man whom Schmitt, at one time considered as a potential candidate for the Centre, had already encountered in Bonn. After 1928, the struggle for leadership between the left and right wings of the Centre Party was decisively won by the Right, which sought to pin the decline in the party's fortunes on its overly close associations with the Social Democrats. Brüning replaced Adam Stegerwald, leader of the Catholic trade unions, as head of the Reichstag delegation. In his initial meetings with Hindenburg and Schleicher, Brüning was at first reluctant to bring down the Müller government, but soon came around to the idea that a cabinet could be formed without a Reichstag majority – that is, without the Social Democrats – if it had the backing of the President. Brüning was committed to resolving the reparations problem once and for all, and even as the Depression deepened he argued, with doctrinaire certainty, that a reduction in public spending and unemployment benefit would achieve the goal of restoring Germany's fiscal sovereignty.[15]

But those around the President wanted to make sure that Social Democrats were not thrown overboard too soon, lest they escape responsibility for this final settlement of the reparations question. The Young Plan, named after the American Owen Young, stipulated that Germany would pay just over two billion marks every year for the next thirty-seven years: the liquidation of the Dawes loan plus interest. For the next twenty years thereafter – that is, until 1987 – Germany would continue to pay two billion marks a year.

The implementation of the Young Plan was dependent on the outcome of negotiations to procure an American loan. The President of the *Reichsbank*, Hjalmar Schacht, although part of the negotiating team, secretly began to sabotage the plan in order to make the government more dependent on the *Reichsbank*, forcing it to repay debts through cutbacks and tax hikes instead of piling on new foreign debts to pay for old ones. The stalling tactics Schacht used in Paris led to a massive run on the mark, quickly revealing the dangers for Germany of any unilateral initiative on the reparations front.[16] In December 1929, when the government none the less seemed willing to accept some of these terms in order to placate Schacht, both the Finance Minister, Hilferding, and his adviser, State Secretary Popitz, resigned in protest. It simply would not have been possible to meet these demands, mainly because of the clamouring for a tax cut by the champions of industry, the DVP.

The Young Plan, including its unpopular reparations provisions, had to be implemented by order of the President; this led to Schacht's resignation. Although Schacht's bid to destabilize the government failed, when the coalition parties could not subsequently agree on the terms of a budget – because the Social Democrats objected to proposed cuts in unemployment insurance – the Müller government resigned, and on the very next day, 27 March 1929, Brüning was appointed Chancellor.

This marked the beginning of the 'late Weimar' system – in fact the beginning of the end for the Republic. With the collapse of the New York stock market and the ensuing banking crisis, Germany's financial lifeline was yanked away, setting in motion the most extreme depression in the history of capitalism. Many of the deep unresolved conflicts which the Republic had faced between 1919 and 1923, papered over in the subsequent brief phase of economic prosperity and relative stabilization, would now re-emerge on an even more massive scale. Even a much more solidly constructed state would have had enormous difficulty in coping with this situation, and the Weimar Republic was an extraordinarily deadlocked and weak state. Geoff Eley has provided a compelling and succinct account of the underlying structural problems of the political order. The basic problem, in his view, was that powerful business and agrarian interests found that coalition-building in a 'pluralist' party system often yielded meagre payoffs, and were increasingly tempted to ditch the whole system:

On the one hand, the political cooperation of the dominant classes and their major economic fractions could no longer be successfully organized within the given forms of parliamentary representation and party government. The usual forms of parliamentary coalition-building consequently became unbearably complicated, so that politics became increasingly fractionalized into a series of maneuvers for influence and control over the high government executive. In the process a gap opened between an increasingly unrepresentative governmental politics, disastrously divorced from any stable basis in popular legitimacy, and a febrile popular electorate, increasingly mobilized for action, but to diminishing effect.[17]

Although Brüning could have counted on the grudging support of a Reichstag majority, mainly because the SPD feared a government even further to the Right, the new Chancellor made it clear that he would be forming a 'government above parties', and was determined to implement a tough package of austerity measures. The theoretical problem that Schmitt would soon confront was that if this plan succeeded, and government was no longer to be based on a majority in the Reichstag, the distinction between temporary measures and laws would become increasingly nominal. For many years now Schmitt had stressed the overriding significance of this distinction. But a government ruling by decree would necessarily put it – and the whole organizational component of the Constitution – into question.

As the presidential system took shape, deep splits opened up within the conservative camp, based on their attitude towards it, stemming largely from the unwillingness of the media mogul and DNVP kingpin Alfred Hugenberg to go along with this attempt to hollow out the Constitution from within. Hugenberg was the former director of the Krupp steel works; during the First World War he had organized funds from heavy industry to pressure the government and public opinion to back a rabid policy of annexations. After the war he built up a press empire which controlled, with few exceptions, nearly all the major bourgeois newspapers. After 1928, under Hugenberg's total control, the DNVP went down the path of increasingly reckless opposition, and eventually into alliance with the Nazis. Although he had pretensions to be a German Mussolini, Hugenberg was unable to turn what was essentially a party of Wilhelmine reactionaries into anything like a mass movement. The internal disintegration of the conservative camp would eventually lead to catastrophic stampedes of its core constituencies over to the Nazis, their erstwhile allies. This recklessness, which went so far as an open attack on Hindenburg, even put an occasional strain on Hugenberg's relations with his friends in heavy industry. One of the main objectives of the Hindenburg clique was to marginalize Hugenberg in order to win the 'moderates' in the DNVP over to a conservative regrouping beyond the party system. Hitler was seen by many of those around Hindenburg as a more reasonable man, with fewer personal ambitions.[18]

Support for Brüning was initially forthcoming from one of the powerhouses of the right-wing press that was not under Hugenberg's control: the Hamburg-based newspaper *Deutsches Volkstum*, edited by Schmitt's friends Wilhelm Stapel and A.E. Günther. This was the paper of the main conservative employers' association, the DHV, which had broken from the DNVP because Hindenburg's strategy of relentless opposition to the Republic completely disregarded powerful middle-class interest groups which were less willing to break with corporatist mechanisms of negotiation. Also providing critical – albeit highly conditional – support were the official representatives of the Gentlemen's Club, who saw Brüning as a transition towards a more completely post-parliamentary system. The reservations about the Brüning government of many of these 'Young Conservatives' had little to do with the Young Plan; after a certain point, Brüning would cease to be useful to them, because his government was ultimately based on the SPD's tacit support for a Reich government led by the head of the Centre Party, and thus the alliance between the Centre and the SPD controlling the Prussian state government. The coalition government in Prussia was the linchpin of the whole Weimar system. Although it was difficult to imagine how the country could be governed without the participation of the Centre Party, its role as a link between a right-wing Reich government and a left-leaning Prussia was an obstacle to any attempt to break with the system altogether.

No one had any idea where this improvised presidential system was heading, and Schmitt's own ambivalences on this point have to be seen in the context of his simultaneous involvement with *Reichswehr* officers, bureaucrats in the Interior and Finance Ministries, various factions at the Gentlemen's Club and the leadership of the Centre party – who all had their own ideas about what presidential rule would bring. Schmitt never completely identified with the outlook of any of the contending players in this parallelogram of forces, and it is difficult to glean from his writings and speeches a fully coherent image of what type of state he thought was emerging.

The evolution of Schmitt's position dovetailed for a while with the exigencies of Brüning's plan to implement draconian austerity measures in the midst of what was turning out to be a major depression. There were still many outstanding questions concerning the constitutionality of the presidential system. The first question was: if the Reichstag rejected these measures, carried a vote of no confidence, and was then dissolved, could the government continue in power until after the new elections, and could it actually proceed to implement these measures in the interim before a new Reichstag had been elected?

On 16 July this scenario came to pass, and not only did Brüning stay in power, he also implemented his financial programme. The constitutional issue was whether the government was violating Articles 85 and 87, which gave the Reichstag control over the budget. Schmitt was not alone in his support for the government's position. The leading liberal authorities on the Weimar Constitution, Gerhard Anschütz and Richard Thoma, agreed that Article 48 gave the President the right to issue decrees with the force of law when the Reichstag was unable to act. But it was Schmitt who was asked to provide the legal argument for using Article 48 to decree, without parliamentary consent, measures of a financial nature. This opened up the question of whether a 'financial state of emergency' could be said to exist. The argument he put forward in a legal opinion from 28 July 1930 represented a substantial departure from his earlier interpretation of what was allowed under Article 48.[19] Previously Schmitt had maintained that the most far-reaching suspension of normal legal procedure could be justified on the basis of its provisional nature, and that all measures implemented during this period were to be sharply distinguished from formal laws which, of course, needed to be passed by the Reichstag. He now claimed that such presidential decrees, although not fully laws, were no longer simply measures, but a new form of legislation. Although he maintained that the distinction between law and measure should not be fully given up, he now considered it difficult to maintain in practice.

Schmitt still held back from denying the ultimately parliamentary nature of legislation. He was careful to insist in his legal opinion that a majority vote in the Reichstag would still lead to the suspension of such decrees, and if it was dissolved, all decrees implemented in the interim could be reviewed by the new Reichstag. It should be said that since the government, in his view, could now repeatedly dissolve a recalcitrant Reichstag, this ultimate control was becoming a *Doktorfrage*.[20] But he still kept open the possibility that the whole presidential system was merely a temporary expedient to govern the country until a party majority could be formed, whereupon the Reichstag would be restored to its former position.

But the difficulties of attempting to stabilize a dire economic situation with a far-reaching programme of structural adjustment led Schmitt to begin to call the very framework of the division-of-powers system into question. In his articles from 1930 on the financial dimension of the Brüning decrees, Schmitt argued that an older *laissez-faire* view, according to which the state should take a hands-off approach towards a self-adjusting economy, had to give way to more activist approaches. He had difficulty believing that fragile and shifting coalition governments could ever set and execute guidelines of national economic policy. Although he considered the Brüning government 'activist', the programme being implemented was in fact beholden to a rigid fiscal orthodoxy, and was innocent of any modern counter-cyclical conception of the budget. Brüning rejected any artificial creation of demand – not only because of the consensus view among economists, which held that such measures would be inflationary, but also because cutbacks and a gold standard were an integral part of his reparations programme. But as the contraction began to affect healthy industries as well, such a rigid adherence to deflationary measures became increasingly irrational from an economy-wide perspective.[21] Despite this unwelcome result, employers by and large supported austerity, as they still do today, because of its restraining effect on wages. Although Schmitt would often write about the dangers of an unbridled capitalist economy, his role in this period was to justify the constitutionality of economic policies which timidly accepted the logic and verdict of the market. Cutbacks in social services and a wage reduction for government workers only had the effect of deepening a depression whose bottom had yet to be reached, and Schmitt became an unloved figure on the Left.

As this scenario unfolded, the Social Democrats and the unions allied to them demonstrated a passivity bordering on paralysis. Although the Social Democrats were the second biggest party in the Reichstag, they had long since lost the taste for rocking the boat of government with principled calls for a no-confidence vote. The role of a real parliamentary opposition had effectively become meaningless, as few parties had an interest in pulling out of governing coalitions of their own making. Although the Depression had taken a devastating toll on the employment level of unionized workers, the almost total absence of strike activity from 1930 to 1933 exposed the degree to which organized labour had been bureaucratically incorporated into various levels of the state, and its inability to act effectively when it was excluded from such power-sharing arrangements.

While the SPD and its unions would not break openly with Brüning, a large section of the conservative professional associations representing government workers began vociferously to protest proposed reductions in their wages. This set them on a collision course with the government and those who publicly defended its measures. The increasingly bitter division within the legal community between supporters of the government and supporters of the right-wing National Opposition (the Nazis plus Hugenberg's DNVP) created an acrimonious atmosphere in conferences organized to discuss the constitutionality of these measures, such as the one held in Halle near the end of October 1931. Alongside coalition party government and overly politicized courts, Schmitt now explicitly portrayed large sections of the bureaucracy as agents of 'polycratic' disorder. His prominent role as a defender of Brüning's emergency financial measures had made him a target of attacks from conservative professional associations. The state bureaucracy was feeling increasingly abandoned by a government which now had no other basis of support than this beleaguered bureaucracy.

Regular personal contacts with the most prominent players in late Weimar politics allowed Schmitt to witness the precarious position of an elite within a modern state with multiple and uncoordinated functions. This lack of direction and coherence allowed what he saw as a swarm of subelites, based in party organizations outside the state, to occupy key positions in the strategic zones within it. In his opinion the institutional entrenchment of a heterogeneous multiparty corporatism was legally sanctioned through the persistence of a nineteenth-century system of division of powers. In the Weimar Republic this problem was aggravated by the pre-eminence of parliament within the division of powers – that is, the absence of any counterbalance to it, apart from the temporary, emergency measures of the President. Schmitt warned that this endless toing and froing between a dysfunctional yet obstructionist Reichstag and a government periodically issuing emergency legislation without a parliamentary majority was creating an opportunity for the judiciary to interpose itself as the final political arbitrator in a state increasingly becoming a bundle of contracts between the most powerful interest groups.

Whatever the merits of Schmitt's case, it should be mentioned that he never thought to include in his portrayal of this 'polycratic rule' all those scheming state secretaries and military officers manoeuvring in the corridors of power.[22] Certainly the Finance Ministry, which Schmitt held up as a bastion of independent statehood, was not included, even though since the mid 1920s it had been doling out massive subsidies to heavy industry, distorting prices throughout the whole economy. His analysis of 'polycratic rule' thus has to be seen in the context of the friend–enemy alignments of the period.[23]

For Schmitt, presidential rule by decree was no longer simply a means to stabilize the division-of-powers system but an organizational necessity for national economic policy. In his writing from this period he tended to associate liberalism not with a belief in government by discussion but with a constitution in which the sphere of politics could be easily delineated from a sphere of self-regulating market relations.[24] He claimed that the central problem of modern politics was that this line dividing the two had broken down and given rise to an uncoordinated interpenetration of economics and politics. To illustrate the magnitude of the problem, he often cited the statistic that in 1928, 53 per cent of Germany's gross national income was controlled by the state in one form or another:

> Here one can proceed from a recognized and undisputed fact that public finance in comparison to the earlier prewar dimensions as well as in relationship to the contemporary free and private . . . economy has assumed such proportions that what lies before us is not merely a quantitative increase but a 'structural transformation'. This will seize hold of all domains of public life, and not only immediately financial and economic affairs.[25]

Influenced by the analysis of Popitz, Schmitt concluded that the self-regulating free market was a thing of the past, and that the importance of 'planning' would grow immensely.[26] In a work published in 1933, he showed a subtle understanding of the role of the state in a modern capitalist economy:

> State power also means, today in an entirely different sense from earlier, simultaneously power over national economic income, and the national economy itself. That means already a power position in itself, but this

moreover results in an irresistible ongoing development of new power positions. Out of this there develops the necessity of a great, long-term plan, even if the purpose of this plan is the restoration of a planless functioning economic system. . . . I am in complete agreement with Hans Freyer that it is not the planners who should rule, but the rulers who should plan.[27]

Schmitt proposed that legal theory had to emancipate itself from thinking in terms of the duality of state and economy as legally separate spheres. He predicted that legal theory would have to come to terms with changes in the relationship between politics and economics brought about by the advent of monopoly capitalism. A more realistic approach to managing a post-*laissez-faire* capitalist economy had to move beyond thinking in terms of the separation of state and society, and differentiate three distinct but connected zones: a nationalized sector – which, in his modest assessment, might consist of only such services as post and public transportation; a purely private sector; and a monopoly sector based on the self-organization of the capitalist class in the commanding heights, organized into syndicates and chambers.[28]

The widening scope and growing necessity of far-ranging political interventions in previously private domains made it all the more important that the commanding heights of the economy be strategically promoted. But Weimar's post-*laissez-faire* economy was a case study in how not to intervene.[29] What made this situation almost intractable was the fact that those who sought to reduce the influence on the economy of corporate interest groups by creating depoliticized zones outside the power of the Reich government were often only compounding the problem of polycratic disorder. The behaviour of the *Reichsbank* under Schacht exemplified the dangers of this process: designed to stand outside the pressures of party politics, it had increasingly become one more among the many semi-independent forces with which the Reich government was forced to negotiate as an equal.[30] As Schmitt saw it, certain regions of the economy did in fact have to be 'depoliticized', while others had to be made more directly subject to political guidance of the right kind; it would take the right kind of government to know which was which.

Schmitt saw the transition to a total state as a Europe-wide phenomenon, but by 'total' he meant the growing involvement of the state in economy and society, not necessarily a state playing a strong, directive role. The term 'total state', as he used it, covered both the emerging corporatist, welfare state and specifically totalitarian regimes. But although he placed them in a common genus, it seemed to him that there was much to be said for the vigour of the Russian and Italian regimes compared to Weimar pluralism. Schmitt was beginning to come to the conclusion that it might not be possible to break the hold of this anarchic, corporatist grip on the economy without breaking with the constitution itself and its underlying class truce.

While Brüning had managed to bend the rules and gain the grudging support of the SPD and unions, this was contingent upon not breaking with earlier settlements – that is, unilaterally changing the federal nature of the Reich in order to restore conservative control over Prussia. Precisely for this reason, the leading representatives of heavy industry in the *Langnamverein* had already openly come out against Brüning, as had the representatives of big agriculture. But even outside heavy industry and subsidized estate agriculture, the Brüning government was fast losing support in the business community, which accused it of pandering to the Social Democrats and the unions. In an article for *Ring* entitled 'Eine Warnung vor falschen politischen Fragestellungen' ('A Warning about Posing False Political Questions') Schmitt cautioned restraint to the powerful elites whose dissatisfaction with Brüning was growing intense, and who were expecting solutions through behind-the-scenes manoeuvres.

> One can approach the problem courageously and, if you like, boldly, and demand a constitutional reform in the authentic political sense, in which one seeks to compel the forces which really dominate the state now to step forward on to the stage as such, ripping down the curtains of pseudo-statehood and making those who have power use it openly, so that responsibility once again becomes possible, so that one can know who is guilty and deal with him. That would certainly be a constitutional reform of the grandest style – not a behind-the-scenes affair but, rather, simply a new constitution. I don't believe that we can speak of such things at present.[31]

The political significance of this cautionary statement should be seen in the light of the contemporary attempts of heavy industry unilaterally to destroy collective bargaining and the compulsory arbitration of the Labour Ministry with massive industry-wide lockouts. Schmitt delivered it as a warning because the public outrage this was creating did not, however, seem to have fazed the lords of steel, iron and coal, and only hardened their conviction that not even their parliamentary representatives would always back them when it came to the crunch.[32] On many occasions over the course of 1930, Schmitt had argued before business groups and in the pages of *Ring* that a solution to their grievances could still be pursued within the framework of the Constitution, and that it would be reckless to think of discarding it:

> in relation to you, I feel myself to be in the position of a mechanic who, while driving, warns that one part must be taken out and replaced by another. . . . More cautiously, I do not wish to say that it involves the car's engine. It does, however, involve a very important part, without which the car will not go, and which it is better to leave alone if one does not want to take one's chances with unforeseeable and dangerous experiments.[33]

Although Schmitt knew Brüning through his earlier involvement in Catholic organizations, he was not especially close to him, nor to the leadership of the Centre Party. He was still in good standing with the party and its press, and was anxious to maintain his reputation in these circles as well. Until the fall of Brüning, he received a good press from the Centre. But since the summer of 1930, support for the government in the general electorate had been diminishing fast. When its financial proposals were rejected by the Reichstag, Brüning thought that by dissolving it he might obtain a more favourable balance of forces in a new Reichstag, allowing him to reduce his reliance on Social Democratic votes. He was spectacularly refuted.

The results of the election of 14 September 1930 demonstrated the toll the Depression was taking on the population, and the hostility to a government whose austerity measures seemed to be making the situation far worse. The Nazis leapt forward from 12 seats to 107, and the Communist Party from 54 to 77. The violent conduct of the Nazis in the streets and in the Reichstag had the effect of making other parties more compliant, and Brüning was able to push through large parts of his financial programme. This session of the Reichstag lasted for only two months and was then adjourned for six, discontinuing it as a regular arm of government.

Anxious not to alienate the DNVP and push it further into its alliance with the Nazis, Brüning kept the SPD out of the government, even though he depended on its support to weather any no-confidence vote. Hindenburg was less concerned than Brüning to operate on a nominally parliamentary basis, and forced him to dismiss all other members of the Centre Party from the Cabinet – except Adam Stegerwald, who stayed on as Labour Minister because his presence was required to maintain the loyalty of the Catholic unions.

As the Depression was reaching its nadir in 1931, with unemployment at about 5,615,000, the city of Berlin became a battleground for violent, armed clashes between Nazi and Communist militias with a heavy toll of dead and wounded. Brüning supported steps taken by the Prussian government against armed and uniformed demonstrations by 'anti-constitutional parties' – that is, the Nazis and the Communists. Although Brüning was not, in principle, against wooing the Nazis, his Interior Minister Groener was eventually forced to take police measures against the violent demonstrations of the SA, in actions that were wildly denounced by nearly the entire bourgeois press as pandering to the Social Democrats in Prussia.[34]

After seven years in office, Hindenburg's term was over, and running for a second pitted him against Adolf Hitler and the Communist candidate, Ernst Thälmann. Hindenburg was not at all pleased to be running as the candidate backed by the Centre and, worse, the Social

Democrats, while all his conservative friends and neighbours from East Prussia seemed to be abandoning him for a corporal who, he was told, came from Bohemia, of all places. Hindenburg's victory in the April 1932 presidential election, although substantial, revealed that fully 37 per cent of the country preferred Hitler. Although many saw the result as a victory for the Republic, General Schleicher came to the conclusion that after Hindenburg's show of strength, the Nazis could now be made more co-operative and, somewhere down the line, be brought into government as a junior partner. But for this to happen, Brüning had to go. Schleicher convinced Hindenburg that the time had come to abandon Brüning, and on 30 May, under heavy pressure from those who had originally brought him to power, he resigned.

Would the Weimar Republic have survived had Brüning been allowed to stay in power? Such counterfactuals are difficult to determine, but according to Trevinarius, a conservative member of his Cabinet, Brüning's objective had been to maintain links with the Social Democrats in order to secure Hindenburg's re-election, use them to get the working class to accept wage reductions, then abandon them for a coalition based on an alliance between the Centre and the Nazis. Brüning had, in fact, arranged Hitler's first meeting with Hindenburg and Schleicher. The ball was already rolling in an unmistakable, if not yet totally irreversible, direction.[35]

11

Legality and Legitimacy

Franz von Papen, a Catholic aristocrat and leading figure in the Gentlemen's Club, was appointed Chancellor. Although he had previously been on the far right wing of the Centre Party, Papen was well respected in the DNVP owing to his impeccable monarchist credentials. The division which had opened up in the conservative camp over the policies of the Brüning government now seemed destined to be closed as DNVP-affiliated ministers were to be brought into government for the first time since 1928. The new Papen government combined the constituencies of old and new conservatism to create a cabinet which, in the midst of the Depression, was a provocative caricature of social exclusion, consisting almost entirely of titled aristocrats.

For a long time Schmitt had believed that the executive had become the natural decision-making centre of a modern state, and involvement with its beleaguered and scheming elites in the last years of the Republic intensified and sharpened this conviction. For all his misgivings about the reactionary conspiracy which had brought down Brüning, he believed that the Papen government represented the last chance for such an elite to reinvent itself as the epicentre of decision, action and organization in the field of modern politics.

Despite his abiding concern with the problem of legitimacy, it should be said that this was from the outset, without doubt, the most unpopular government in modern German history. Violently attacked by the SPD and the double-crossed Centre Party, it was also rejected – albeit less violently – by the moderate right-wing DVP, representing a significant segment of business opinion outside heavy industry.

The fall of Brüning sent shock waves through the Centre Party,whose leaders sensed that the fate of the Italian Popolaris under Mussolini might be in store for them.[1] Determined to avoid this fate, the archconservative Prelate Kaas, the party's official leader, sought to intensify negotiations with the Nazis, in order somehow to get back into government. Schmitt, who had been lauded for supporting Brüning, was now considered a renegade, and was bitterly attacked in the party press. From this point on, none of his articles would be published in the Centre-affiliated press, and he was confined to publishing almost

exclusively in 'conservative revolutionary' journals. Reconciliation in
the conservative camp was purchased at the expense of the Centre's
bitter hostility to the new government.

The establishment of the Papen government also split the ranks of
the so-called National Opposition, leaving the Nazis on the outside
barely tolerating a government in which some of their erstwhile reactionary allies were well represented. Even this 'tolerance' of the Nazis
towards Papen had a price: the ban which had earlier been imposed
on Communist and Nazi militias was lifted from the SA and the SS
on 14 June 1932, making the latter, *stricto sensu*, no longer 'anti-
constitutional'. The number of dead from street battles between
Communists and Nazis skyrocketed from seventeen in June to eighty-
six the following month. Schmitt was much more cautious than his
patron Schleicher about the advantages of dealing with the Nazis as
partners. Elections had been scheduled for 31 July, and during the
campaign Schmitt argued in a publication now under the control of
the General, *Tägliche Rundschau*, that a vote for the Nazis was courting
disaster; but from the wording of his argument it is clear that he was
addressing it to those who had already begun to vote Nazi or were
now tempted to; he was being drawn willy-nilly to this end of the
political spectrum:

> Anyone who allows the National Socialists to obtain the majority on 31 July,
> even if he is not a National Socialist and sees in this party only the lesser of
> evils, is acting foolishly. He gives this ideologically and politically immature
> movement the possibility of changing the Constitution, introducing a state
> church, dissolving the unions, etc. He hands Germany over to this group.
> Therefore, while it was previously justifiable, considering the circumstances,
> to promote Hitler's resistance movement, on 31 July it would be thoroughly
> dangerous, because 51 per cent gives the NSDAP a 'political premium' of
> unforeseeable consequences.[2]

In 1932 it became obvious that the status quo could collapse at any
moment, and Schmitt was not alone in adopting what could be
described as a manifestly cavalier attitude towards the Constitution. In
his mind, interpretative trends in constitutional law going back to the
early 1920s were partly to blame for the Constitution's increasingly
indeterminate status in political life. What he considered the earlier
theoretical error of not clearly distinguishing laws and executive measures had given rise to a sort of customary right, on the basis of which it
was now possible for government decrees to substitute for laws no
longer forthcoming from a dysfunctional Reichstag. The only remaining distinction, in his view, was that decrees issued by the government
could never change the Constitution, while qualified majorities in the
Reichstag could still change individual provisions of it. In retrospect, it

now seemed clear to him that when the Constitution was first being framed, the failure to approve the originally conceived provision placing the emergency powers of the President under stricter parliamentary control resulted in a large constitutional grey area, a gap, which was now being filled by the precedent of executive authorization.

But a constitution with such large grey areas, so dependent on precedent to reveal its 'inner principles', could be only a tentative framework, and had to remain open to revisions which would impart greater coherence to the whole. At this time Schmitt still insisted that this was not the emergence of a new constitution; rather, it was the protection of the existing one under unforeseen circumstances, but the meaning of this distinction was become increasingly tenuous.

Schmitt's subtle theoretical splitting of the Constitution into an essential and a less essential part enabled the new government to justify its constitutional programme. Perhaps surprisingly, then, he did not embrace most of the reactionary constitutional revisions proposed by the Papen government, particularly the introduction of an upper house to guarantee permanent conservative control over the state. Much of the impetus behind this almost farcically reactionary agenda came from old monocled conservatives who viewed Prussia as their state by birthright, and were unreconciled to the postwar loss of their status privileges. The most aggressive representative of this element was the Interior Minister, Gayl, who, more than any other member of the Papen Cabinet, unflinchingly advocated the most aggressively reactionary measures. This class type was still prominent in the DNVP, and the party's participation in any national government was conditional upon restoring conservative hegemony in the Prussian state, which was now, by a parliamentary manoeuvre, still in the possession of the Weimar coalition. If they could not achieve this in an alliance with the Centre Party, they wanted it done by pure authoritarian means – the out-and-out reconquest of the Prussian bureaucracy.

Schmitt was somewhat unenthusiastic about this reactionary forward charge. His opposition to the creation of an upper house which would provide the organizational basis for a conservative reconquest of the state was particularly explicit:

In the history of modern constitutions, the second chamber – that is a chamber not based on universal suffrage – has previously had the function of restraining and retarding. It is supposed to secure permanence, continuity and stability against a revolutionary first chamber based on the universal suffrage of the essentially propertyless masses. In our case, the first – that is, the chamber based on universal suffrage – is incapable of any action. If now a second chamber is conceived as a restraint and a counterpoise to a first chamber incapable of acting, then it is an ill-conceived institution; something which is in itself incapable of acting does not need to be restrained.[3]

While Schmitt could never bring himself to support schemes so absolutely out of step with the times, and thus lacking any popular legitimacy, he would find himself working more intimately with this government than with the previous one. It should be said, however, that not even significant differences in political motive between Schmitt and those who were moving more or less in the same direction on this issue can change the fact that his little project was effectively working in tandem with a bigger one. Until 1933 he was willing to believe that these conservative gentlemen were the agents of a great political renewal – that is to say, he imputed to them goals which they did not have and could not achieve.

In the civil-war atmosphere of Berlin in the summer of 1932, Schmitt finished a book entitled *Legalität und Legitimität*[1] ('Legality and Legitimacy'), in which he argued that the Reich government must be able to ban the actions of anti-constitutional parties. He said that the existence of parties with massive militias at their disposal had created an almost revolutionary situation in which the distinction between the normal and the exceptional had become so thoroughly effaced that the question of what the normal procedures were could no longer be answered except politically.

Legalität und Legitimität began by pointing out that the Weimar Republic had now reached a point where parliament, the courts and the executive could all plausibly claim to be the highest authority in the state. But before a decision could be reached on the basis of the wording of the Constitution, it was necessary to clarify the criteria of legitimation specific to each of these powers of government.

In essentially feudal political communities based on entrenched rights and privileges, legitimate political decisions took on a judicial form. These were political communities where independent powers were often only nominally subject to centralized authority, and maintained a right of resistance which could be exercised during litigation with other powers. The contemporary tendency in conflict-ridden, 'pluralistic societies' to reduce government to arbitration created new opportunities for this older mode of legitimation to re-emerge. When the state is carved up into spoils among contending powers, such powers will come to rely upon a politicized judiciary to review the terms of the contracts over the spoils, because they will no longer tolerate decisions from a strong form of government which would eliminate their growing 'right of resistance'.

What were the conditions for the elimination of this right of resistance upon which the territorial monopoly of legitimate force is based? For classical liberals, the theoretical solution to this problem was that the right of resistance could be alienated to a state exercising its power through general laws, which – in contrast to the arbitrary quality of royal decrees – generated binding obligations in conformity with reason. In the nineteenth century this trust in legality had been based on the assumption that parliamentary majorities would not violate the basic rights of individuals. This in turn was based on the assumption that the politically active population was homogeneous, not divided into permanent factions with interests apart from those of the community in general.

Schmitt argued that when the assumption of a homogeneous national will underlying the opposition of parties is abandoned, governing coalitions based on a parliamentary majority find it difficult to present their interparty compromises as laws which all are obliged to obey. This is because the obligation to obey a majority which could previously claim to represent a uniform whole cannot be simply transferred to majorities which are merely statistical aggregations of constituencies, provisionally mobilized around the friend–enemy oppositions of party politics. Indeed, he suggested that it was difficult to understand what the basis of obedience to the law would be in a 'pluralist system' where semi-independent corporate bodies, associations and parties have partially emancipated themselves from an enclosed, uniform and compulsory order. Without the latter, 'the primordial problem of "resistance to tyrants", that is, against injustice and the misuse of state power, remains, and any functionalist-formalist hollowing out of the parliamentary state will not solve it.'[5]

Schmitt claimed that the obligation of obedience to the law would disappear if law were simply the product of anything a qualified majority could agree to on a given day. In order to be democratically legitimate, a qualified majority has to be able to present its actions plausibly as in accordance with the best interests of the minority, or at least as not preventing a minority from becoming a future majority: 'A material principle of justice must always be presupposed, even if it is only the principle that all opinions and movements be given a chance to form a majority.'[6] Even the obligation to obey a majority based on such a purely procedural principle of justice as this would none the less be conditional on certain assumptions concerning what in the Constitution could be suspended or altered. But Schmitt argued that the trust in the legislator for which the right of resistance was forgone evaporates if a majority could legally come to power and then proceed to change the Constitution, and so block off this legal path to power for the minority left behind. This problem assumes massive proportions when parties explicitly committed to replacing the Constitution have a chance of forming a government. According to Schmitt, despite the tenuous legitimacy of the majority upon which it is based, such a government would derive from the mere occupancy of power, a certain 'political surplus-value':

This political premium is in peaceful and normal times relatively calculable; in abnormal times entirely incalculable and unforeseeable. [This premium] is of a threefold nature: first, it emerges out of the concrete interpretation and treatment of such indeterminate and discretionary concepts as 'public safety and order', 'danger', 'emergency', 'necessary measures', 'anti-constitutional activity', 'peaceful intention', 'vital interest', and so on. Secondly, the legal occupant of power has the presumption of legality on his side in disputed cases which naturally always arise with the use of such indeterminate concepts in difficult conditions. Thirdly, and finally, his commands for the time being are immediately executable, even if complaints and the protection of courts are foreseen.[7]

Schmitt rejected the idea put forward by his former student and Social Democratic theorist Otto Kirchheimer that the procedural principle of equal chance to form a government could be extended to parties programmatically committed to destroying the Constitution, as long as there were safeguards preventing them from subsequently keeping other parties from forming a government. Schmitt argued that this principle provided no way out of the problem of political surplus-value, the premium which accrues to whoever is in government; and he considered it a sign of the impending collapse of the state that by default, the courts were being entrusted with this problem. He maintained that it was the government, not the courts, which must be allowed to discriminate against those parties which, if they legally came to power, would shut this door of legality behind them – they would be the enemies of the Constitution.

It is clear from the following passage that not only did Schmitt still put the Communists and the Nazis in this category – contrary to the line of the Papen government – but that because of the simple fact that the Nazis were far more likely to be included in some future government, he actually saw them as representing the greater, more immediate danger:

[Concerning] the numerous commentaries and judicial decisions on the legality or illegality of National Socialist organizations . . . on the 'peacefulness' of their assemblies, I would like to emphasize that when it comes to National Socialists, Communists, godless or whoever, the decisive answer to these sorts of questions, if they are given in a juristically objective form, should in no way be discerned from individual articles of the Constitution.[8]

The attempt to curb potential abuses by raising the qualified majority in the Reichstag to two-thirds in the case of a constitutional revision did not address the real problem of legitimacy, because heightened numerical hurdles cannot specify any inviolable principles of the Constitution. Such principles, Schmitt now argued must take precedence over the organizational norms of the first part of the Constitution, which do not by themselves reveal how they should be read when difficult questions of interpretation arise. Yet the problem was that the material principles set out in the second part of the Constitution lacked any connection to its value-neutral organizational component: 'The Weimar Constitution is literally split between the value neutrality of its first and the value plenitude of its second component.'[9] Although he presented this as a dramatic discovery, Schmitt had claimed as far back as *Verfassungslehre* that the constitutional *Rechtsstaat* lacked a co-ordinating principle between the section which organized the political will of the community and the section which limited it in the name of individual freedoms: in simple terms, was the validity of the law based on the legislative will organized in the first section, or in the bundle of rights and goals laid out in the second?

Whereas Schmitt had previously argued that the organizational part of the Constitution took precedence over the controversial principles articulated in its first section, he now argued that the basic rights, the bourgeois core of this second section, provided the Constitution with its ultimate principles, and thus a perspective from which to interpret the division of powers spelled out in the organizational part. Schmitt's claim that the bourgeois core of the rights-based section had to take precedence over the procedural section, in which the collective will was organized, implied that popular sovereignty was not the ultimate source of the Constitution's legitimacy. Although this was the opposite of the position he had taken in *Verfassungslehre*, the break was not yet acknowledged.

Prewar legal positivism had held that the universal rights of man defined the limits of state power *vis-à-vis* private individuals, but what the state gave, it could also take away, as long as the limitation of such rights was done by legal statute. Trust in the rule of law was so great that legislation limiting a basic right was described as the 'concretization' of that right in legal form. But the disturbingly demotic political complexion of postwar parliaments had led to widespread sentiment in German legal circles that some limits, embodied in inviolable rights, had to be imposed on parliament, especially now that the monarchy's power of veto had been removed. Schmitt, too, argued that in a democracy it is difficult to protect anything from a majority, even though this is often necessary.

But because the basic rights section of the Weimar Constitution contained – apart from traditional bourgeois rights and freedoms – a motley assortment of social demands, not all its provisions could be given equal weight, because this section contained principles which simply could not be reconciled – first and foremost, the contradiction between a bourgeois *Rechtsstaat* and socialism. The attempt to come to some compromise on this point had created unanticipated problems of interpreting the status of these provisions as limitations on the prerogative of the legislator. Habermas has recently argued that the existence of such complex material norms in a constitution has created serious problems for democracy based on a division of powers:

> Although basic rights originally consisted of 'defensive' rights that grant liberties and keep an intervening administration within the bounds of law, they have now become the architectonic principles of the legal order, transforming the content of individual, or 'subjective' liberties into the fundamental norms that penetrate and shape 'objective' law, albeit in a conceptually unclarified manner.[10]

Furthermore, when such general bourgeois freedoms are mixed up with very particular provisions protecting unions and other specific corporate groups, an undesirable consequence invariably ensues: general freedoms are seen as being simply 'concretized' by any act of legislation, while the already concrete protection of this or that group cannot be touched by the legislator except by altering the Constitution.

In Schmitt's view, the core of this second component had to be pruned down to the essentials. What, then, were the essential basic freedoms? Not everything could be conceived as a basic right; unless corporate bodies have secured an imprescriptible right of existence, these must be individual rights. Such rights could be seen as approaching the status of natural rights. In this work, as in *Verfassungslehre*, Schmitt was very clear about what type of society formed the material basis of this minimal set of individual liberties: 'These freedoms circumscribe the social structure of an individualistic social order whose maintenance and safeguarding should be served by the organizational regulation of the state.'[11] In specifying the status of these 'individualistic' basic freedoms in a political order, he drew upon the writings of the one contemporary he considered to be his teacher, the recently deceased Frenchman Maurice Hauriou:

> [These freedoms] have, as an outstanding French theorist of public law, Maurice Hauriou has explained, a '*superlégalité constitutionelle*', which is raised not only above the usual simple laws, but also over the written constitutional laws, and excludes their replacement through laws of constitutional revision.[12]

Again, Habermas provides a succinct account of the problem which Hauriou, Schmitt and others were confronting:

> [O]nly with the establishment of the Weimar Republic did the political bases for the assumed autarchy of private law disappear. It was then no longer possible to contrast private law as the realm of individual freedom with public law as the field in which state coercion has effect. Already on the defensive, civil law jurisprudence was stimulated by these developments to reflect on those non-legal background assumptions that had provided the tacit under-

lying premises for the now wavering distinction between private and public law.[13]

Schmitt concluded *Legalität und Legitimität* by acknowledging that there was no way of denying that the framers of the Constitution had intended the Reichstag to be the legislative power, not a government, lacking a parliamentary majority and authorized by the President to act in a legislative capacity. Although he attempted to present rule by presidential decree as a practice in conformity with the fundamentals of the *Rechtsstaat*, he simultaneously suggested that perhaps the Weimar Constitution was simply no longer a constitution of the nineteenth-century parliamentary type, because properly interpreted, it entrusted its protection more to the executive than to parliament.

Every viable constitution confers upon a particular institution far-ranging discretionary powers to ensure that a political community will not drift away from its original mandate. The interpretation of this mandate becomes the central political issue in periods of great historical transformation, because the question of whether it has been revoked by 'history', 'the people' or, in an earlier era, by 'God' himself, is inescapable. Schmitt felt that in the twentieth century, as in the sixteenth and seventeenth centuries, the relationship between rulers and ruled would be revolutionized by the executive. In the introduction to *Legalität und Legitimität* he sought to convey the significance of the Papen government, and whatever came after, in the context of a history-making redefinition of the relationship between state and subject, as well as his uncertainty about the direction of these changes: 'The governmental as well as the administrative state are ... instruments of radical changes, whether reactionary or revolutionary, and comprehensive planned, long-range transformations.'[14]

When a whole form of government, a constitution, is about to give way, the language of legality is eventually discarded by those who think that their turn is coming. The war of incommensurable standards of legitimacy was now moving towards a day of reckoning, and the momentum was overwhelmingly on the Right; but in what direction – 'reactionary or revolutionary'; and who would rule – top hats or brown shirts; and with what mandate? Schmitt gave no sign of knowing the answers to the questions he was posing.

Trial and Endgame

On 20 July 1932, ten days after Schmitt had finished *Legalität und Legitimität,* Papen placed the whole of Prussia under martial law, alleging that its Social Democratic-led Braun–Severing government could no longer withstand the Communist menace, and that it was to be dissolved and replaced by a commissar appointed by the Reich. The Social Democratic-led government had been a minority government since state elections on 24 April in which more than 50 per cent had voted either for the Nazis or for the Communists. But since no new majority could be formed, the incumbents declared that they were a caretaker government, and would not step down. Papen attempted to demonstrate before the election that he was moving strongly against the Left, but the imposition of a Reich commissar was also another step in the strategy of taming the Nazis: although the police measures taken by the deposed Braun–Severing government of Prussia against the Nazis would cease, a Prussia ruled directly by the Reich could not fall, through elections, into the hands of the Nazis.

Schmitt was certainly aware of at least the existence of these plans, if not the details, when he finished *Legalität und Legitimität.* On 25 July, only five days after the Reich government openly sought to depose the 'other government' in Berlin, the Braun–Severing government, Papen announced in a Cabinet meeting that Schmitt would justify this move in a forthcoming article.[1] He might even have played a role in convincing Hindenburg of the constitutionality of this course of action.

This strike against Prussia was a breach of what Schmitt had for a long time considered to be the truce underlying the Constitution, and with this step the presidential system had crossed the Rubicon. Previously Schmitt had maintained that the real problem was not the Constitution but a system of party competition and collusion which had worked its way into the state apparatus and disruptively reprogrammed its functions. But as early as 1931 many in Schmitt's network were coming to the conclusion that sidestepping the Reichstag through Article 48 was not enough, and that further steps had to be taken against 'Red Prussia'.

A major source of instability in Prussia, and in the Republic as a whole, was right-wing alienation from a polity in which organized labour had small but solid footholds in the state, thus preventing the 'right kind' of structural adjustment – that is, one in which the burdens were borne principally by the working class, and not – as happened repeatedly in Weimar – by conservative constituencies as well. Geoff Eley points out that this was a situation with a dangerous precedent:

> the closer analogue to Italy in 1918–1922 is the Germany of 1930 to 1933, when the situation of the SPD was highly reminiscent of the Italy Socialist Party's ten years before. It provoked the right to anger and anxiety with the same immobilizing combination of characteristics: entrenched reformism, obstinately bunkered in the defensive apparatus of social legislation, labor law and local government influence which blocked the necessary measures of ruthless capitalist stabilization.[2]

Although it was only one of fifteen historic states, Prussia occupied two-thirds of the surface of the entire Reich, and contained three-fifths of its population. This is where the Social Democrats and unions were the most entrenched, being far weaker on the Reich level, and in the eyes of the Right this was the crux of the federal problem. The shift in Schmitt's legal views on the federal nature of the Constitution was in large part motivated by this partisan evaluation. Although he had initially regarded proposals for a constitutional revision by executive decree of the federal relationship between Reich and Prussia as legally dubious and politically unnecessary, by the end of 1931 he was becoming receptive to the idea that the Weimar Constitution needed to be purged of an unwieldy federal structure inherited from the old Bismarck Reich. It is possible to argue that this change of position was not purely opportunistic, as his unitarist conception of the state was difficult to reconcile with the federal structure inherited from the old Prusso–German monarchy.

Under the old monarchy, the Reich government did not possess fully developed attributes of statehood, ultimately because it did not have the power to levy income taxes. Bismarck's intention had been effectively to hamstring it by making it reliant on regressive sales taxes. Even while the Weimar Constitution was being written, attempts had been made by those representing the Reich to abandon a federalism which had lost its historical, as well as fiscal, justification. At the time, the principal obstacle to such plans had been Bavaria, which bargained hard to preserve its independence. After the war, in his duties at the Reich Finance Ministry, Popitz had tirelessly advocated a centralized regime of tax collection as the foundation of a more concentrated statehood.[3] The necessity of reparation payments accelerated this process of concentration. Even before he became chief aide to the Finance Minister, Hilferding, Popitz had been willing to draw fire from the business community, including the DVP, for his ideas; but the evolution of the presidential system shifted the focus of his political diagnosis and proposals for reform sharply rightwards. After his retirement, he came into increasing contact with businessmen, and became convinced that the tax burden had to be shifted from their shoulders; consequently, the costs of social welfare would have to be shifted on to local government, which would be left to support the needy out of property taxes. As few would be able to do this, such services would be drastically cut back. Despite his conclusion that the self-regulating market was a thing of the past, Popitz saw the new role of the state not in terms of public works but as a means of holding wages down and creating other such 'incentives' for capital investment.[4]

Early in 1931, as chairman of a study group on financial reform, Popitz had proposed that on a fiscal level the Reich should incorporate the intermediate federal states, thus creating a direct taxing and spending relationship to the municipalities. Popitz's proposals came at a time when the *Länder* (the federal states) and municipal governments were in a deep fiscal crisis brought about by the collapse of the economy and the subsequent ballooning social welfare costs. Unlike Schmitt, the more conservative Popitz couched his political programme in the language of the nineteenth-century bourgeois ideal of municipal self-government based on sound local budgets controlled by those who paid property taxes. Only those municipalities which could maintain themselves on this basis would retain self-government. The idea behind this plan to eliminate the intermediate power of the *Länder* was to shift costs downwards and power upwards.[5] Of course, Prussia would be the first state to be slated for downsizing in Popitz's plan.

Both Popitz and Schmitt moved in governing circles on the Reich level whose functions and jurisdictions overlapped and conflicted with counterpart Prussian ministries, not so firmly in the control of people like themselves. Popitz proposed that a revamped Reich limit itself to controlling the *Reichswehr*, the courts and police forces in big cities and industrial regions. The question of who controlled the 85,000 policemen in Prussia – roughly the same number as in the *Reichswehr* – was critical for the men around Hindenburg, because as things now stood, it was not clear whom they would obey in the event that they received conflicting orders. For Schmitt, this uncertainty demonstrated that Germany was on the verge of ceasing to be a state. As he put it in a later work: 'The kernel of the modern state is in its executive. . . . The most important of all monopolies, the monopoly of arms, is in its hands and belongs essentially to it.'[6] Despite the obvious fact that in the existing political context the dissolution of Prussia as a separate federal state was directed at the Social Democrats, the unions and the local welfare state, even the Social Democrat Hermann Heller recognized that the maintenance of the state government of Prussia, representing two-thirds of the population of the Reich, alongside a Reich government quartered in the same city, was both a colossal waste and a threat to the unity of the country:

> The dualism of Prussia and the Reich has dangerous consequences which in their totality are threatening to German democracy. As a result of the fact that Prussia has in its hands a massive administrative apparatus, a party might believe that it is able to renounce its power and responsibility within the Reich, to the degree that it is secure in its influence over the [Prussian] administration and especially the police.[7]

Although the dangers and inconveniences of the Reich/Prussia dualism were evident to many, dissolving whole layers of the Prussian administration and police inevitably raised the question: on whose terms? Since the Right held the reins of power at Reich level through the ever more powerful office of the President, any attempt at this point to undercut the independence of the Prussian state apparatus was bound to be a strike against the Left, the remains of the Weimar coalition in Prussia, and ultimately the political settlement upon which the whole Constitution was based.

Even before the Papen government's strike against Prussia, Schmitt might have thought that Popitz's plan to dissolve the Prussian state and bring its municipalities directly under the control of the Reich, although ideal, would be impossible to pull off, even considering the string of constitution-bending precedents which the presidential system had behind it. Although Article 18.1 gave the Reichstag the power to change the borders of any of the federal states, a two-thirds majority was necessary; even if the government could issue decrees with the force of law, almost no one claimed that this applied to issues requiring more than a simple majority; otherwise the Constitution itself could be changed in such a fashion.

But because the Prussian state government was now no longer based on a majority in the *Landtag*, and no new majority could be formed, the possibility had opened up that the Reich might be able to impose its will unilaterally on the 'other government' residing in Berlin. The Prussian government, for its part, claimed that it was only following the example of the Reich in denying a 'negative majority' the right to make Prussia ungovernable, and sought an injunction from the Reich Court in Leipzig to prevent the imposition of commissarial rule. The Prussian Social Democrats sought to avoid any mass actions against this coup from above that might scare away conservative state governments which were also opposed to unilateral changes in the federal status quo, but did not want to be seen as standing side by side with the Social Democrats.[8] Although no injunction was granted, this time the Reich

Court did not simply let the Reich have its way and a trial was scheduled for October.

Schmitt was called upon to represent the Papen Cabinet's claim that only the Reich, not a state government, could decide which parties were 'anti-constitutional', and thus could be discriminated against. He would argue that the Prussian government did not have the same right as the Reich President to impose such repressive measures, because while the latter occupied a position above parties, no government representing the interest of a party should have at its disposal the 'political surplus-value' to persecute its enemies in another party.[9] Behind all the legal technicalities of the case, Schmitt identified this as the political crux of the controversy. He made his point straightforwardly in an article which appeared on 29 July in the *Deutsche Allgemeine Zeitung*: 'There is no doubt that the essential point of controversy in the case concerns the political evaluation of two parties, the National Socialists and the Communists.'[10] During the proceedings Schmitt found himself adopting lines of argument which expressed a growing abandonment of previous inhibitions:

> It was an issue of the Reich government changing its manner of handling the National Socialist Movement, not so as to howl with the wolves, or to take the wind out of their sails or the like. It was in the first instance a simpler and more immediate matter of being just and objective, and lifting the insulting equivalence between a movement which millions of Germans not only sympathized with, but voted for, and the Communist Party.[11]

Perhaps Schmitt's views were simply changing to meet the needs of the case, but many of his arguments were now being used by friends and associates to discuss the National Socialist cause more sympathetically. On the Left, former friends and students increasingly came to view him in a sinister light. Otto Kirchheimer, perhaps the most talented of Schmitt's former students, portrayed him in dark colours, while also suggesting that most assessments of his political significance were illusions of the political moment:

> Over the course of this year [1932] Schmitt has, in the domain of the intellect, fallen into a reputation as nasty as that of Schleicher in practical politics. He has become a man of darkness, to whom one attributes just about everything, a state oracle that 'obviously' must be standing behind all plans, intentions and calculations.[12]

The raw, acrimonious atmosphere both inside and outside the courtroom would strain Schmitt's usually easy-going temperament. While previously he had been arguably far less anti-Semitic than most of his contemporaries on the Right, this was beginning to change. By some accounts, he appeared less convincing speaking before a court than his adversaries, some of whom were Jewish, and some of the frustration he felt towards them led to an occasional private anti-Semitic outburst, despite the fact that his main partner in representing the Reich at Leipzig was Erwin Jacobi, a Jewish legal scholar and a representative of Schmitt's position on Article 48 from the early 1920s.

The trial was destined to be a landmark event – not only because of the fateful nature of the proceedings, and the attendant publicity, but also because some of the best-known legal minds in Germany were representing both sides. Adding to the tension was the presence in the court of people, 'friends and enemies', who had quite often been on the opposite side of controversies, and now saw this one as bringing it all to a head. Schmitt – together with Professors Jacobi and Bilfinger – represented the Reich. Article 48.1 allowed the President to employ force to ensure a federal state's compliance with Reich laws; the only requirement was the President's assessment of non-compliance. But the decision could subsequently be challenged before the State Court, and this is exactly what occurred; in the meantime, the decree was suspended by the caretaker Prussian government. The plaintiffs consisted of parties which had a stake in making sure that Article 48 could not be used to suspend a state government: Prussia, the Prussian Centre Party, and Bavaria. Representing Prussia was the Social Democrat Hermann Heller, formerly a friend of Schmitt's but now a personal enemy; Gerhard Anschütz, author of the standard work on the Weimar Constitution; and Arnold Brecht, director of the Prussian Interior Ministry. The Centre Party was represented by Hans Peter, and Bavaria by Hans Nawiasky. The plaintiffs denied that the condition of non-compliance with Reich law was present and argued that the purges of the Prussian bureaucracy were unconstitutional, motivated by the government's plan to strike a deal with the Nazis.

Although this trial provided the opportunity for Schmitt to establish himself as the foremost constitutional legal scholar in the country, he had always rejected the idea that a court could sit in judgement over a political conflict. But in this case, if the Reich had tried to reject the jurisdiction of the court, and attempted to impose a commissar, the result would have been an at least four-sided civil war. Now he was going to have to tailor his arguments to a court which appeared to be playing the role of Guardian of the Constitution.

The ruling of the court on 25 October indeed confirmed Schmitt's worst fears about political justice: on the one hand the court ruled that the Prussian government had been unlawfully suspended; on the other, it also ruled that the Reich had the right to install a commissar in Prussia. In Schmitt's view, such a 'Solomonic' judgement not only did not resolve the conflict, it made the question 'who controls Prussia?' even more confusing: there were now three governments in Berlin: the

Reich national government, the commissarial government imposed by
the Reich on Prussia, alongside the still official Braun–Severing government. Although it paved the way for the Nazi seizure of power, this
decision – ironically – was greeted as a victory by those who supported
the Republic and as a defeat for those who supported Papen. It was, if
not the former, then certainly the latter, in that it convinced Hindenburg that from now on things had to proceed with a more outward
respect for legality.[13] Schmitt believed that because the government
had not clearly emerged as master of the situation, it would be
impossible to strike with a free hand against the remains of the Weimar
system without simultaneously strengthening the Nazis. He considered
the ruling a political and personal defeat.

But there was one alternative to a Nazi coalition government left
within the limited framework of the presidential system. Even before
the verdict, a fault line had opened up between General Schleicher
and his entourage on the one side, and Papen and Interior Minister
Gayl on the other, over how to respond to the results of the elections
on 31 July which had clearly expressed the widespread hatred in the
population for the Cabinet of barons around Papen. Since the Nazis
had polled 38 per cent and the Communists 14.5 per cent, it was
impossible to form a majority government even with the participation
of all the parties in the political space between them. Moreover, since
there was no question of support for a Papen Cabinet from either the
SPD or the Centre, the government was based on a very slender
conservative cross-section of the electorate. Adding to the government's
problems was the breakdown of negotiations with the Nazis caused by
the fact that Hitler had now acquired an even stronger position. When
the Reichstag began to convene on 12 September, Papen dissolved it
before a vote of no confidence could be initiated.

An election was supposed to be held sixty days after dissolution, and
a conflict over what to do next broke out between Schleicher and
Papen, a man who until then had been his political creature. Papen –
and, more insistently, Gayl – were in favour of declaring a state of
emergency, indefinitely suspending the Reichstag, then implementing
revisions of the Constitution which would guarantee permanent conservative control over the state. Papen and Gayl openly professed their
attachment to monarchism, but claimed that they would not push for
an immediate restoration of the Hohenzollerns. Their reservations had
a lot to do with the fact that however unpopular monarchism was, the
still living – and thus unavoidable – Wilhelm II was even more so.
Papen and Gayl confined themselves to an attempt to implement more
immediate changes which would set the stage for the final elimination
of the Republic. These changes included making the franchise age-
weighted and indirect, while establishing an appointed upper house of

life senators as a counterweight to a demoted Reichstag. Although it was directed at the Left, the Papen–Gayl plan would also have resulted in an irreparable break with the Nazis, whose electoral strength would have been considerably diluted if these revisions had been implemented – particularly raising the voting age to twenty-five. Schmitt felt that such a course of action would be a reckless provocation to most of the country. Indeed, these proposals were so widely and vehemently opposed that it soon became clear that the days of this government were numbered.

There seemed to be one alternative left before one might have to start 'howling with the wolves'. Previously Schleicher had been just as willing as Papen to send the Reichstag packing, but Schmitt now advised him directly on how to stand apart from the discredited Papen by maintaining a semblance of constitutionality. Popitz, Minister Without Portfolio in the Cabinet and member of the newly imposed Reich commissarial government in Prussia, agreed that it would be more prudent to postpone the elections only temporarily. Schleicher was now looking for someone who could be the front man in a new government which would have a broader base of support in the population. In a scheme to bring down Papen, Eugen Ott, leader of the *Wehrmacht* office in the *Reichswehr* Ministry, informed the Papen Cabinet that at its present strength the *Reichswehr* could not simultaneously handle war on both the foreign and domestic fronts. The timing of Ott's announcement was intended to lead to Papen's downfall, which it did. By December Schleicher had convinced Hindenburg to withdraw his support from the discredited Papen and have himself named Chancellor, bringing an end to the attempt at a gentlemen's counter-revolution from above.

Along with another officer, Marcks, Ott was a close confidant of Schleicher, and the liaison between Schleicher and Schmitt. For a couple of months, as a political adviser to this circle of military men, Schmitt exercised a degree of political influence which he would never subsequently attain. In a speech to a group of businessmen on the tenth anniversary of Mussolini's March on Rome on 23 November, before Schleicher came to power, he claimed that the time had now come for the 'quantitative total state' – that is, multiparty corporatism – to be replaced by the 'qualitative total state'; here he had Schleicher, and more distantly Mussolini, but not yet Hitler, in mind.[14] Although this was the furthest Schmitt was willing to go as long as the Weimar Constitution still stood, it demonstrates that he was now willing to come to terms with a new kind of post-constitutional regime.

Advised by Schmitt, Schleicher committed himself to a plan more ambitious than another holding action; this so-called *Querverbindung* plan drew heavily on ideas current in national revolutionary circles, and was conceived as an attempt to break through the stalemate to which the presidential system had come, by broadening its base of support in the population after three years of catastrophic implosion. The idea was that after this destabilizing bid to push the political system too far and too fast to the Right, the President should once again become a *pouvoir neutre*. Bendersky describes the 'national-revolutionary' objectives of this government:

> He would try to create a national front extending from the Socialists and Catholics to the left wing of the Nazi Party. The goal would be to rally the popular anti-capitalist forces, which had been traditionally divided by class, ideology, and religion behind a massive program of social reform and public works projects that would not just counteract the economic crisis but produce a national revival.[15]

This, at any rate, was the rhetoric of the short-lived regime cranked out by the Schleicher mouthpiece *Tägliche Rundschau*, edited by Hans Zehrer. Presenting an almost Marxist-sounding analysis of the economic crisis, the editorial team called for a 'revolutionary' alliance between the military and the new middle classes to break with the world market and introduce planning. After the trial Schmitt threw his support behind the Schleicher regime, which he perceived as the last chance to hold back the Nazis.

The Schleicher government represented a weird and brief pause in the slide towards total confrontation with parliament. Indeed, there were signs that the new government foresaw the eventual restoration of the legislative role of the Reichstag. Realizing that the Papen government's unrelenting hostility towards the SPD and the unions had immeasurably increased the weight of the Nazis in any political equation, Schleicher even made some friendly-sounding overtures to the Left. While the SPD leadership was justifiably wary of the man who had led the charge against the Braun–Severing government in Prussia, the SPD-aligned union federation was more sympathetic. In retrospect Schmitt attributed responsibility for the failure of this missed opportunity to the SPD leadership, whose unwillingness to discard every last principle looked to him like sheer obstinacy:

> Many unionists sympathized with Schleicher at that time. . . . But Schleicher could make little use of it, because at the decisive moment a purely doctrinaire and ideological view prevailed against him – above all due to Breitscheid. A little while before, I had a nocturnal conversation with a mutual acquaintance. What obstinacy! For Breitscheid, world history stopped when the defence Minister was a general, not a civilian. And now this same General – who, whenever possible, appeared in uniform – was supposed to become Chancellor. There are certain things that just won't do.[16]

The other prong in the strategy of the short-lived Schleicher government was the attempt to split the Nazi Party and bring the main representative of its left wing, Gregor Strasser, into the government. Strasser was arguably the second most popular man in the party, enjoying the support of its more socially radical and plebeian North German membership. His advocacy of public works to relieve unemployment and his rejection of the strategy of a civil war against the unions separated him from Hitler, who was anxious not to alienate the business community. More importantly, Hitler was concerned not to let his grip on the party slip by allowing an independent power centre around Strasser to crystallize.

There was little chance that this plan, with its far-fetched conception of political alliances, could have succeeded, even if its economic proposals represented a long-overdue reversal of an obtuse fiscal conservatism. Its mild reformism, and the apparent drift back to parliamentary government, antagonized big business. But what really sank this government was its attempt to end agricultural subsidies for East Elbian landlords. This was too much for Hindenburg, whose own family estate stood to be affected by this 'Bolshevik' experiment. He soon lost his patience with Schleicher's seemingly endless series of manoeuvres.

In a sense, Schleicher's plan typified a way of thinking that was natural to those whose idea of politics was limited to scheming in the corridors of power. His attempt to get union support for a *Reichswehr* government should be seen as a feeble attempt to put this 'national revolutionary' conception into practice. Despite his deep involvement with this short-lived government, Schmitt was sceptical about the *Querverbindung* plan's prospects of success, mainly because of the SPD's opposition to anything that smacked of military government.

Schmitt had decided to leave Berlin as early as November, probably because of the disappointing Reich Court verdict. It seems that despite his subsequent engagement on behalf of Schleicher, the life of politics very near the centre of power had suddenly become too tense for him, and he now planned to resume the tranquil life of a scholar, far away from 'the elites': 'This Berlin is a vacuum between east and west, a passage, through which a draft is channelled. The Berliners take this current to be the breath of the world spirit, and feel that they are in a world-historical role.'[17] This was the voice of disappointment, masquerading as contempt. Very soon he would be drawn back into this vacuum, desperate to play precisely this role.

Although Schmitt's involvement in shadowy, behind-the-scenes intrigues had strained his relations with many Catholic and liberal circles, in the academic community his national reputation as one of the leading constitutional legal theorists was now firmly established. Many of the top universities – Leipzig, Munich and Cologne – had approached him over the previous year, and in November he tentatively accepted a position from Cologne which was to begin on 1 April 1933. But his decision to leave the Handelshochschule was intertwined with other motives: its director, Moritz Bonn, was Jewish and liberal, and the new Reich Commissar for Prussia had slated the college for cutbacks. He might now have wanted to put some distance between himself and those who too conspicuously represented the dying Republic. Three weeks after the Court's decision, Schmitt accepted an offer from Cologne for a position beginning the next summer.

In January 1933 the Schleicher government began to unravel in the face of near-unanimous opposition from the Reichstag, which was determined, in the event of Hindenburg's death, to make sure that Schleicher would not become President, as the Constitution stipulated. Apart from the Communists and the DNVP, the entire Reichstag backed a Nazi-proposed constitutional amendment to ensure that the presidency would devolve upon the President of the Reich Court, and this amendment was passed with an overwhelming majority. In Schmitt's eyes, this final victory for political justice represented the final negation of government within a Weimar framework.

Schmitt was the target of an open letter by the leader of the Reichstag Centre faction Prelate Kaas, who advised the Schleicher government not to follow the recommendations of Schmitt and his followers – well known, according to the Prelate, for their sophistical rationalizations of breaches of the Constitution. Schmitt was furious; he wrote a letter to the Centre's newspaper *Germania* demanding a retraction. While he tried to muster up support for his rebuttal from his powerful friends, Popitz informed him in a telephone conversation that because of his reputation he might have to be sacrificed – that is, dropped as the regime's unofficial legal adviser.[18]

Schmitt's diary from this month conveys his feeling of desperation, and clearly indicates that he was not looking forward to the future and had little idea what his role would be in whatever regime came next.

[Entry for 22 January 1933]
I was deeply sad and depressed. Ott wants to dissolve [the Reichstag] and have new elections. I fear the dead end of parliamentarianism, Social Democracy and polyocracy. Braun and Kaas lead to Hitler. That is their triumph. Drank a lot of heavy Burgundy and the conversation broke up.

[Entry for 26 January 1933]
Walked home sadly around 6.00 accompanied by the young SA man Dietrich Schäfer, who wrote me a nice Christmas letter on the Leipzig judgement. He spoke of the innocence of the SA, who were waiting in vain for Hitler's appointment and thought that the present government could defeat the

Communists only through terror, but would not be capable of it. That only
the National Socialists could do, but not for long.

[Entry for 27 January 1933]
Dinner at Marcks' . . . Marcks is deeply depressed. Something unbelievable
has happened. The Hindenburg myth is at an end. The Old Man was finally
only a MacMahon. Dreadful situation. Schleicher stepping down, Papen or
Hitler is coming. The Old Man has finally gone mad. In a fearfully cold
night went back home around 11.00.[19]

Burnt out, bitter and anxious, Carl Schmitt stumbled into the Hitler
era. However much the strategies he supported had contributed to the
collapse of the Weimar Republic, it was a result for which he, at least,
had not consciously aimed. Although he was open to hard-Right
agendas of political renewal – Fascism certainly; perhaps, in his wildest
dreams, something even more radical – he could not bring himself to
discard a constitutional framework with which he had wrestled for so
long, struggling – often successfully – to have it seen in the light of his
own conceptions. It is true that he had argued that a constitution could
not form an enclosed, self-referential system, since many of its most
important provisions are necessarily 'weak links', points of potential
political interpretation and reinterpretation. But he had invested a
great deal in the idea that such constitutional frameworks should have
an authority in political life which places them above party conflict,
moderating even fundamental oppositions like 'left' and 'right'. During
the Weimar Republic Schmitt repeatedly shifted ground, pulled in two
different directions: at one pole an image of an architectonic constitutional form, holding together a world out of joint; at the other a more
partisan vision of catastrophe and the phoenix-like rise of a new elite.
Unable to see the Nazis as a force for renewal, he was also unwilling to
support efforts to stabilize the Republic, as this would have put him on
the other – the 'left' – side of the political fence. Failing, perhaps, to
sense the necessity of making a decision here, he put his trust in
ineffectual conspiracies.

13

The National Socialist Revolution

A month after being deposed, Papen began negotiating with Hitler in meetings arranged by the Cologne banker Kurt von Schröder over the terms of a Nazi–conservative coalition government. Papen was able to convince Hindenburg that although Hitler would receive the chancellorship, he would be flanked by men of the old guard who would watch his every move. With Schleicher losing his grip on power, Schmitt was out of the loop and heard about Hindenburg appointing Hitler to the chancellorship over the radio at the Café Kutschera. He later wrote in his diary that he was 'irritated and yet somehow relieved; at least a decision.'[1] That night, while a giant torchlit parade passed through the Brandenburg Gate, Schmitt had a visit from an anxious friend: Wilhelm Stapel, editor of *Deutsches Volkstum*.[2] Both Stapel and his colleague at the paper, A.E. Günther, had been great believers in the Hindenburg myth – the idea that the President was the rallying point of a conservative restoration, otherwise known as the 'conservative revolution'. While they had been willing to see the Nazi movement as part of this wider 'revolution', Hitler as Chancellor at first appeared to undermine the balance of forces upon which their whole project was based.

Hindenburg's decision to appoint Hitler Chancellor resulted in the rapid marginalization and disintegration of the circle around Schleicher within which Schmitt had played such a prominent role. Schmitt's efforts to reposition himself in the midst of a cataclysmic changing of the guard gave him a penetrating first-hand insight into the friend–enemy dynamics of the new Germany. In the preceding period he had addressed the crisis of traditional elites, their inability to occupy the strategic positions of power in modern politics and reinvent themselves as a new breed of modern rulers. He had not previously thought that Fascist-style one-party rule was even an option in an advanced industrial country like Germany, with its highly organized interest groups, particularly its unions. The spectacle of the very rapid, total destruction of the latter must have made a very deep impression on him. It provided a powerful demonstration that an 'elite' had emerged – as he had predicted four years earlier in Barcelona – from 'the social and cultural abyss'. He had never previously seen the Hitler gang in this light, and could not immediately overcome the feeling that they were simply unfit to be the sole rulers of a great European state. But after a few months of caution in 1933, it dawned on him that National Socialism in power represented the unexpected, even perverse resolution of what he had earlier identified as the main problems of political order in age of mass politics. This conviction was the basis of his relationship to National Socialism, even when one allows for the role which naked ambition and opportunism played in his decision to cleave to the new order. But this 'solution' came at a high price in the light of his own central concerns: although he expressed no moral reservations about the course of events in his writings, he viewed the subordination of the state to the party and the disintegration of the state into party fiefdoms with growing misgivings.

It seems that even a few days after the Reichstag fire on 27 February and the smashing of the Communist Party, Schmitt had not yet abandoned his reservations about the direction of events, because his name did not appear on a petition, signed by three hundred professors and published on 3 March, calling on the universities openly to support the new order. It is probable that at the time he had not yet given up on the possibility that Schleicher and the *Reichswehr* might depose it in a *coup d'état*.[3] On 5 March, Hitler sought to consolidate his grip on power and demonstrate Nazi supremacy over his conservative allies in the coalition by staging an 'election' which, in an atmosphere of storm-trooper terror and intimidation, would give his party a resounding popular mandate for their revolution. By 24 March the Nazis had coerced all the remaining parties, with the exception of the Social Democrats, into supporting the Enabling Act which stipulated that from now on laws could be passed not only by the Reichstag but by the government as well. The tenuous distinction between laws and measures based on the division of powers had finally been eradicated, and Schmitt saw this as the sign that the old constitution, although not formally abrogated, no longer existed.

No one in Germany or in the outside world denied that this was the new government of the German people: there was no government in exile which could lay claim to being the real, legitimate government; and except for those who were the victims of the Gleichschaltung, it was a shrinking minority which now felt resolutely opposed. There was nothing out of the ordinary in Schmitt's sympathy for the new regime, and the idea that all his previous writings have to be seen in the light of an all-too-typical 'decision' not to abandon career and country out of concern for the victims of oppression is far-fetched. When one is trying to form a judgement about Schmitt's stance in 1933, one should bear in mind that almost everybody who left National Socialist Germany at the time had been forced out on political or 'racial' grounds: the number of people who did not fall into these proscribed categories, who left out of sheer moral revulsion, can probably be counted on one hand. If later developments under this regime compel us to revise our perception of the boundaries of moral responsibility, these had not yet happened in 1933. When Schmitt was much older, he rationalized his decision with what were often compelling arguments:

> As a positive jurist a fully new situation began for me with the Enabling Act. I would like to know what Hans Kelsen would have done in my situation, since he is a convinced positivist. I know it: he always emphasized that the matter is over for a positive, scientific jurist the moment the dice fall.[4]

But the matter does not end here. Schmitt did not decide to obey merely on the Hobbesian grounds that subjects owe obedience to the power which protects them. He went far beyond this, seeking to find a place at the heights of this political system. In the revised version of *Der Begriff des Politischen* which came out in 1933, Schmitt emphasized the significance of the political oath as a vector of the potential 'totalization' of politics, the point at which it becomes all-encompassing fate.[5] Whatever is true in this claim, the accompanying feeling of being enveloped and swept along by history also enabled him to rationalize everything he would do from now on.

Schmitt's support for this seizure of power was made easier by the fact that it had the appearance of being legal from the vantage point of the old constitution, even if – as he had pointed out in earlier works – such transitions are never legal affairs. Had this appearance been lacking, a full-frontal collision with state officialdom, committed to upholding the law, would have been probable. The normally destructive initial phases of a revolution were thereby avoided. But because it did not smash the state apparatus but, rather, superimposed its own structures upon it, this new order did not yet have a definitive constitutional form.[6]

At a conference of legal scholars held in Weimar from 26 March to 1 April, Schmitt argued not only that the Weimar Constitution was dead, but also that the Enabling Act was now the provisional constitution of a new German state which, through plebiscitary acclamation, had acquired a national legitimacy far clearer, in his opinion, than the one which had sanctioned the establishment of the Republic in 1919. His article 'Das Gesetz zur Behebung der Not von Volk und Reich' was his first sign of open support for the regime, but a note of reservation was still apparent; not only did he point out the ambiguity surrounding President Hindenburg's position within the new order, he also omitted to mention by name either of the governing parties or, for that matter, Hitler.[7] Again, one should not assume that it was because of fear, or opportunism, or even the belief that one must simply obey the powers that be, that Schmitt began to warm to the Nazi seizure of power: not only was it turning out to be the successful culmination of the presidential system, but the wave of enthusiasm which swept over large parts of the population was beginning to look to him like that formless, mass acclamation of a sovereign nation which could turn any usurpation into an authentic revolution.

On 1 April Schmitt received a telephone call from Popitz, who was still Minister Without Portfolio as well as Reich Commissar over the Prussian Ministry of Finance, asking him to participate in a committee composing a *Reichsstatthaltergesetz*. Both Schmitt and Popitz saw this as an opportunity to reverse at one stroke the untenable settlement imposed by the High Court in October. For Schmitt it was particularly satisfying to see his position vindicated, and this was why he began to think that he might have a place in 'the movement' after all. The new law would put the relationship between the Reich and the federal states on a much more centralized footing by dissolving their existing governments, abolishing their parliaments and placing them under the rule of a commissar appointed by the Interior Minister of the Reich. Even though the political leadership of the whole Reich would be in the hands of the party, the administrative elite of Prussia would be allowed to maintain its independence from the party through a privileged, direct relationship to the top. This power-sharing formula, he hoped, would be the basis of the unwritten constitution of the new regime.

Although Schmitt saw certain things moving in a very promising direction, he had initial misgivings. Perhaps because he had been so closely involved with cliques who were now rapidly losing ground, he could not at first identify completely with the direction in which things were moving. The 1 April 1933 entry in his diary registers his awareness of the political myopia of the outflanked Franz Papen, an embodiment of the precarious fortunes of his whole caste:

> Papen, personally sympathetic, struggles for his political existence. We talked about the Statthalter of the Reich in the Länder. Papen thinks that the final goal is a Reich monarchy, and that the Statthalter has to be a placeholder for the monarchy. Naive.[8]

On 3 April, the committee drafting the *Reichsstatthaltergesetz* met to discuss proposals. In his diary Schmitt described those in attendance – Papen, Popitz, and other state secretaries from the Reich Interior Ministry – as sombre and anxious in the extreme. The outstanding question was the status of the Prussian federal government under the new law. Goering arrived at the meeting a little later, and immediately made it clear that Prussia would be directly subordinated to the Chancellor. Schmitt remarked in his diary that Goering's succinct and forceful manner was a positive contrast to the petulant indecision of

the others. In a very revealing indication of his attitude towards the
new masters, he described Goering as 'somewhat Wilhelmine, perhaps
the right type for these times'.[9] 'Wilhelmine' for Schmitt was, to say the
least, a rather ambivalent label, synonymous with theatrical pomp.
Despite his initial efforts to see them in a better light, he was not often
tremendously impressed by the personal stature of the leading members of the new elite.

On 7 April Schmitt was allowed to attend a meeting at which Hitler
was going to present his political programme before about a hundred
representatives of the traditional state elite. In a room filled with
members of the General Staff, Admiralty, bureaucrats from the *Reichswehr* and Reich Interior, Schmitt sat across and at only a little distance
from the Führer, who appeared to him 'like a bull in the ring'.[10] He
later portrayed the scene with details which capture the political
moment almost to perfection:

> Then the Führer appeared. The military sat there with steely faces and
> wanted to hear what he had to say. In a certain sense it was the exact
> opposite of the mass public to which Hitler was accustomed and, on the
> other hand, also the opposite of those private circles in which he could draw
> everyone in. . . . Hitler began his speech; it was at least twenty minutes to half
> an hour before one had the feeling that he was moving towards takeoff. He
> knew that moment exactly, and spoke directly to his audience – the contact
> was uncanny; the almost medial dependency on the audience, on applause,
> on 'inner applause'. But here everyone sat with iron countenance, not
> applauding, listening to everything with iron rationality and precision. He
> did not connect, and no ray was emitted – nothing.[11]

Schmitt's perception of Hitler is perhaps the most enigmatic aspect of
his relationship to National Socialism. Only occasionally did he mention Hitler in his writings from this period, but this was not – as he
would claim after the war – because he considered him too crude to
merit mention. The real reason was that Hitler was an utterly uncanny
object of fascination for him: how exactly could this man, born in the
same year as himself, coming out of nowhere, seemingly so pitifully
ignorant, have seen through the façade of the European status quo,
effortlessly shattering it at its weakest links? The young Nicolaus Sombart recalls that Schmitt was one of the few in the world of 'inner
emigration' who took Hitler seriously – indeed, as a mythical figure.
Over the course of their many walks through Berlin, Schmitt struggled
to convey Hitler's significance to his sceptical adolescent companion:
'He is a Golem. One must take the tag which lies under his tongue, on
which lies his secret code. Then one has him in one's power.'[12]

After leaving Berlin for Cologne in early April, Schmitt began to
discuss the meaning of recent events with those whom he had known
in a personal and intellectual capacity from Berlin and Bonn. These

discussions had less of that stone-cold rationality which distinguished the ones he had attended in Berlin. Schmitt owed his smooth transition into the new order to his contacts in the Interior Ministry. Ensconced in these settings, he could come to accept the movement, and even admire Hitler. But this essentially collaborative attitude soon gave way to an exuberant affirmation of the 'national revolution'. The willingness of those he met in Cologne to put aside earlier inhibitions and let themselves be moved by the groundswell of national enthusiasm must have been a transformative experience for Schmitt.[13] In Cologne he spoke with many for whom this 'breakthrough' had an eschatological significance: the poet Kurt Eschweiler, the scholar of canon law and opponent of political Catholicism Hans Barion, and his friend A.E. Günther from *Deutsches Volkstum*. Both *Deutsches Volkstum* and *Europäische Revue* had come around to seeing the Nazis not just as a useful battering ram against Weimar but as the leading force in a historic breakthrough to a new national and European order.[14] Their position differed from that of those conservatives who were still embittered by their failed attempt to domesticate the Nazis. At a conference at the Maria Laach Benedictine monastery, when Edgar Jung, speechwriter for the now irrelevant Vice-Chancellor Papen, openly expressed his dismay at the Nazis' sheer ingratitude towards their conservative partners, Schmitt was said to have muttered: 'This man is ripe for the concentration camps.'[15] Schmitt explained to Stapel that because of his decision to contribute his services and reputation to the 'National Revolution', there would now be three groups who, from this point on, would consider him an enemy: conservative supporters of Hugenberg, the Catholics and the Jews.[16]

Shortly thereafter Schmitt received a letter from Martin Heidegger which urged him to join the party, and with his new perspective on things he was now ready to sign up; on 1 May both men waited in long queues to become party members. Despite the massive influx of new members, which soon resulted in a moratorium, Schmitt and those who jumped on board were going beyond the call of duty: neither Popitz nor Jünger, nor most of Schmitt's other friends, nor even a majority of those who taught in the law faculties, ever became members, and he was in no danger of losing his position if he had chosen not to do so. But despite his brief attempt to retreat from politics after the trial, he was no longer content to be just a professor, and while Popitz belonged to an honoured old elite still entrenched in the state apparatus, there was no way Schmitt could have had anything like the same proximity to these 'world-historical events' except by joining the party.

His involvement with Cologne was marred by controversy from the beginning. The mayor of the city in 1932 – none other than Konrad Adenauer – had expressed his opposition to Schmitt early on, but this can in part be attributed to his bad reputation in the Centre Party.[17] Shortly after he arrived in Cologne he became embroiled in another controversy which revealed that he was now quite willing to 'howl with the wolves'. Hans Kelsen had recently come to Cologne, having been forced to flee from an increasingly menacing anti-Semitic atmosphere in Vienna. After his arrival, he had taken part in the effort to bring Schmitt to the department by writing to him on more than one occasion, despite Schmitt's well-known and undiplomatic criticisms of his views – one of the sticking points in Schmitt's negotiations with the university was his insistence that his salary should not be lower than Kelsen's.[18] Not long after the Nazi seizure of power, the universities underwent large-scale purges. While he was on holiday in Sweden, Kelsen was dismissed on both 'racial' and political grounds. A petition circulated among the faculty to have him reinstated; while it expressed sympathy for the new regime, the petition stated that it would be a huge blow to the university to lose such an internationally renowned scholar. It argued that the new law specifically exempted veterans, and that Kelsen fell into this category.[19] Schmitt, who had spent the war in offices, archives and cafés, felt no compunction about being the only member of the legal faculty not to sign this petition.

But this is only the tip of the iceberg; his involvement in the academic Gleichschaltung went far beyond a commonplace indifference to the misfortunes of others. A very large percentage of professors of law were being removed from their positions, creating ideal opportunities for academic 'empire-building'.[20] In this vacuum, Schmitt's advice on new appointments could make or break a career. He used this opportunity to promote his own career by playing Cologne off against other interested universities, ultimately hoping for an offer from the prestigious Berlin University. A letter to him from the Prussian Kultusminister, Wilhelm Ahlmann, reveals not only Schmitt's success at playing his cards in this game, but the degree to which he personally embodied the presence of the new regime in the academy: 'You know that the restructuring of Cologne University. . . . is in the first instance connected to your person. . . . Our intention was and is to strengthen your position further through corresponding offers of appointment.'[21]

On 11 May the local Nazi newspaper paid tribute to Schmitt, and gave him a title which both friends and enemies would thereafter use to depict his relationship to the Third Reich: 'Crown Jurist'. On 31 May he wrote the first of a number of pieces which were so completely infamous that they distinguish Schmitt from the legions of those scurrying to find a position in the new order. In this article in a party publication, entitled 'Die deutschen Intellektuellen' ('The German Intellectuals'),[22] Schmitt mercilessly attacked all those intellectuals who had recently fled the country: first for having left and then for presuming to judge events from the outside. For this supreme presumption, he declared, they were forever barred from returning. In one of the many low points of this tirade, he referred to Albert Einstein as a 'poison-filled German-hater'. Many of those who had known Schmitt from before, and been forced to flee Germany like hunted animals, rightly considered this to be a shameless mockery of their plight; it would not quickly be forgotten, and from now on, the 'émigrés' would be among his worst enemies.

The path leading Schmitt back to the centre of power began with his nomination on 31 July to a position in a newly created advisory council for the state of Prussia, the so-called *Staatsrat.* Popitz, who had been nominated shortly before, had arranged for Schmitt to be recognized in this way for his work on the *Reichsstatthaltergesetz.*[23] Even much later, Schmitt described his nomination to this largely powerless upper house as the greatest honour of his life. While the legitimacy of unelected advisers had been denied in the classic age of parliament, Schmitt claimed that National Socialism recognized that the relationship between a political counsellor and those who held power was truly the nerve centre of a properly constituted state. He certainly had a great deal of experience in the last years of Weimar in the role of secret adviser.[24] Early on he sensed that in the Nazi regime the problem of who had the ear of the leader would assume some of the significance it had once carried in ancient dialogues on tyranny. He hoped that the new regime might come to rely on a special relationship between a Crown Jurist and a 'tyrant'. One could say, then, that it was not only for Hobbesian reasons that he cleaved to the new order; there were what one could roughly call 'Xenophonic' reasons. Carl Schmitt now regarded the well-counselled tyrant as the best of all rulers, and during these early years of the regime he was willing to wager that it was possible to reinvent this advisory relationship in modern tyrannies.[25]

As a Rhinelander of obscure origins, the title of *Staatsrat* also appealed to him, on a deeper psychological level, because it seemed to mean that he had finally reached the innermost chamber of 'Prussia', that previously uncanny and inaccessible fortress.[26] His feeling of being at the centre was confirmed by the spectacular swearing-in ceremony of this council, held on 15 September and attended by almost the entire resident population of party, state, academic and ecclesiastical dignitaries – 'the great and the good', so to speak.[27] Goering, who liked to surround himself with aristocrats and highbrows, had filled the *Staatsrat* with people who could at least symbolize a portion of the state that was not completely broken up into party fiefdoms. Significantly, Hitler chose to snub the whole affair, and sent a statement which, while congratulating the newly sworn in members, warned that 'the Party cannot become the preserver of the states [*Länder*] of the past, but must become their liquidator in favour of the Reich of the future'[28] – a blunt early indication of the irrelevance of this whole affair.

But Schmitt did not come to Berlin only to participate in the ceremonial trappings of power. His nomination to the *Staatsrat* was soon followed – as he had been led to expect – by the offer of a position in the law faculty of the University of Berlin, and despite entreaties from Cologne to stay, once again he could not resist the spell of the capital. While he was a professor at the Handelshochschule he had lived in the shadow of this more prestigious institution, the most prestigious university in the whole of Germany, located in the government quarter. He took the position made vacant by the forced retirement of Hermann Heller, a man for whom he had developed an obsessive hatred. Heller died in exile in Spain the following year. Another personal enemy of Schmitt's – Eric Kaufmann, a right-wing nationalist of Jewish origins – was also forced to retire. Before 1933, the fact that they had both held jobs at the University of Berlin, had contributed to the resentment and hostility Schmitt felt towards them. Now they were getting their comeuppance. Such personal and professional windfalls made these high times for Schmitt. He now seemed to be well ensconced in both the state and the academic apparatus.[29]

In October Schmitt was the keynote speaker at a conference in Leipzig attended by hundreds of scholars from many European countries.[30] His recently published book on the structure of the new regime, *Staat, Bewegung, Volk* ('State, Movement, People'), was widely read, and to many outsiders it looked as if he was close to occupying a position similar to Gentile's in Italy – more or less the official theoretician of the regime. The theme of Schmitt's lecture was the necessity of a fundamental break with the practice and whole conceptual framework of the *Rechtsstaat*. He thought it would be possible to bring the party around to his particular conception of a legal practice subject to political 'necessity'. He was the main theoretician of the *Rechtserneuerung* ('legal renewal') project in the newly created Nazi legal establishment, and occupied strategic positions in these party-dominated journals and forums. By the end of the year he seemed to occupy a near-optimal location within the force fields running through state, university and party.[31] Even before his re-entry into the political arena, Schmitt understood the dynamic of these fields. In July, when *Staat, Bewegung, Volk* was published, it was already clear to him that the impossibility of defining the relationship between state and party in such a regime in precise procedural terms also made it impossible to conceptualize the legal order in terms of older, more systematic criteria.

Schmitt sought to portray the new regime as an architectonic order consisting of three distinct elements: state, movement and people. He defined the 'state' as the administrative apparatus, the 'movement' as the political leadership organizing and acting in the name of the 'people'. The 'people' was that region of the new political system which was once a legally and institutionally distinct 'civil society', and now consisted of a multitude 'living in the shadow and under the protection of decisions reached in the higher regions of the political order'.[32] There was little populist-*völkisch* euphemism in this brutally realistic description, identifying the true role of the people under National Socialism. With a certain curious detachment, he was announcing an event of world-historical significance: popular sovereignty, obliterated in substance, had been simultaneously transvalued into a symbolic code of total domination.

But this conception of state, movement and people also contained a succinct factual description of the hierarchy of power which had replaced the old division of powers: the Nazi 'movement' in alliance with an independent but subordinate state bureaucracy, and a non-political and servile judiciary handling affairs in a residual sphere of private law. Although the division-of-powers framework of the old *Rechtsstaat* was gone, Schmitt still considered it an important task to work out a flexible scheme for determining the boundaries between the administrative sphere of the old state-based elite and the political sphere of the new party elite. This book was an attempt to give a theoretical principle to the *ad hoc* balance of powers sanctioned by the law which he had helped to frame, the *Reichsstaathaltergesetz*, and have it adopted by the 'movement' as the basis of the new order.

The book's other objective was to place National Socialism within a wider political genus. In Schmitt's view this tripartite categorization of state, movement and people was the defining characteristic of all the political communities which had broken with the constitutional standards of the nineteenth-century *Rechtsstaat:* – National Socialist Germany, Fascist Italy, and Bolshevik Russia. We have already seen how greatly Schmitt admired Italian Fascism, but the inclusion of Bolshevik Russia in this series is, to say the least, rather surprising in a work written for official Nazi consumption. Although his principal contrast was between the more statist Fascism and the more 'movement'-dominated National Socialism, the inclusion of the Russian radical brother suggests that the category to which National Socialism belonged was not so much 'Fascism' in the generic sense of a counter-revolutionary mass movement as a larger genus in which counter-revolution and revolution were no longer clearly distinguishable. This was the genus 'total state–total politics', which included roughly the same kinds of regimes subsumed under the later term, 'totalitarianism', but without any of the later pejorative connotations.

Despite the direct genealogical relationship between National Socialism and Italian Fascism, the distinction between them was one of the
central points of *Staat, Bewegung, Volk*. Schmitt had to formulate his
case carefully, and avoid the impression that he preferred the head of
state, Mussolini, to the party chief, Hitler. But tactical discretion was
not the only reason why he portrayed National Socialism as the greater
of the two. He considered National Socialism more radical precisely
because it gave priority to an openly political 'movement' over the
neutral 'state'. In the twentieth century the state was losing its monopoly of the political, and Schmitt rather boldly portrayed National
Socialism in the light of his own ideas as a movement based on the
recognition that the concept of the state presupposed the concept of
the political, by which he meant that the state no longer had a
monopoly of legitimate violence. While this relativization of the state
under the pressures of Weimar mass politics had assumed the form of
polycratic disintegration, National Socialism promised to reintegrate
the masses into a new kind of political totality which was something
more than a state in the classical sense.

In Schmitt's view, the attempt to dissolve the distinction between
state and society was what distinguished National Socialism from Italian
Fascism. The Fascist Party was a legally incorporated organ of the state;
in contrast, neither the NSDAP as a whole, nor any office within it, was
incorporated as an organ of state. The leading positions in the party,
the *Führer* and the chief of the SA, were connected to the state by
personal union. In fact, the whole field of relations between the Nazi
movement and the state bureaucracy was structured and traversed by
personal bonds. This dynamic of personalization was dissolving the
boundaries of the whole division-of-powers system, and the normative
standards based on it.

But Schmitt was not content simply to let things stand in this
completely indeterminate condition. While he saw National Socialism
as more radical than Italian Fascism, he remained temperamentally
closer to the statism of the latter. It was not uncommon for Nazi
ideologues to scorn the neo-Hegelian statism of Italian Fascism, and
Schmitt had to tailor his arguments accordingly. His idea was to shore
up the boundaries between state and party, and while Italy was in some
sense a model for him, making the Nazi party an organ of state along
Italian lines would only have worsened the problem of polycratic
disorder. In Italy this problem had been brought under control because
the state elite had not only rallied to Fascism but, in so doing, had
successfully made it their own party. No such fusion was possible in
Germany, and Schmitt wanted to make sure that National Socialism
remained more a 'movement' open to ideas from outside – his ideas
– and less a party with a fixed programme and ideology. Indeed, he

preferred to describe National Socialism as a 'movement' rather than as a 'party' because he believed that while a 'movement' could reform and modernize the state, a 'party' was something which emerged out of the disintegration of the state. He believed that even in a one-party regime, the party would always be a semi-independent, competitor bureaucracy trying to control and penetrate the state while maintaining its independence.

The Unity Law of December 1933 seemed to address some of the issues posed in Schmitt's discussion of party–state relations. It decreed that 'state and movement are bound into a unity but not fused into one another', and referred in passing to the dangers of mixing the two.[33] But Hitler completely rejected the 'Schmittian' interpretation of this law; he, too, placed great significance on the fact that the law distinguished between the movement and the state, but denied that the term 'movement' implied any qualification of the leading role of the Nazi Party.[34]

At the time Schmitt also wanted to distinguish himself from all those in the state elite who saw preserving their autonomy merely as a step towards re-establishing their hegemony. He was very well acquainted with these people, and although he deeply respected their status traditions, their failure to adopt any bold course of action in the last years of the Republic had made it clear that they were not up to the challenge of directly ruling a modern state. In his analysis of this failure, Schmitt gave a totalitarian twist to a theme from Max Weber: without charismatic leadership, the modern state would become a directionless bureaucratic machine. The appointment of Adolf Hitler on 31 January 1933 demonstrated that the powerful dignitaries of the Finance and Interior Ministries and presidential staff did not constitute a real political elite. Schmitt declared this an event with far-reaching consequences for political philosophy: 'On this 31st of January, the Hegelian bureaucratic state of the nineteenth century, which was distinguished by the unity of bureaucracy and the state-bearing layer, was replaced by another state construction. On this day, therefore, one could say: "Hegel died".'[35]

Although the meaning of this verdict seems clear enough, it was delivered with a certain ironic reserve. In fact, shortly after this text was written, Schmitt would come to see Hegel not as a dead dog but as a previously untapped source of intellectual renewal, someone who had offered a precocious vision of a new kind of political totality. The young Hegel was the theorist of the phoenix-like resurrection of the state in the eye of an overwhelming storm – that is to say, the ideologist of a conservative reconciliation of state and revolution. In a letter to a friend in 1960 Schmitt recounted how in the middle of April 1936 he had the opportunity to interview his hero, Mussolini, in the Palazzo

Venezia, and put to him a question concerning the status of Hegel in contemporary totalitarian regimes:

> The conversation concerned the relationship between state and party, and Mussolini said, with a pride clearly directed at National Socialist Germany: 'The state is eternal, the party transitory; I am a Hegelian!' I noted: 'Lenin was a Hegelian, so I will allow myself the question: where is the world-historical residence of Hegel's spirit? In Rome, in Moscow or perhaps still in Berlin?' He answered, with a charming laugh: 'I give this question back to you!' Whereupon I answered: 'Then naturally I must say: in Rome. . . .' This discussion with him was a great intellectual pleasure, and remains unforgettable to me in all its details.[36]

In the first years of the Nazi regime, Schmitt sought to present the disintegration of the norms of the *Rechtsstaat* as a welcome development for jurisprudence. Law in this 'post-Hegelian' political order would no longer be based on a precise and predictable code which ensured the security of property and the integrity of the individual. He no longer saw the growing indeterminacy of legal procedure as the disruption of a normal condition. During the early years of the regime, when he enthusiastically supported National Socialism, he believed that the abandonment of fixed rules of procedure was a dialectical breakthrough to an order based on the untrammelled imperatives of political necessity. A passage from Hölderlin's *Patmos* captured the experience of this 'breakthrough' – not just for Schmitt, but for Heidegger, Jünger and many others: 'Where the danger is, there also grows the delivering power.'

Despite his flirtation with Hegel, the vast distance separating Schmitt in these years from the whole spirit of Hegel's political philosophy was clearly on display in a 1935 meeting of the BNSDJ at which he presided. It was proposed that the term 'man' be eliminated from Article 1 of the Civil Code:

> The legal concept of 'man' in the sense of Article 1 of the Civil Code conceals and falsifies the differences between a citizen of the Reich, a foreigner, a Jew, and so on. Replacing scientific abstraction as something remote from reality, thinking in concrete terms, seeing equal as equal and above all unequal as unequal, and emphasizing the differences among men of different races, nations and occupational estates in the sense of God-given realities – that is the main goal of National Socialist academic jurists, not just of those who are organizationally led by Carl Schmitt. . . .[37]

The Social Democratic newspaper *Neuer Vorwärts*, now in exile in Prague, referred to the conclusions of this conference in an article entitled 'Carl Schmitt Abolishes Man'.[38]

And this is where the contrast with Hegel was at its most extreme: Hegel saw Napoleon's great world-historical deed as the enactment of rational codes of law, based on the integrity of the abstract legal person. For Schmitt, National Socialism was a movement fated to reverse this legal 'depoliticization' of the world set into motion by the rational state.

14

The Revolution in Legal Thought

Carl Schmitt sat on the governing board of the BNSDJ, the main Nazi legal organization, and was one of the editors of its very prestigious journal. As head of the academic division his position in this organization was unique, because unlike other members, who answered to Reich inspector Walter Raeke, he answered directly to Hans Frank, head of the whole Nazi legal establishment, later Governor General of Poland (and later still sentenced to death at Nuremberg).[1] Schmitt's ambition to shape the agendas and idioms of his discipline made it necessary for him to consolidate his position over other influential centres of legal theory. He also belonged to the governing council of the Munich-based journal *AfDR*, and as Munich was the site of the Brown House, the Nazi Party headquarters, his contacts with the head of its Cultural-Political Office, Philip Bouhler, kept many of those within the party who resented Schmitt's privileged positions at bay. With these various footholds Schmitt was for a while a formidable institutional force, without doubt the leading scholar in his field.[2]

Schmitt was all the more pre-eminent in a field which had been purged of nearly all his older colleagues. Those who had not been driven out on 'racial' or political grounds – Gerhard Anschütz, Conrad Bornhak, Rudolf von Laun, Richard Schmidt, Paul Schön, Rudolf Smend, Richard Thoma and Heinrich Treipel – promptly retired and dropped out of public view altogether. Schmitt, young and promising in the early Weimar years, was now old enough to be an adviser and mentor to a younger generation which swamped the numerous purged and vacated departments of law. The discipline was open to colonization by those who could most effectively project their formulas and ideograms into the corridors of power, and make them stick as powerholder jargon. But Schmitt's bid to become the founder-legislator of his discipline collided with the politico-professional aspirations of others; for the party's chief ideologist, the Altkämper Alfred Rosenberg, the influx of academically trained minds into the party brought with it the threat of a humiliating marginalization; an earlier convert to the Nazis, law professor Otto Koelreuter, doggedly sought to diminish Schmitt in the eyes of party bigwigs; Reinhard Höhn, a young rival in the subdiscipline of administrative law, pursued Schmitt with the cloak-and-dagger methods of the SS. Since the stakes were so high, the competition became literally breakneck.

Schmitt's function in these early years of the regime was to provide some intellectual orientation to a legal community confronting the problem of how to know which laws were still valid. This was not easy, because no attempt was ever made to abrogate the Civil Code, so most of its provisions were left standing. But the constant stream of conflicting measures issued by different party and state officials made it difficult to know whether a judgement was to be based on the existing legal statute, some principle of political expediency, or what amounted to the same thing: the tenets of Nazi ideology. Schmitt initially experienced this growing incoherence of legal procedure as an emancipation from the cramped formalism of positivist jurisprudence, and thought that political guidelines set out in general clauses could provide a way of conceptualizing legal rules which would be more open to interpretation based on 'political necessity':

> In legal theory and practice we are already at the point where the theoretical question is posed . . . as to whether a word or a concept of the legislator can be binding in a really calculable way. We have had the experience of every word, every concept, becoming immediately disputable, indeterminate, and labile. . . . If we consider it in this way, today there are only indeterminate legal concepts. . . . The fiction and illusion of a law issued in such a way that all cases and situations can be construed in advance according to the facts of the case, and would be subsumable under the law, cannot be revived. Today, even the thought of an attempt at a gapless codification or normativization would be unimplementable.[3]

As leader of a national *Rechtserneuerung* project, Schmitt sought to be the one to articulate a distinctively National Socialist legal philosophy. Such a philosophy had to represent a total break with the norms of the *Rechtsstaat*, and he made it clear that even one of its fundamental principles – *nulla poena sine lege* (no punishment without a law) – would have to be completely rethought, if not discarded. In the aftermath of the Reichstag fire, the Nazis had forced the passage of a law making politically motivated arson a capital offence, the so-called *lex Lubbe*. The principle forbidding retroactive punishment was so deeply ingrained that the Nazis were unable to obtain from the courts the legal lynching they wanted.

Soon afterwards Schmitt declared that such judicial conservatism was a scandal, and revealed the need for new guidelines of judicial practice radically distinct from the norms of the European *Rechtsstaat*. In criminal law the principle of *nulla poena sine lege* encapsulates the formalism of the *Rechtsstaat* principle, and he focused on it in his attack because its application generates outcomes which even today often offend the popular sense of what constitutes a just punishment:

Everyone understands that it is a requirement of justice to punish crimes. Those who, in the Van der Lubbe case, constantly spoke of the '*Rechtsstaat*' did not place primary importance on the fact that an evil crime found a just punishment. For them the issue lay in a different principle, which, according to the situation, can lead to the opposite of a just punishment, namely the *Rechtsstaat* principle: no punishment without a law, *nulla poena sine lege*. [By contrast, those] who think justly in a case see to it that no crime remains without a punishment. I pit this *Rechtsstaat* principle *nulla poena sine lege* against the principle of justice, '*nulla crimen sine poena*' (no crime without a punishment). The discrepancy between the *Rechtsstaat* and the Just State then becomes immediately visible.[4]

Schmitt argued for a distinctive position within the field of Nazi jurisprudence: most academic jurists, even those much closer to the mainstream of Nazi ideology than Schmitt, tended to maintain that the *Rechtsstaat* was a timeless ideal which needed to be stripped of its inessential, liberal accretions in order that an authentic National Socialist *Rechtsstaat* could take shape. He rejected this conception, arguing that a 'relativistic' liberal formalism was inherent to the very ideal of the *Rechtsstaat*, and that the latter needed to be replaced by a state in which 'equity' – substantive, goal-orientated justice – could override any legal rule when necessary.

Although Schmitt did not make the comparison, it is instructive to consider of Thomas Hobbes's views on this issue. Hobbes had argued that because the letter of the law could always be used to thwart the intention of the legislator, decisions on the basis of the letter of the law had to be subject to equitable review in Chancery. The formula of equity is *salus populi suprema lex esto*: public safety is the supreme law; it is supreme because it is based on a political community's right to exist. Hobbes argued against those – like the great common lawyer and parliamentarian Edward Coke – who claimed that the meaning of treason or felony was determined by legal statutes; by contrast, according to Hobbes, treason and felony were 'crimes in their own nature without help of statute'.[5]

But even if one compares Schmitt's view of the theory behind Nazi criminal justice with Hobbes's definition of equity, the historical context was now so dramatically different that behind the formal resemblance there was a near-complete opposition of political purpose: while both men saw legal language as prone to radical indeterminacy, Hobbes, unlike Schmitt, argued that it would be wise for the sovereign power to reduce this to a minimum by formulating and publishing all the laws in clear English prose, and to strip the statutes of lawyer-Latin jargon. And while Hobbes believed that equity was the only relief from the often viciously unjust penalties of an archaic legal practice, Schmitt described the existing body of criminal law as a Magna Carta for criminals.[6]

At the second meeting of the BNSDJ Schmitt formulated new guide-lines of legal practice for judges which would help them to know what standard of interpretation was to be applied in a case. The objective of these guidelines was to enable judges to refer to 'the tenets of the movement' whenever a judgement on the basis of the relevant statute would clearly be politically unacceptable.[7] General clauses usually come into play when the facts of a case cannot be subsumed under a legal norm, whereupon a judge is compelled to ground his decision in a broad guideline spelling out the principles of the law. Schmitt had previously been hostile to the idea that a judge could invoke such broad guidelines in refusing to apply a statute, or in voiding it as unconstitutional; but he was now confident that although judges would no longer be bound to statutes, the judiciary was in no position to encroach on political matters. Judges could still exercise a certain discretion in those cases which did not have political consequences, but it was entirely up to those in the party and the state to decide what was political, and therefore beyond the jurisdiction of the courts.

For Schmitt, this *ad hoc* supplementation of the Civil Code expressed the needs of a social order which was still based on private property, but whose inner principles could no longer be coherently expressed in general legal norms. Although he occasionally expressed concern that this mode of legal practice was in danger of degenerating into a condition of total formlessness, Schmitt believed that the age of the legal code was over. But his views on the predicament of private law were always those of a jurist trained in public and constitutional law, and just as in his view the norms of the Civil Code no longer mirrored new realities, Schmitt thought that drafting a new constitution would contradict the spirit of 'the movement'.[8] Even in his Weimar writings Schmitt was attracted to the idea of a parsimonious encapsulation of the real constitution of a state in an 'institutional minimum'. This was the Archimedean point from which one could interpret the otherwise indeterminate relationships between legal norms. His case against premature codification was based on his belief that for a long time to come it would be difficult to express the improvisational practice of this regime in legal language. In this he was right: just as the Civil Code remained as the basis of private law, the Weimar Constitution was suspended but never formally abrogated. The Third Reich existed from beginning to end in a 'state of exception'.

Since the early 1920s Schmitt's proposed solutions to the crisis of legal form had oscillated between an emphasis on the significance of a legally ungrounded political decision and an emphasis on an inviolable deep legal structure. This oscillation revealed his disorientation in the face of the breakdown of the intellectual syntheses and distinctions embodied in nineteenth-century legal codes. In the uncoordinated

interpenetration of state and society, he saw forces undermining the
distinctions between the normal and emergency condition of political
life, between laws and administrative measures, between public and
private law, and finally between domestic and international law. In his
'decisionist' writings the breakdown of a 'gapless' legal system was
theoretically radicalized by ascribing a higher theological significance
to legally ungrounded 'sovereign' decisions. But this 'decisionism'
coexisted uneasily with, then gave way to, an increasingly strong conviction that there must be an ultimate source, an underlying substratum
of meta-legal relationships, and that this deepest level of the legal
system could not be represented either as a merely 'valid' norm – the
positivist solution – or as the legislative act of a sovereign – the
decisionist solution. Although in *Die Diktatur* and *Politische Theologie* he
had sought to identify decisionism with an authoritarian restraint on
popular sovereignty, this very emphasis on the will could easily accommodate his subsequent qualified acceptance of popular sovereignty –
as in the 'will of the people'.

In *Über die drei Arten des rechtswissenschaftlichen Denkens*[9] ('On the
Three Kinds of Legal-Theoretical Thought') Schmitt formulated his
vision of the whole *Rechtserneuerung* project as an attempt to move
beyond the duality of positivism and decisionism. Although he subsumed positivism under the wider category of 'normativism', he
pointed out that positivism was actually an intellectually incoherent
hybrid of normative and decisionist modes of thought. Decisionism
could not, therefore, provide an alternative to positivism because, like
positivism, it holds that a legal rule is valid not according to substantive
anterior criteria of legitimacy, but in part simply because it is enacted.

Schmitt pointed out that while Pindar's expression '*nomos basileus*'
conveyed an ancient, venerable belief in the superiority of the rule of
law over the rule of men, if by law Pindar meant only an aggregate of
statutes, it would be impossible to explain why such an aggregate would
ever be more majestic, more legitimate, than the arbitrary will of men:
no one would say of such an aggregate that it was 'king'. We find the
same vision of law as a source of authority more rational than the will
of men – or most of them – in Plato's *The Laws*:

> For wherever in a state the law is subservient and impotent, over that state I
> see ruin impending, but wherever the law is lord over the magistrates and
> the magistrates are servants to the law, there I descry salvation and all the
> blessings that the gods bestow upon a state.[10]

In *Über die drei Arten*, Schmitt unveiled his alternative to positivism and
decisionism, calling it 'concrete order thought'. His portrayal of this
makes it seem as if he was now groping for a new variant of natural
law, having previously rejected it as an anachronism.[11] In *Verfassungslehre*

he had claimed that in the modern world there were two theories which addressed the problem of the legitimacy of an entire legal system: a legal system could be legitimate because its immanent principles conformed to an anterior natural law; or it could be legitimate because the legislative power within this legal system is authorized by the sovereign will of the people. He now believed that the National Socialist revolution had made it easier to reject the decisionist idea that the will of people 'living in the shadow and under the protection of decisions reached in the higher regions of the political' was the source of the legitimacy of a political order.[12]

In *Der Nomos der Erde*, published after the war, Schmitt formulated the antithesis between nomos and popular sovereignty much more clearly:

> The well-known saying concerning the nomos as the ruler, and the ideal that the nomos should rule, meant something entirely different in Aristotle than it does in the usual contemporary view. Aristotle says the nomos must, in opposition to the democratic resolutions of the people, be definitive.[13]

Schmitt was now criticizing not just the idea of a unified sovereign people as the ultimate author and subject of a legal order, but the very idea of a state-based, positive legal order. It is indicative of how far he was willing to move from his earlier steadfast conviction that sovereign statehood was the indispensable presupposition of coherent legal-political reasoning that he now attributed the decline of older modes of 'concrete order' legal thought to the rise of 'one order absorbing all orders within itself'[14] – that is, the sovereign state. This shift coincided with a valorization of the pre-state, 'Germanic' traditions of feudal law, which had never previously appeared in anything he had ever written. In *Der Nomos der Erde* Schmitt was willing to join the chorus of those who portrayed the reception of an abstract Roman law as resulting in the corruption of a more concrete, 'Germanic' jurisprudence. Previously this view, heavily influenced by Gierke's 'association theory', had been an anathema to him, and his endorsement of it here was probably a concession to right thinking.[15] In the previous decade his intellectual affinities on this had been summed up by a reviewer: 'The clarity and rigour of Roman law has formed the character of this philosopher and jurist, and its voice is expressed in every line he writes. For the Romanist Carl Schmitt, that softer kind of German law is an alien world.'[16] In any event, after this book, Schmitt never again called into question the value of the inherited traditions of Roman law.

Schmitt's criticism of the 'statist' conception of law cannot, however, be explained simply in terms of a concession to the political climate of ideas, striking departure as this was from his earlier position. The idea of a new form of legal-political order, 'beyond the state', appealed to him now because it suggested a possible way out of the previously only half-acknowledged theoretical problems which stemmed from his earlier conception of constitution. In a state-based conception of the law, the only reference points for legal decisions are the foundational norms of the constitution and the positive laws enacted by the constitutionally authorized legislator. He had previously argued that in a modern democratic state, the constitutional system derived its legitimacy from the 'people' in its role as constituent power. In earlier writings he counterposed this ultimate founding will to a foundational norm, but it was never entirely clear why the will of the people was any less abstract and fictional a reference point than this foundational norm. More disturbingly, one could plausibly argue that it was the same thing expressed in two different ways. In *Über die drei Arten*, he tacitly acknowledged that the popular will – indeed, any decisionist hypostatization of the will – could be just as 'hypothetical', or 'unconcrete' a construct as Kelsen's Basic Law. Reversing this entirely, he now subscribed to Maurice Hauriou's 'realistic' criticism of the idea of popular sovereignty: to put it simply, it could not be reconciled with the fact that government could never be exercised by 'the people'.[17]

Schmitt now portrayed positivism, as well as his earlier decisionism, as two complementary results of the same process: the disintegration of an underlying 'common law'. This was not 'common law' in the narrower English sense, but 'common law' in the broader sense of law not sharply separated into public and private and not made by legislation, which in modern democracies had become the instrument of the 'self-organization' of society. Although he did not use the term 'common law' in this sense until shortly after *Über die drei Arten* was written, his 'concrete order' theory was an attempt to open up the problem of the politico-historical presuppositions which shape this 'common law'. He found in the word 'nomos' a term which captured this conception of law as something historical yet not the product of 'social construction'; something made, yet not made to be an instrument. He quoted a passage from Hölderlin which, he felt, poetically captured the authentic meaning of 'nomos':

> The Nomos, the law, is the cultivation, in so far as it is a form, in which man
>   encounters himself and the god
> The church, and the law and the old inherited statutes
> Which, stronger than any artifice, holds together the living relations
> In which a people encountered itself and encounters the time.[18]

In the *Verfassungslehre*, it was the sovereign people who 'gave' the constitution: the German verb 'to give' is *geben*, and the people were portrayed in that work – as they were in all theories of popular sovereignty from the time of the French Revolution – as a *verfassungs-*

gebende power – a constitution-giving power. But the key term in this passage from Hölderlin is not *geben* but *begegnen* – not 'to give', but 'to encounter', an infinitive devoid of any demotic voluntarism. The people were now only a *verfassungs-begegnende* power, 'living in the shadow and under the protection of decisions reached in the higher regions of the political'. Whatever Hölderlin's original intention, this was how he was now being interpreted by Schmitt. At the time, Heidegger interpreted Hölderlin to make similar points.

This interpretation of Hölderlin also put Hegel's political philosophy in a new light. In *Staat, Bewegung, Volk*, Schmitt had claimed that Hegel's political philosophy was superseded because it depended upon the existence of an enlightened bureaucracy as the governing class of the rational state. In *Über die drei Arten* he cancelled this verdict: he now portrayed Hegel as the philosopher whose conception of the origin and ground of the legal order avoided both normativism and decisionism. It is true that the late Hegel of *The Philosophy of Right* was much closer to Schmitt on this issue than the young Hölderlin, an enthusiast for the Jacobins.

> Another question readily presents itself here: who is to 'give' the constitution? This question seems clear, but closer inspection shows at once that it is meaningless, for it presupposes that there is no constitution there, only an agglomeration of individuals. . . . In any case, it is absolutely essential that the constitution should not be regarded as something made, even though it has come into being in time. It must, rather, be treated as something simply existent in and by itself, and therefore divine, and so as exalted above the things that are made.[19]

But the Hegel who had given conceptual form to Hölderlin's poetic vision of law arising out of a people encountering itself in history was no longer merely the official philosopher of the Prussian bureaucracy.

> Hegel's state [as in 'status'] . . . is neither the mere sovereign decision, nor the 'norm of norms', nor a variable combination of these two conceptions of the state, alternating between the state of emergency and legality. It is the concrete order of orders, the institution of institutions.[20]

As we have seen, Schmitt was a great admirer of the French scholar of administrative law Maurice Hauriou, one of the founders of modern 'institutionalism'. Despite his attempt to align his views with a supposedly 'Germanic' tradition of jurisprudence, he totally ignored the most influential contemporary school of self-styled Germanist legal thought, which was heavily influenced by Gierke's association theory. He found the closest approximation to his own views in French institutionalism, and in *Über die drei Arten* he sought to avoid what he considered the self-governing implications of the word 'association' by using the more authoritarian term 'institution' instead. It is often difficult to capture the meaning of the specialized idioms of a discipline, particularly when they are no longer in circulation; why did Schmitt identify so strongly with French 'institutionalism' while rejecting Gierkian 'association theory' based on the idea of the juristic personality of corporations? In German, the term 'association' – *Körperschaft* – refers to a group of persons legally constituted as members of an artificial private body. According to Gierke, the state could only recognize, not create, such associations. The closest equivalent to 'institution' in German is *Anstalt*, which refers to a hierarchical organization that exercises *Anstaltsgewalt* over its users, who do not have membership rights. A passage from Weber's *Economy and Society* clarifies the original meaning of 'institution', and suggests why Schmitt had an affinity for the term:

> In substance, [the concept of institution] is of ecclesiastic origin, derived from late Roman ecclesiastic law. The concept of institution was bound to arise there, in some manner, as soon as both the charismatic conception of the bearer of religious authority and the purely voluntary organization of the congregation had finally yielded to the official bureaucracy of the bishops.[21]

'Institutionalism' appealed to Schmitt because it provided a language in which law could be understood non-normatively, as the transparent expression of the dynamic requirements of political institutions, or 'concrete orders' which precede and form the necessary presuppositions of legal reasoning. The significance of this relationship of precedence and presupposition is that it can justify overriding and altering legal rules whenever the existence of such 'concrete orders' are at stake. But it was no longer just the organizations which comprised the state that could exempt themselves from the jurisdiction of the courts; under National Socialism the legal distinction between public and private was losing its significance, and terms like 'concrete order' could be used to justify restricting or nullifying personal liberty and contractual freedom over whole regions of social and economic life. The legal theory of the Nazi period, without exception, sought to provide formulas which would expedite this *ad hoc* suspension and nullification of legal rules. This does not mean that Schmitt's formulations in this work were purely opportunistic: even before the Nazis seized power, he had come to the conclusion that as long as a regime maintained the historically necessary relationship between the spheres of public and private, norm and exception – ultimately, politicization and neutralization – it was legitimate. As he had put it earlier, the ability to get this relationship right was what distinguished the 'qualitative total state' (Fascist) from the 'quantitative total state' (the pluralist welfare state).

In *Verfassungslehre* and *Legalität und Legitimität* Schmitt had argued that the constitution of a *Rechtsstaat* was split between a section which specified how the public will was expressed and a section which protected personal liberty and property. By the time he wrote the latter he could no longer clearly identify which of these was the foundation of the legal system. He sought to solve this conundrum by explaining how the authority of law originates neither *ex nihilo* from the legislative power of the state, nor from a natural law which was valid before the establishment of this legislative power. According to Hauriou, to argue that the legislative power of the state created *ex nihilo* the liberty and property rights of its subjects was to portray the origin of the state as 'a juridical miracle'. Yet in Schmitt's view, in an era of mass politics and technological wonders it would be a sheer anachronism to set any natural-law limits to political power.

In his Weimar writings Schmitt had repeatedly argued that unless legislation took place within the strict limits of the division of powers, all the qualities which distinguish law from an administrative measure, and legitimate authority exercised in its name, would be lost. But his real concern was not the preservation of the division of powers, but the social order which the division of powers was designed to protect. In *Verfassungslehre* and *Legalität und Legitimität,* he argued that the individual freedoms externally embodied in the right to own and alienate property constitute a system of meta-legal presuppositions which positive laws could not violate without undermining that which makes laws just and obedience to them obligatory. In *Über die drei Arten,* bourgeois society receded into the background, for the obvious reason that under National Socialism it could no longer be evoked as the basis of political legitimacy, and the interpretative key of legal reasoning. But if bourgeois society no longer provided the material principle of justice under National Socialism, what had replaced it? Schmitt provided no answer to this question. Although he claimed that uncovering the concrete order of presuppositions, which could not be expressed in the form of rules, was the only way to understand the immanent principles of legitimacy within a legal system, he portrayed this concrete order in rather vague terms.

Schmitt was heading towards a politico-theoretical cul-de-sac. His use of terms like 'concrete order' expressed an ideological fantasy that the right relationship between public and private could be secured by a regime which was the guardian of the ultimate sources of legal authority, and yet, like the prince in medieval Thomism, not subject to the law. In a later work, the ideological dimension of this attempt to portray an explosively unstable, instrumentalized legality as a 'concrete order' of authority comes across vividly:

> *Gouverner c'est légiférer* . . . I take this formula in its compelling simplicity as a significant symptom allowing us to recognize how far the constitutional concepts of Locke and Montesquieu have been surmounted, and how far

our juristic thinking is once again tied to the pre-constitutional traditions of European intellectual history. A concept of law which sees legislation as an affair of government approaches the concept of law held by Aristotle or Thomas Aquinas. According to this great philosopher, law is essentially an act of government; it is, as Thomas said, 'not the reason of any kind of men, rather in a specific sense the practical reason of those who lead and govern the community'.[22]

The reference to Aquinas concealed the essential issue: law as any act of any official from a horde of governmental and para-governmental agencies, addressed to this or that group of subjects, revocable at will, even retroactive in effect, cannot generate legal obligations – not just because it is unpredictable, but because inconsistent and reversible decisions addressed to a heterogeneous assortment of legal subjects cannot be rationally justified by an indivisible sovereign will, nor by a purely procedural standard of fairness, and arguably not even by any coherent, substantive criteria of justice.

Despite his earlier, increasingly disingenuous insistence on maintaining the balance-of-powers system within the Weimar Republic, Schmitt had for some time effectively provided arguments promoting the transfer of legislative power to the executive, and he was now writing in a situation where this delegation had reached the extreme point. The difference between a law and an SS memo was collapsing. Only later would it dawn on him that this was the point at which jurisprudence as the science of interpreting the meaning of laws becomes irrelevant; and, even further, that it was the point at which the relationship between legality and legitimacy also ceases to have any significance, simply because legality can at this point *always* be overridden by a government invoking the higher legitimacy of its action. He was about to be thrown overboard by a dynamic of ever more brazen assertions of legitimacy.

15

Flight Forward and Retreat

The bloody spectacle of the Röhm purge demonstrated that Schmitt's position in the Third Reich was not nearly as secure as it had seemed. In June 1934 Schmitt published an essay *Staatsgefüge und Zusammenbruch des Zweiten Reiches* ('State Structure and Collapse of the Second Reich'), in which the 'National Revolution' was portrayed as the victory of the spirit of the Prussian army over bourgeois liberalism – that is, as the successful culmination of Bismarck's struggle against the *Rechtsstaat*. Of all the pieces he ever wrote, this was the most conventionally conservative and 'Prussian' in spirit. The central role which Schmitt attributed to the military did not reflect only his ongoing ties to these circles but also, perhaps, his expectation that such men would soon be making their move against the most unruly elements in the party, perhaps even curbing Hitler in the process. Despite all his good fortune within the party, up to June 1934 there is evidence to suggest that he was in contact with senior officers seeking his advice on the possibility of a *coup d'état*.[1]

On 21 June 1934 the *Reichswehr* Minister, General Werner von Blomberg, threatened Hitler with a coup if no action was taken against the intolerable challenge posed by Ernst Röhm and the SA to the autonomy of the military. On 25 June the crisis had gone so far that the Army Chief of Staff, Freiherr Werner von Fritsch, put troops on a state of alert. Hitler, backed into a corner, was able a week later to make the most out of this crisis, and unleashed a wave of terror in which Röhm and his followers were slaughtered in *razzias* led by Goering and Himmler. This in itself would have been a welcome development for those, like Schmitt, who were not enamoured of the streetfighter type. But it came at a heavy price, because Hitler skilfully used this crisis not only to crush plebeian mutiny in the ranks but also to bring erstwhile conservative allies to heel, and settle scores with those who were still thinking about a *coup d'état*. General Schleicher, who had not resigned himself to being sidelined, was brutally murdered along with his wife.

Schmitt's position within the regime had been based on his ability to form an intellectual bridge between the movement on the one side, and the military and civilian state elites on the other. This crisis threatened to undermine his position, not just because of suspicions that he might still be linked to Schleicher's entourage – after all, he had been quite conspicuously involved in many of the General's political manoeuvres – but also because the Nazis would no longer be needing anyone to man this position. But he did not give up easily. On the heels of the Röhm affair, he published an article praising the purge as a form of 'revolutionary justice'. Carl Schmitt was the only major jurist in the country to do so, and he hoped that by distinguishing himself in this manner he could counter any suspicion that he had bet on the other side even for a moment.

Of all Schmitt's writings during the Third Reich, this article, entitled 'Der Führer schützt das Recht' ('The Leader Protects the Law'), was later considered the most shameless, because of its nakedly apologetic purpose. It has recently been suggested by Helmut Quaritsch, who clearly wishes to 'rehabilitate' Schmitt, that the arguments of this article were so transparently absurd that they have to be considered as something close to intentional parody.[2] This is completely false: Schmitt took himself far too seriously to write anything which was not meant to be taken seriously. Even though his purpose was to rationalize a murderous purge, and even though he wrote the article because he feared for his life, its argument was consistent with everything he had previously written under National Socialism and, however iniquitous, it was far from 'absurd'.

Quoting Hitler, he argued that the true leader is always a judge. This did not entail any revision of his earlier criticism of political justice, as the sort of 'justice' he was referring to here was not the ordinary sort, administered by courts nominally bound to the law. A reference to the opinion of Dufour – who, with Hauriou, was one of the fathers of French administrative jurisprudence – clarifies the real meaning of his claim that Hitler could directly administer summary justice. According to Dufour, the government can exempt itself from judicial review when it must 'defend society against enemies, inside, outside, open, con-cealed, present and future'.[3] Schmitt argued that this sort of action should not be retrospectively legalized, as the regime was now attempt-ing to do; this was entirely consistent with his view that settling accounts with a political enemy should not be done with legal pretexts.

On the question of summary justice, Thomas Hobbes was not so far away from the principle articulated in this article: Chancery as supreme court, equity as supreme law, king as supreme judge – this was the Hobbesian formula of government. But again, the difference is as profound as the similarity. For Hobbes, there was a natural-law limit to the king's summary justice: an armed rebel could be killed without trial, but not an unarmed subject. At least some of those butchered in the so-called 'Night of the Long Knives' fell into the latter category. Even if Schmitt did not endorse such excesses, he could provide no reason why they, too, were not in conformity with 'revolutionary justice'.

If he did have more general misgivings about some of the barbaric excesses of Nazi criminal law – and this is not unlikely – he chose to express them in a singularly perverse form. Indicative of the intellectually bizarre atmosphere of the times is that fact that he argued in an interview which appeared in the party newspaper *Der Angriff,* entitled 'Können wir uns vor Justizirrtum schützen?' ('Can We Protect Ourselves from Judicial Error?'), that the Inquisition provided a model of humane justice for all ages.

> It was a terribly humane measure when Pope Innocent III created the 'Inquisitorial Law'. The Inquisition was probably perhaps the most humane institution conceivable, since it came from the standpoint that no one accused could be condemned without a confession. When, in the course of a century, the practice of the Inquisition degenerated into torture, because one wanted a confession, and had to extort it, that is indeed a dark chapter of cultural history, but seen in terms of legal history, even today the idea of Inquisition can hardly be touched.[4]

In a land ruled by men who took a very dim view of the Catholic Church, Schmitt invoked the Inquisition as a model for the SS. A residual and idiosyncratic Catholicism had served him well as a theoretical fellow traveller, but to save himself now he would have had to throw all this overboard, and become a wide-eyed, true believer. Not for want of effort, he found this difficult to do.

The honeymoon between National Socialism and those scholars of the first rank who embraced it did not last long. Like Heidegger, Schmitt briefly felt that he could be the intellectual architect of the new order. It is tempting to look back and see such intellectuals as they saw themselves – as important actors on the stage of history. Much more so than Martin Heidegger or Gottfried Benn, Schmitt did have a real political impact, even if his role was always minor. It is unlikely that Hitler had anything more than the faintest idea of who he was; under National Socialism, ingenious legal reasoning became increasingly dispensable. Yet outside Germany, left-wing and liberal émigrés often perceived him to be the official philosopher of the regime, and a great many Italians, including many at the top, colluded in this immense overestimation of his domestic role and stature. Even though such intellectuals seemed for a while to be riding high, the political momentum of National Socialism in power eventually bypassed all those who were not able to defend themselves in the intellectually raw environment of the party. In comparison to Mussolini's Italy,

where right-thinking intellectuals were co-opted and pampered, Nazi
Germany was ruled by a man who gazed at ideas from outside the
brutal mental prison of *Mein Kampf*, with ferocious incomprehension.

The struggle to hold on to his powerful – albeit precarious – positions
within the academic and political arena was taking its toll on Schmitt's
temperament, unnerving him and bringing out the harshest and most
paranoid aspects of his personality. Even as early as the beginning of
1934 Schmitt seemed to an old student, Paul Adams, like a different
man:

> The condition of Carl Schmitt is terrible. In Munich he certainly treated me
> very well. New to me was his abrupt manner of denigrating my views and
> their explanations. . . . Politically he will never be accepted by the National
> Socialists. His style, his genius, his fundamentally solitary existence will always
> cause offence. It would have been better if he had gone to Munich and
> existed on the periphery.[5]

At a time when the Nazis were shaking off come-lately fellow travellers,
Schmitt's pre-1933 associations – and even his post-1933 writings – were
drummed up to call into question his faith in National Socialism.
Leading the charge were those who greatly resented Schmitt's celebrity
status within the Nazi legal establishment, and saw themselves as
unjustly passed over. Within the ranks of academic jurists, Otto Koelreuter, theorist of a 'National Socialist *Rechtsstaat*', spearheaded these
efforts. Alfred Rosenberg, the party's dull-witted official ideologist, had
early on sought to discredit Schmitt with charges of statism and
Catholicism. But by far the most effective opposition came from Höhn
of the SD, the SS office on the lookout for ideological deviation.
Although Schmitt was an incomparably greater thinker than his
opponents in the party, he possessed an original and independent
mind – he could not bring himself to abandon his own ideas completely
for ideas which struck him as absurd and shallow. For this reason, he
and those like him were ultimately not adaptable enough to survive the
gruelling scramble to hold on to the best positions.[6]

This is not to say that Schmitt was intellectually unaffected by this
inner Gleichschaltung. Alongside his domestic adversaries, he was
beginning to feel personally threatened by Jewish émigrés like his
former friend Waldemar Gurian. Gurian's articles in Swiss newspapers,
written under the pseudonym Paul Müller, sought to discredit Schmitt
in the eyes of the party by pointing out his past affiliations with the
Centre Party, his previously close relationship with many Jews, and his
essentially opportunistic nature. Gurian sarcastically upbraided the
Nazis for not realizing what a slippery character they were dealing
with.[7] Schmitt's enemies within Germany seized upon these disclosures,
as Gurian had hoped they would. Schmitt was beginning to form

paranoid and desperate ideas about the forces at work behind these intrigues, coming from so many directions, involving people determined to bring him down.

In 1936 he came up with a plan to evade this impending encirclement. Hoping to protect his gravely threatened position, he organized a conference whose theme was the elimination of contaminating Jewish influences on German jurisprudence. He probably believed that if the exclusive object of National Socialist demonization was 'the Jew', then this might divert attention from less important issues – like the fight against those suspected of Catholic sympathies. In fact, Höhn opposed Schmitt's planned conference on the grounds that the 'Jewish Problem' had already been solved, and accused Schmitt of bringing up old issues to divert attention from the necessity of a struggle against the Church.[8]

Before 1933, whatever traces of anti-Semitism Schmitt exhibited were entirely conventional, and there are absolutely no grounds for thinking that his later views were somehow there in nuce. It is often assumed that people are anti-Semites either because of some deep psychological defect or, conversely, because of cynical opportunism. While the opportunistic motive was present, and abundantly evident to all those who knew him, after the passage of the Nuremberg Laws Schmitt realized that the anti-Semitism of National Socialism was not simply demagoguery to stir and distract the masses, but one of the central concerns of the movement. His intellectual strategy under the Nazis was always to find the point of fundamental philosophical agreement between himself and the movement, and to present this point of contact as its historic mission. Whatever calculated exaggerations were involved in his attempted demonstration of ideological rectitude, he, too, now believed that there was in fact a Jewish problem, and that it needed to be 'solved' if Europe was to be saved. No longer able to rely simply on the occasional anti-Semitic allusion, in 1935 he hailed the Nuremberg Laws as 'Die Verfassung der Freiheit' ('The Constitution of Freedom').[9] This being said, one cannot neatly distinguish these new-found 'convictions' from paranoia and a cynical willingness to do whatever it would take to prevail. But while Schmitt was willing to accept and justify the relentless civic degradation and expulsion of the Jews, it is inconceivable that in 1936 he was thinking of anything approaching a 'Final Solution'.

Schmitt was willing to stoop very low for allies in his struggle to ward off the encirclement spearheaded by Heydrich. Julius Streicher was probably one of the most notorious Jew-baiters in a country where there was now plenty of competition. The lowbrow, lurid, vaguely pornographic ravings of the paper he edited, Der Stürmer, were so demented that they regularly created a certain embarrassment within the party itself. Although the anti-Semitism which Schmitt would profess at this conference and in the future had a different style and intellectual basis from Streicher's, to stave off impending defeat he was at this moment willing to consort with this most outrageously unsavoury character.

As the keynote speaker at this ill-attended event, Schmitt opened the conference with a quotation from Hitler: 'In that I defend myself against the Jews, I struggle to do the work of the Lord.'[10] He maintained that although the Nuremberg racial laws were now in place, further vigilance was necessary, because the whole of German jurisprudence was contaminated by Jewish influences. On an earlier occasion he had made the claim that the problem was not individual Jewish figures, but a whole way of thinking about law: 'There are peoples who exist only in "the Law", without soil, without a state, without a church; to them normative thought is the only rational juristic thought, and any other mode of thinking is inconceivable, mystical, fantastic or laughable.'[11] But Schmitt insisted that this Jewish threat to German jurisprudence could not be understood in terms of some biologically conceived racial difference; this would be to put the Jews on the same level as the Japanese and the Magyars, highly esteemed peoples in the National Socialist racial order. By contrast, he portrayed Jews across the ideological spectrum as representing a *political* threat to European peoples. In his view, the history of the Jewish Diaspora in Europe was a history of the Jews' concealed, ultimately disastrous attempts at infiltration. Shocking as these views are, they are not so far from the diagnosis of Curtius in 1932: 'We do not fight the Jews, but the destruction: not the race, but the negation.'[12] Curtius, of course, could not have anticipated the meaning this might have in 1936, but it should be remembered that before 1933, Schmitt wrote nothing remotely similar.

In the lecture Schmitt gave at this conference, he claimed that the Jews represented a threat from two directions: 'Jewish chaos and Jewish legality . . . anarchist nihilism and positivist normativism . . . raw sensualist materialism and abstract moralism'.[13] Although the first terms of these anti-Semitic binaries seemed to contradict the second terms, in his mind they belonged together: legalism was the façade behind which lurked anarchy, 'the mystery of lawlessness'. This association was present at many levels in his later writings. In Schmitt's mind the Jewish Diaspora was Janus-faced, embodying everything and its opposite – legalism and anarchy; normativism and nihilism; moralism and raw sensualism – oppositions stemming from their essentially free-floating, abnormal condition as a diasporic people. Consequently, there would be two fundamentally different 'kinds' of Jews whom he saw embodying the iniquitous spirit of their people: liberal rationalists like Spinoza and Kelsen; and those exotics who had managed to infiltrate the citadels of conservative power, like the sixteenth-century Cabalist Isaac Abravanel, Benjamin Disraeli and F.J. Stahl.[14]

This conference was little more than a call for a well-organized intellectual pogrom. Schmitt declared that the 'unholy' Jewish presence in German jurisprudence could be exorcized only if it could be clearly determined, once and for all, who was a Jew and who was not. It was important, he maintained, not to compare the views of Jewish and non-Jewish authors, even when these 'seemed' to converge. Perhaps Schmitt thought that if the role and presence of Jews in German legal culture could be precisely delimited, libellous, indirect insinuations of Jewish influence could be curtailed. But even if this was his intention, the way he chose to execute it guaranteed that the consequences would be further to poison the intellectual atmosphere. His proposed solution was that all writings by Jews should be taken out of circulation in libraries and put in a carefully guarded 'Judaica' section. Any references to the views of Jewish scholars should be prefaced by some mention that they belonged to this enemy people. Many of these proposals were soon adopted.

By the end of 1936 it was clear that Schmitt's 'flight forward' strategy had failed to reverse the decline in his political fortunes. He was soon forced to resign from his official positions in the party legal establishment. It has often been claimed that this resulted in a certain 'internal emigration' expressed in hints and esoteric allusions. But thanks to intervention by Goering and Frank on his behalf, Schmitt, although disgraced, was hardly persecuted. In a letter addressed to the editorial board of the SS paper *Schwarze Korp*, Goering made it clear that they were immediately to cease any further attacks on Schmitt: 'Without wanting to take a position on the factual accusations which are in themselves not unjustified, I must emphatically state that it is not acceptable for well-known personalities, who have been called to high public office through my trust, to be defamed in this way by your journal.'[15]

Whatever disillusionment Schmitt experienced, his academic position in Berlin still placed him at the summit of his profession. Moreover, he comforted himself that he was still '*Staatsrat*', and he clung to this title, always preferring it to 'professor'. He was not about to abandon all this to enter the world of real émigrés, whom he hated more than even his domestic adversaries, and who now certainly rejoiced at the news of his downfall. His fascination with the centres of political power kept him in Berlin, and until the very end of the war, like Heidegger, he laboured to discern the meaning of the world-historical catastrophe which National Socialism was setting in motion. The Third Reich would never conform to Schmitt's vision of a new kind of enclosed political totality, but would lurch from crisis to crisis, driven by a growing lack of internal co-ordination which was kept below the surface only by a string of real and ideologically defined 'successes'. He would only ever perceive the enormity of these unfolding crimes through the rather narrow lens of the 'crisis of the state'.

But he was beginning to see menacing shapes and phantasms through this theoretical prism. Political language in Nazi Germany was saturated with the jargon of mythology, and Schmitt was well equipped to take advantage of the possibilities of this medium. According to Nicolaus Sombart, he could write in two registers: a conceptual prose in which problems were sharply posed, and another in which these same problems floated in a stream of concealed associations around images and symbols.[16] While in earlier works references to the mysteries of evil were an undercurrent, an interplay of tone and allusion, they now began to press closer to the surface, periodically erupting, as he sought to form a more vivid picture of the enemy.

The Leviathan Myth

Carl Schmitt had initially supported the Nazis because he believed that they were poised to solve the problem of the 'pluralistic' disintegration of the secular state, as a neutral, higher power in an age of mass politics. From 1933 to 1935, he had argued that the new regime was bringing an end to an era of crisis by moving beyond the legal-rational form of state to a new kind of order, ruled by an openly partisan 'movement'. This initial affirmation of the 'movement' against the 'state' coincided with a diminishing interest in Hobbes, the great theorist of the state as a neutral apparatus, and with a much greater estimation of Hegel than is evident in anything he had ever written before.

Even after his humiliating defeat, he did not immediately change his verdict on Hobbes as a theorist of a defeated cause. Months before, he had even written an essay on Hobbes's depiction of the state as machine – 'Der Staat als Mechanimus bei Hobbes und Descartes' ('The State as a Mechanism in Hobbes and Descartes') – in which he suggested that this metaphor was a symptom of an eventually fatal neutralization. He claimed that although this mechanical metaphor had a greater plasticity in the seventeenth century, when it was still possible to think of a body as a living machine governed by a central intelligence, it would later lose such associations and turn into an image of a static apparatus, an instrument to be conquered, used and destroyed by 'society'. The state, Schmitt implied, was vulnerable to pluralistic disintegration, because the machine metaphor was a clear signal, to anyone looking for weak links in this edifice, that behind the terrifying mythic scaffolding the state was merely a man-made construction, to be built and demolished at will. It was on this point that he compared Hobbes unfavourably to Hegel: '[Hegel] has no kinship with this "mortal God" of Hobbes's philosophy of state. On the contrary, [Hobbes's] "deus mortalis" is a machine whose "mortality" is based on the fact that one day it may be shattered by civil war or rebellion.'[1] Schmitt pointed to the apparent paradox that Hobbes chose, despite this metaphor of the state as a machine, to portray his commonwealth on the cover of his greatest work, in the form of a giant man, and then to entitle this work

'Leviathan', the mythological sea monster referred to in the Book of Job. He insisted that Hobbes failed to use any of the mythic associations around the term 'Leviathan' to qualify his mechanistic conception of the state:

> Looked at closely, the use of the Leviathan to represent Hobbes's theory of the state is nothing other than a half-ironic literary idea born out of a fine sense of English humour. Only the enormous striking power implicit in the image of the mythical beast has led to the mistaken notion that this is the central idea of Hobbes's theory of the state. The sentences and the words that Hobbes uses to describe it do not leave any doubt that he did not take this image to be believable, conceptually, mythically or demonically.[2]

Helmut Schelsky, one of Schmitt's students at the time, replied to this essay, arguing that Schmitt had failed to grasp Hobbes's affirmation of political action – an affirmation which, he claimed, could not be grasped by trying to impose a system on Hobbes's thought. Schelsky suggested that those who adhered to a 'political theology' could never fully grasp the secular, action-orientated nature of political thought. Schmitt responded diplomatically to these charges in a series of lectures, later published as *Der Leviathan in der Staatslehre Thomas Hobbes* (*The Leviathan in the Political Theory of Thomas Hobbes*). In this book he simply discarded his earlier claim that this symbol possessed only an ironical meaning. The new interpretation was based on the assumption that, on the contrary, 'Leviathan' was indeed 'the central idea of Hobbes's theory of the state', because it revealed the actual political intention of Hobbes's work: the struggle to defeat 'political theology'.

But in this work, 'political theology' no longer meant the analogical relationship between political and theological concepts. Schmitt now associated it with the Judeao-Christian belief that a secular polity could never legitimately have full jurisdiction over religious communities directly subject to God. Since the mid-1920s he had been moving towards the idea that the division between state and Church provided the inspiration and the mould for the later division between state and society. In this sense, he now strongly identified with Hobbes's struggle, and qualified this only by asserting that Hobbes had failed, an assertion contained in the subtitle of this book: *The Meaning and Failure of a Political Symbol*.

Schmitt now argued that Hobbes's decision to entitle his greatest work 'Leviathan' was an attempt to depict the forces arrayed against the newly forged early modern state by evoking some of the powerful and complex associations which this name carried; and that these associations played a significant role in the historical reception of Hobbes's thought. Hobbes's decision to name his political construction after a figure of biblical mythology has to be seen in the light of a desperate struggle, over the millennia, to establish an enclosed, secular polity against a myriad of sinister, indirect forces, seeking to prise the state open at its weakest links. He insinuated that European Jewry was at work here.

Schmitt claimed that an understanding of the later diasporic Jewish tradition of Leviathan interpretation provided an insight into the awesome forces of destruction which this stateless people hoped to unleash on the heathen world. He implied that Hobbes's brief allusions to this symbol represented an attempt to confront the threat of the stateless, by giving this symbol a new meaning. From the outset it is clear that Schmitt was attempting to put the prevailing anti-Semitism on a more intellectually respectable basis.

> [Less] well known are the interpretations that arose in the Middle Ages, in which the unique, totally abnormal condition of the Jewish people in relation to all other peoples became discernible, a condition that cannot be compared to that of any other people. Here we are confronted by the political myths of the most astonishing kind and by documents often fraught with a downright magical intensity. They are produced by Cabalists and naturally have an esoteric character. . . . According to such Jewish-Cabalistic interpretations, the Leviathan represents 'the cattle upon a thousand hills' (Psalms 50:10), namely the heathen. World history begins as a battle amongst the heathen. The Leviathan symbolizing sea powers, fighting the Behemoth, representing the land powers. . . . But the Jews stand by and watch how the people of the world kill one another. This ritual slaughter is for them lawful and 'kosher' and they therefore eat the flesh of the slaughtered peoples and are sustained by it.[3]

Schmitt suggested that Hobbes, in his own way, was seeking to counter a Cabalistic mythology in which the Leviathan is finally subdued and then devoured. It is clear from later writings that the medieval Cabalist he had in mind was Isaac Abravanel, last in a line of medieval Jewish philosophers. Abravanel lived from 1437 to 1508, in the time of the great discoveries, and was the treasurer first of the King of Portugal and then of the King of Castile. Schmitt thought he saw in the writings of this Cabalist the iniquitous spirit of the Jewish Diaspora staring him in the face. Abravanel had predicted that after the heathen powers had destroyed themselves in a great war, a Messianic age would begin in which all the kingdoms of the world would be liquidated, and the once proud nations would be reduced to being servants of the Jews, forced to 'herd the cattle and sheep and cultivate their fields and vineyards'.[4]

Leo Strauss argued, in a book written a year after Schmitt's was published, that although 'the Messianic Age for Abravanel is a period rich in miracles, [including] the resurrection of the dead', this age of universal peace was not an otherworldly but an earthly utopia. Strauss pointed out that Abravanel's vision of Messianic times was based not on Scripture but, rather, on an anarchic strand of ancient political thought:

> He took up from Seneca the criticism of civilization, urban life, coercive government, private property – all products of the rebellion against the natural order instituted by God. Life in accordance with nature is life in the field: roaming families owning things in common in the desert under God's miraculous providence.[5]

In contrast to Maimonides, Abravanel denied the legitimacy of kingship in Israel and argued for the rule of judges – priestly interpreters of God's will, with no executive power: an essentially stateless theocratic confederacy. Strauss insisted that this, too, came not from the Hebrew Bible but from contemporary Papist justifications of ecclesiastic rule.

Significantly, the point of departure for Schmitt's interpretation of Hobbes in the light of 'the Jewish Question' was a passage from an earlier work by Strauss on Spinoza, which compared Spinoza's views on religion and politics to those of Hobbes. It is very possible that Strauss, in his book on Abravanel, was responding to Schmitt's discussion of his own ideas, particularly the way in which Schmitt had drawn on his ideas to argue an anti-Semitic case. What were the issues in this only partially concealed dialogue? First, it is important to identify the exegetical basis of this dialogue in *Leviathan*. For a modern reader of *Leviathan*, it might seem curious that Hobbes devoted so much space to discussing passages in the Old Testament which address the decision of the Jewish confederacy, living until then under the direct rule of God – that is to say, the priestly judges ruling in his name – to 'depose' God, and submit to a king in the manner of the Gentiles. This was their attempt at becoming a state – an attempt which would ultimately fail. Schmitt's reference to Strauss's interpretation of Hobbes's political agenda highlights the significance of this seemingly obscure matter:

> [Strauss] remarks in this context that Hobbes regarded the Jews as the originators of the revolutionary state-destroying distinction between religion and politics. That is correct only insofar as Hobbes opposed the typically Judeo-Christian division of the original political unity. The distinction between secular and spiritual power was, according to Hobbes, alien to the heathens because to them religion was part of politics; the Jews brought about unity from the side of religion.[6]

It is significant that both Schmitt and Strauss agreed that the central problem in Hobbes's political theory was 'the typically Judeo-Christian division of the original political unity'. This identification of Judaism and Christianity was no passing comment on Schmitt's part: he made it clear that he agreed with Hobbes that not only Presbyterian sects but also the Roman Catholic Church were the inheritors of this 'state-destroying distinction'.[7]

Schmitt and Strauss were not the first to think that this was the decisive issue in interpreting Hobbes. In *The Social Contract*, Rousseau argued that this opposition, and the problem of restoring 'the original political unity', ultimately came down to the question of whether or not it was possible for any Christian people ever to establish an enclosed secular polity against the power of independent estates, in particular the clergy; and in his opinion, Hobbes was the first to see the problem clearly:

> Wherever the clergy constitutes a body, it is master and legislator in its domain. There are, therefore, two powers, two sovereigns, just as everywhere else. Of all Christian Authors, the philosopher Hobbes is the only one who correctly saw the evil and the remedy, who dared to propose the reunification of the two heads of the eagle, and the complete return to political unity, without which no state or government will ever be well constituted. But he ought to have seen that the dominating spirit of Christianity was incompatible with his system and the interest of the priest would always be stronger than the state. It is not so much what is horrible and false in his politics, but what is correct and true which has made it odious.[8]

In all these references to the problem of restoring 'the original political unity', the opposition between state and Church is interchangeable with – and slides into – the opposition between state and society: both 'Church' and 'society' designated politically ungovernable regions where unruly powers and passions were at work. In Schmitt's opinion, the religious community had become the archetypal form of the anarchic 'partial association':

> The 'private' sphere is thus withdrawn from the state and handed over to the free – that is, uncontrollable and invisible – forces of 'society'. Those mutually heterogeneous forces formed the party system whose essential core, as J.N. Figgis identified perceptively, was composed of Churches and trade unions. From the duality of state and state-free society arose a social pluralism in which 'indirect powers' could celebrate effortless triumphs.[9]

The seemingly anachronistic opposition between religion and politics came alive in his mind because he could now visualize the emancipation of society from coercive government as the advent of that grim and terrifying Messianic age portrayed by Abravanel: the return to a subpolitical human nature.

Despite the brevity of Hobbes's allusions, Schmitt claimed that the Leviathan was the esoteric centre of his whole political theory, because it was the name given to the only kind of polity which could solve this problem. And the name itself was important, because the associations it evoked had fateful consequences for the outcome of this enterprise. The question was 'whether the Leviathan stood the test of being the politico-mythical image battling the Judeo-Christian destruction of the natural unity, and whether he was equal to the severity and malice of such a battle'.[10]

This restoration of natural unity *from the political side* meant the construction of a myth which would make the state once again appear as an awe-inspiring higher power, a total polity which could dissolve all 'partial associations' when necessary. In the twentieth century the unbridled forces of civil society defeated Hobbes's misbegotten Leviathan, which was not equal to this battle. Schmitt believed that in an age of mass mobilization, an increasingly complex interpenetration of politics and economics, and the decline of an interstate order based on sovereign states, mythological representations of authority were once again needed to orientate the theory and practice of total political systems. The thrust of Schmitt's reinterpretation of the Hobbesian project is a polemical valuation of the 'state' in relation to a series of terms against which it can be set in the form of a binary opposition: 'social movement', 'religion' and 'party'. A subdued note of disappointment about National Socialism, as an amalgamation of all three, can be discerned in the inter relationship of these oppositions.

Schmitt could with some justification see the struggle for a 'total state' – that is, the political retotalization of 'partial associations' – as the common ground between himself and Hobbes. But his insistence that the mythic representation of this total polity was important for Hobbes seems to lack any textual basis, a point which he almost conceded.[11] He expressed, in fact, a certain disappointment that Hobbes did not seem to make much use of the impressive drawing on the cover, nor, more significantly, of his mysterious title, mentioning the Leviathan only in passing, and giving only a glimpse of its basis in Scripture:

> Hitherto I have set forth the nature of man, whose pride and other passions have compelled him to submit himself to government, together with the great powers of his governor, whom I compared to Leviathan, taking that comparison out of the two last verses of the one and fortieth of Job, where God, having set forth the great power of the Leviathan, calleth him the King of the Proud. 'There is nothing', saith he, 'on earth to be compared with him. He is made so as not to be afraid. He seeth every high thing below him, and is king of all the children of pride.[12]

Despite the often tendentious direction of his reading, Schmitt was probably correct in assuming that Hobbes sensed that troubling implications flowed from portraying the state as an entirely man-made, artificial construction – a machine – and that it would be better that a subject should keep in his mind's eye the image of a monster of irresistible power. While it might be thought that Hobbes made these biblical allusions to the Book of Job only because he wanted to ingratiate himself with a public steeped in biblical discourse, this surely does not explain why he used such provocative appellations as 'Leviathan' and 'Mortal God'. 'Leviathan', even if it had lost much of its diabolic meaning in the seventeenth century, was certainly not the most obvious name for a 'Christian Commonwealth'. 'Mortal God' was, in a sense, even more scandalous, outrageously implying that any regime which effectively protected its subjects, even one which persecuted the godly, was Christlike. Hobbes's enemies could plausibly infer that his intent was to put his 'Mortal God' in the place of Christ, the real mortal God. Indeed, Hobbes knew that the interpretations of Scripture in *Leviathan* were by far the most provocative part of the argument:

> That which perhaps might most offend are certain Texts of Holy Scripture, alleged by me to other purpose than ordinarily they used to be by others. But I have done it with due submission, and also (in order to my Subject) necessarily; for they are the Outworks of the Enemy, From whence they impugne the Civill Power.[13]

The opposition to almost the whole tradition of Christian conceptions of the relationship between religion and the state is so extreme that at one point Hobbes conceded, shockingly, 'How we can have peace while this is our religion, I cannot tell.' Schmitt now clearly endorsed this view: 'Whoever defends the rights of the state against the claims of the God-invoking Pope, of Presbyterians and Puritans, cannot simply relinquish the divinity to his opponents and to the Church.'[14]

The Judeao-Christian tradition paves the way for liberalism by turning the state into an instrument of those – from churches to trade unions – who strive to exempt themselves from its full jurisdiction. One of the central objectives of this work was to establish that Hobbes had sought to ward off the possibility that the state, as he portrayed it, could be seen by those who submitted to it as simply an instrument of their own private ends. Again, it is possible that Schmitt was responding to Leo Strauss on this point. Strauss had argued, in a book on Hobbes just a year earlier, that Hobbes, in conceiving of the state as the artifact of atomized individuals, had effectively established the essential foundations of a later liberal conception of the state as an instrument of society.[15]

Schmitt argued that although the European state did eventually succumb to this fate, Hobbes had sought to avoid this possibility by portraying the sovereign as a terrifying mythological animal. That ephemeral collective agency 'the people', which establishes the sovereign as their exclusive representative, dissolves immediately after enacting this founding covenant of submission into a dissolute and powerless multitude: a popular sovereignty asserted, only to be negated without

remainder. This reprivatization is the precondition for the maintenance of the mythic, monstrous stature of the sovereign, who must
appear as greater than each if he is to appear as greater than all.

But while Hobbes had merely toyed ironically with this mythic
allusion, Schmitt improbably portrayed it as the central idea, because
he sought to eliminate the dangers to the unity of political order
inherent in the residual role which a natural law based on individual
security and consent played in Hobbes's theory, and the only way to do
this – as Hauriou had pointed out – was to portray the origin of the
state as a 'juridical miracle'. The modern 'total state' needed to assume
a mythic form because, much more radically than Hobbes's relatively
modest political construction, it had severed its basis in any underlying
natural-law limitation on political power.

The warning contained in this work was that Hobbes's construction
was not equal to the severity and malice of this battle against 'political
theology'. Schmitt claimed that although in *Leviathan* Hobbes had
argued for the imposition of uniform public worship, he unwittingly
opened up a crack in his case which would later be widened by
liberalism into a gaping chasm. Schmitt argued that Hobbes had
qualified this subjection of religion to the state by arguing that compulsory state religion was only a matter of external observance, not of
inner faith. It was out of this qualification, and the ensuing division
between inner faith and outward obedience, that liberalism – and,
later, legal positivism – was able to develop.

But did Hobbes in fact insist on the necessity of a state religion?
Although he was originally a strong supporter of the established
Church, he shed no tears over its abolition by Parliament and, under
Cromwell, sympathized with Independency, the view that ministers
should be supported by their congregations, not the state:

> And so we are reduced to the Independency of the primitive Christians, to
> follow Paul, or Cephas, or Apollos, every man as he liketh best. Which if it
> be without contention and without measuring the doctrine of Christ by our
> affection to the person of his minister (the fault which the Apostle repre-
> hended in the Corinthians), is perhaps the best.[16]

More serious than this simple oversight on Schmitt's part was an
almost unbelievable omission. He simply failed to point out that
Hobbes had put a much more radical natural-law qualification on
sovereignty than the one involving religious uniformity: in contrast to
Locke, Hobbes argued that those conscripted or condemned to die
acted in conformity with the natural law of self-preservation when they
attempted to escape, despite the legally unlimited nature of sovereign
power. Since the whole point of the covenant of submission was self-
preservation, security from violent death, the obligation to obey

stopped at this point, even if no right of resistance could be based on this qualification:

> Upon this ground a man that is commanded as a soldier to fight against the enemy, though his sovereign have right enough to punish his refusal with death, may nevertheless in many cases refuse without injustice, as when he substituteth a sufficient soldier in his place; for in this case he deserteth not the service of the commonwealth. And there is allowance to be made for natural timorousness, not only to women (of whom no such dangerous duty is expected), but also to men of feminine courage. When armies fight, there is on the one side or both, a running away; yet when they do it not out of treachery, but fear, they are not esteemed to do it unjustly, but dishonourably. For the same reason to avoid battle is not injustice, but cowardice.[17]

One would think that for someone who had defined politics in relation to the possibility of having to face violent death at the hands of an enemy, this qualification would represent the more decisive contribution to 'liberalism'.

Anxious to defend Hobbes's reputation, Schmitt claimed that it was the Jew Spinoza who had in fact provided the original philosophical foundations of liberalism. Spinoza supposedly accomplished this by stealthily distilling, out of Hobbes's prudent attempt to secularize political authority, a full-blown, radical defence of a completely neutral, demythified state. Spinoza's attempt to turn religion into a purely private affair was merely the first of a series of historic neutralizations which eventually left the individual free to determine his political obligations in the light of cold self-interest.[18]

But however much he wanted to deflect the blame on to Spinoza, Schmitt acknowledged that the evil could be traced back to Hobbes. The Englishman's distinction between external compulsion and inner freedom contained *in nuce* not only the later distinction between state and society but, more importantly, the inversion of the hierarchy between them.

In the civil and religious wars of the seventeenth century it was natural to think of man as an evil being in whom the light of reason flickered dimly, if at all. In the eyes of the theorists of Absolutism, any society which man formed in the shadows of the Baroque court could make no claim to represent anything higher than the public power perched far above it. It was only in the next century, as the memory of these terrible wars receded, that this mythic aura faded, making it possible for society to assert its existence as an enlightened public. The 'public sphere', the source of light and rationality, was no longer seen as embodied in the state, but in the diffuse discourses of society. Schmitt claimed that Hobbes's conception of the state as a mechanical apparatus was the unacknowledged ancestor of the eighteenth-century

Enlightenment vision of the ideal state as a purely secular instrument of society:

> In Condorcet the state of the Absolutist princes of the European continent, especially France, is presented as having performed its historic task for more than a century, the police having provided well for public security and order . . . Condorcet therefore no longer sees man as radically evil and wolf-like, but as good and educable. In this phase of the rationalist doctrine, the compulsory and the educational work of the system was regarded as historically timebound, a transient affair; at any rate, it was expected that the state would make itself superfluous. In other words, the dawn of the day when the great Leviathan would be slaughtered was already visible.[19]

Schmitt could plausibly claim that Hobbes had sought to design a polity which would appear as something more than an association of individual subjects, and that there was an irresistible tendency to imagine this surplus of the whole over the parts mythically. But even if this explains why Hobbes might have dabbled in mythic symbolism, it does not, of course, explain why he chose the specific figure of the Leviathan. In exploring this point, Schmitt offered an explanation as ingenious as it was textually baseless.

In Cabalistic mythology the Leviathan appears as the mightiest creature of the deep, locked in battle with a terrestrial counterpart, the Behemoth. Schmitt pointed out that Hobbes's decision to designate the Leviathan, the sea monster, as the symbol of this sovereignty, and Behemoth, his counterpart on land, as the symbol of civil war and chaos, was not based on any Scriptural reference: if anything, on some intuitive level, the attributes seem to be inverted. Behemoth was perhaps the more natural choice for a symbol of an Absolute state based on a territorial monopoly of violence. According to Schmitt, it was only the historical fact that in the seventeenth century the English state was becoming the pre-eminent maritime power of the world which explains the seemingly counterintuitive selection of the Leviathan as the mythic name given to the European state in the century of its genesis:

> For several years in the middle of the seventeenth century it appeared as if Cromwell's dictatorship would make England become both a centralized state and a great sea power. The image of the sea monster Leviathan as a symbol of the English state held for a brief historical moment, and it is a curious coincidence that the *Leviathan* appeared in 1651, the same year as the Navigation Acts were passed.[20]

Schmitt suggested that Hobbes's theory of sovereignty would not be taken up in his own country because its programme was much closer to the Absolutist ideal of the continental land powers; yet on the Continent, the alien associations around the image of a sea monster somehow prevented Hobbes's programme from being properly understood.

However implausible this idea might seem, the opposition of land and sea is not irrelevant when we interpret Hobbes's political thought: when he wrote *Leviathan*, it is quite probable that Hobbes subscribed to the conception of territorial waters developed by Selden in his famous rebuttal of Grotius's *Mare Liberum*, entitled *Mare Clausum*. If one considers the symmetry of the following oppositions – closed/ open; land/sea; state/society – the direction of Schmitt's interpretation becomes at least more intelligible. Schmitt was suggesting that Hobbes had attempted to superimpose the 'closed' Baroque apparatus of French–Spanish continental Absolutism on to a social order 'opened up' by its revolutionary turn towards the sea, the indispensable medium of existence for a society entering into a dynamic condition of perpetual economic motion. To put it another way: 'Leviathan' was the name of a failed attempt at a totalization of the ultimately contradictory elements of state and society, symbolized by land and sea.

Conversely, Hobbes had chosen to characterize the origins and course of the English Revolution as Behemoth, symbol of anarchy and civil war; but this land animal was a singularly inappropriate image for the seafaring energies which the Revolution unleashed. In early modern Europe, two new parallel political worlds came simultaneously into being: a territorial world of war, diplomacy and taxation based on the Absolutist state form, and a wide-open maritime world of colonization, slaving and piracy which Parliamentary England would increasingly come to dominate. In Schmitt's view the most dynamic agents in this Atlantic arena of stateless war and commerce had directly influenced the outcome of the English revolutions of the seventeenth century, because they were also the most radical adherents of a militant puritanism. The political settlements which emerged from these revolutions represented the definitive negation of continental Absolutism: the English Commonwealth did not become a state in the continental sense of a power legally distinct from society, and this constitutional peculiarity was the domestic manifestation of its unique position as a power both inside and outside the continental European interstate system.

Schmitt's suggestion that Hobbes's decision to entitle his greatest work 'Leviathan' should be seen in the context of a uniquely English historical moment was an imaginative – even brilliant – *aperçu*, however textually baseless it may have been. But his attempt to connect, by insinuation, his earlier reflections on the Jews as the instigators of the state–society split to this portrayal of the unique nature of the English polity went far beyond interpretative licence: as one encounters the suggestion that the power of the Jewish Diaspora was somehow

promoted by the British Empire, because both embodied forces inter-
stitial to a continental European state-based political system, it is
difficult to avoid the conclusion that one is reading a highbrow version
of the *Protocols of the Elders of Zion*. Whatever else can be said on behalf
of Schmitt's interpretation, it is undeniable that on a certain level he
was turning Hobbes into a mouthpiece for his own views on the nature
of the war looming on the horizon, and the fate of European Jewry in
this war.

The work examined in this chapter is a mythological account of the
origins and crisis of the classical European state, and the prospects for
a totalitarian resolution of this crisis. Schmitt had come to believe that
political thought had an ineradicably mythic dimension. Even though
he had earlier recognized the significance of mythically conceived
programmes of total transformation, he had viewed them from a
certain critical distance. But now he had chosen to write about a theme
which had bewitched him, and from which he no longer had any
critical distance: the so-called 'Jewish Question'. Here a pseudo-relig-
ious arcana could provide effortless, imaginary solutions to many of the
problems which he had addressed in earlier writings: the relationship
between the modern state and civil society; the rationalization of the
European state seen as a process of secularization; and the tension
between salvaging a classical state-centred political world and breaking
through to a new world of totalitarian political orders. A passage from
Politische Romantik, written by a younger Carl Schmitt, provides a near-
perfect description of the jarring combination of rational and mythological perspectives which he brought to bear on these problems in his
work on Hobbes:

> In the conception of a mysterious power exercised behind the scenes,
> concentrated in the hands of a few men, allowing them invisibly to direct the
> history of men ... in such constructions of 'the mysterious', a rationalist
> belief in the conscious domination of men over historical events is mixed
> with a demonic-fantastic fear of a monstrous social power, and often even
> with a secularized belief in providence.[21]

Less than twenty years after this was written, in 1937, this damning
indictment of political mythology had found its target.

Diaspora, Utopia, Katechon

Carl Schmitt was always struck by historical parallels between the early modern era and the twentieth century, seeing in his own times epoch-making upheavals of comparable proportions: 'All historical knowledge receives its light and intensity from the present.' Both the early modern era and the one through which he was living experienced a profound transformation in the relationship between the Jewish Diaspora and European Christian peoples. Of particular interest to Schmitt were the parallels between the contemporary expulsion of the Jews from Germany and the comparable fate which had befallen them in the fifteenth century in Spain, before its century of European hegemony.

In 1935 he pored over a book entitled *Die Vertreibung der Juden aus Spanien*,[1] written by the Romanian-born Jewish author Valeriu Marcu, who was then living as an exile in the South of France.[2] The work is a masterpiece of historical imagination, sympathetically portraying the tragic plight of the forcibly assimilated 'Maranos' in the most militantly Catholic monarchy of Europe. Despite his sympathy, Marcu made it clear that he thought that the expulsion of the Maranos from Spain was historically inevitable, because of an insurmountable distance separating even the most assimilated Jews from an authentically Christian polity. In his view there was a fundamental difference in how diasporic Jews and Christians, even those who were no longer observant, imagined salvation, and this expressed itself in a different vision of the political community: 'The emotional axis of the Christian was the revealed, that of the Jews, the awaited Messiah.'[3] Schmitt believed that the radical opposition between Christian and Jew posited in this formulation had far-reaching political consequences: 'What Bruno Bauer called Judaisization is the establishment of this condition of waiting, which is instituted for an unforeseeable duration, in an ever more comfortable waiting chamber.'[4]

Marcu had claimed that the Jews rejected the whole arcana of the Christian state, because they rejected the view that anything could be known about the Redeemer and the moment of his arrival. No longer having a political community of their own, they rejected all miracles and Messianic prophecy, and generally regarded the role of religion in the states under which they lived in coldly instrumental terms. As Schmitt, rather more harshly, put it later: 'The Jews understand the logic, tactics and practice of an empty legality better than any Christian people, since the latter cannot cease to believe, against the law, in love and charisma.'[5]

Marcu wrote that despite the fact that the Maranos were the most economically dynamic element in Spanish society, their brutal expulsion hardly seemed to be avenged by the subsequent course of history. Schmitt, no doubt, reflected upon the contemporary relevance of these passages:

> Only the general abhorrence of the Hebrews provided the Monarchy with this seemingly entirely unpolitical, seemingly entirely disinterested instrument which enabled the King to subject and level the grandees, the aristocracy, the provinces, and even the clergy.[6]

> The peninsula was not acquainted with the Bartholomew's Day Massacre and the French civil war, nor the mania of witch burning, nor the furies of Germany's Thirty Years War. The Holy Office quickly ended its work in the first two decades and then remained as a decorative, threatening instrument. The Inquisition became with time the most humane court on the continent.[7]

Schmitt went further than Marcu in portraying the Jews expelled from Spain as a subversive element in the rest of Europe, opening up dangerous historical paths. He emphasized the role of many successive generations of assimilated Jewish thinkers in deepening the cleavage between state and society – that is to say, weakening the state by promoting the emancipation of civil society. He sought to relate this to Strauss's observation that the Jews undermined their own state by splitting religion off from it, establishing a zone where unregulated prophecy could flourish. Schmitt now believed that the spectre haunting Europe had not been born in 1848: it was an ancient spirit of criticism and rebellion which had reappeared in the modern world in the unruly force fields of civil society.

Schmitt held that 'authentic' Christianity could be distinguished from its Jewish predecessor by its anti-utopian eschatological vision of history; this, however selective, was the concept of Christianity which had to be upheld against all the various proponents of a utopian 'New Jerusalem'. It should not be thought that Schmitt saw the European 'Jewish Problem' as simply a clash of religions. The issue, for him, was the direction of modernity as a history of secularization: was the historical process of secularization which began with the early modern sovereign state destined to end in stateless 'utopias'? Stripped of all esoteric symbolism, this, for him, was the real political meaning of the Jewish Question. In his opinion, the only nineteenth-century figure who had understood this properly was the Young Hegelian Bruno Bauer:

> He correctly understood from his Hegelian conception of history that it is a question not of emancipation but of secularization. But please follow the sequence! One cannot without further ado promenade out of the ghetto into the modern world. For that one must first pass through the stage of Christianity.[8]

'Authentic' Christianity was anti-utopian because it did not promise justice in this world. The Christian saviour was not a lawgiver, but an abrogator of the old laws. By contrast, Judaism, even as it dissolved into purely secular currents, invariably gave a whole new meaning to secularization: humanity was progressing through a long-term legalization of conflict to a distant, far-off, but this-worldly kingdom of peace: to a New Jerusalem. As Schmitt explained sadly to his young companion, Nicolaus Sombart: 'From 1789 it seemed to be decided that the leading cultural nations answered the question of the meaning of history in terms of Judaism.'[9]

Schmitt saw himself as Hobbes's kindred spirit, because he believed that he, like Hobbes, had struggled to preserve a residually Christian moment in his conception of political order. If Messianic expectations were not to sink into 'the spirit of utopia', salvation had to be a distant light on the horizon. In this world men must live in fear and insecurity – not because, as Hobbes thought, this was simply the human condition, but because fear and insecurity were the preconditions of political virtue.

In his reflections on Hobbes, Schmitt simply ignored the Englishman's relentless, 'this-worldly' materialism, and focused on what was still residually Christian in his political thought: after all superstition had been stripped away, a state could still be said to be Christian if it officially held only one proposition to be true: that Jesus is the Christ, that is, the promised redeemer.[10] Barbara Nichtweiss explains why this Hobbesian 'political theology' appealed to Schmitt:

> [Schmitt] apparently trusts that the statement 'Jesus is the Christ' exhibits its force even 'when it is pushed to the margin of a theoretical structure, seemingly even when it is pushed outside of the conceptual framework altogether'. With Hobbes – and also probably with Schmitt as well – this 'pushing away' into the marginal realm signifies 'making the effect of Christ undangerous; to de-anarchize Christianity, but to allow it, in the background, a certain legitimating effect.[11]

In this way Hobbes had sought to 'neutralize' endless doctrinal strife within Christendom, and Schmitt, as he often did, subtly reversed the intention of a Hobbesian theme, affirming where Hobbes sought to

negate. He claimed that only in the light of this ultimately parsimonious, 'institutional minimum' of political theology was it now possible to
avoid seeing history as something that would end in grimly frivolous
utopias.

Only after the war did Schmitt claim that there was a Scriptural basis
for this view in Paul's second epistle to the Thessalonians.[12] Paul's
letter of ministry to the early Christian community in Thessalonika is
noteworthy because it does not portray a conventionally conceived
apocalyptic scenario. Its purpose was to censure those in Thessalonika
who had rejected conventional sexual behaviour and abandoned voca-
tions in ecstatic expectation of the immanent end of the world. Paul
was forced to explain to this community that there were no signs that
the end of the world was nigh. One would know when that day was
coming, because it would be preceded by certain events which had
clearly not yet taken place. First there would be a 'falling away', then
'the lawless one' would reveal himself, placing himself above all others,
and claiming to be God.

The verses in this letter which interested Schmitt concerned not
Christ but a more shadowy figure, the 'Katechon', which in Greek
meant the 'restrainer', and in the Luther Bible is translated as the
'Aufhalter', from the verb aufhalten. The sixth verse of the second
chapter of this letter reads: 'And ye know what restraineth him, until
he reveals himself in his time'; the seventh continues: 'The mystery of
lawlessness doth already work, only there is one that restraineth him
now until he be taken out of the way: and then shall be revealed the
lawless one, whom the Lord Jesus will slay with breath of his mouth
and bring to nought with the manifestation of his coming.'

Not only is there no other reference in the whole of Scripture to
such a figure, but the force being restrained was described with an
equally unprecedented phrase: the 'mystery of lawlessness'. Paul sought
to convince those in Thessalonika who were preparing themselves for
an apocalypse in which the powers of this world would be cast down
that in truth the Roman Empire under Claudius was the force holding
back the evil powers of the cosmos. Only after this restraining force was
destroyed would the lawless one finally reveal himself, and as he would
soon thereafter be destroyed, nothing good could come from pretend-
ing already to be living in these last days. Paul, writing centuries before
Constantine's conversion, could not have foreseen a Christian
'Katechon'.[13]

A passage from Derrida identifies the significance which this
deferred eschatology assumed in Schmitt's thought:

[A] chance is left for the future needed for the coming of the other, for the
event in general. For, furthermore, who has ever been sure that the expecta-

tion of the Messiah is not from the start, by destination and invincibly, a fear, an unbearable terror – hence the hatred of what is awaited? And whose coming one would wish both to quicken, and infinitely to retard, as the end of the future?[14]

If this 'Katechon', this '*Aufhalter*', was the central figure in any authentic Christian, anti-utopian conception of world history, then Hobbes could somewhat more plausibly be construed as a Christian. But what is noteworthy about the role of this figure as depicted in the epistle is its essentially conservative function of holding the existing world, the status quo, in place. Although Schmitt was always ambivalent about what in the status quo should be preserved, as a man of the Right he would never embrace its total liquidation, and it is never completely clear whether he thought that the main danger came from a total liquidation or a total legalization of the status quo; perhaps he felt that, paradoxically, the result would be the same.

In the light of this 'Katechon' conception, the series of restraining figures from Schmitt's earlier writings – 'commissarial dictator', 'sovereign', 'Defender of the Constitution', 'Leviathan' – falls into a coherent pattern. Yet it is unlikely that *Führer* belongs to this pattern at all, or if it does, it does so only in a paradoxical way. As he originally conceived it, the world-historical role of National Socialism was not that of an '*Aufhalter*' at all but, rather, the opposite, an '*Aufbrecher*' – the one who breaks through. One should recall that for many, this latter term captured the initial groundswell of enthusiasm for the Hitler regime, and was applied as a label to those like Carl Schmitt, Martin Heidegger and Gottfried Benn who, in 1933, felt that they were the interpreters of this 'breakthrough'.[15]

As we have seen, throughout his life Schmitt often abruptly shifted position and allegiance, but in a way, this contrast between '*Aufhalten*' and '*Aufbrechen*', 'restraining' and 'breaking through', are the poles of an oscillation, a restless movement without synthesis. In 1932, this seemed to Leo Strauss to be a tension-ridden political project, full of promise, 'which did not yet have a name'; not too many years later, National Socialism had demonstrated its historical impossibility.

The International Order and World War

Carl Schmitt's role as a theorist of and commentator on the destruction of the German *Rechtsstaat* had come to an ignominious end. In any event, it is arguable that nothing of any theoretical interest could now be written on the subject. The situation on the outside was different. The re-emergence of a rearmed Germany under Nazi rule led to the rapid hollowing out of the precarious international legal settlements underpinning the Versailles Treaty and the Geneva-based League of Nations. Schmitt immediately recognized that the intensifying international disorder was reopening problems of legal theory which had been foreclosed on the domestic front. The deepening of a world Depression, and the international ascendancy of the far Right from Spain to Japan, gave him the opportunity to develop his criticisms of the postwar international regime along increasingly radical lines. His writings from 1937 to 1942 analyse the crisis of interwar geopolitics, and reveal the constitutive tension in his evaluation of National Socialism: 'restraining' or 'breaking through' – '*aufhalten*' or '*aufbrechen*'. The problem, in a nutshell, was whether the classic European interstate system centred on the sovereign state was in terminal crisis and, if so, towards what kind of international political order, if any, was a world on the brink of war moving.

Schmitt had managed to keep his prestigious academic position in Berlin owing to the intervention of Goering on his behalf, and this thereafter became the principal locus of his intellectual activity. Although from 1933 on he had been associated with the Kaiser Wilhelm Association for the study of International Public Law, until 1937 he did not often write on the state of international politics, at this time a subject less likely to incite the wrath of party ideologues. But his enemies within the party establishment kept a close eye on him. An SD operative, in describing Schmitt's plan to establish an institute of international relations in Italy in co-operation with Costamagna and with the approval of Mussolini, could barely conceal his frustration at Schmitt's ability to use his extensive foreign connections to slip away from impending encirclement:

This institute is supposed to deal with international legal questions from a German–Italian perspective against Geneva, Locarno, Versailles and the orientation of the Western powers on the Abyssinian question, etc. It really involves a very subtle plan by Carl Schmitt. After he saw he was excluded in all ways from shaping National Socialist domestic legal life, he now seeks a new field of activity in which he would like to avoid his complete marginalization, hoping eventually to regain the momentum.[1]

But the turn towards foreign policy was not simply a tactical manoeuvre; in *Der Begriff des Politischen*, Schmitt had already registered the significance of the breakdown of the traditional barriers separating foreign and domestic politics. In his speech at Gentile's Italian Institute of German Studies, he claimed that even the language of political theory would need to be realigned to explain this process and the related emergence of a new topology of the political:

Aristotle's concept of politics was essentially determined from the perspective of *domestic* politics. In the eighteenth century, politics was primarily conceived as *foreign* policy, while for domestic politics, the expression 'police' arose out of the same Greek etymological root, 'politea'. The nineteenth-century liberal-democratic state conceived of politics . . . as *domestic* politics, namely as *party politics*. With the end of the liberal cycle and the beginning of a new era of integral politics, the previously dominant theoretical representations of the structure of politics have proved unsatisfactory: the necessity of finding new concepts arises. One cannot in fact assume that one can return through a kind of pendulum movement back to the eighteenth-century [primacy of] foreign policy; even the concept of foreign policy acquires, in the epoch of integral politics, a new depth and total significance.[2]

Before Germany's spectacular military and diplomatic breakthroughs in 1938, the tone and range of references in Schmitt's writings on international relations suggest a participation in a wider European scholarly discussion on international jurisprudence, and if one wanted to maintain one's standing in this community, it was important to write things which did not seem to be obvious propaganda. In this context Schmitt sought to present German foreign policy as based on classical conventions governing war and neutrality, which institutions like the League of Nations were allegedly endangering. Even though the political context was now dramatically different, his line of argument was not, at this point in time, essentially different from his approach during Weimar.

Schmitt still maintained that the central insurmountable problem in interpreting international law was '*quis judicabit?*' – who decides on its content and enforcement, when states are still seen to be in some way sovereign, despite the League of Nations. The contemporary problem in international law was this 'in-between' condition in which the status of the sovereign state was unclear. Either the League was an irrevocable federation which unconditionally abolished war between member states, or it was a revocable alliance based on the will of sovereign states which had *jus belli*, the right to settle their own affairs through war, and recognized rights as neutrals in wars between other sovereign states. But even in his Weimar writings on the subject, he had occasionally suggested that a 'homogeneous' community of states would represent a welcome supersession of this 'decisionistic' dichotomy, which had, after all, resulted in a fratricidal European war. The problem in Weimar was that this element of homogeneity was unattainable within the framework of the Versailles Treaty, by which Germany was kept in an unstable condition of semi-statehood. In Schmitt's Weimar writings, homogeneity and equality went together, but by the mid-1930s this association was beginning to vanish. He referred in one essay published in 1936 to a speech by Hitler which referred to a European 'family of nations', counterposing this to the League of Nations, a framework within which Europe could never achieve 'self-determination'.

Schmitt wrote *Die Wendung zum diskriminierenden Kriegsbegriff*[3] ('The Turn towards a Discriminatory Concept of War') before Germany's 1938 breakthroughs. It thus captures Germany's position immediately prior to its bid for regional and then European domination. By its tone and range of references it constituted an attempt to participate in a wider European scholarly discussion on international jurisprudence. The argument that the League of Nations sanctions policy jeopardized the integrity of neutrals should be read in particular in the context of a larger European reception, where neutral opinion still mattered.

Schmitt argued that the traditional European customary law of nations was organized around a concept of war as a legitimate instrument of settlement between states which met a minimal standard of 'civilization'. This made possible relatively precise distinctions between war and peace, soldier and civilian, and finally belligerents and neutrals. But the symmetry and objectivity which distinguished the classical juristic concept of war as a diplomatically initiated and terminated armed conflict between states was recklessly abandoned in the aftermath of the First World War for a discriminatory perspective which portrayed armed conflict between states as on the one side a crime committed, and on the other a punishment meted out.

Legitimating this turn towards a discriminatory, split conception of war was the just war doctrine. While political communities have always felt that justice was on their side, with the consolidation of the early modern system of sovereign states it had come to be understood that there was no authority or standard on earth which could definitively determine which of the warring parties was in the right. As the intensity of religious–moral fanaticism in the sphere of interstate relations decreased, it was possible to organize and conceptualize war as a tête-à-tête between states and on this basis, to develop loose but effective diplomatic and legal conventions to regulate its conduct.

An essential precondition for the plausibility of this older, relatively tolerant, non-discriminatory concept of war was the presence of neutral powers, with recognized rights. The modern just war doctrine was an ideological weapon by which the leading powers of the League of Nations sought to appropriate from their defeated enemies the defining attribute of sovereignty, the right to settle claims through war. But in so doing they dissolved the traditional boundaries institutionally separating war and peace: without a symmetrical, unified conception of war, a military action can be arbitrarily classified in the new international legal jargon as a pacification measure (e.g. the Franco–Belgian military occupation of the Ruhr), a crime (German resistance to this occupation), or indeed, if the League of Nations neither sanctions nor condemns the action, as falling into a sort of conceptual no-man's-land (e.g. the Japanese invasion of Manchuria). So, too, the traditional distinction between belligerents and neutrals is made more precarious to the extent that international sanctions applied against a violator state are theoretically binding on all non-belligerent members of the international community: neutrality is possible only in relation to other sovereign states among whom war is a legitimate institution. Schmitt cited an English scholar of international law, Fischer Williams, who referred to the particularly wretched condition of neutrals in Dante's Inferno to suggest that when the Enemy is a lawbreaker like the rebel Prince of Darkness, no one should imagine that he who claims neutrality in the struggle against him will be spared the worst of fates.[4] Schmitt concluded that the just war doctrine, by delegitimating neutrality, paves the way for the transition to total war.

He reviewed a cross-section of French and English literature which attempted to resolve this contradictory state of affairs. The French authors were inclined to support a legislative supremacy of the League of Nations over previously sovereign states, thereby transforming them into federated members of a dramatically empowered international community. The English, by contrast, took the seemingly more modest course of proposing that an international court be established to adjudicate between disputing states. Schmitt argued that neither type of proposal forthrightly addresses the full consequences entailed by such dramatic inroads into the legitimacy of classical sovereignty: nothing can overcome the elementary fact that a war between states can never be impartially conceptualized as a relation between a crime and a punishment. The question of *quis judicabit?* cannot be easily avoided.

Although Schmitt had claimed a few years before that this sort of decisionism had been superseded in the domestic construction of the

Reich, he still apparently considered it essential for an international order. As long as Germany's foreign policy was directed primarily towards rectifying perceived injustices of the Versailles system and the attempt by the League of Nations to legalize this status quo, he continued to blame the contemporary disruption of interstate relations on postwar innovations which curtailed sovereignty. But he was coming to the conclusion that the conceptual confusion surrounding the definition of war and neutrality in contemporary international relations was symptomatic of the structural decline of traditional conventions based on sovereignty, and that in this sense it was irreversible.[5]

Whatever propagandistic intention there was in this analysis, it is puerile to think that demonstrating this intention refutes the case being made. The question '*quis judicabit?*' is inseparable from another question, which is almost never clearly posed today: what is 'war', as distinct from 'peacekeeping', 'sanctions', and other punitive measures implemented in the name of international law? While Schmitt exhibited an obvious opportunism in aligning his views with his government's foreign policy objectives, he was also becoming dissatisfied with a 'decisionist' definition of war on the theoretical grounds that it was becoming increasingly difficult simply to identify 'war' with military conflict, or with reference to the increasingly insignificant moment of the formal declaration of hostilities. War, which could no longer be equated with actions or declarations, had to be defined in relation to an existential enemy, whose presence now determined the real meaning of 'war', beneath any particular military action, or declaration of intent. (The meaning of this becomes clearer when we think of the undeclared, all-pervasive nature of the Cold War.) Schmitt had not yet formed a full picture of the ultimate friend–enemy alignments of the coming period, but he sensed that they were about to explode the old interstate system.

In 1937, what were Schmitt's views on the particular conflicts which were threatening to spill over and converge into a new world war? Clearly he supported the German reoccupation of the Rhineland. He certainly would have supported the Anschluss with Austria, although, curiously, he never mentioned this issue. His support for strengthening the Berlin–Rome Axis came from a long-standing opposition to the Versailles Treaty and his admiration for the Italian regime. His arguments defending the rights of neutrals were put forward to justify non-compliance with the sanctions which the League of Nations placed on Italy to punish it for its 1936 invasion of Ethiopia, a member state of the League. Until the late 1930s he was probably more cautious in his sympathy for the trailblazer of interwar revisionism, Japan, the first country to leave the League of Nations, if only because its impact on European politics was still uncertain and remote.

These were all positions one would have expected Schmitt to take. What is far more surprising is his complete silence on the Spanish Civil War. Not only was Spain the main theatre of military activity for the Axis powers at the time, but one would have thought that Schmitt would have been more sympathetic – if not enthusiastic for – the cause of Franco's Nationalist rebels. In the Nationalist camp the militant Catholicism of Donoso Cortes had fused with the equally militant Fascism of the Falange. Schmitt had delivered his speech 'Das Zeitalter der Neutralisierungen und Entpolitisierungen' from a podium in Barcelona, and was well known in right-wing circles in Spain. Perhaps the reason for his silence is that he wanted to avoid confirming suspicions in Germany that his political sympathies were Catholic in inspiration. But this is unconvincing: the level of open German support for the Nationalist cause against the Republican government was so great that it is hard to imagine how Schmitt would have been risking anything by at least mentioning Spain. Furthermore, even after the war, when he could write what he wanted, his single published reference to the Civil War dates from 1963.[6] Even though it might seem hard to believe, perhaps Schmitt was genuinely disturbed by the launching of an armed rebellion by Franco, however much he might otherwise have preferred a Nationalist over a Republican government. All one can say for certain is that Italian and German military intervention in Spain would have been hard to justify on the basis of the arguments in this work.[7]

Die Wendung zum diskriminierenden Kriegsbegriff, originally delivered as a paper at an *AfDR* conference in October 1937, had been very well received, and Schmitt seemed to be experiencing a modest reversal of fortune. The Reich Foreign Minister, Ribbentrop, sent him a letter in June 1938 congratulating him for expressing the German position so convincingly.[8] But even outside Germany, in Switzerland, Schmitt's 'classical' conception of strict neutrality was well received by reviewers who felt that international obligations might draw historically neutral countries into the fray.[9]

This brief period in which Nazi foreign policy could justify itself on such grounds came to an end soon after the invasion of the Sudetenland. The British appeasement policy behind the Munich agreement intended to keep the Third Reich from any further annexations which would destroy an already deeply endangered balance of power, or at least see to it that this process would be directed against the Soviet Union. When the *Wehrmacht* marched into rump Czechoslovakia and established the 'Protectorate of Bohemia and Moravia', Schmitt concluded that with this step the conventions of the historic European interstate system based on the sovereign state had finally given way.

While he had previously always distinguished between domestic and international law, with the intention of calling the status of the latter into question, ironically it was these developments which prompted him systematically to address for the first time the question of whether domestic and international law had a common, ultimate source. In an essay entitled 'Über die zwei grossen "Dualismen" des heutigen Rechtssystems'[10] ('On the Two Great "Dualisms" of Contemporary Legal Systems'), he began his inquiry into these 'dualisms' by posing a question about the status of international private law. From a domestic perspective, was it public or private law? The question could be more precisely formulated: did its 'validity' depend upon agreements between sovereign states, who were free to not abide by them, or was what made it valid somehow 'prior' to the state and its positive laws, and therefore irrevocable for the same reasons that the individual freedom to own and alienate property is often tacitly assumed to be the irrevocable foundation of a legal system, not a condition created by laws?

The distinction between public and private law comes from Roman law, and subsequently became the central theoretical opposition of European legal and political thought. But as Max Weber pointed out: 'the exact criteria of this distinction are surrounded by controversy'.[11] In 'Über die zwei grossen "Dualismen"' Schmitt asked what the relationship was between the distinction of public and private law on the one hand, and domestic and international law on the other. The early modern emergence of the sovereign state was a development within a wider European legal system, despite claims to legal autarky by the newly emergent 'Mortal Gods'. An older political map representing an originally feudal terrain of overlapping, crisscrossing and permeable jurisdictions was replaced over the course of time by a newer map representing the now more familiar world of the uniformly demarcated jurisdictions of sovereign states. During this legal–political transition, figuratively represented in Hobbes's image of the emergence of 'Mortal Gods', states became not just in degree but qualitatively distinct from the private subjects who came to belong to their self-enclosed domestic legal systems. Schmitt argued that although the attribution of 'sovereignty' to a state depends upon it being recognized as a legal subject of international law – as an agent which can make 'lawlike' agreements with other states – it is difficult to conceptualize how the obligations arising out of membership of this informal international legal community enter into self-enclosed domestic legal systems, and for the very same reason: the attribution of sovereignty. He claimed that this gap between the international and domestic sides of a wider legal system based on the sovereign state undermined the possibility of coherently conceptualizing the status of international private law, and thus of binding international law *tout court*. Schmitt was now increasingly inclined to see a problem in 'the sharp antithesis of the primacy of international law or of domestic law [which arises] out of this decision-istic conception of the state and its form of legality'.[12]

This was directly related to the issue of the ultimate and common source of both international and domestic law. Schmitt argued that this dualism, as well as the dualism of public and private law, derived their meaning from a concept of the state whose necessary counterpoint was an international, private 'common law', embodied in conventions which a state must respect if it is to be recognized as civilized and fully sovereign. In recognizing these conventions, a nineteenth-century state simultaneously recognized the limits of its domestic legislative preroga-tive, that is, the substantive distinction between public and private. Schmitt described the global economic framework which the interstate order based on the norms of the European *Rechtsstaat* had always tacitly presupposed: 'Behind the foreground of an international law whose subjects are exclusively states . . . a universal international law in the economic domain comes to be established on the basis of the world-wide validity and currency of liberal-democratic constitutional law.'[13]

But as law in the era of parliamentary ascendancy came to be exclusively equated with statutes enacted by national parliaments, it became increasingly difficult to conceptualize the status of such inter-national private-law conventions. The existence of formally enclosed legal systems was none the less compatible with a European interstate order as long as it was tacitly understood that legislation could not abrogate an underlying order of rights embedded in a much wider system of private law. Before the nineteenth century it was understood that the rights embedded in this wider legal system had not been created, only recognized and confirmed in statutes:

> In the eighteenth century, international legal custom was seen without further ado as 'part of the Law of the Land' [in English in the original] on the basis of a natural-law conception of Common Law. The state-ness of the law was not yet the decisive conceptual criterion, as a result of the dominant common-law conceptions. Common Law [in English in the original] and natural law could slide into one another.[14]

The status of this international private 'common law' – law not made but only recognized by states – becomes increasingly precarious as enacted statutes become the exclusive source of law, creating the conditions for legislation to become an instrument of social construc-tion, with no substantive boundaries. The dissolution of this inter-national private common law calls into question the boundary separating the inside from the outside of a national legal system. Schmitt argued that there has to be some kind of 'common law' to mediate this legal relationship between inside and outside, because without this mediation, international order is an impossibility. The transformation of obligations, of *auctoritas interpositio*, stemming from international private law, into domestic state law becomes increasingly difficult to conceptualize. This so-called 'transformation' problem is still, both in the European Union and in international trade rounds, a political and legal issue of considerable importance. Schmitt approached it within the very different context of the intertwined political and economic implications of German hegemony over Europe.

The question in his mind was what its form would be after the world market had collapsed, ceasing to be an economic unit under the informal direction of the Anglo-Saxon powers:

> Liberal constitutionalism ... guaranteed primarily the private, state-free character of trade, the basis of world free trade. Out of this emerged a non-state, private connection and community over and beneath the boundaries of states, which supported the world economic system, world trade and world market. When this uncontrolled private trade comes to an end, so too the method of British or Anglo-Saxon world domination comes to an end.[15]

From 29 March to 1 April 1939 two conferences were held at the Christian Albrecht University of Kiel – one in honour of the twenty-fifth anniversary of the Institute for Politics and International Law; the other a gathering of National Socialist professors of law. Both events were chaired by a friend of Schmitt, the university's rector, Paul Ritterbusch.[16] These conferences were attended by some of Schmitt's most prominent colleagues, including figures from outside Germany. It was here that he laid out an entirely new vision of geopolitical order. These conferences and Schmitt's paper provided a model for the way German professors could make themselves useful to the war effort by providing concepts and catch phrases for educated opinion. As the Nazi regime smashed its way to European hegemony, grant-seeking, fief-building academics from a whole range of disciplines came together to generate a body of literature which portrayed Germany's war aims in an ennobling, world-historical light. During all phases of the war, Schmitt positioned himself expertly in this wide interdisciplinary space.

He could now look back at the moments of exhilaration and disappointment which he had so far experienced in his career under the Nazis, and see them as intellectually invigorating encounters with a merciless *Weltgeist*:

> Even today, the great problems of the twentieth century are still approached in the Western democracies with lines of inquiry from the age of Talleyrand and Louis Philippe. By contrast, in Germany the legal-theoretical discussion of such problems is at an advantage. We have purchased that through experiences which were often hard and bitter, but the advance is indisputable.[17]

Schmitt attempted to explain the significance of the war in politico-juridical terms: the collapse of the nineteenth-century British Empire-based world system generated profound legal indeterminacies surrounding the now anachronistic boundaries between sovereign states. This catastrophe would come to an end only when the disintegrating Westphalian interstate order was reorganized into gigantic continental security blocs, each dominated by a leading power. As he later came to envisage it, such a bloc would circumscribe a continental economic order, thus providing the foundation for a continental legal system. He called this bloc a *Grossraum* ('Large Space').

From a letter written months after the conference to a French friend, Pierre Linn, it was clear that Schmitt was bracing himself for a new world war:

> That today *Grossräume* are forming, and thus a war is flaring up, is in no way worse and more terrifying than other earthquakes in earlier centuries. *Deos video ascendentes.* Why should I fear the Behemoth more than the Leviathan? Your great military and maritime author Castex, whom I read with tremendous pleasure, also says that world history is a battle between land and sea. *La mer contre la terre.* Until Christ returns, the world will not be in order.[18]

In the published versions which followed, Schmitt elaborated on his new vision of German regional hegemony over Central Europe. His book *Völkerrechtliche Grossraumordnung* ('The Order of Large Spaces in International Law') can be read as an extension of the leitmotiv of Franz Naumann's *Mitteleuropa*, written during the First World War, but totally transformed in direction by the immanent possibility of a Nazi-dominated Europe. Schmitt claimed that the only way a world war could be avoided was if Germany declared that Central Europe was off-limits to other powers, in emulation of the American Monroe Doctrine, which stipulated that the United States had the right to protect the entire Western hemisphere from what it perceived to be hostile encroachment. On 14 April 1939, after the invasion of the rump Czechoslovakia, President Roosevelt declared that there should be no more annexations in Europe. On 28 April Hitler responded by saying that America had no business meddling in European affairs, and that Germany now claimed a right under a doctrine exactly like the one claimed by the United States in its sphere of influence. He declared, in conclusion: 'We Germans now advocate precisely this doctrine for Europe.' Schmitt could consider this a spectacular confirmation, but he was advised in a phone call from Hans Frank not to quibble about an acknowledgement of this citation.[19]

The first edition of *Völkerrechtliche Grossraumordnung* was published before the signing of the Molotov–Ribbentrop Pact. Its conception of German regional hegemony was relatively 'modest', and did not yet foresee any system of direct rule over the remaining states of Eastern Europe. With the signing of this pact, the scope of this *Grossraumord-nung* widened considerably, but did not yet entail German domination over the entire Continent. On 4 March 1939 Ribbentrop referred to the Monroe Doctrine in meetings with the American Deputy Secretary of State, Sumner Welles, claiming that the division of Poland was an affair that concerned Germany and the Soviet Union, not the Western powers. By June of the following year, nearly the entirety of Western Europe was occupied or on the verge of being occupied by German armies, and Schmitt rapidly transformed his original conception of regional hegemony, put forward in Kiel, into a conception of a giant, German-dominated Fortress Europa extending from East Central Europe to the Atlantic.[20]

One should not assume that Schmitt rejoiced every time the *Wehrmacht* smashed through enemy lines. The desperate situation of Serbians living in occupied and dismembered Yugoslavia must have been deeply troubling to both Schmitt and his Serbian wife. A passionate admirer of French literary culture, he did not relish the moment of France's humiliating defeat. In a letter to Ernst Jünger, now stationed in occupied Paris as an officer working for the German army's censorship bureau, Schmitt narrated a fable which had been told to him by his friend, the Yugoslav writer and former ambassador Ivo Andrič. It captures the unease which both Schmitt and Jünger felt in the face of this too cheaply won victory:

> Marko Kraljevič, the hero of a Serbian national epic, encountered at daybreak a Turkish hero. They fought with each other from early morning to around evening. They were covered with filth and blood. Finally, Marko Kraljevič succeeded in killing the Turk, and tore his breast open. There he saw that the Turk had two hearts. On the second heart sat a snake, who said to Marko Kraljevič: 'You are lucky that I did not wake once during your entire fight.' Then Marko Kraljevič cried: 'Woe is me . . . I have defeated a hero who was stronger than me.'[21]

Despite their misgivings, both Jünger and Schmitt reaped the cultural benefits of victory. The occupation of France opened French salons and publishing houses to Germans who prided themselves on their taste for such things. Through Jünger, Schmitt had the pleasure of meeting all the notorious collaborators on the French literary scene – Céline, Brazillach, Drieu la Rochelle. In the atmosphere of the Occupation, he could move through Paris, technically as an official of the Prussian state, without feeling any of the inhibitions which foreigners usually feel in that city.

For Schmitt, France was the classical, the original European sovereign state: its fall represented the end of an era.[22] In earlier writings on international law he had argued that there could be no coherent interstate order if the legal autarky of sovereign states was abandoned, and the right to decide on war and peace was handed over to the League of Nations. He none the less conceded that a structural transformation in geopolitical relations was taking place which made a return to prewar conventions based on a non-discriminatory concept of war between sovereign states improbable.

In *Völkerrechtliche Grossraumordnung*, Schmitt finally broke his residual theoretical allegiances to the sovereign state as the cornerstone of international order. He now recognized that the European system of sovereign states which had emerged out of the rubble of feudalism was experiencing its own terminal crisis, as new technologies of warfare and communication – aircraft and radio waves – created modes of organizing political space which conflicted with and relativized the importance of boundaries based on the two-dimensional co-ordinates of territorial sovereignty. Only those powers capable of organizing the economic and political life of whole continents could occupy the strategic positions in these emergent, highly dynamic – indeed, messy and diverse – geopolitical fields:

> The great spatial problems of world political reality – spheres of influence, extraterritorial claims, bans on the extraterritorial claims of powers from other regions, zones of all kinds, spatial demarcations on the high seas (administrative zones, danger zones, blockade, sea patrol, convoy) the prob-lem of colonies ... international law protectorates, dependencies – all this [diversity] falls victim to the indiscriminate either/or of state territory or non-state territory.[23]

Schmitt envisaged the emerging reorganization of political space along the lines of a vast geographical zone integrated by a shared political history, embracing a large number of satellite states, which would constitute the *Grossraum* for a guardian power, a Reich. A Reich was not, in his view, a state in the conventional sense, as its field of political action extended far beyond its own territorial borders. In contrast to the politically neutral, territorial and bureaucratic entity of the state, it possessed a dynamic political and historical 'idea' which determined what constituted a threat to the collective security of the wider *Grossraum*. The second-class satellite states, which Schmitt had once seen as the embodiment of political reason, were now nominal entities: no longer sovereign, they would be honeycombed by a vast network of military bases, radio towers and patrolled airspaces, con-trolled by a Reich.

In its original form the Monroe Doctrine was the prototype of the *Grossraum* order. The principle of the doctrine was that the entirety of the Western hemisphere was republican, and constituted a world apart from a decadent Europe of dynastic wars. As American power expanded over the course of the nineteenth century, this doctrine acquired all the authentic features of a *Grossraum* principle: a planetary conception of political spaces delineated by a strategic vision, as interpreted by a guardian power.

This nineteenth-century American vision of a world divided between continents and hemispheres, each with their own political orders, appealed to Schmitt, and he compared it favourably to the British Empire, a hotchpotch of heterogeneous possessions strewn over the surface of the world. The British Empire did not constitute a *Grossraum* united by a coherent principle of political legitimacy, but a colonial empire based on the rapidly disappearing international conventions of the previous century. The nineteenth-century world economy had been loosely integrated by the British domination of the high seas and strategic canals – that is, 'free trade'. A limited, British-sanctioned access to overseas colonies had provided an avenue through which a handful of other powers could be incorporated into this system, effectively stabilizing the European balance of power. This balance of power preserved the sovereignty of various small and medium-sized states, keeping them from falling too completely into the sphere of influence of a more powerful neighbour. It was this order – based on static territorial boundaries between states, on a sharp distinction between fully sovereign states and colonies, and finally on an internationally accepted convention whereby the *terra firma* was organized into politically enclosed spaces, but the seas were 'free' – which was in the process of collapsing.

In 1940, as Germany, Italy and Japan confirmed the Three Power Pact, the world did seem to be dividing up into several *Grossräume*, and the question was what the US response would be. Schmitt saw the alternative before America as either to acknowledge the disintegration of the old order based on British colonialism, or to drift into a war with the undefined purpose of 'restraining' these transformations. It is clear from his published writings that at the beginning of 1941 he wanted to limit the war to a struggle against the British Empire, and hoped that neither America nor the Soviet Union would be dragged into this conflict.

In 1940 the Molotov–Ribbentrop Pact was still in effect, and there were even signs that the USA might go along with a redivision of the world along the lines implied by the *Grossraum* principle. On 6 July the US Secretary of State, Stephen A. Early, announced in London's Hyde Park that there 'was no intention on the part of this government to intervene in any territorial problem in Europe or Asia. This government would like to see and thinks there should be applied, a Monroe Doctrine for each of those continents.'[24] It seemed only rational to

Schmitt that in the twentieth century Britain could no longer maintain its hegemonic position, after the disintegration of the open world economy of the nineteenth century and its liberal *laissez-faire* norms.

In Schmitt's opinion the new world powers were Germany, the USA, Japan, and perhaps the Soviet Union as well. Schmitt's writings on international law were well received in Japanese government and pro-government circles, strengthening the intellectual credentials for a Japanese Monroe Doctrine – an idea which, for obvious reasons, could be used to great propagandistic effect. Schmitt in turn expressed admiration for the Japanese military liquidation of the outposts of European colonialism in Asia and the Pacific, seeing in it the further confirmation of his *Grossraum* concept. But the subsequent Japanese air raid on Pearl Harbor meant that all of a sudden the USA was at war with Germany and Italy, after the European Axis Powers declared war on the USA, upholding an alliance with Japan which brought them very little. This almost inexplicable German declaration of war was the brainchild of Hitler's extraordinary underestimation of American power. The USA would now be gearing up for an assault on 'Fortress Europe'.

Schmitt was intensely distressed by this rapid and total alteration of the political equation, and his writings from 1942 to 1943 reveal hostility and grudging respect for American power, as it seemed to emanate inexorably over the whole world, cracking open the Axis empires:

> Today, in 1943, the USA seeks to establish itself in Africa and the Near East; on the other side of the globe, it reaches up into China and Middle Asia. It spans the entire earth with a system of airforce bases and runways, and proclaims an American Century for our planet. With that, all conceivable boundaries, however broadly conceived, are eliminated.[25]

For Schmitt, the ideological justification for an American Century was an obnoxious and anachronistic claim still to represent the freedom of the New World against a corrupt and unfree Old World. As he saw it, the geopolitics of any coming American Century would be a combination of a Monroe Doctrine for the Western hemisphere with a worldwide pan-interventionism. Defence of American interests and freedom, he predicted, would eventually necessitate sending American troops to fight on the Yangtze, on the Volga and on the Congo.

It is clear that in Schmitt's view the main enemy and obstacle to any possible European *Grossraum* was America, not the Soviet Union. From 1939 to the invasion of the Soviet Union in 1941, he mentioned the 'universalism' of the 'Bolshevik world-revolutionary East' only once, in passing. In his opinion the Molotov–Ribbentrop Pact formed the outermost boundary of any viable European *Grossraum*, and he considered Hitler's subsequent invasion of the Soviet Union an absolutely disastrous overstepping of the boundaries. Hitler had just invaded the Soviet Union when the final, third edition of this book was published, and Schmitt was never compelled to clarify whether he considered 'the Russians' inside or outside Europe. Operation Barbarossa was in its very first phases, and the concluding comment from the Preface, dated 28 July 1941, expresses a fear of being overwhelmed by this new turn of events: 'May the reader understand when I give this essay the motto: "We are like sailors on a continual journey and no book can be anything more than a logbook."'[26]

Schmitt never wrote anything justifying the war on the Eastern front, and this is a significant detail in the life of a man who stood on the Right in what Nolte has called 'the European civil war'. The feeling that with the invasion of the Soviet Union, and the ensuing war of enslavement and genocide, the possibility of a postwar international order based on the *Grossraum* principle had been undermined can be discerned from his bitter comments on the course of the war, recalled by Nicolaus Sombart: 'Hitler's historical task: overcoming the Versailles Diktat, through land war. But now we carry on a war of racial annihilation in the East and a worldwide sea war in the West.'[27]

In 1942 Schmitt wrote a book, as if he was telling his daughter Anima a story entitled *Land und Meer*[28] ('Land and Sea'). It was written after Operation Barbarossa had been launched. He recognized that this was the fateful turning point which would bring down the world around him, whoever emerged victorious. But his own thinking had been so intimately inflected by the dynamic of the National Socialist *dérapage*, now moving inexorably towards disaster, that he did not pull back even at this point. Like many in the political elite, he feared that Hitler was on course for catastrophe, yet he feared defeat, and a terrible punitive vengeance, even more. As he explained to the young Sombart:

> From an Anglo-Saxon perspective we are pirate – the enemy of humanity. Pirate – that means not the individual, but the ship and its entire crew, from captain to the ship hand. If the ship is captured, everyone will be hanged: captured together, hanged together, with the exception of those in chains. Pardon will not be given.[29]

In *Land und Meer* National Socialism was not explicitly mentioned – partly because of the storybook quality of the narrative, but perhaps also partly because Schmitt was tired of the game of appropriating and reinterpreting its catch phrases, lowering the literary tone of his work. Aspects of Nazi rule over Europe might have troubled him, but like many others he steeled himself, wanting to believe that this giant empire was something more than an inferno of war, deportations and murder. He had a filtered awareness of what was going on, and endeavoured to portray these unmentionable events as the birth pangs of a new world order. As he saw it, this war was about the redivision of the planet, the violent seizure of land, oceans and skies by powers engaged in what could be described as a historically new round of primitive accumulation.

Schmitt began his story with a justification of the language of political mythology. Although modern physics no longer considers the four elements of earth, water, air and fire to be elements properly speaking, he suggested that these ancient categories have retained their symbolic power because they represent modes of political organization and agency. In the collective imagination of a people, the transition from one mode of life to another can be grasped through these elemental categories. Although human beings were originally terrestrial, unlike other animals they can alter their relationship to the world, leaping from one element to another, and recombining them in historically new forms:

> Man has the energy to historically conquer his existence and consciousness. He knows not only birth, but the possibility of rebirth . . . He can choose, and in certain historical moments he can even choose through his own action and his own accomplishment, the element, which he commits to as a new total form of historical existence.[30]

It is through the prism of a particular element that spatial relationships are imagined by whole political communities. Schmitt claimed that when the great pioneering powers of Europe struck out towards the world oceans, this immeasurable broadening of the known world resulted in a qualitatively new conception of physical space. The opening of the world oceans created the cultural context in which the universe could be conceived of as an infinite, empty space. This perspectival shift transformed fundamental intuitions of space in European art, literature and philosophy, and created the cultural environment in which new modes of political thought, action and organization flourished: 'The painting of the Renaissance replaced the space of Medieval Gothic painting; the painter now sat before the men and things painted by him in a space which perspectively disclosed an empty depth.'[31]

Released from the limits and inhibitions of traditional spatial intuition, the ruling classes of Europe were mentally equipped to become the masters of the world. In *Elements of Law* Hobbes had identified the same connection Schmitt was now making between this transformation in the conception and organization of space and the growth in the power of European civilization:

> For from the studies of these men hath proceeded, whatsoever cometh to us
> for ornament by navigation; and whatsoever we have beneficial to human
> society by the division, distinction and portraying of the face of the earth;
> whatsoever also we have by account of times, and foresight of the course of
> heaven; whatsoever by measuring distances, planes, and solids of all sorts;
> and whatsoever either elegant or defensible in building: all of which sup-
> posed away, what do we differ from the wildest of Indians?[32]

The experience of seemingly limitless, inhumanly empty, oceanic passages opened up the possibility of a nihilism on a much deeper level
than was ever possible in antiquity. The response to the challenge this
posed manifested itself in the boundless energies of early modern
'primitive accumulation'. The driving forces, the agents of this world-
historical transformation, inhabited the wild society of merchant inter-
lopers, pirates and whalers. The Atlantic world of piracy, colonization
and slaving formed a vast arena of mercantilist warfare among the
major European powers. The sea had a special significance in Schmitt's
political imagination as a zone of unbounded freebooting. Some of
these associations are conveyed in a passage from Melville's *Moby Dick*:
'Consider, once more, the universal cannibalism of the sea, all of whose
creatures prey upon each other, carrying on eternal war since the world
began.' For Schmitt, Melville was the Homer of the Atlantic Ocean.[33]

The front lines of the religious and civil wars racking early modern
Europe, pitting Catholic Spain against Calvinist powers, extended into
the Atlantic, and were fought out there with unrestrained ferocity:

> The corsairs of the sixteenth and seventeenth centuries ... play a great
> historical role. They stood as active fighters in the great world conflict
> between England and Spain. By their enemies the Spaniards they were
> designated common criminals and armed robbers, and hanged when they
> were caught. ... Hundreds and thousands of English men and women
> became at that time corsair capitalists.[34]

There was a clear insinuation of a contemporary parallel: Germany in
the twentieth century was in a comparable historical position to England in the seventeenth, and what from one side might look like bestial
crimes committed by pirates who, if caught, were to be hanged, could
be seen from another side as the actions of the pioneers of a historical
breakthrough. But the parallels did not stop there: the fanatical political determination of such pioneering powers were also comparable
across the centuries. Calvinism enjoyed an elective affinity to the most
dynamic forces behind this early modern *Raumrevolution*, radicalizing
the milieu of Atlantic seafaring. It was an activist election myth of
'elites' who saw themselves as saved from a meaningless and damned
world. Calvin proposed that this certainty of being saved was what gave
world history its order and meaning, and provided the impetus for the

most energetic political enterprises: 'It is, in the jargon of modern sociology, the highest degree of the self-consciousness of an elite, which is sure of its level and historical moment.'[35]

England had emerged from this interstate and religious struggle victorious, because its new ruling classes had successfully turned the political direction of state power towards the maritime theatre of war and commerce. Schmitt portrayed this as the emergence of a new nomos of the earth. The Greek word 'nomos' is usually derived from the word for 'divide', but Schmitt argued here that its original meaning could be better understood from the German verb which, he claimed, derived from the same etymological root: *nehmen* – to take. Ancient and medieval legal codes exhibited a cognizance of this original meaning because it was better, even if mythically understood then, that the order of property and authority in a community was based on an original act of appropriation and distribution of the land. This *Land-nahme* – 'land grab' in plain English – was the primitive appropriation which established the dimensions and internal divisions of a political community, mine and thine; and Schmitt argued that world history could be seen as a succession of these epic appropriations and distributions of the elements, creating the geo-elemental substratum of political order:

> Every fundamental order is a spatial order.... At the beginning of every great epoch, therefore, there stands a great appropriation of the land. In particular, every important change and displacement of the picture of the world is bound up with world political changes and with a new division of the earth, a new appropriation of the land.[36]

The interstate order of modern Europe had been based on the opposition between Christian and non-Christian peoples, later conceived in terms of civilized and uncivilized. These oppositions expressed an ongoing world-historical expropriation of non-European peoples and territories, and – again in an unmistakable allusion to the contemporary war – Schmitt pointed out that none of the colonial powers of that time had recognized the rights of the original inhabitants of the lands they seized. Despite the brutal wars fought between European states, by civilized convention they were understood to form a collectivity, even a family, of nations. Germany was excluded from the most powerful and privileged positions in this new order, and its landlocked and provincial horizons were expressed in its rejection of Calvinism.

In this 'Westphalian' state system the terrestrial surface of the earth was divided up between the European powers, but Schmitt claimed that there was a great gaping lacuna in this political system: the sea belonged to no one, or everyone, and in effect to just one: the British

Empire. This division between the politically enclosed and divided surface of the earth, where European conceptions of war and peace reigned, and the world oceans, which were *res omnium*, was recognized in the conventions of interstate and private law from the early modern period to the present.

Schmitt maintained that a new planetary *Raumrevolution* had begun with the mastery of electrical power, radio waves and the development of mechanized flight. This was opening up a politically unoccupied and unorganized space, and the possibility of its appropriation by powers holding the decisive technologies. Element-straddling polities were emerging out of the occupation of previously open seas and skies:

> As the airplane came, a new third dimension, appearing alongside land and sea, was conquered. Now man is lifted above the surface of the land as well as the sea, and receives in his hand a wholly new means of transport, [as well as] a weapon. The range and measures are further transformed, and the possibility of human domination over nature and other men ascends into unforeseeable domains.[37]

As control of the skies increasingly became decisive for strategies of power projection, the old interstate order based on the division of land and sea, and all its conventions, was crumbling. The First World War had been essentially a nineteenth-century war in which no fundamental historical stakes were involved. Schmitt perceived this war as different in that it involved the total opposition between distinctive forms of political existence. The end of the British Empire was the beginning of another world order arising out of war and primitive accumulation: *Land-*, *See-* and *Luftnahme*. This was not, strictly speaking, an 'apocalyptic' vision, nor was it based on any 'political theology':

> Only in struggle can the new nomos arise. Many see in it only death and destruction. Some believe that they are experiencing the end of the world. In reality we are experiencing only the end of the former relationship between land and sea. . . . Even in the cruel war of old and new powers, just measures arise and meaningful proportions form. Here, too, gods are and rule/ Great is their measure.[38]

A new understanding of space as a field of human energy, activity and organization was emerging, with far-reaching consequences for the shape and scale of polities. Schmitt referred to 'a contemporary German philosopher' – Heidegger – who had captured the significance of this *Raumrevolution* as a paradigm shift which promised to overcome the nihilism of empty space: 'Die Welt ist nicht im Raum, sondern der Raum ist in der Welt'[39] ('The world is not in space; rather, space is in the world'). Even if these new representations of space had not yet been grasped in coherent conceptual form, Schmitt believed that changes in material, elemental being always precede changes in consciousness, and that the latter were coming too:

> But historical forces wait for science, no more than Christopher Columbus waited for Copernicus. Each time, through the impulse of new historical forces, new lands and seas enter into the horizon of the collective consciousness, the spaces of historical existence are transformed. At that moment arise new measurements and dimensions of political-historical activity, new sciences, new orders, new life or reborn peoples. Seneca: 'The hot Indus and the cold Araxes converge, Persians drink from the Elbe and Rhine. Thetis will reveal new worlds. And Thule will no longer be the outer edge of the earth.'[40]

The clash and fusion of the elements had become a key to interpreting a war which had lost its significance for Schmitt as a struggle between ideologies. The language of elemental mythology substituted for – but also concealed the erosion of – the language of historical justification.

Whatever the idiom, Schmitt's writings on international law in this period are on one – obvious – level propaganda. His portrayal of the unimaginably grim and violent landscape of German-occupied Europe as the model of a new world order makes it understandably difficult to identify the real theoretical issues these writings address. But the substance of much of what Schmitt wrote on this issue at this time can and should be separated from the political projects they announce and define. In the works discussed in this chapter, Schmitt returned to a cluster of problems which he had explored in the 1920s, when he relentlessly criticized the attempt to legalize the international status quo after the First World War: the criminalization of war, the proliferation of extraterritorial zones within nominally sovereign states, the increasingly problematic status of sovereignty itself as a foundational premiss of legal order, and the particularly intense form that this crisis assumed in postwar Germany. He believed that all these developments were aspects of the protracted disintegration of a distinctive, European geopolitical civilization based on the balance of power. The war and the postwar deadlock that followed had led to a startling decline in the material power of Europe as a whole within an emerging American-centred world market, without giving rise to any viable redistribution of world power. Schmitt's writings accurately tracked a vector of development in world politics which threatened to bring an end to the canonical status of European geopolitical forms, and outlined a project for their transformation in an era of the redivision of the planet by regional superpowers.

19

The Law of the Earth

By 1943, after the crushing Red Army victory at Stalingrad, mythopoeic depictions of an immanent world-historical 'breakthrough' gave way to more sober assessments of the near future. Although Schmitt began to re-evaluate the tendency of the war, it still seemed probable that Germany could emerge from it intact and still the strongest power on the Continent. But controlled retreat on the Eastern front, and a possible diplomatic accommodation with the West, meant getting rid of Hitler. Although it is likely that he was entertaining such thoughts, his support for a coup would probably have been conditional upon whether it could be pulled off without plunging the country into a civil war. His friend Johannes Popitz was involved in the plot to assassinate Hitler, the objectives and details of which Schmitt knew nothing, even though he and his wife were living with the Popitzes after their own apartment had been bombed. As far as generals and state secretaries were concerned, this little professor did not have much to contribute to the prospects of an extremely dangerous enterprise.

During 1943 and 1944 Carl Schmit was frequently abroad, lecturing in Budapest, Bucharest, Madrid and Lisbon on the role of jurists in these difficult, transitional times. It is possible that his lecture tour was intended by those in the regime who had given him permission to speak abroad to be a labour of academic diplomacy, signalling to friendly regimes that a change of orientation might be coming as a result of the worsening military situation.

In its quiet conservatism, Schmitt's lecture represents a significant – albeit temporary – departure from a political trajectory stretching back to 1933. Indicative of a dramatic retreat from more radical agendas is the fact that Schmitt spoke on the contemporary relevance of Savigny, theorist of the *longue durée* in European jurisprudence and someone who had, in his view, struggled to preserve a classical inheritance in an age enamoured of legislative experimentation. The title of this lecture, published as an essay shortly afterwards, was 'Die geschichtliche Lage der europäischen Rechtswissenschaft' ('The Historical Condition of European Jurisprudence').[1] The question Schmitt posed to his audience was whether it was still possible to speak of a common tradition of

'European' jurisprudence, or even of Europe as a region defined by a common historical experience. He argued that the most decisive experience in the formation of Europe as a political civilization had been the centuries-long process of the reception of Roman law, a selective and conflictual transformation of local legal tradition:

> Through the labour of jurists from all European countries, Roman law became a common vocabulary, the speech of a juristic community, a recognized model for the labour of juristic conceptualization, and, through this, the spiritual and conceptual Common Law [in English in original] of Europe.[2]

Roman law was not something that could be counterposed to common law; rather, it was something which had shaped this common law, and imparted to it Europe-wide uniformities. Schmitt maintained that this included even those countries which retained the core of their own distinctive legal traditions. R.C. van Caenegem, in his history of private law, provides a succinct description of this long historical process:

> *Ius commune* is to be contrasted to *ius proprium*, the 'particular' law which was in force in its countless variations in the various countries, regions and cities of Europe, in the form of customs, ordinances and charters. The study of Roman law in the Middle Ages might have perhaps limited itself to purely academic research like our own approach (for instance) to ancient Egyptian law. Over the centuries, Roman legal doctrine permeated legal practice . . . and the medieval learned law thereby influenced the development of law to a greater or lesser extent in all parts of Western Europe.[3]

These common-law traditions, shaped and filtered by the reception of Roman law, were endangered by the rise of legislation as a continuous activity and mode of government. Schmitt repeated a point that he had made some years before: when the legitimacy of laws comes to be derived exclusively from the will of the legislator, the common traditions of European private law – once given the status of natural law because they were not 'made' in the same sense as modern legislation – begin to dissolve: 'Our fathers and grandfathers threw an antiquated natural law to one side, and saw in the transition to what they called 'positivism' a great historical progression from illusions to reality.'[4] Positivism represented a turning away from these traditions. Schmitt claimed that Savigny had recognized that if the will of the legislator expressed in written statutes became the only source of law, this would eventually make jurisprudence an anachronism, because this will would always be in a constant state of flux and dynamic evolution.

In the twentieth century, war, revolution and economic crisis gave rise to a form of accelerated legislation delegated to the executive through frequent and permanent enabling laws. Decrees or measures ousted laws as the most direct expression of this legislative will. In Schmitt's opinion, Savigny had anticipated this danger at the beginning of the legislative age, when he argued that the inner unity of the laws could never be grasped if an unlimited power to legislate generated ever more laws. Whereas it was once believed that the enduring validity of a law was what made it rational, the ever shorter intervals between manifestations of the legislative will necessarily undermined this belief.

The most striking thing about this lecture was its denigration of the political will – not just the political will as expressed in parliament, but the political will *tout court*. In making his criticism of 'legislation', Schmitt took up a distinction from Savigny which had been central to conservative thought since the nineteenth century, but had never previously appeared in his writings. He claimed that in an essay entitled 'The Vocation of Our Times', Savigny had grasped the 'non-intentional emergence' of real law, and counterposed it to the teleological – that is, goal-orientated – nature of legislation.[5] Again, van Caenegem explains the significance of Roman law in this context for both Savigny and Schmitt: 'The triumph of the *Corpus iuris* is to be explained first and foremost by its prestige and its intrinsic doctrinal quality: Roman law was authoritative "non ratione imperii, sed imperio rationis" (not by reason of power but by power of reason).'[6]

This depiction of Europe as the outcome of a long civilizing process of Roman law reception was in diametrical opposition to Schmitt's portrait of the genesis and rebirth of Europe in a world war of elements. The idea that the word nomos was related to *nehmen*, 'to take' – and that a *Landnahme*, an act of almost revolutionary violence, was the meta-legal origin of law – was tactfully omitted in this lecture, delivered to conservative audiences for whom this would not have been a comforting message: after all, in establishing title to property, what was once taken can be taken again. Although Schmitt would soon return to speculating on the original meaning of 'nomos', it is another example of how rapidly he could shift ground when he perceived that the main threat to him and what he thought he stood for was coming from a new direction.

Schmitt now argued that the vocation of jurisprudence was not just the guardian but the actual source of law, in the sense that the labour of juristic interpretation was what imparted rational form to diverse legal materials. He made it explicit in this lecture that the 'accelerated' legislation of the twentieth century represented above all a threat to the vocation of jurisprudence. However true this was, it is arguable that he was no longer in the best position to make this point. Perhaps there was an element of self-criticism involved, but this is unlikely. What is more likely is that he less modestly perceived his own career as in some way personally embodying the whole predicament of European jurisprudence.

The brief Eurocentric era in world history was coming to a cataclysmic end. Schmitt envisaged an unpromising postwar landscape: instead of a rational division of the world between a handful of historically defined geopolitical systems, the world was about to be partitioned between two ideologically defined superpowers, striving for universal hegemony. By 1945 he had almost finished *Der Nomos der Erde* (which would be published only in 1953), in which he outlined the history of the rise and fall of a geopolitical civilization organized around inter-state conventions which regulated war and peace within Europe, and ratified the ascendancy of Europe as a whole over the non-European world. This was the interstate civilization of the *jus publicum Europaeum*. He sought to present his idea of a European *Grossraum* as a solution to the epochal crisis of the system of international legal conventions by which the status of public and private, war and peace, ultimately land and sea, had been distinguished from the seventeenth century to the beginning of the twentieth.

In articles from the late 1930s, Schmitt had argued that during these centuries international law came to recognize only enclosed sovereign states as legal subjects – that is to say, European international law was based on the recognition of a sharp boundary between public and private, and between the inside and outside of a state. Both these boundary principles were transgressed and shattered – 'destructively' by the exponentially expanding claims of society on the state, but also 'constructively' by economic and military planning on ever larger scales.

Hobbes had described the confusion generated by indeterminable, permeable and overlapping political boundaries as the 'Kingdom of Darkness'. In the twentieth century the German Reich was the extreme, exemplary case of an 'unenclosed and unenclosable' political space in which the relationship between state, nation and constitution remained fluid and undefined. As a latecomer as a nation-state, with ethnically problematic borders, both Germany's emergence as a half-hegemonic power and its catastrophic military defeats put its existence as a 'normal' state within the European interstate order at risk. Seen in an epochal context, this breaking open of the German state, the most extreme case of the crisis of the European state as an enclosed legal system, put into question the very meaning of the word 'law'. Schmitt thought that when the jurisdictional boundaries and prerogatives within and between states become indeterminable, the very nature of law becomes increasingly difficult to determine.

In *Der Nomos der Erde*,[7] Schmitt sought to flesh out his account of the origins and nature of law. The central argument is an elaboration of an idea put forward in *Land und Meer*: the very possibility of legal relations is dependent upon an original act of collective appropriation of land which establishes the material matrix – literally the ground – of these legal relations:

A *Landnahme* [appropriation of the land] establishes right in two directions: towards the inside and towards the outside. Towards the inside – that is, within the group – appropriation of the land, the first order of all possession and property relations, is created with the first division of the ground. . . . Every appropriation creates towards the inside a kind of supreme property of the community in its entirety, even if the later division does not maintain this pure communal property, and recognizes a fully free private property of the individual. . . . The *Landnahme* is both externally (with respect to other peoples) and internally (for the ground and property relations within a land) the Ur-type of constitutive legal procedure. It creates the most radical legal title there is, *the radical title* in the full and comprehensive meaning of the phrase. . . . This distributional law . . . is naturally no positive law in the sense of later state codification, or the system of legality of a later state constitution; it is and remains the real kernel of an entirely concrete, historical and political event, namely the appropriation of the land.[8]

The significance Schmitt attributed to an appropriation of the land in defining radical title had nothing to do with the Nazi cult of the soil. Determining the criterion of possession of land, the radical title, prior to the allocation of the formal title of property had been one of the central problems of pre-nineteenth-century natural-law theory. Even Kant, who brought this tradition to a close, argued that dominion of the land 'is the highest condition of the possibility of property and all further public and private right'. But this dominion had only the status of a conceptual condition in Kant's theory of law; Rousseau, more sensitive to the painful gap between legality and legitimacy, was willing to address the establishment of this dominion as a real event, not just a conceptual condition, and derive from this the most discomfiting consequences – so discomfiting, in fact, that the following passage, which appeared in the Geneva Manuscript of *The Social Contract* was simply omitted from the later, better-known version:

On Real Estate: But as the force of the state is incomparably greater than that of each private individual, public possession is by that very fact stronger and more irrevocable, without being more legitimate, at least in relation to Foreigners. For in relation to its members the state is the master of all their goods through a solemn convention, the most sacred right known to man. But with regard to other states it is so only through the right of the first occupant, which it derives from the private individuals, a right less absurd, less odious than that of conquest, and yet which when well examined proves scarcely more legitimate.[9]

The crisis of the sovereign state deepened and radicalized the problem of the meta-legal underpinnings of the legal system because, according to Schmitt, it had put into question the nomos of the entire earth, the right of whole peoples collectively to possess the ground, a portion of the earth, and enclose it against others. Contemporary normative theories of justice, by and large, bypass this problem of the radical title, because any attempt to address it brutally underscores the difficulties of extending the principles of distributional justice beyond the limits of enclosed, 'homogeneous' polities. The settlement and enduring occupation of territory, even when it entails the expulsion of aboriginals, transforms arbitrary facts on the ground into a sacrosanct title. Schmitt initially posed this ultimate question of distributional justice in an attempt to justify and explain the wave of annexations, partitions, genocide and forced expulsion which National Socialism had set in motion. However ethically bankrupt his vision of a new international order, the course of the war and the final destruction of the German Reich had given him an undeniable insight into the arbitrary nature of the title by which any people encloses a portion of the earth for itself.

20

Finis Germania

Carl Schmitt was prepared – or so he thought – for the final destruction of the Third Reich. At some point in 1944 he realized that Germany was going to lose the war, before many of his friends and associates had come to this increasingly obvious conclusion. After his friend Popitz was executed early in 1945 for his involvement in the plot to kill Hitler, perhaps he even considered himself, in his own way, an enemy, not just a critic, of the Nazi regime. In the maelstrom of the final months of the war, Schmitt began to register the enormity of the Judeocide more directly, and in the correspondence between him and Ernst Jünger, both men sought to distance themselves from it – not for the sake of the Jews, but for the sake of those who persecuted them. In February 1945, Jünger recalled Flavius Josephus' account of 'obstinacy of the Jews in the siege of Jerusalem'. The attempted extermination of the Jews had served only to set their Old Testament morality at loose in the world at large. Schmitt replied with a quotation from Bruno Bauer: 'But in the end God created the Jews, and if we kill them all, we will suffer the same fate'.[1] As odious casuistry, such responses are beneath comment. Mytho-historical parables, medium of exoneration and estrangement, convey here a deranged corollary of a thesis from *Der Begriff des Politischen*: the enemy defines the horizon of a political project; he must be respected, since the attempt to destroy him destroys the project, politically annihilating the annihilator.

By 22 April 1945, the Red Army encirclement of Berlin was complete. Inside Berlin were two million civilians. On the outskirts of the city, a million German troops – a half-trained, rag-tag army of the very old and very young – mobilized for a last-ditch, suicidal defence of the city. Schmitt participated in this enterprise as an air-raid warden. By 28 April, the Soviet General Konev's tanks and infantry were moving in on the Tiergarten, near the centre of the city, now only a mile from the Soviet forces approaching Berlin from the north. In a bunker located between these two pincers, Hitler and some of his closest associates had already killed themselves. On 2 May the red flag was finally flying over the Chancellery, and the fighting had come to an end. Although there is little evidence of what Schmitt was up to during the last days of the Third Reich, it seems that after a brief encounter with the Soviet occupying forces, he was allowed to pass into the American zone.

A completely bombed-out, ruined city, foreign occupation and disclosures revealing the unprecedented nature of Nazi crimes were not enough to deter Schmitt from writing, that summer, a rather lengthy legal opinion on the impending war crimes trials. By August 1945 he had finished *Das internationalrechtliche Verbrechen des Angriffskrieges und der Grundsatz 'Nullum crimen, nulla poena sine lege'*[2] ('The International Legal Crime of War of Aggression and the Fundamental Norm "No Crime, no Punishment without Law"'), which was intended to assist in the legal defence of businessmen – the notorious Friedrich Flick in particular – against the accusation of having been involved in the preparations for a war of aggression. With considerable erudition, Schmitt demonstrated that since there was no clear international legal consensus during the period from 1919 to 1939 on whether the initiation of a war by a sovereign state was a criminal act, a businessman surely could not be held criminally accountable for his involvement in preparing for such a war. This was a line of argument which one might have expected Schmitt to have put forward at the time. What is new is the total revulsion expressed towards the genocidal policies of the Nazis – actions which, he claimed, could be punished, even though there was no law which explicitly addressed them, or any precedent for judging them. Scepticism towards such a late demonstration of outrage is, of course, entirely justifiable. But Schmitt maintained clearly and unequivocally that no one could be acquitted of crimes of genocide by saying that they were simply following the orders of superiors. Even though this work was written for the purposes of bolstering the case for the defence on the narrow issue of initiating a war of aggression, it was so categorical on the issue of genocide – and, by implication, on the use of slave labour – that it would actually have undermined the defence of someone like Flick, not to mention the more incontrovertibly culpable. The following passage reveals why Schmitt's text was ultimately of no use to the defence:

> Of an essentially different nature are the second kind of war crimes, which must be distinguished here. They are atrocities in the specific sense of planned killings and inhuman cruelties, whose victims are defenceless people. They are not military actions, yet they stand in a specific relationship with the war of 1939, because they were committed in preparation or during this war and are characteristic manifestations of an inhuman mentality which finally culminated in the war of 1939. The rawness and bestiality of these crimes exceed the normal human capacity of conception. They spring out of the bounds of all the familiar dimensions of international and criminal law. . . . That is all self-evident. Anyone who would, with respect to these crimes, raise the pretext of 'nullum crimen', and seek to refer

to previous provisions of criminal law, puts himself in an objectionable light.[3]

At this point Schmitt was probably willing to concede that the crimes of the Third Reich were worse than the Allied treatment of Germany. But in this book he sought to separate the charge of genocide from the charge of having begun a war of aggression because there was no law at the time which forbade this; thus any punishment of Germany on these grounds would violate the principle *nulla poena sine lege*. This, of course, was the very principle which Schmitt, in the aftermath of the Reichstag fire, had declared defunct. Convincingly or not, he was trying to distinguish the interstate nature of the war – which, in his view, had to be judged on the basis of criteria specific to this form of conflict – from the perpetration of crimes too horrible to mention.

Thinking that he, too, had in his own way been victimized by the Nazis, Schmitt was surprised to be arrested by American soldiers and held for interrogation as a potential defendant at Nuremberg. Detained for nearly two years, he became deeply embittered with the victors' justice, retracting his initial concession that the genocidal crimes of the Third Reich had been worse than the firebombing of German cities and the subsequent mass expulsion of Germans from Eastern Europe. His hostile opinion of the new dispensation grew more vehement as he was interrogated by Robert Kempner, an émigré who had lost his position in the Prussian Interior Ministry in 1933 as a result of Goering's purges of the Prussian bureaucracy. From his cell, it appeared to Schmitt that the Americans had installed returning Jewish émigrés, hellbent on vengeance, as the new rulers of the country:

> I have been imprisoned, my most intimate property, my library, has been confiscated, and I have been locked up in a cell as a criminal; in short, I have fallen into the hands of this mighty American empire. I was curious about my new masters. But I have until this very day, five long years, not yet once spoken with an American, but only with German Jews, with Herr Loewenstein, Flechtheim and the like, who were not at all new to me but, rather, for a long time well known to me. A peculiar master of the world, these poor modern Yankees, with their ancient Jews.[4]

In his postwar notebooks, Schmitt deliriously suggested that God knew about the retaliation Germany would suffer when he let 'hundreds of thousands' of Jews die in death camps, and that the retaliator would in turn eventually suffer the same fate: 'As God allowed hundreds of thousands of Jews to be killed, he simultaneously saw the revenge that they would take on Germany; and that which he foresees today for the avengers and those demanding restitution, humanity will experience in another unexpected moment.'[5] This is the ranting of a humiliated and broken man; had he been perfunctorily 'de-Nazified', like almost all his colleagues, his mind would probably not have dwelt upon such grim thoughts. But his truculence cannot be seen simply as some kind of psychological defence mechanism. In a letter to Jünger, he argued more dispassionately that Hitler was simply not as bad as everyone was now making him out to be: 'Kniebelo [Hitler] was a criminal, but neither the greatest (for the greatest crimes the world spirit chooses other tools) nor the last, and one can no longer live off the struggle against the dead Kniebelo.'[6]

The experience of internment was undoubtedly the lowest point of Schmitt's entire life. After a long period of ambivalence towards Catholicism, even Christianity, one could say that in the misery of his internment, he found religion again. In his cell he felt a despair far deeper than anything he had expressed in the last chapter of *Politische Theologie*: while he had previously drawn on theological themes to make political arguments, he was now on occasion veering towards a literal belief in a Christian Saviour. But his mind, true to form, could not focus on any tangible image of deliverance; for Schmitt, religion was a language for expressing the presence of an irresistible evil:

> The annihilation of the enemy is but the attempt (the claim) of a *creatio ex nihilo*, of a new world from a *tabula rasa*. Anyone who wants to annihilate me is not my enemy, but my Satanic tormentor. The question of how I should behave towards him can no longer be politically but only theologically answered. Dialectical theology of the most concrete kind arises when the annihilator claims to want to annihilate only the annihilator.[7]

Schmitt saw the new West Germany – with its re-education, occupation zones and Atlanticism – in a distinctly apocalyptic light. Although many have argued that his relationship to National Socialism was purely opportunistic, the fact that he was one of the very few major intellectuals who refused to sign the certificate of de-Nazification demonstrates that his opportunism had limits. He was not willing to adapt if this meant that he had to criticize his whole life's work as ideologically contaminated. When Robert Kempner asked him during cross-examination whether he felt complicitous with what had transpired under the Nazis, Schmitt gave a response which precisely conveyed his attitude to the whole issue of complicity in history:

> Schmitt: That will always be the case when someone takes a position in such a situation. I am an intellectual adventurer.
> Kempner: Intellectual adventure is in your blood?
> Schmitt: Yes, and so thoughts and ideas emerge. I take the risk. I have always paid my bills, and have never played the shirker.
> Kempner: And when what you call the search for knowledge ends in the murder of millions?
> Schmitt: Christianity also ended in the murder of millions. But one doesn't know that until one has experienced it for oneself.[8]

In detention, Carl Schmitt had time to reflect on the meaning of the almost unbelievable events of the past thirty years, and his own role in them. These reflections appeared in a collection of essays, published in 1950, *Ex Captivitate Salus*. He began by confessing how utterly exposed he felt when an old friend, also a returning émigré, said to him that although his ideas seemed clear enough, who he was remained a mystery. This question bored into him only because he had become so deeply invested in the highly stylized identities which he ascribed to his vocation that there was no longer an easy answer to the question of who was the man behind his writings: 'That was a terrible accusation – to say that what you think and say may be interesting, but who you are – your self, your essence – is murky and unclear.'[9] In this book Schmitt addressed, for the first and last time, this question: who was Carl Schmitt? Typically, he chose to present his situation in a world-historical context, and rise above what he thought were the pettier questions of personal responsibility. The sentiment running through all his reflections – widely shared by right-wing European intellectuals after the war – was that great agendas of renewal, however flawed in practice, had been shattered, and that as a consequence Europe was finished. This was the experience of defeat, and Schmitt explored its various facets in an elliptically autobiographical fashion.

The first facet was the political suicide committed by the Prussian elite. In retrospect, he concluded that the very establishment of the German Reich under Prussian leadership had put the historic European interstate order into question by generating a disruptive concentration of power at its centre. Prussia's elites were incapable of solving this problem of Germany's relation to Europe, and sought to stave off defeat by playing a deadly game of *va banque*. Schmitt had witnessed at close quarters how this elite had entered into an alliance with the Nazis, then utterly lost itself in the bargain. The penultimate moment of this collective self-destruction was the botched attempt by an element of this elite to assassinate Hitler, followed by the execution of all those involved, including Popitz, the man who symbolized this elite in his mind. The postwar decree issued by the Allies abolishing the state of Prussia was simply the terminal point of a longer process.

He explored another Europe-wide aspect of this experience of defeat by contrasting the seemingly improbable pair De Tocqueville and Spengler. Spengler had introduced the post-World War I German public to the idea that the court of world history had passed judgement on Europe, which was now sentenced to sink into an age of iron. Schmitt pointed out that this was also the central visionary insight, albeit less crudely formulated, of Alexis de Tocqueville. De Tocqueville's whole political outlook was shaped by the experience of accumulated defeats: a class defeat, which had unleashed the spectre of mass democracy; a national defeat – less troubling to him, since he did not live to see 1871; a still nearly unimaginable European defeat at the hands of Russia and America, appearing only as a speck on the horizon; and finally, a religious defeat as he came to understand that the convergence of all these developments signalled the end of the Christian era in history.

After the First World War, Schmitt claimed that this image of world-historical decline had induced a mood of existential panic among right-wing European intellectuals. Despair and disorientation led either to a retreat from politics or to a giddy embrace of political movements like Fascism, which had popularized the fashionable pessimism of the cafés and transformed its catch phrases into an activist, perversely optimistic programme of political renewal. It should be said that Schmitt was not the only one of his contemporaries to adopt a posture of aristocratic pessimism after a period of deep complicity with Fascism. In his assessment, a whole generation of the European Right had failed to understand the theological stakes of the historical moment they were experiencing. In an oblique yet self-aggrandizing gesture of self-criticism, he acknowledged that he, too, had failed at the time to understand the significance of the figure of the Katechon, 'the Restrainer', in the age of the masses – that is, in the age of the Decline of the West. This was the closest he came to a critical reflection on his role in Weimar and after.

Schmitt's unwillingness to criticize himself was no mere psychological idiosyncrasy – it was a political decision. Despite his ambivalence towards its ideology, Schmitt had been willing to embrace National Socialism because it seemed to represent a solution to what he had identified as the main problems of political legitimacy in an age of mass politics; and until it was absolutely clear to him that the war was a lost cause, his reservations about National Socialism concerned only its most self-destructive tendencies. To say that he was less enthusiastic about the early Federal Republic would be an understatement. Behind the rhetoric of equality, he saw in the platitudes of the new Constitution a licence to discriminate against those who were not willing to be re-educated. Democracy itself was to blame for poisoning the atmosphere in the sphere of the political:

> The platform of democratic equality is only the springboard for new inequalities. That is De Tocqueville's real fear. The consequential equality is never real, and only in a single fleeting second true: in the moment in which the old privileges are removed and the new are not yet openly consolidated – that is, in the barely tangible moment of transformation from the old discriminations to the new, that fabulous interval in which neither the Nazis persecute the Jews, nor the Jews persecute the Nazis.[10]

Even though many of his students would play a leading role in shaping the Constitution of the Federal Republic[11], Schmitt believed that it represented an intellectually sterile attempt to restore the *status quo ante*. The new Constitution embodied all the political flaws of its Weimar predecessor: a High Court as the Guardian of the Constitution on the basis of a refurbished natural-law ideology; a Christian and Social Democratic welfare state firmly anchored in the Constitution; and a tacit acknowledgement of Germany's nonexistence as a state.

In this last respect, the 'restorationist' Bonn Constitution must now have seemed to him decisively inferior to the Weimar Constitution. Schmitt believed that the destruction of the German Reich was the most extreme case of the wider deterioration of the political form of the European state, divided between an Atlantic and a Warsaw Pact order. He wrote to Jünger that the annihilating impulse behind legal positivism was now fully exposed in Kelsen's latest formulations on the fate of Germany:

> He writes that since 1944 Germany no longer exists in international law, is no longer present, no longer a subject of law, juristically nothing, entirely nothing, nothing other than nothingness. Except that the Allies, if it suits them, can create a new, totally different legal subject, in no way way identical to the past, and can give it the name 'Germany', which proves nothing against the nothing.[12]

In the struggle between these two geo-ideological blocs, Schmitt's identification with 'the West' would always be lukewarm. He saw the collapse of pro-Western parties in Czechoslovakia in 1948 as a warning for their counterparts in Germany: 'When even the little Czechs went so wrong with their hasty option for the West, what will happen to us Germans, when we seek heedlessly to decide between East and West, and promote a false decisionism.'[13]

Schmitt's hostility towards Atlanticism was long-standing, and obviously did not entail any sympathy with the Soviet Union. He believed that the Cold War system of all-pervasive antagonism between the Free World and Communism was based on the liquidation of Europe's unique interstate political civilization. He would only ever tacitly admit that the attempt to establish a German-dominated European *Grossraum* was the single most decisive factor in bringing this about. Even in the misery of his cell, his mind was too politically charged for him to stop thinking about what Germany could do to get out from under the crushing, damning verdict of total defeat. He scribbled down a condensed political programme in his notebook:

> 1. Frontal struggle against the idea of the just war; open demonstration of its historical, juristic, and moral falsity; its character as an instrument of civil war etc. Hopeless?

2. Positivistically-patiently hollowing out; Underhanded normalization; Sabotage through collaboration of the foundations of the Nuremberg judgement; conscious and planned playing the worm in rotten wood; Porzia-method of taking them at their word.

3. A combination of these two possibilities with divided roles.[14]

These three possibilities, taken together, can be seen as a testament to Schmitt's entire career on the political front; they identify the alternating roles, tactics – even identities – which he assumed in the wars of his time. Classicist and intellectual adventurer, Catholic and Fascist, *Aufhalter* and *Aufbrecher*, Fox and Lion: from 1919 to 1945, Carl Schmitt was an explosively unstable combination of these opposing possibilities. *Complexio Oppositorum.*

Conclusion

After nearly two years in detention, Carl Schmitt returned, a defeated man, to his native Plettenberg. He was stripped of his academic position, and effectively barred from ever holding one again. His library had been confiscated. In 1950 his beloved wife died of cancer. Apart from the sister who took him in, most of the people he had known initially stayed clear of this notorious figure, a living reminder of a traumatic, still too recent past. Despite his tendency to advertise his misfortunes loudly to anyone who would listen, he did not easily succumb to adversity. He was determined to resume correspondence with friends and former colleagues, establish discussion circles and generally re-enter intellectual life. Soon people began to trickle into his modest home in Plettenberg, which Schmitt would later name 'San Casciano' after Machiavelli's residence in exile. Within a few years he became the centre of an intellectual freemasonry embracing many of West Germany's most prominent conservative academics. Although he was a taboo figure in the postwar Federal Republic, he none the less exercised a strong – albeit indirect – influence on the design of its Constitution. A pension was eventually arranged for him by a circle of prominent industrialists, and he lived in modest comfort until he died in 1983 at the age of ninety-five, having lived under four German regimes.

Schmitt's postwar life largely falls outside of the scope of this study. I can justify ending it decades before he died in terms of intellectual interest: although he remained prolific, much of what came later consists of footnotes to earlier works. During the Weimar Republic he possessed an extraordinarily multifaceted mind. His intellectual range perhaps diminished a little during the Nazi period as the previously central problems of democracy and constitutional law no longer had any domestic purchase; but this foreclosure on the home front precipitated a shift of focus, and his writings on international law from this period successfully tapped into the live wires of world politics. It was the politically neutralized atmosphere of the early Federal Republic which finally extinguished this protean intelligence and led to the premature hardening of his mind. Even when he was critical of the new status quo, later in life Carl Schmitt was more conventionally reactionary: reconciled to the Church (after the death of his wife), critic of the welfare state, self-proclaimed defender of Old Europe in a post-political consumer society. During the last decades of his life he became a living period piece, to all appearances an intellectual invalid from an antediluvian world.

One of the central assumptions of this study was that the ideas of Carl Schmitt took shape in the intertwining timelines of civil and world wars, and that understanding his thought requires retracing the path of his interventions on the constantly shifting battlefields of the inter-war era. But the question then arises: is it even possible for such a figure, so embedded in his own time, to leap out of the grave and speak, or be spoken of, in the present tense. The question is particularly appropriate in this case, because Schmitt always insisted that actuality is the decisive criterion for historical judgement: 'All historical knowledge receives its light and intensity from the present; all historical representations and constructions are filled with naive projections and identifications; only a consciousness of our own historical situation will provide historical insight.'[1]

But the question of Schmitt's contemporary relevance – of what, to use the Crocean expression, is living and dead in his thought – must be posed carefully. The 'present', in this sense, is an unstable category, and the light it sheds on the life and times of the defeated is often harsh and inconstant. Defeat can bury whole intellectual traditions, blocking off the path of empathetic excavation. Determining the contemporary actuality of Carl Schmitt immediately raises the problem of the continuity between the present and the interwar era; are the categories, sites, and stakes of the wars of today close enough to those of Schmitt's time to warrant transposing lines of thought drawn from his work on to contemporary contentions?

I will argue that Schmitt's accounts of the hollowing out of liberal democracy, and the nature of war and peace in a New World Order, are, at very least, timely antidotes to the inebriating consensus which surrounds these big issues today. Indeed, he is arguably alone in having developed a body of theoretical work which focuses directly on these issues. The potential significance of this figure on the contemporary intellectual map is only beginning to be appreciated. Let me try to anticipate the foci of this future reception.

The 'enemy' is the central orientating co-ordinate of strategic action; as the stark embodiment of potentially catastrophic defeat, he concentrates the mind in the sphere of the political. Schmitt attempted to capture the harsh objectivity as well as the phantasms of the political – that is to say, the necessity of conflict and the surplus of violence and passion. His formulations can be directed at models which reductively represent political conflict in terms of rational choice models of market competition. The fundamentals of this approach are laid out in the model developed by Anthony Downs: elections are like contests for market shares in which the preferences of individual voters are pre-given, and parties position themselves at some point along a continuous and narrowly bounded left–right spectrum in order to maximize votes. Under these assumptions, the direction of political competition will always converge on a winning centre because this is always where the most votes are. These assumptions capture the strategic universe of media-staged electoral contests in the leading liberal democracies – the USA first and foremost – and go a long way towards explaining why victory today invariably goes to the most unctuous, telegenic centrist.

But it cannot explain why this centre now moves ever rightward, regardless of which party wins an election. Schmitt's portrayals of political conflict bring to light what exactly is at stake in contests for power when the direction of the political system is up for grabs, and powerful vested interests can be overwhelmed by disruptive shifts in the centre of political gravity: elections are only one stage of a wider, multitheatre struggle for hegemony; voter preferences are actively shaped by partisan mobilization; the divisions within a left–right political spectrum, as well as the distance between its extremes, can widen to the point of civil war whenever defeat threatens to bring not the comfortable life of loyal opposition, but permanent marginalization, political death or worse; fleeing from the centre can therefore be strategically rational; the winning party is sometimes the one which can mobilize a mass base along an emergent crosscutting dimension, scrambling an older scheme of partisan identification. The degree to which any of these 'Schmittian' tendencies is at work in a particular political system will vary, but even when they are checked they exist as never entirely excluded possibilities of regroupment.

How are these possibilities affirmed or negated in contemporary conceptions of democracy? The views of Schmitt's most intelligent contemporary nemesis, Jürgen Habermas, are particularly illustrative of what is at stake. Schmitt's hyperpolitical deconstruction of the language of consensus brings to light the pervasiveness of partisan rule interpretation at all levels of communicative action, even in a constitutionally stabilized political system. Diametrically opposed in intention, Habermas's work explores the spheres of disinterested communication in a political system, the fair procedures of an 'endless conversation' which monitor and domesticate the power of bureaucracy and money. Habermas argues that this approach has the advantage of bringing to light the norms out which meaningful democratic consent can emerge; these norms of communication, not the mythology of a homogeneous demos, are the legitimating centre of gravity in a democratic political system. Schmitt claimed that democracy is popular sovereignty, and that this sovereignty presupposes the 'homogeneity' of a people. According to Habermas, Schmitt posited the existence of a mythologically homogeneous people as an unlimited sovereign power, in order to justify shattering the whole constitutional system. I have argued that this is simply a misinterpretation of Schmitt's conception of 'homogeneity', which has no intrinsic anthropological meaning; 'homogeneity' indicates the minimal threshold of political unity beneath which 'the people' dissolves into warring parties, each claiming to represent the whole. Although Schmitt feared the slide into this civil war condition, in his own way he recognized that it is only in the struggle between parties vying for hegemony over 'the people' that the latter is mobilized as an agent, and becomes something more than the empty signifier of an imagined community.

The shrewdest insights into democracy are not always made by friends of the people. The truth in Schmitt's polar opposition of liberalism and democracy is historically variable: in some periods these are the terms of a more or less harmonious historic alliance; in others, one term can be seen as the negation of the other. *Fratelli, coltelli.* To the extent that neoliberalism is a liberal doctrine, the relationship between these two terms today is probably about as complex and antagonistic as it was during the Weimar Republic. Mainstream political discourse has not acknowledged this because, in the meantime, democracy has shed much of its original, ancient meaning as a political system in which all power is in the hands of an assembled people. The standard justification for this semantic corruption is that ancient forms of direct democracy cannot be resurrected in a modern context of a complex division of labour and private liberties. But the significance of Schmitt's conception of democracy is that it elides this sharp ancient–modern dichotomy of direct versus representative government. Even if it is impossible to establish a political system in which a permanantly assembled people governs itself, Schmitt suggested that a political system is authentically democratic to the extent that it is open to periodic 'emergencies' in which the people can swing into action as an independent semi-legislative power. Demonstrations, gigantic rallies and general strikes are events which keep alive, and in motion, the original constituent power of the people. Democracy takes on its real meaning in the exceptional situation. Although Schmitt was no friend of the council democracy which sprang up in the aftermath of military defeat, the memory and institutional residues of this revolutionary episode continued to inform his understanding of democracy until the end of the Weimar era, even as he attempted to give it a more plebiscitarian form. Schmitt, following Machiavelli, recognized the role of the class struggle in catalyzing popular government. From this perspective it is arguable that the relentless decline of these forms of popular power over the last two decades – and the related decline of belief in the efficacy of public power of any kind – is a ruinous development for democracy.

Neither the Downsian market model of elections as the strategic aggregation by parties of the preferences of individual voters, nor the more idealistic Habermasian model of inviolable constitutional rules of consensus formation, has convincingly explained the meaning of democracy in the absence a self-organizing, sovereign people. Let us recollect the evocative image of democracy as an explosively high-energy political system put forward by Schmitt, who viewed the phenomenon with both fear and admiration: 'Out of its endless, elusive, groundless power emerge ever new forms, which it can at any time shatter, never limiting itself.'[2] This power is frozen, neutralized or extinguished in the core regions of world capitalism, a development which has made the entire world safe from democracy.

Schmitt wrote at a time when a civil war had generated a political spectrum which was far too wide and internally volatile to be contained by a system of institutionalized compromise and corporatist bargaining. The crisis of parliamentarianism which he diagnosed was a crisis of overpoliticization. Nearly the exact opposite holds true today, as government by discussion languishes under an unprecedented degree of consensus around a narrow band of economic fundamentals. While Schmitt's critique of the involution of parliamentarianism remains valid, what has more recently colonized or replaced the classical debating and resolving chamber in the West is neither corporatist bargaining, which he opposed, nor the politics of nationalist myth, which he endorsed, but more venal forms of electoralism – a frothy, money-soaked, sound-bite politics, fruit of an ongoing privatization and neutralization of public power.

There have been other times in which democracy in this sense has been simultaneously turned back and transformed into what were, normatively speaking, perversions of itself: if we take only Europe, the 1850s – and then, far more dramatically, the 1930s – witnessed potentially tide-turning counter-offensives. We are living through a comparable era, in which the patterns of social conflict and collective agency, which gave the world-historical democratic trend a sharp, egalitarian edge, have been decisively checked – not, this time, by an organized political counter-offensive *à la* Cortes or Mussolini, but by a historically unprecedented neutralization of public power *tout court*. The related neutralization of democracy has made the transition to it a relatively safe process in large parts of the world, which now get the vote at the very moment when, it is claimed, there is nothing left for government to do but prepare their citizens for life in the world market.

One of the central, little-theorized sociological transformations in Western societies over the past twenty-five years has been the decline of the masses. The low-level legitimation crisis of the democracy in this period is the harvest of this decline: not over- but, rather, depoliticization; not the multidimensional expansion of public power but, rather, its constriction and immobilization. Neoliberals regard this as a positive development. Certainly the widespread belief that 'civil society' is impervious to political transformation, and that the role of democracy is listlessly to tilt this 'civil society' back and forth for ever, contributes greatly to the now deeply institutionalized neoliberal slant in the politics of just about every country in the world. The uniform message of official and academic utterance on politics today – that there is no responsible alternative – is the harvest of a 'neutralization' on a scale which Schmitt would have found difficult to imagine.

Roberto Unger has argued that the straitjacketing of political alternatives we experience today is only an intensification of features built into the very design of Western constitutions:

> Two features have dominated the modern Western constitutional tradition: a style of constitutional organization of government slowing politics down, for the sake of freedom connected with private property, and a set of practices and institutions helping to keep society at a relatively low level of political mobilization. Democratic experimentalism demands that we replace both these sets of political and constitutional conventions.[3]

Unger's iconoclastic critique of these traditions of Western constitutionalism is reminiscent of that of Schmitt, who invoked the idea of the people as a groundless *pouvoir constituant* in order to loosen constitutional restraints on the exercise of executive power. The Left can invoke this idea in its original, radical democratic form, as a concentrated public power capable of reining in the powers of private property. Those who thought of democracy as a dangerous, overreaching and unstable political system, even from an enemy perspective, have more to say about the meaning of radical democracy than an effete, incorporated and culturalist Left.

Schmitt's relevance to commentary on international relations should be even more readily apparent. Here we leave behind the world of the rule of law and enter the state of nature – that is, a zone where the fictions of legality can be particularly pernicious. More effectively than anyone else he called into question the stability of an international order in which all states are subject to incipient forms of international government, but only to widely varying and often unspecified degrees: his polemics capture the vaguely Kafkaesque ring of a jargon which declares war between states to be abolished, and invokes the highest ideals of humanity to justify 'police operations' and sanction regimes against outlaw governments.

The geopolitical jargon of the metropolitan power elite is now 'internationalist'. This provides some cold comfort for those on the Left who are grateful that at least this jargon is not 'nationalist' or, in America-speak, 'isolationist'. This is essentially Habermas's reasoning in justifying the participation of the German Social Democratic–Green government in the NATO bombing of the rump Yugoslavia. In the very title of his article 'Human Rights Politics Equal Power Politics: The Self-Empowerment of NATO Should Not Become the Rule', Habermas implicitly acknowledged Schmitt's claim that the one who decides on the exception to the rule, is effectively sovereign. Although he expressed some misgivings about the legality of the NATO attack, and was unsure whether the bombing was intensifying or alleviating the humanitarian crisis, he comforted himself with these thoughts:

> Shoulder to shoulder with the old democracies, who are more formed by traditions of reason than we [Germans] are, Ministers Fischer and Scharping refer to the idea of a process of domesticating the natural relations between nations through human rights. And thus the transformation of international law into the rights of a world citizenry is put on the agenda. Legal pacifism wants to not only foreclose the possibility of war between sovereign states, it wants to abolish it completely in a thoroughly legalistic cosmopolitan world order. From Kant to Kelsen these traditions also existed here [in Germany]. But today, for the first time, a German government is taking them seriously.[4]

Habermas dismisses the idea that the Kosovo intervention can be explained in terms of the more squalid motives of US and NATO power projection because it was simply too risky in a pure power-political calculus; thus one is compelled to accept the authenticity of the stated humanitarian intention. He does not seriously consider the idea that this humanitarian rhetoric might be the expression of a violent, sanctimonious hubris in the face of 'rogue states', who will no doubt conveniently continue to provide all sorts of occasions for 'exceptional' measures into the foreseeable future. The precedent is now established that when NATO has a just war to fight, even the foundational norms of international law can be suspended.

Habermas does not subscribe to the just war theory, nor endorse its moralizing paroxysms. Indeed, his claim is that only the further evolution of a cosmopolitan world legal order can neutralize the self-righteous fanaticism of sovereign belligerents by subjecting interstate conflict to the compulsory arbitration of international authorities. Cautiously optimistic, he predicts that current trends promise eventually to bring to a close the millennia-long epoch of warring states. Certainly he has some misgivings about the practice of American-

initiated humanitarian interventions launched without the authorization of the Security Council; but he is convinced that an interstate
pacification process will unfold through the constitutional structure of
the United Nations, and that this will be facilitated by expanding the
permanent membership of the Security Council, and eventually
empowering the now powerless General Assembly.

In essays from the 1920s and 1930s on the fate of the League of
Nations, Schmitt eloquently argued against comparable, Kantian
notions of a long-term legalization of the international order. Habermas has recently offered a spirited counter-attack, taking on Schmitt's
criticisms of this tradition, in an essay entitled 'Kants Idee des ewigen
Friedens aus dem historischen Abstand von 200 Jahren' ('Kant's Idea
of a Perpetual Peace from a Distance of 200 Years').[5] He directs his fire
at what he takes to be Schmitt's chief contention: that the universalism
of international law violates the principle of sovereignty. But this whole
line of attack misses Schmitt's more essential point: international law is
suspect for Schmitt not because it is universal in its scope, but, rather,
because it never will be, since powerful states, or whole alliances of
states, will either have their privileges ensconced in international law,
or evade its jurisdiction on what they deem to be vital mattters of
security. Habermas seems to conflate the idea of an international legal
community with the immeasurably harsher realities of the American-
headquartered New World Order, and fills in the gap with a weak
Kantian assumption that with luck, things are moving in the right
direction. He does not ask whether there are historical moments, even
whole eras, in which one can legitimately call this assumption into
question. Although he points to Nuremberg, Bosnia and Somalia as
instances of a promising trend, he neglects to mention when he thinks
that the United States will ever be a subject of international law to the
same degree as Iraq, for example, is today.

Even if one does not share the view that Machiavellianism is the last
word in politics, scepticism about the long-term prospects of a legal
domestication of power can play an important demystifying role. As
long as law is dependent on armed bodies of men, there is an
undeniable moral integrity to antinomianism. As Rousseau pointed out
in his 'Essay on the Origins of Inequality', when, in the long – perhaps
never to be completed – transition from the state of nature to the truly
civil condition, law is used to anchor privileges more firmly than was
ever possible in the state of nature, nostalgia for the more primitive
condition is never entirely illegitimate.

But what can one learn from reading Schmitt on force and fraud in
international relations that cannot be learned from that grand and
uncompromising moralist Noam Chomsky? After all, Chomsky's truculence in the face of *bien-pensant* 'internationalism' is untarnished by any

wicked Machiavellianism. The enlightenment which comes from reading Schmitt is, by contrast, sobering, even disquieting; famously, he
made the claim that our perception of violence is structured by a
partisan schema which divides people into friends and enemies, and
that this division is rarely made on the basis of pure human rights
criteria, or truly impartial criteria of utility; anyone who has ever
believed strongly in a cause – indeed, anyone who has looked with
detachment at one scene of human misery and boiled over in rage at
another – will recognize, upon reflection, the significance of this
insight.

Schmitt's formulations are responses to questions arising out of a
harsh partisan vortex; they register the shocks of an ongoing state of
emergency, near-revolutionary levels of political tension; they are
chronicles of an interwar high politics, of winner-take-all contests for
the future. To return to the question posed at the beginning of this
Conclusion: how, then, can they be relevant in the shock-absorbent
world of contemporary liberal democracy? Perry Anderson argues that
one of the defining characteristics of postmodernity is the closure of
the political as a relatively autonomous sphere in which collective
agents could take shape around hegemonic projects.[6] From this perspective, Schmitt's writings are modernist texts *par excellence*. They
contain a number of sharp, composite images of an era characterized
by the simultaneity of the non-simultaneous. They are attempts to
capture the experience of the end of several overlapping eras in
European history at an explosive convergence of turning points: an age
of class struggles escalating into civil wars extending from 1848 to the
1920s; an Indian summer of aristocratic and *haut-bourgeois* forms of life
on the eve of their destruction; a seemingly irreversible devaluation of
the dominant political traditions of the *belle époque*: conservatism,
liberalism and moderate socialism. Trends measured in decades were
in turn subsumed by ones measured in centuries and millennia: the
exponential growth of the modern European state as a warmaking, tax-
collecting and redistributive machine breaking out of the original
dimensions of the classical sovereign polity; the obsolesence of
inherited traditions of Roman jurisprudence; the ongoing, accelerating
de-Christianization of the European mind, unleashing spectres of nihilism. Schmitt believed that human nature itself was coming into sharper
focus in this time out of joint, in this state of emergency. The pathos of
this moment, with its immense wars of the spirit, can seem remote and
anachronistic in an age of diminished expectations, cancelled alternatives, and closed political horizons. Lurking behind the contemporary
interest in Carl Schmitt is the sense that this present cannot last for
ever.

Notes

1 The Young Carl Schmitt

1. Joseph Bendersky, *Carl Schmitt: Theorist of the Reich* (Princeton University Press, Princeton, NJ 1983), p. 6. This is the best-known intellectual biography of Schmitt. It contains a great number of astute observations, and while the book is admirably free of axe-grinding, it tends – too much, in my opinion – to present Schmitt in the role of an intelligent and beleaguered conservative nationalist, often downplaying the extremely unusual, radical side of his mind.
2. Ibid., p. 4.
3. Ibid., p. 7.
4. Paul Noack, *Carl Schmitt: eine Biographie* (Propyläen Verlag, Berlin 1993), p. 18. Noack's biography is a very good portrait of Schmitt the man. It does not, however, provide a critical discussion of Schmitt's writings.
5. Quoted from ibid., p. 21.
6. Carl Schmitt, *Über Schuld und Schuldarten: eine terminologische Untersuchung, Strassburger Inaugural-Dissertation* (Breslau 1910). With few exceptions, I use the German original even when an English translation exists. I have translated titles into English in parentheses, but page-number citations refer to the German text. Except where indicated, translations are my own.
7. Carl Schmitt, *Gesetz und Urteil* (C.H. Beck, Munich 1969), 2nd edn.
8. Ibid., p. 32.
9. Carl Schmitt, *Der Wert des Staates und die Bedeutung des Individuums* (C.H. Beck, Munich 1969), 2nd edn; cited from Noack, *Carl Schmitt*, p. 32.
10. Ibid.
11. Manfred Dahlheimer, *Der deutsche Katholizismus 1888–1936* (Verlag Ferdinand Schöningh, Paderborn 1999), p. 51. This is the best and most comprehensive treatment of Schmitt's relationship to German Catholicism. The author concludes that Schmitt kept his distance from the various forms of contemporary German Catholicism.
12. Schmitt, *Der Wert des Staates*, p. 32.
13. Noack, *Carl Schmitt*, p. 35.
14. Walter Lacqueur, *Weimar* (Putnam, New York 1974).
15. See Ellen Kennedy, 'Politischer Expressionismus: Die kulturkritischen und metaphysischen Ursprünge des Begriffs des Politischen von Carl Schmitt', in Helmut Quaritsch, ed., *Complexio Oppositorum* Duncker & Humblot, Berlin 1988), pp. 233–51.
16. See Hugo Ball, *The Critique of the German Intelligentsia* (Columbia University

Press, New York 1993). Indeed, Ball's polemic against Prussia, Protestantism and the Jews, written while he was a paid literary agent of the Entente in Switzerland, bordered on paranoid delirium, and Schmitt later felt the need to distance himself from this extravagant Bohemian, Dadaist convert to Catholicism.

17. In a tribute to the poetry of a friend, the minor Expressionist poet Theodor Däubler, Schmitt depicted the war as a manifestation of the unleashed power of the Antichrist, by which he meant a modern European society hell-bent on re-creating the world through technology, and thus attempting to usurp the place of God. Although he would later cultivate this apocalyptic style, in this essay the dark and foreboding horizon is a politically shapeless and mediocre Expressionist construct.

18. Michael Löwy, *Georg Lukács: From Romanticism to Revolution* (New Left Books, London 1979).

19. Hans Mommsen, *The Rise and Fall of Weimar Democracy* (University of North Carolina Press, Chapel Hill 1996), p. 26.

20. Friedrich Neumann, *The Rule of Law under Siege* (University of Chicago Press, Chicago 1996), pp. 30–31.

21. Mommsen, *The Rise and Fall of Weimar Democracy*, p. 47.

22. Bendersky, *Carl Schmitt*, p. 22.

23. Diary entry from 8 November 1918, cited from Dirk Hoeges, *Kontroverse am Abgrund* (Fischer Wissenschaft, Frankfurt am Main 1994) p. 132.

24. Gary Ulmen, *Politischer Mehrwert* (Weinheim, 1991), cited from Noack ed., *Complexio Oppositorum*, p. 41.

25. Letter from 21 August 1976, cited in Piet Tommissen, 'Baustein zu einer wissenschaftlichen Biographie', in Quaritsch, ed., *Complexio Oppositorum*, p. 78.

26. Max Weber, *Politics as a Vocation and Science as a Vocation* (Oxford University Press, New York 1946); Carl Schmitt, *Politische Romantik* (Duncker & Humblot, Leipzig 1925), 2nd edn.

27. Ibid., p. 227.

28. Ibid., pp. 113, 143, 191.

29. Ibid., p. 140.

30. Ibid., p. 138.

31. Ibid., p. 21.

32. Exemplary in this respect is the consistently superficial treatment of Schmitt's ideas in Stephen Holmes, *The Anatomy of Antiliberalism* (Harvard University Press, Cambridge, MA 1994).

33. Before the war, the only contemporary German Catholic of distinction to have criticized Romanticism, polemically contrasting it to a purer classicism, was the lay Catholic essayist Karl Muth (Dahlheimer, *Der deutsche Katholizismus*, p. 63).

34. Schmitt, *Politische Romantik*, p. 13.

35. Ibid., p. 35.

36. Schmitt referred to Marx's attack on Romanticism in *The Holy Family*, claiming that the 'realism of this Hegelian revolutionary turned against the "Christian" spiritualism and devaluation of reality, against the "lack of objectivity", without being able to grasp this contradictory and multifaceted enemy with a succinct concept' (ibid. pp. 35–6).

37. Ibid, pp. 70–71.

38. Georg Lukács, review of *Politische Romantik, Archiv für die Geschichte des Sozialismus und der Arbeiterbewegung* 8, 1928, pp. 307–8. Lukács qualified this otherwise highly sympathetic review by stating that Schmitt had failed to flesh out his identification of Romanticism with the German bourgeoisie with a more detailed class analysis.

39. Schmitt, *Politische Romantik*, p. 172.

40. One has only to compare him to the most talented figure in this whole milieu, Ernst Jünger, to understand this: the very title of a book like *Der Krieg als inneres Erlebnis* ('War as Inner Experience') (Velhagen & Klasing, Bielefeld 1933) graphically demonstrates this point. Certainly Schmitt was a vivid prose stylist and a literary connoisseur. It was the overly promiscuous use of the rhetoric of the beautiful and sublime to which he objected.

41. Schmitt, *Politische Romantik*, p. 36.

42. Charles Maurras, *Romantisme et Révolution* (Nouvelle Libraire Nationale; Paris 1925).

43. Schmitt, *Politische Romantik*, p. 19.

44. Some of the underlying assumptions about national character in this work can be more clearly discerned in a much later essay:

> The specificity of the French mind is characterized by concepts like classicism, rationalism, *clarté*, and *mesure*. Classicism and rationalism are by common conception seen to be nearly a monopoly of the French.
>
> This distinctive intellectual habitus was the product of the political role which jurists had played in the history of that nation. The juristic flavour of his conception of classicism is unmistakable, and suggests the reasons for his affinity for la Grande Nation.
>
> As with no other people, the French legist was the pathbreaker and spokesman of national unity in great moments of historical struggle and civil war. The French mind is therefore a juristic mind and the French language more than any other a juristic language, because French national development was decisively influenced by the French legists. ('Die Formung des französischen Geistes durch den Legisten', in *Staat, Grossraum, Nomas: Arbeiten aus den Jahren 1916–1969*, ed. Günter Maschke (Duncker & Humblot, Berlin 1995.)

45. Schmitt, *Politische Romantik*, pp. 224–5.

46. 'Briefe von E.R. Curtius an Carl Schmitt (1921–22)', in *Archiv für das Studium der neueren Sprachen und Literaturen*, cited from Hoeges, *Kontroverse am Abgrund*.

47. Carl Schmitt, *Die Diktatur* (Duncker & Humblot, Munich 1921).

48. 'Briefe von E.R. Curtius an Carl Schmitt (1921–22)', in *Archiv für das Studium der neueren Sprachen und Literaturen*, cited in Noack, *Carl Schmitt*, p. 174.

49. Thomas Mann, 'Von deutscher Republik', in *Gesammelte Werke*, vol. XI (S. Fischer, Frankfurt am Main 1960).

50. Karl Mannheim, *Konservatismus* (Suhrkamp, Frankfurt am Main 1994).

51. Günter Maschke, *Der Tod Carl Schmitts* (Karolinger, Vienna 1987), p. 20. This often disturbing collection of essays provides penetrating insights into Schmitt's life and work.

52. William Chace, *The Political Identities of T.S. Eliot and Ezra Pound* (Stanford University Press, Palo Alto, CA 1973), p. 127.

53. T.S. Eliot 'Make it New', *Criterion* 7 (1924), cited from ibid., p. 114.
54. Schmitt, *Politische Romantik*, p. 19.

2 Dictatorship Sovereign and Commissarial

1. Paul Noack, *Carl Schmitt: eine Biographie* (Propyläen Verlag, Berlin 1993), p. 54.
2. Ibid., p. 46.
3. Ibid., p. 29.
4. Peter Caldwell, *Popular Sovereignty and the Crisis of German Constitutional Law* (Duke University Press, Durham, NC 1997). This work provides a very useful overview of debates in German constitutional law from the Weimar period. I have drawn upon it extensively in my discussion of the national organization and politics of the courts under the Weimar Republic. But the author seems to be unable or unwilling to reconstruct the line of Schmitt's thought on these subjects, so concerned is he to 'refute' Schmitt, and impute to him views the author believes he should have had but, as a matter of fact, didn't. To mention only one example: he insists that Schmitt subscribed to a '*völkisch*' nationalism, and does not cite passages from *Verfassungslehre* ('Constitutional Theory') which incontrovertibly prove the opposite.
5. Carl Schmitt, 'Diktatur und Belagerungszustand. Eine Staatsrechtliche Studie', *Zeitschrift für die gesamte Staatsrechtswissenschaft*, vol. 38, 1916, pp. 138–61.
6. Heinz Hürten, *Reichswehr und Ausnahmezustand: ein Beitrag zur Verfassungsproblematik der Weimarer Republik in ihrem ersten Jahrfünft, Rheinisch-Westfälische Akademie der Wissenschaften, Vorträge G222*, p. 15 (Westdeutscher Verlag, Opladen 1977). This study provides an excellent account of the role of Article 48 in the politics of the early Weimar Republic.
7. This law was never passed, allowing the massive discretionary power of the President to be defined by precedent.
8. Niccolò Machiavelli, *The Prince and the Discourses* (Carlton House, New York 1962), p. 202.
9. Carl Schmitt, *Die Diktatur* (Duncker & Humblot, Leipzig 1921), p. 18.
10. Schmitt did not dwell on the arguments of Junius Brutus, but it is important to consider them more carefully, as they constitute what Schmitt would soon call a 'political theology', and one that was diametrically opposed to the 'political theology' with which he would much later come to identify. Junius Brutus argued that his conception of kingship was sanctioned by biblical precedent. The Jews' decision to bring an end to their condition as a loose tribal confederacy under the direct rule of God – i.e. of the priesthood – and to have a king above them in the manner of the Gentiles, did not entail an abrogation of the people's earlier direct covenant of submission with God. By this precedent – now valid in all Christendom – the degree to which the people – i.e. the civil and clerical magistrates acting in their name – are subjected to the Prince is radically attenuated. As an indication of the significance that this line of argument assumed in the early modern Frondes, Hobbes had to write at great length in *Leviathan* that God had let himself be deposed by the Jewish people and, in so doing,

had sanctioned the subjection of all magistrates, civil and clerical, to the direct unattenuated will of the sovereign.

11. Jean Bodin, *Six Books of the Republic*, cited by Norberto Bobbio in *Democracy and Dictatorship* (University of Minneapolis Press, Minnesota 1989), p. 93.
12. Schmitt, *Die Diktatur*, p. 35.
13. Ibid., p. 40.
14. Carl Schmitt, 'Absolutism' (1925) in *Staatslexikon der Görres Gesellschaft*, reprinted in Günter Maschke, ed., *Staat, Grossraum, Nomos: Arbeiten aus den Jahren 1916–1969* (Duncker & Humblot, Berlin 1995), p. 98.
15. Cited from Montesquieu in Schmitt, *Die Diktatur*, p. 106.
16. Ibid., p. 137.
17. Karl Marx, *The Eighteenth Brumaire of Louis Napoleon* (Progress, New York 1963), p. 66.
18. Schmitt, *Die Diktatur*, p. 142.
19. Ibid., p. 200.
20. Quotation from Condorcet cited in ibid., p. 204.
21. Ibid. Schmitt conveyed his image of the nature of these 'new conditions' while citing the opinion of Justice Minister Schiffer, who had maintained in 1920 that a military commander could theoretically order the use of poison gas and aerial bombardment to restore order.
22. Schmitt, *Die Diktatur*, p. vii.
23. Ibid., p. 203.
24. Ibid., p. 105.
25. Ibid., p. 199.
26. Carl Schmitt, 'Die Diktatur des Reichspräsidenten nach Artikel 48 der Weimarer Verfassung', reprinted with *Die Diktatur*, 1924 edn, p. 241.
27. Ibid., p. 238.

3 The State of Emergency

1. *Briefe von E.R. Curtius an Carl Schmitt*, cited from Paul Noack, *Carl Schmitt, eine Biographie* (Propyläen Verlag, Berlin 1993), p. 55.
2. There are repeated references in Schmitt's writings to the uncomprehending hostility of official theologians towards lay Catholic writers like Cortes, and himself. The later fate of Charles Maurras perhaps also struck him as typical of this conflict.
3. This is not to say that Schmitt had an instrumental relationship to Catholicism in the way that one could say Charles Maurras did; indeed, I will argue later that this is what most sharply distinguishes him from Maurras.
4. Günter Maschke, *Der Tod Carl Schmitts* (Karolinger, Vienna 1987).
5. Heinz Hürten, *Reichswehr und Ausnahmezustand: ein Beitrag zur Verfassungsproblematik der Weimarer Republik in ihrem ersten Jahrfünft*, Rheinisch-Westfälische Akademie der Wissenschaften, Vorträge G222 (Westdeutscher Verlag, Opladen 1977), p. 13. Schmitt's own writings reflected this difficulty in defining what an emergency is, i.e. whether it is a really existing condition to which the state then responds, or whether it is simply a condition which nominally ensues every time the state suspends the law. This slipperiness is characteristic of a jargon which flourished in Weimar, in which 'hard and resolute' decisions were valorized. From some of these early Weimar writings Schmitt

earned the reputation of being a 'decisionist', but he adopted this 'decisionist' idiom largely as a reaction to the exclusive emphasis on general norms
in positivist and neo-Kantian legal theories. The 'decisionism' to which he
adhered did not rely on any existential psychology. It was based on the very
plausible assumption that there existed political conflicts which were, if not
irreconcilable, then still incapable of being resolved through negotiation
or by reference to general norms.

6. Hürten, *Reichswehr und Ausnahmezustand*, p. 13.
7. Carl Schmitt, 'Vergleichender Überblick über die neueste Entwicklung des
   Problems der gesetzgeberischen Ermächtigungen' (1936), in *Positionen und
   Begriffe* (Duncker & Humblot, Berlin 1988), 2nd edn, pp. 214–29.
8. Max Weber, *Economy and Society* (University of California Press, Berkeley
   1978), p. 657.
9. This use of the word 'gap' was popularized by Bismarck during the Prussian
   constitutional crisis of the 1860s.
10. Carl Schmitt, *Politische Theologie* (Duncker & Humblot, Munich 1922), p. 9.
11. Although Schmitt did not cite anyone, his definition is rather close to even
    the wording of a passage in Hegel's *Philosophy of Right*. In this work the
    sovereign, and his right to decide arbitrarily, occupied a central role in a
    rationally organized state. Hegel says that the sovereign is:

    the personality of the state, its certainty of itself ... [which] supersedes all
    particularities, cuts short the weighing of arguments and counter-arguments
    (between which vacillations in either direction are always possible) and
    resolves them by its 'I Will', thereby initiating all activity and actuality. (G.W.F.
    Hegel, *Philosophy of Right* [Cambridge University Press, Cambridge 1987],
    para. 279)

12. Precisely such a gap gave Article 48 of the Weimar Constitution its unfore-
    seen and fateful significance: in the last paragraph, reference was made to
    a law which, in the future, would be passed by the Reichstag regulating the
    implementation of emergency powers. Even leading constitutional legal
    scholars, like the liberal Anschütz, maintained that until the return of
    normal conditions, closing this gap through the passage of this law would
    be inopportune, and that until then Article 48.2 provided sufficiently clear
    restrictions on potential abuses. The law referred to in the last paragraph
    of the article, specifying the scope of Reichstag control over government
    emergency powers, was never passed.
13. Schmitt, *Politische Theologie*, p. 9.
14. Ibid., p. 20.
15. Weber, *Economy and Society*, p. 948.
16. The problem Schmitt was addressing is an extreme case of a now familiar
    issue in legal theory. H.L.A. Hart identifies it as arising, even in the normal
    course of legal reasoning, out of the essentially 'open-ended' texture of the
    legal language of even very precisely worded statutes:

    Even when verbally formulated general rules are used, uncertainties as to the
    form of behaviour required by them may break out in particular concrete
    cases. Particular fact situations do not await us already marked off from each
    other, and labelled as instances of the general rule, the application of which
    is in question; nor can the rule itself step forward to claim its own instances.

(H.L.A. Hart, *The Concept of Law* [Oxford University Press, Oxford 1979], p. 46)

According to Hart, this problem cannot be resolved by attempting to freeze the meaning of legal terms, because there is an irreducible moment of decision in the specification of the meaning of a statute.

17. Schmitt, *Politische Theologie*, p. 37.
18. Ernst Nolte, *Der Faschismus in seiner Epoche* (R. Piper & Co Verlag, Munich 1963), pp. 68–71.
19. Ibid., p. 84.
20. After the war, Cortes became a familiar name among intellectuals of an extremely reactionary persuasion. See Manfred Dahlheimer, *Der deutsche Katholizismus 1888–1936* (Verlag Ferdinand Schöningh, Paderborn 1999), p. 203.
21. 'Discours sur la Dictature', in *Oeuvres* de Donoso Cortes, vol. 1 (Briday, Lyon 1877), p. 352.
22. My translation of a passage from Donoso Cortes, *Der Staat Gottes* (F.A & Co. Verlag, Leipzig 1933), p. 121. In a letter to J.B. Schweitzer (London, 24 January 1865), Marx explained the abnormal context in which a Donoso Cortes might have found Proudhon so terrifying:

> His coming forward in the National Assembly, however little insight it showed into existing conditions, was worthy of every praise. After the June insurrection it was an act of great courage. In addition it had the fortunate consequence that M. Thiers, by his speech opposing Proudhon's proposals, which was then issued as a special publication, proved to the whole of Europe on what a pedestal of children's catechism the intellectual pillar of the French bourgeoisie was based. Indeed compared with M. Thiers, Proudhon expanded to the size of an antediluvian colossus. (Karl Marx, Class Struggles in France [International Publishers, New York 1934]

23. Cortes, *Der Staat Gottes*, p. 127.
24. Carl Schmitt, 'Donoso Cortes in Berlin, 1849' (1927), in *Positionen und Begriffe*, p. 85.
25. Ibid., p. 77.
26. Carl Schmitt, *Römischer Katholizismus und politische Form* (Jakob Hegner, Hellerau 1923).

4 Catholicism and Nationalism in Modern Politics

1. Andreas Koenen, *Der Fall Carl Schmitt* (Wissenschaftliche Buchgessellschaft, Darmstadt 1995), pp. 31–7. This book is a treasure trove of biographical information on Carl Schmitt. Unfortunately, its central thesis – that Schmitt believed that the restoration of the medieval Catholic German Reich was part of the Divine plan of salvation – is simply false, and often skews the focus of the book towards nonexistent associations. Fortunately, the author is scrupulous enough to provide a mass of evidence to disprove his own thesis.
2. The violently anti-Catholic Adolf von Harnack had once characterized the Church in this way to encapsulate its politically protean nature. Schmitt

simply changed the valences of the term (Manfred Dhalheimer, *Der deutsche Katholizismus 1888–1936* [Verlag Ferdinand Schöningh, Paderborn 1999]), p. 111).

3. Joseph Bendersky, *Carl Schmitt: Theorist of the Reich* (Princeton University Press, Princeton, NJ 1983), p. 53.

4. Kurt Toepner, 'Der deutsche Katholizismus zwischen 1918 und 1933', in *Der Zeitgeist der Weimarer Republik*, ed. Hans Joachim Schoeps (Stuttgart 1968).

5. Ibid.

6. Koenen, *Der Fall Carl Schmitt*, p. 39. The Deutsche Windhorstbund proposed Schmitt as a Centre candidate on 24 February 1924.

7. Schmitt was hardly a typical member of the right wing of the Centre Party, which was, by and large, monarchist in its sympathies, if not fanatically so.

8. Koenen, *Der Fall Carl Schmitt*.

9. Other prominent German Catholic intellectuals of the time, like Max Scheler and Othmar Spann, were more recognizably Catholic in their commitment to establishing a universally valid hierarchy of values. Schmitt ignored them. Indeed, the only German theologian ever to have directly 'influenced' him was his friend Erik Peterson, born Protestant, who later converted to Catholicism. Peterson's exegesis emphasized the significance of the juridical dimension of New Testament pronouncements. Each man's respective conceptions of the relationship of politics and theology in an eschatological perspective reveal the influence of the other, in a pattern of affinity and diametrical opposition. To put it crudely, Schmitt became increasingly insistent on seeing theology in a political light, while Peterson consistently upheld the rightness of the opposite perspective.

Schmitt later claimed that the ideas which went into *Römische Katholizismus* originated in conversations with Franz Blei. Perhaps the latter's idea of the Church as a worldly political institution, his contempt for both a half-educated clergy and Catholic laymen who wanted to integrate the Church into the mainstream of modern society, provided certain points of engagement and departure for Schmitt's own formulations. But it is hard to believe that at this time the specifically political ideas of Schmitt's work owed much to Blei, who was very much a Catholic of the German Romantic sort.

10. Dahlheimer, *Der deutsche Katholizismus*, p. 32.

11. Ibid., p. 161.

12. *Action Française* was widely considered highbrow: Proust, Rodin, Gide and Apollinaire were subscribers. Outside France T.S. Eliot and the young Walter Benjamin could be counted among its readers. Schmitt had been an avid reader of *Action Française* publications since his stint in the censorship office charged with handling enemy propaganda, and his interest continued to grow after the war.

13. Ernst Nolte, *Der Faschismus in seiner Epoch* (R. Piper & Co. Verlag, Munich, 1963), p. 112.

14. Ibid.

15. Carl Schmitt, *Römischer Katholizismus und politische Form* (Jakob Hegner, Hellerau 1923), p. 38.

16. Nolte, *Der Faschismus*, p. 71.

17. The most interesting figure on the Left in this context is, of course, Walter

Benjamin. In *Theses on History* (Suhrkamp, Frankfurt am Main 1995) he suggested that this eschatological moment had to be conceived in a revolutionary, not Schmittian or counter-revolutionary sense. In his role in the wartime censorship office Schmitt had come across Ernst Bloch's *Spirit of Utopia*.

18. The accusation that Schmitt held this Maurrasian view came originally from Heinrich Getzeny in 'Katholizismus des Seins oder Katholizismus des Geltenwollens', *Schildgenossen* 7, 1927, pp. 341–6. See also Helmut Quaritsch, ed., *Complexio Oppositorum* (Duncker & Humblot, Berlin 1988), p. 60.
19. Dahlheimer, *Der deutscher Katholizismus*, p. 531.
20. Gurian to Erik Peterson 20 September 1926, in Barbara Nichtweiss, *Erik Peterson: Neue Sicht auf Leben und Werk* (Freiburg 1992), cited from Koenen, *Der Fall Carl Schmitt*, p. 626.
21. Schmitt, *Römischer Katholizismus und politische Form*, p. 7.
22. Ibid., p. 130.
23. Ibid., p. 13. Schmitt's identification of the Church with the 'world empire' and, even more, the posited resemblance to the British Empire, is revealing in that later he would come to see precisely such 'universalism' as the antithesis of a rationally organized political world.
24. Ibid., p. 14.
25. E.R. Curtius, *Der Deutsche Geist in Gefahr* (Deutsche Verlags-Anstalt, Stuttgart/Berlin 1932), p. 50.
26. In fact this idea of a Complex of Opposites was in part an attempt to address Curtius's criticism of Schmitt's stark contrast between Romantic and dictator: Schmitt's claim that the rhetoric of the Church constituted a language of political authority 'falling into neither discourse nor dictate' contains a probable reference to this criticism.
27. Schmitt, *Römischer Katholizismus und politische Form*, p. 17. Dahlheimer contrasts two pictures of human nature – 'Homo homini lupus' (Hobbes) versus 'Homo naturaliter familians et amicus' (St Thomas) – to convey this point.
28. Ibid., p. 21.
29. Ibid., p. 34.
30. Ibid., p. 65.
31. Georges Sorel, *Reflections on Violence* (Collier Books, New York 1950), p. 124.
32. Schmitt, *Römischer Katholizismus und politische Form*, p. 56.
33. Ibid.
34. Ibid., p. 37.
35. Ibid., pp. 57–8.
36. Ibid., p. 37.
37. Ibid., p. 70.
38. Ibid., p. 75. Schmitt rarely used the term 'Abendland', and never as a way to refer to Western Europe in opposition to the Bolshevik East. 'Abendland' in this latter sense was a buzz-word among the right-wing, Catholic literati of Bonn.
39. Quoted in ibid., p. 77.
40. Ibid., p. 80.
41. Interview with Schmitt by Dieter Groh, in Koenen, *Der Fall Carl Schmitt*, p. 60.
42. Schmitt, *Römischer Katholizismus und politische Form*, p. 53.

43. Carl Schmitt, 'Absolutismus' (1926), in Günter Maschke, ed., *Staat, Gross-raum, Nomos* (Duncker & Humblot, Berlin 1995), p. 98.
44. Schmitt, *Römischer Katholizismus und politische Form*, p. 66.
45. Quoted from Dahlheimer, *Der deutsche Katholizismus*, p. 452.
46. Carl Schmitt, *Die Kernfrage des Völkerbundes* (F. Dümmler, Berlin 1926).

5 The Legitimation Crisis of Parliament

1. Carl Schmitt, *Die geistesgeschichtliche Lage des heutigen Parlamentarismus* (Duncker & Humblot, Munich 1926).
2. This is the title of the English-language translation of this work by Ellen Kennedy. 'Crisis of Parliamentary Democracy' is a misleading translation because not only is there no mention of democracy in the original title, but it links parliament and democracy in a way that runs counter to Schmitt's whole argument. I think a more literal translation – 'The Intellectual – Historical Condition of Contemporary Parliamentarism' – would have been better, albeit somewhat awkward.
3. Schmitt never adopted Sorel's understanding of democracy as a government of mediocre notables. This was closer to his understanding of liberalism. In the French Republic, democracy could be attacked as bourgeois; less plausibly so in the Weimar Republic.
4. Schmitt, *Die geistesgeschichtliche Lage des heutigen Parlamentarismus*, p. 7.
5. M. Guizot, *The History of the Origin of Representative Government in Europe* (Henry G. Bohn, London 1852), p. 264.
6. Schmitt, *Die geistesgeschichtliche Lage des heutigen Parlamentarismus*, p. 10.
7. Schmitt, *Die geistesgeschichtliche Lage des heutigen Parlamentarismus*, p. 7.
8. When he was discussing the classical liberal ideas of Constant, Guizot, Mill and De Tocqueville, Schmitt's tone was either sympathetic or gently ironic. He reserved his vitriol for modern-day legal positivism and 'pluralist' theories.
9. Dieter Grimm, *Deutsche Verfassungsgeschichte, 1776–1866* (Suhrkamp, Frankfurt am Main 1988), p. 116.
10. Schmitt, *Die geistesgeschichtliche Lage des heutigen Parlamentarismus*, p. 35.
11. Ibid., p. 22.
12. Carl Schmitt *Verfassungslehre* (Duncker & Humblot, Munich 1928), p. 79.
13. Ibid., p. 231.
14. Terry Eagleton, *The Ideology of the Aesthetic* (Blackwell, London 1990), p. 318.
15. Wyndham Lewis, *The Art of Being Ruled* (Black Sparrow Press, Santa Rosa 1989), p. 132.
16. Georges Sorel, Reflections on Violence (Collier Books, New York 1950), p. 186.
17. Schmitt, *Die geistesgeschichtliche Lage des heutigen Parlamentarismus*, p. 71.
18. Ibid.
19. Ibid., p. 81.
20. Ibid., p. 74.
21. Antonio Gramsci, 'The Modern Prince', in *Selections from the Prison Notebooks* (International Publishers, New York 1980), p. 126.
22. Quoted from Schmitt, *Die geistesgeschichtliche Lage des heutigen Parlamentarismus*, p. 88.

23. Ibid., p. 89.
24. Richard Thoma, 'Zur Ideologie des Parlamentarismus und der Diktatur', *Archiv für Sozialwissenschaft und Sozialpolitik* 53, 1925, pp. 212–17, reprinted in appendix to the translation of *Die geistesgeschichtliche Lage* by Ellen Kennedy: *The Crisis of Parliamentary Democracy* (MIT Press, Cambridge, MA 1987).
25. Schmitt, *Die geistesgeschichtliche Lage des heutigen Parlamentarismus*, p. 5.

6   Status Quo and Peace

1. Carl Schmitt, 'Reichspräsident und Weimar Verfassung', *Kölnische Volkszeitung* 198 (15 March 1925), p. 1.
2. Ibid.
3. Andreas Koenen, *Der Fall Carl Schmitt* (Wissenschaftliche Buchgesellschaft, Darmstadt 1995), p. 125.
4. Joseph Bendersky, *Carl Schmitt: Theorist of the Reich* (Princeton University Press, Princeton, NJ 1983), p. 85.
5. Carl Schmitt, 'Zu Friedrich Meineckes *Idee der Staatsräson*' (1926), in Carl Schmitt, *Positionen und Begriffe* (Duncker & Humblot, Berlin 1940), p. 48.
6. Carl Schmitt, 'Das Rheinland als Objekt internationaler Politik' (1928), in *Positionen und Begriffe*, pp. 20–33.
7. Carl Schmitt, 'Völkerrechtliche Probleme des Rheingebiets' (1928), in ibid., pp. 97–109.
8. Ibid.
9. Carl Schmitt, 'Status Quo and Peace' (1925), in ibid., pp. 37–43.
10. Carl Schmitt, 'Völkerbund und Europa' (1928) in ibid., pp. 80–97.
11. Ibid., p. 96.
12. Ibid., p. 91.
13. Hans Mommsen, *The Rise and Fall of Weimar Democracy* (University of North Carolina Press, Chapel Hill 1996), p. 272.

7   *Rechtsstaat* and Democracy

1. A couple of works have recently been published on debates in Weimar constitutional law focusing on the contributions of Schmitt, Hans Kelsen and Hermann Heller. One is the previously mentioned indispensable work by Peter Caldwell, *Popular Sovereignty and the Crisis of German Constitutional Law* (Duke University Press, Durham, NC 1997), the most recent is David Dyzenhaus's *Legality and Legitimacy* (Oxford University Press, Oxford 1997), which combines the vices of intellectual sloppiness and unbearable moralizing.
2. Caldwell, *Popular Sovereignty*, p. 150.
3. Ingeborg Mauss, 'Volk und Nation im Denken des Aufklärung', *Blätter für deutsche und internationale Politik* 5, 1994, p. 607.
4. Carl Schmitt, 'Der bürgerliche Rechtsstaat' (1928), in Günter Maschke, ed., *Staat, Grossraum, Nomos: Arbeiten aus den Jahren 1916–1969* (Duncker & Humblot, Berlin 1995), p. 45.
5. Aristotle, *Politics* (Penguin, Harmondsworth 1975) Bk 3, ch. 4, p. 105.

6. Dieter Grimm, *Deutsche Verfassungsgeschichte, 1776–1866* (Suhrkamp, Frankfurt am Main 1988), p. 12.
7. Carl Schmitt, *Verfassungslehre* (Duncker & Humblot, Leipzig 1928), pp. 8–9.
8. J.H. Schar, *Legitimacy in the Modern State* (Transaction Books, New Brunswick 1981), p. 23.
9. Hans Kelsen, *Problem der Souveranität und die Theorie des Völkerrechts* (Mohr, Tübingen 1928), pp. 97–8.
10. A great irony arises when one contrasts the views of Kelsen and Schmitt: although Kelsen was a true democrat, popular consent could play no role in his conception of a legal system; while Schmitt, who had a rather more idiosyncratic idea of democracy, considered popular consent the key problem of legal theory in a democratic age.
11. H.L.A. Hart, *The Concept of Law* (Oxford University Press, Oxford 1979), p. 107.
12. Schmitt, *Verfassungslehre*, p. 11.
13. Ibid., p. 80.
14. Alexis de Tocqueville, *Democracy in America* (Vintage, New York 1958).
15. Dieter Grimm, 'The Future of the Constitution', cited in Jürgen Habermas, *Between Facts and Norms* (MIT Press, Cambridge, MA 1995), p. 390.
16. Schmitt, *Verfassungslehre*, p. 22.
17. Ibid., p. 31.
18. Ibid., pp. 172–3.
19. Friedrich Neumann, *The Rule of Law under Siege* (University of Chicago Press, Chicago 1996), p. 33.
20. Schmitt, *Verfassungslehre*, p. 153.
21. Ibid., p. 243.
22. Ibid., p. 314.
23. In fact he indicated his preference for a moderate solution to this problem by repeated references to Aristotle's conception of *politea*: moderate democracy as the best form of mixed government (ibid., pp. 202, 216, 228).

8 The Crisis of Political Reason

1. Joseph Bendersky, *Carl Schmitt: Theorist of the Reich* (Princeton University Press, Princeton, NJ 1983), p. 35.
2. Ibid., p. 57. It should be pointed out, however, that by the late 1920s the two colleges were slowly becoming more intimate.
3. Ibid., p. 61.
4. This is one of the reasons why many of those who were forced to leave the country in 1933 would portray him as especially villainous. He was probably one of the few figures on the Right with whom they had ever come into intellectual contact.
5. Ellen Kennedy, 'Carl Schmitt and the Frankfurt School', *Telos* 71, Spring 1987, pp. 37–67. Although this article is informative, it makes some highly implausible assertions: Kennedy, self-stylized defender of liberal democracy, claims that Schmitt's significant intellectual influence on Kirchheimer and Neumann demonstrates that left- and right-wing criticisms of the Weimar Republic were motivated by the same antiliberal animus. The problem with this kind of argument is that any two points on the political spectrum can

be connected in this way, and nothing interesting is demonstrated. Unfortunately, the impassioned responses to Kennedy by Professor Martin Jay and others in subsequent issues of *Telos* were so concerned to deny any possible influence by Schmitt on the Frankfurt School that they tacitly accepted the premiss of Kennedy's argument.

6. Walter Benjamin, *Gesammelte Briefe* (Suhrkamp, Frankfurt am Main 1997), vol. 3, p. 558.

7. Carl Schmitt, *Der Begriff des Politischen* (Duncker & Humblot, Berlin 1963), 4th edn.

8. A recently published book by Heinrich Meier – *Carl Schmitt and Leo Strauss: The Hidden Dialogue* (University of Chicago Press, Chicago 1995) – traces the path of these alterations through the successive editions of the work between 1927 and 1933. Meier demonstrates that Schmitt moved from a concept of the political as an autonomous domain to one in which the political is an intensification of enmity. He shows how Leo Strauss's criticisms of the 1932 edition were incorporated into the 1933 edition. But in no way do any of these changes demonstrate Meier's extraordinary thesis: that behind a deceptive secular disguise, Schmitt was a Catholic fundamentalist who believed that all politics eventually came down to a struggle between Christ and Antichrist. There were quite a few people who openly wrote in this apocalypse-mongering style at the time; Schmitt was simply not one of them, and had he been, he would not have gone to such elaborate lengths to conceal his views. Schmitt's relationship to theology is more complex than Meier's thesis can allow for. The changes introduced between 1927 and 1933, far from indicating Schmitt's continuing allegiance to an antisecular political theology, overwhelmingly demonstrate the opposite: the growing importance of this worldly idea of a 'total state'.

9. Schmitt, *Der Begriff des Politischen*, p. 20.

10. Leo Strauss to Carl Schmitt, 4 September 1932, cited from Meier, *Carl Schmitt and Leo Strauss*, p. 125.

11. Schmitt, *Der Begriff des Politischen*, p. 24.

12. Quoted from ibid., pp. 24–5.

13. Ibid., p. 67.

14. Carl Schmitt, 'Machiavelli' (1927), in Günter Maschke, ed., *Staat, Grossraum, Nomos: Arbeiten aus den Jahren 1916–1969* (Duncker & Humblot, Berlin 1995), p. 103.

15. Noticing, perhaps, that such a formulation might appear difficult to reconcile with Christian teaching, Schmitt sought to cover his exposed flank with a little creative exegesis. He argued that the enemy whom we are commanded to love was not the public enemy of a political community – *hostis* – but only the private enemy – *inimicus*. Quite apart from the fact that distinctions which could be expressed in Latin might have had no counterpart in the languages in which Scripture was originally written, it is inconceivable that such a distinction would have made sense to anybody in the early Christian communities. Schmitt probably came across this distinction between *hostis* and *inimicus* in the works of Cicero, who did in fact distinguish between the robber-band and the legitimate enemy [*legitimus hostis*] with whom one signs legal treaties: Cicero, *De Officiis* (Heinemann, London 1975), III, 108.

16. Plato, *Collected Dialogues* (Princeton University Press, Princeton, NJ 1973), p. 1227.
17. Meier, *Carl Schmitt and Leo Strauss*, p. 22.
18. For a rigorous discussion of the implications of this 'intensification model' of the political, see Uwe Justus Wenzel's contribution to *Die Autonomie des Politischen*, ed. Hans-Georg Flickinger (VCH Verlagsgesellschaft, Weinheim 1990).
19. Herfried Münkler, *Im Namen des Staates: Die Begründung der Staatsräson in der frühen Neuzeit* (S. Fischer, Frankfurt am Main 1987), p. 36.
20. Schmitt, *Der Begriff des Politischen*, p. 47.
21. Meier, *Carl Schmitt and Leo Strauss*, pp. 26–7. Meier astutely identifies the shift in rhetorical strategy between the 1927 and 1932 editions.
22. Cited from Paul Noack, *Carl Schmitt: eine Biographie* (Propyläen Verlag, Berlin 1993).
23. Carl Schmitt, *Ex Captivitate Salus* (Greven Verlag, Cologne 1950), p. 89.
24. Schmitt, *Der Begriff des Politischen*, 3rd edn, p. 12.
25. Ibid., 2nd edn, p. 40.
26. *Widerstand*, Heft 12, 1932, pp. 369–75.
27. Schmitt, *Der Begriff des Politischen*, p. 64. Meier cites the bit about 'necessary intellectual presuppositions' (*Carl Schmitt and Leo Strauss*, Ernst Niekisch, p. 52), but leaves out the rest.
28. Quoted from Schmitt, *Der Begriff des Politischen*, p. 57 fn.
29. Leo Strauss to Carl Schmitt, in Meier, *Carl Schmitt and Leo Strauss*.
30. Schmitt, *Der Begriff des Politischen*, p. 64.
31. Carl Schmitt, *Aufzeichnungen der Jahre 1947–1951* (Duncker & Humblot, Berlin 1991), p. 220.
32. Jacques Derrida, *The Politics of Friendship* (Verso, London and New York 1997), p. 84.
33. Schmitt, *Aufzeichnungen der Jahre 1947–1951*, p. 36.
34. Schmitt, 1963 preface to *Der Begriff des Politischen*, p. 17.
35. Schmitt, *Der Begriff des Politischen*, p. 46.
36. Ibid., p. 71.
37. Ibid., p. 74.

9   The Elites: Between Pluralism and Fascism

1. Carl Schmitt, 'Donoso Cortes in Berlin, 1849' (1927), in *Positionen und Begriffe* (Duncker & Humblot, Berlin 1940), p. 77.
2. Carl Schmitt *Ex Captivitate Salus* (Greven Verlag, Cologne 1950), p. 35.
3. Andreas Koenen, *Der Fall Carl Schmitt* (Wissenschaftliche Buchgesellschaft, Darmstadt 1995), pp. 87–95. The information here on Schmitt's position on the social and academic map of Berlin, and his network of connections, comes from the extraordinarily detailed account provided by Koenen.
4. Paul Noack, *Carl Schmitt: eine Biographie* (Propyläen Verlag, Berlin 1993), p. 99.
5. Carl Schmitt, *Der Hüter der Verfassung* (Duncker & Humblot, Berlin 1931), p. 81. Although Schmitt had no specialist knowledge of economics, he was an astute observer of the political significance of economic developments.

During his years at Bonn his intuitions on these matters might have begun
to take on a more concrete form in discussions with his colleague, Joseph
Schumpeter. Whatever the source of his ideas about the economy, his
knowledge of capitalism as an economic system was so deep that even as he
began to sense the need for a radical break with economic orthodoxy, he
never took seriously the corporatist and pseudo-socialist jargon fashionable
in broad circles of the Weimar Right.

6. Koenen, *Der Fall Carl Schmitt*, p. 95.
7. Ibid.
8. Popitz as a professional bureaucrat and theoretician is the subject of two
   very useful works: Hildemarie Dieckmann, *Johannes Popitz – Entwicklung und
   Wirksamkeit in der Zeit der Weimarer Republik* (Lutz, Berlin 1960); Arwed
   Bentin, *Johannes Popitz und Carl Schmitt: Zur wirtschaftlichen Theorie des totalen
   Staates in Deutschland* (C.H. Beck, Munich 1972).
9. Cited from Helmut Quaritsch, *Positionen und Begriffe* (Duncker & Humblot,
   Berlin 1989), pp. 102–3. This book provides an interpretation of some of
   the essays in Schmitt's collection of the same title published in 1940.
10. Ibid., p. 106.
11. Kurt Sontheimer, *Antidemokratisches Denken in der Weimarer Republik* (Nym-
    phenberger Verlagshandlung, Munich 1962), 3rd edn, 1992.
12. Klaus-Peter Hoepke, *Die deutsche Rechte und der italienische Faschismus* (Droste
    Verlag, Düsseldorf 1968).
13. Joseph Bendersky, *Carl Schmitt: Theorist of the Reich* (Princeton University
    Press, Princeton, NJ 1983), pp. 135–6.
14. Michael Mann forthcoming work on Fascism.
15. Koenen, *Der Fall Carl Schmitt*, pp. 60–61.
16. Ibid., p. 112.
17. Ibid., p. 163.
18. Quoted from ibid., p. 175.
19. Quoted from ibid., p. 177.
20. By 'inner' Schmitt distinguished such literary–cultural discontents from
    political and social protest.
21. Schmitt, *Ex Captivitate Salus*, p. 19.
22. Quoted from Wilhelm Neuss by Piet Tommissen, 'Bausteine zu einer
    wissenschaftlichen Biographie', in Helmut Quaritsch, ed., *Complexio Opposi-
    torum* (Duncker & Humblot, Berlin 1988), p. 92.
23. Hoepke, *Die deutsche Rechte und der italienische Faschismus*, p. 32.
24. Carl Schmitt, *Politische Theologie II: Die Legende der Erledigung jeder politischen
    Theologie* (Duncker & Humblot, Berlin 1970).
25. Erwin von Beckerath, *Wesen und Werden des faschistischen Staates* (Springer,
    Berlin 1927).
26. Carl Schmitt, review of Erwin von Beckerath's *Wesen und Werden des faschis-
    tischen Staates* (1929), in Schmitt, *Positionen und Begriffe*, p. 110.
27. Ibid., p. 112.
28. In the Appendix to Carl Schmitt, 'Staat als konkreter an geschichtliche
    Epoche gebundener Begriff' (1941), in Carl Schmitt, *Verfassungsrechtliche
    Aufsätze aus den Jahren 1924–1954* (Duncker & Humblot, Berlin 1988), p. 385.
29. Noack, *Carl Schmitt*, p. 154.
30. Karl Mannheim, *Ideologie und Utopie* (F. Cohen, Bonn 1929).

31. Jacques Derrida, *The Politics of Friendship* (Verso, London and New York 1997), p. 107.
32. Koenen, *Der Fall Carl Schmitt*, p. 54.
33. Carl Schmitt, 'Das Zeitalter der Neutralisierungen und Entpolitisierungen', in Schmitt, *Positionen und Begriffe*, p. 121.
34. Ibid., p. 121.
35. Ibid.
36. Ibid.
37. Schmitt, *Ex Captivitate Salus*, p. 27.
38. Schmitt, 'Das Zeitalterder Neutralisierungen und Entpolitisierungen', p. 124.
39. Ibid., p. 129.
40. Ibid., p. 368.
41. Leo Strauss, 'Notes on *The Concept of the Political*' (1932), reprinted with Carl Schmitt, *The Concept of the Political*.
42. Schmitt, 'Das Zeitalter der Neutralisierungen und Entpolitisierungen', pp. 130–31.
43. Ibid.
44. Carl Schmitt, 'Donoso Cortes in Berlin, 1849' (1927), pp. 75–85.
45. Carl Schmitt, 'Der unbekannte Donoso Cortes' (1929), in *Positionen und Begriffe*, p. 116.
46. Ibid., p. 119.
47. T.S. Eliot, *After Strange Gods* (Harcourt & Brace, New York 1934), pp. 45–6.
48. Schmitt, *Ex Captivitate Salus*, p. 90.
49. Leo Strauss, 'Comments on *The Concept of the Political*'; emphasis added.
50. Letter from Ernst Jünger to Carl Schmitt, 14 October 1930, in Helmut Kiesel, ed., *Ernst Jünger – Carl Schmitt Briefe 1930–1983* (Klett–Cotta, Stuttgart 1999), p. 7.
51. Ernst Jünger, *Die totale Mobilmachung* (Junker & Dunnhaupt, Berlin 1934), 2nd edn.
52. Waldemar Gurian, *Um des Reiches Zukunft: Nationale Wiedergeburt oder politische Reaktion?* (Herder & Co., Freiburg 1932).
53. Carl Schmitt, *Hugo Preuss – Sein Staatsbegriff und seine Stellung in der deutschen Staatslehre* (J.C.B. Mohr, Tübingen 1930).
54. Ibid., p. 28 fn.
55. Von Bruch, 'Deutsche Hochschulelehrer als Elite', in *Zeitgeist der Weimarer Republik*, ed. Hans Joachim Schoeps (E. Klett, Stuttgart 1968).
56. Schmitt, *Hugo Preuss*, p. 15.
57. Ibid., p. 16.
58. Mannheim, *Ideologie und Utopie*.
59. Schmitt, *Hugo Preuss*, p. 25.

10 Presidential Rule and Judicial Activism

1. Earlier, on 8 November 1923, the Reich Court had ruled that on the basis of Articles 153 and 242 of the Constitution, creditors who had been wiped out by hyperinflation could make a claim for compensation. When the government tried to respond to this by having a law passed in which the nominal value of the currency was established as legal tender for all debts, the Reich Court threatened to disobey any such law. Incidents such as this

strengthened Schmitt's conviction that judicial activism was a threat to effective government.

2. Carl Schmitt, 'Das Reichsgericht als Hüter der Verfassung', *Die Reichsgerichtspraxis im deutschen Rechtsleben. Festgabe der juristen Fakultäten zum 50jährigen Bestehen des Reichsgericht*, vol. 1, 1929, pp. 154–78.

3. Benjamin Constant developed the concept of a 'pouvoir neutre et intermédiaire' to define the role of the monarch in the constitution of Restoration France. As Kelsen would point out, this was an idea rooted in the pre-democratic age of early constitutionalism.

4. Peter Caldwell, *Popular Sovereignty and the Crisis of German Constitutional Law* (Duke University Press, Durham, NC 1997), p. 146.

5. Carl Schmitt, *Der Hüter der Verfassung* (Duncker & Humblot, Berlin 1931), pp. 12–13.

6. Caldwell, *Popular Sovereignty*, p. 147.

7. Ibid.

8. Ibid., p. 160.

9. Schmitt, *Der Hüter der Verfassung*, p. 1.

10. Hans Kelsen,'Wer soll der Hüter der Verfassung sein?', in *Die Wiener rechtstheoretische Schule* (Pustet, Munich 1968).

11. Ibid.

12. Andreas Koenen, *Der Fall Carl Schmitt* (Wissenschaftliche Buchgesellschaft, Darmstadt 1995), p. 125. The article referred to here is the original piece from 1929, not the book version.

13. Ibid.

14. Hans Mommsen, *The Rise and Fall of Weimar Democracy* (University of North Carolina Press, Chapel Hill 1996), p. 282.

15. Ibid., p. 293.

16. Ibid., p. 272.

17. Geoff Eley, 'Conservatives and Radical Nationalists in Germany', in *Fascists and Conservatives*, ed. Martin Blinkhorn (Unwin Hyman, Boston, MA 1990), pp. 53–4.

18. Mommsen, *The Rise and Fall of Weimar Democracy*, p. 359.

19. Carl Schmitt, 'Verfassungsrechtliche Gutachten über die Frage, ob der Reichspräsident befugt ist, auf grund des Art 48 abs. 2 RV finanzgesetzvertretende Verordnungen zu erlassen', in Joseph Bendersky, *Carl Schmitt: Theorist of the Reich* (Princeton University Press, Princeton, NJ 1983), p. 124.

20. Ibid., p. 144.

21. Mommsen, *The Rise and Fall of Weimar Democracy*, p. 395.

22. Heinrich Muth 'Carl Schmitt in der deutschen Innenpolitik des Sommers 1932', *Historische Zeitschrift*, Beiheft 1, Beiträge zur Geschichte der Weimarer Republik (1971) pp. 75–147.

23. Ibid.

24. Schmitt, *Der Hüter der Verfassung*, p. 73.

25. Ibid., p. 81.

26. Ibid., p. 80.

27. Ibid., p. 370.

28. Carl Schmitt, 'Gesunde Wirtschaft im starken Staat', *Mitteilungen des Vereins zur Wahrung der gemeinsamen wirtschaftlichen Interessen in Rheinland und Westphalen*, Heft 21 (23 November 1932), pp. 13–32.

29. Schmitt, *Der Hüter der Verfassung*, p. 91.

30. Ibid., p. 107.
31. Carl Schmitt, 'Eine Warnung vor falschen politischen Fragestellungen' (1930) in *Der Ring*, Jg. 3, Heft 48 (30 November 1930), pp. 253–6.
32. Mommsen, *The Rise and Fall of Weimar Democracy*, p. 95.
33. Carl Schmitt, in '*Langnamverein Berichte*', 1930, p. 964, cited in Paul Noack, *Carl Schmitt: eine Biographie* (Propyläen Verlag, Berlin 1993), p. 126.
34. Mommsen, *The Rise and Fall of Weimar Democracy*, p. 419.
35. Ibid., p. 358.

11   Legality and Legitimacy

1. Hans Mommsen, *The Rise and Fall of Weimar Democracy* (University of North Carolina, Chapel Hill 1996), p. 467.
2. Carl Schmitt, 'Der Missbrauch der Legalität', *Tägliche Rundschau*, 19 July 1932.
3. Carl Schmitt, 'Gesunde Wirtschaft im starken Staat', *Mitteilungen des Vereins zur Wahrung der gemeinsamen Wirtschaftlichen Interessen in Rheinland und Westphalen*, Heft 21 (23 November 1932).
4. Carl Schmitt, *Legalität und Legitimität* (Duncker & Humblot, Berlin 1988), 4th edn.
5. Ibid., p. 32.
6. Ibid., p. 31.
7. Ibid., p. 35.
8. Ibid., pp. 50–51. At the time when this was written, there was considerable sympathy in bourgeois public opinion for Nazi and DNVP accusations that the police, under Prussian Interior Minister Severing, were soft on the Communists. The fact that Schmitt did not explicitly identify with this widespread sentiment at this point is surely noteworthy.
9. Ibid., p. 52.
10. Jürgen Habermas, *Between Facts and Norms* (MIT Press, Cambridge, MA 1995), p. 247.
11. Schmitt, *Legalität und Legitimität*, p. 60.
12. Ibid., p. 60.
13. Habermas, *Between Facts and Norms*, p. 396.
14. Schmitt, *Legalität und Legitimität*, p. 12.

12   Trial and Endgame

1. Paul Noack, *Carl Schmitt: eine Biographie* (Propyläen Verlag, Berlin 1993), p. 138.
2. Geoff Eley, 'Conservatives and Radical Nationalists in Germany', in Martin Blinkhorn, ed., *Fascists and Conservatives* (Unwin Hyman, Boston, MA 1990), p. 56.
3. Arwed Bentin, *Johannes Popitz und Carl Schmitt: Zur wirtschaftlichen Theorie des totalen staates in Deutschland* (C.H. Beck, Munich 1972), p. 20.
4. Ibid., p. 27.
5. Ibid., p. 22.
6. Carl Schmitt, 'Die Machtpositionen der modernen Staates' (1933) in

Verfassungsrechtliche Aufsätze aus den Jahren 1924–1954 (Duncker & Humblot, Berlin 1958), p. 367.

7. Hermann Heller, 'Die neue Ordnung des Reiches', in *Gesammelte Schriften* (Sijthoff, Leiden 1971), p. 397.

8. Hans Mommsen, *The Rise and Fall of Weimar Democracy* (University of North Carolina Press, Chapel Hill 1996), p. 451.

9. Schmitt's assertion that the Papen government could claim to be 'above parties' was based on the manifestly implausible assumption that impartiality was the same thing as being widely hated by the whole population, and all its parties. The idea that legitimacy in a modern state had to be based on the will of the people was fading from his mind.

10. Carl Schmitt, 'Preussen contra Reich vor dem Staatsgerichtshof', *Stenogrammbericht der Verhandlungen vor dem Staatsgerichtshof in Leipzig vom 10 bis 14 und vom 17 October 1932* (Berlin 1932).

11. Ibid.

12. Cited in Heinrich Muth, 'Carl Schmitt in der deutschen Innenpolitik des Sommers 1932', *Historische Zeitschrift*, Beiheft 1, Beiträge zur Geschichte der Weimarer Republik (1971), p. 138.

13. Mommsen, *The Rise and Fall of Weimar Democracy*, pp. 485–6.

14. Carl Schmitt, 'Gesunde Wirtschaft im starken Staat', *Mitteilungen des Vereins zur Wahrung der gemeinsamen wirtschaftlichen Interessen in Rheinland und Westphalen*, Heft 21 (23 November 1932).

15. Joseph Bendersky, *Carl Schmitt: Theorist of the Reich* (Princeton University Press, Princeton, NJ 1983), p. 183.

16. Dieter Groh and Klaus Figge, 'Interview mit Carl Schmitt für die Sendung *Zeitgenossen* des Südwestfunks' (1 February 1972), published in Piet Tommissen, *Over en in zake Carl Schmitt* (Duncker & Humblot, Berlin 1996), p. 89.

17. Quoted from Manfred Dahlheimer, *Der deutsche Katholizismus 1888–1936* (Verlag Ferdinand Schöningh, Paderborn 1999), p. 453.

18. Noack, *Carl Schmitt*, p. 162.

19. Cited from ibid., p. 156.

13 The National Socialist Revolution

1. Andreas Koenen, *Der Fall Carl Schmitt* (Wissenschaftliche Buchgesellschaft, Darmstadt 1995).

2. Ibid., p. 221.

3. Ferdinand Hermens, *Zwischen Politik und Vernunft: Gesammelte Aufsätze aus drei Welten* (Duncker & Humblot, Berlin 1969), pp. 158–9.

4. Dieter Groh and Klaus Figge, 'Interview mit Carl Schmitt für die Sendung *Zeitgenossen* des Südwestfunks' published in Piet Tommissen, *Over en zake Carl Schmitt* (Duncker & Humblot, Berlin 1996), p. 169.

5. Carl Schmitt, *Der Begriff des Politischen* (Hanseatische Verlaganstalt, Hamburg 1933), p. 21.

6. Carl Schmitt, *Staat, Bewegung, Volk: Dreigliederung der politischen Einheit* (HAVA, Hamburg 1933).

7. Carl Schmitt, 'Das Gesetz zur Behebung der Not von Volk und Reich', *Deutsche Juristen-Zeitung*, Jg. 38, Heft 7 (1 April 1933), pp. 455–8.

8. RW Hauptstaatsarchiv, cited from Paul Noack, p. 171.

9. Ibid. cited from Noack, Carl Schmitt, *Carl Schmitt: eine Biographie* (Propyläen Verlag, Berlin 1993), p. 173.

10. Ibid., p. 175.

11. Groh/Figge interview, p. 108.

12. Nicolaus Sombart, *Jugend in Berlin* (Carl Hanser Verlag, Munich 1984), p. 250. The chapter on Schmitt in this work provides the best psychological portrait of Schmitt in the secondary literature, by someone who knew him very well. Sombart recollects incidents which vividly capture the disconcerting and unusual cast of Schmitt's mind: though the Golem was a familiar figure in the film and literature of the Weimar era, it would not perhaps have occurred to most to identify Hitler with a Jewish mythological figure. The only fault in this otherwise outstanding work is Sombart's outrageous and bizarre theory that the interpretative key to Schmitt's political thought, and even his personal life, is an uncomprehending fear of women, seen as the mythic enemy of the German male. While this suggestion does not even warrant a refutation as a characterization of Schmitt's work, it should be pointed out that Sombart's account of life in the Schmitt household refutes his own insinuation of misogyny: Schmitt appears as exceedingly deferential to his wife, and informal – indeed, unpatriarchal – with his daughter.

13. Koenen, *Der Fall Carl Schmitt*, p. 351.

14. Ibid., pp. 271–7.

15. The anecdote comes from Karl Löwith, and is cited from Manfred Dahlheimer, *Der deutsche Katholizismus 1888–1936* (Verlag Ferdinand Schöningh, Paderborn 1999), p. 477.

16. Ibid., p. 367.

17. Ibid., p. 321.

18. Ibid., p. 365.

19. Bernd Rüthers, *Wissenschaft als Zeitgeist-Verstärkung?* (C.H. Beck, Munich 1989), p. 67.

20. By 1938, roughly 45 per cent of professors and lecturers in the law faculty had lost their position (ibid., p. 61).

21. Ahlmann to Schmitt, 21 June 1933, *RW Archiv*, cited in ibid., p. 366.

22. Carl Schmitt, 'Die deutschen Intellektuellen', *Westdeutscher Beobachter*, Jg. 9, no. 126, 31 May 1933.

23. Koenen, *Der Fall Carl Schmitt*, p. 188.

24. Carl Schmitt, 'Die Bedeutung des neuen Staatsrat', *Westdeutscher Beobachter*, 17 July 1933.

25. Carl Schmitt, 'Das Gespräch über die Macht und den Zugang zum Machthaber', *Gemeinschaft und Politik*, Jg. 2, Heft 10 (1954), pp. 9–15. The best discussion of these questions – how should the greatest minds of an age conceive of tyranny, and on this basis what are the prospects of collaboration? – can be found in the now famous exchange and correspondence between Leo Strauss and Alexandre Kojève, published in Strauss's *On Tyranny* (Cornell University Press, Ithaca, NY 1968).

26. Ernst Jünger knew Hitler and his type well, and kept his distance from the new regime. Sensing the dangers of collaboration, he advised Schmitt to turn down the chance to become *Staatsrat*, leave the country, and finish an opus on legal theory at the home of his in-laws in Serbia (Helmut Kiesel,

ed., *Ernst Jünger – Carl Schmitt Briefe 1930–1983* [Klett–Cotta, Stuttgart 1997], p. 679).

27. Helmut Koenen, *Der Fall Carl Schmitt*, p. 442.
28. Ibid., p. 444.
29. Ibid., p. 503.
30. Ibid., p. 495.
31. Ibid.
32. Schmitt, *Staat, Bewegung, Volk.*
33. Koenen, *Der Fall Carl Schmitt*, p. 523.
34. Ibid., p. 524.
35. Schmitt, *Staat, Bewegung, Volk*, pp. 31–2.
36. Schmitt to Jean-Pierre Faye, 5 October 1960, cited from Koenen, *Der Fall Carl Schmitt*, p. 777.
37. Reported in *Frankfurter Zeitung*, 19 November 1935; cited in Koenen, *Der Fall Carl Schmitt*, p. 538.
38. *Neuer Vorwärts*, 29 December 1935.

14　The Revolution in Legal Thought

1. Andreas Koenen, *Der Fall Carl Schmitt* (Wissenschaftliche Buchgesellschaft, Darmstadt 1995), p. 502.
2. Ibid., p. 552.
3. Carl Schmitt, *Staat, Bewegung, Volk: Dreigliederung der politischen Einheit* (HAVA, Hamburg 1933), p. 43.
4. Carl Schmitt, 'Nationalsozialismus und Rechtsstaat', *Juristische Wochenschrift* 63, 1934, pp. 713–18. Interestingly, this contrasting of the *Rechtsstaat* with the Just State was Slavophile in origin, and was used in the nineteenth century to distinguish Western liberalism from the Russian popular community.
5. Thomas Hobbes, *Dialogue between a Philosopher and a Student of the Common Law* (University of Chicago Press, Chicago 1987).
6. Carl Schmitt 'Der Führer schützt das Recht', in *Positionen und Begriffe* (Duncker & Humblot, Berlin 1940).
7. Carl Schmitt, 'Neue Leitsätze für die Rechtspraxis', *Juristische Wochenschrift*, Jg. 62, 1933, p. 2793.
8. Koenen, *Der Fall Carl Schmitt*, p. 490.
9. Carl Schmitt, *Über die drei Arten des rechtswissenschaftlichen Denkens* (HAVA, Hamburg 1934).
10. Plato, *The Laws*, in *Collected Dialogues* (Princeton University Press, Princeton, NJ 1973).
11. Leo Strauss considered Schmitt's criticisms of decisionism here to be a tacit concession that the only real alternative to positivism was a pre-modern version of natural right. Although Schmitt's use of the word 'nomos' points in this direction, it also simultaneously points to the historical origins and political presuppositions of the phenomenon of legal order – a sort of natural right without naturalism. In his postwar notebooks, he argued that in the modern world, the language of natural right had ceased to be believable: 'Natural right is a deceptive, anachronistic term in the era of

natural sciences . . .' (Carl Schmitt, *Aufzeichnungen der Jahren 1947–1951* [Duncker & Humblot, Berlin 1991], p. 195).

12. Habermas's claim that Schmitt's conception of popular sovereignty is connected to his later Nazism is implausible; it cannot be reconciled with the fact that he simply dropped the Rousseauian problematic after he became a Nazi.

13. Carl Schmitt, *Der Nomos der Erde* (Duncker & Humblot, Berlin 1950, 3rd edn 1988), p. 37.

14. Ibid.

15. Schmitt no doubt knew that the early modern 'reception' of Roman law had gone much further in Germany than in the rest of Europe outside the Mediterranean zone. 'Germanic' customary law had a greater influence on the Code Napoléon, drawn in large part from the customary laws of northern France, which – like England but unlike Germany – remained outside the Roman law zone.

16. Freiherr von Soden, 'Kritik der Kritik', *Allgemeine Rundschau* 23, 1926, cited from Manfred Dahlheimer, *Der deutsche Katholizismus 1888–1936* (Verlag Ferdinand Schöningh, Paderborn 1999), p. 300.

17. Kenneth Dyson, *The State Tradition* (Oxford University Press, Oxford 1987), p. 163.

18. Schmitt, *Über die drei Arten*, p. 17. This translation is not meant to suffice for those who are interested in Hölderlin's poetry. I wish only to draw attention to the significance of the word 'encounter'.

19. G.W.F. Hegel, *Philosophy of Right* (Cambridge University Press, Cambridge 1987).

20. Schmitt, *Über die drei Arten des rechtswissenschaftlichen Denkens*.

21. Max Weber, *Economy and Society* (University of California Press, Berkeley 1978), p. 714.

22. Carl Schmitt, 'Vergleichender Überblick über die neueste Entwicklung des Problems der gesetzgeberischen Ermächtigungen' (1936) in *Positionen und Begriffe*, p. 228.

15 Flight Forward and Retreat

1. Paul Noack, *Carl Schmitt: eine Biographie* (Propyläen Verlag, Berlin 1993), p. 185.

2. Helmut Quaritsch, ed., *Positionen und Begriffe* (Duncker & Humblot, Berlin 1989), p. 101.

3. Carl Schmitt, 'Der Führer schützt das Recht', in *Positionen und Begriffe*, p. 201.

4. *Der Angriff*, 1 September 1936, cited from Andreas Koenen, *Der Fall Carl Schmitt* (Wissenschaftliche Buchgesellschaft, Darmstadt 1995), p. 703.

5. Adams to Günther Krauss, 3 December 1934, cited from ibid., p. 628.

6. This story of Schmitt's 'encirclement' is told with little variation in several of the above-mentioned works which deal with his Nazi period.

7. Waldemar Gurian, 'Entscheidung und Ordnung' (1934) *Schweizerische Rundschau*, 34 Jg., pp. 566–76.

8. Koenen, *Der Fall Carl Schmitt*, p. 708.

9. Bernd Rüthers, *Wissenschaft als Zeitgeist Verstärkung?* (C.H. Beck, Munich 1989), p. 96.

10. Carl Schmitt, 'Das Judentum in der deutschen Rechtswissenschaft', in 'Die deutsche Rechtswissenschaft im Kampf gegen den jüdischen Geist' (*Deutsche Juristen-Zeitung*, Jg. 41, Heft 20 (15 October 1936), pp. 1193–99.

11. Ibid.

12. E.R. Curtius, *Der Deutsche Geist in Gefahr* (Deutsche Verlags-Anstalt, Stuttgart/Berlin 1932), p. 85.

13. Ibid.

14. Schmitt had mentioned Stahl, defender of the Prussian state in the deeply reactionary 1850s, in his Weimar writings on a couple of occasions, always associating him with De Maistre and his ilk. But as a Jewish convert to Christianity, Stahl could now be vilified as an infiltrating agent of corruption and revolution, nesting in the citadels of the old Prussian state. After 1935 Schmitt was not above writing like a typical Nazi hack in identifying Stahl with Karl Marx, and insisting on calling him Stahl-Jolson.

15. Goering to the editorial board of the *Schwarze Korps*, 21 December 1936, cited from Koenen, *Der Fall Carl Schmitt*, p. 752.

16. Nicolaus Sombart, *Jugend in Berlin* (Carl Hanser Verlag, Munich 1984).

16   The Leviathan Myth

1. Carl Schmitt, 'Der Staat als Mechanismus bei Hobbes und Descartes', p. 100. This has now been translated by George Schwab as an accompanying essay along with *The Leviathan in the Political Theory of Thomas Hobbes: The Meaning and Failure of a Political Symbol* (Greenwood Press, Westport, CT 1996). All references come from this translation of the essay and the longer work.

2. Ibid., p. 94.

3. Ibid., p. 69.

4. B. Netanyahu, *Abravanel* (Jewish Publication Society of America, Philadelphia 1968), p. 234.

5. Leo Strauss, in *Isaac Abravanel: Six Lectures* (Cambridge University Press, Cambridge 1937).

6. Schmitt, *Leviathan in the Political Theory of Thomas Hobbes*. Shortly before Schmitt published these lectures on *Leviathan* Strauss had finished his own, rather more rigorous work on Hobbes, where he restated the position which Schmitt had attributed to him:

   The Old Testament set up the rule of priests, i.e. a form of government which is bound to issue in Chaos, as the Old Testament record itself shows. ... That is to say the Old Testament laid the foundation for the dualism of power temporal and spiritual which is incompatible with peace, the demand *par excellence* of reason. As regards Christianity it originated in a rebellion against the civil sovereign and therefore was forced to sanction the dualism of the two powers. Holding the view of the Bible which he did, Hobbes was compelled to try his hand at a natural explanation of the Biblical religion. The fundamental difference between paganism and Biblical religion consists in this: that whereas pagan religion was part of human politics, Biblical religion is part of divine politics, the kingdom of god. (Leo Strauss, *The Political Philosophy of Thomas Hobbes* [Oxford University Press, Oxford 1936]).

7. Erik Peterson, a former friend and colleague from Bonn, with whom Schmitt used to discuss theological questions, wrote from Rome, where he lived in voluntary exile, on the tendency of this line of argument: 'The polemic against the *potestas indirecta* has a meaning only if one has renounced Christianity and has decided for Heathenism.'

8. J.-J. Rousseau, *The Social Contract* (Harper & Row, New York 1984).

9. Schmitt, *Leviathan in the Political Theory of Thomas Hobbes*, p. 73.

10. Ibid.

11. How seriously should Schmitt's allusions to Scripture be taken – are they there to generate a spurious aura of arcana, or do they play some more essential role in the structure of the argument? Martin Leutzsch has examined Schmitt's biblical references exhaustively, and identified a pattern of rather cavalier indifference to the protocols of Scriptural exegesis:

> He is not a Bible reader in the same sense as, say, Thomas Hobbes. References to the Bible are rare in his publications, and the Bible is not *ratio scripta* for him as it is for the jurists and theologians of the early modern period. (Martin Leutzsch, 'Die Wirkungsgeschichte', in *Die eigentlich katholische Verschärfung* [Wilhelm Fink Verlag, Munich 1994])

12. Thomas Hobbes, *Leviathan* (Hackett, Indianapolis, IN/Cambridge 1994), ch. XVIII, p. 210.

13. Hobbes, 'Epistle Dedicatory to the *Leviathan*'.

14. Schmitt, *The Leviathan in the Political Theory of Thomas Hobbes*, p. 32.

15. Strauss, *The Political Philosophy of Thomas Hobbes*. Schmitt, no doubt, read Strauss's book only later, but it is probable that his contacts with Strauss from 1932 on allowed him to anticipate his thesis. Schmitt actually wrote a letter of recommendation to the Rockefeller Foundation which allowed Strauss to leave Germany, and pursue his research on Hobbes at Oxford.

16. Hobbes, *Leviathan*, ch. XLVII, p. 482.

17. Ibid., pp. 142–3.

18. It is hard to make sense of this claim on the basis of anything Spinoza actually wrote. Precisely because Spinoza did not conceive of political authority as arising out of an original, collective experience of fear, he could argue that the most powerful state would be the one in which subjects perceived their own power as inseparable from the power of the state. Because for Spinoza the 'goal' of the state was not simply security but liberty and power, there was room in his theory for a conception of political virtue in which dying for a political cause was, under certain circumstances, no longer an act of irrational hubris. Another passage from the *Tractatus Theologico-Politicus* reveals that Spinoza was often temperamentally closer to the republican Machiavelli than to the monarchist Hobbes: 'For men whose consciences are clear do not fear death or beg for mercy like criminals, since their minds are not tormented by remorse for deeds of shame; they think it a merit, not a punishment to die for a good cause, and an honour to die for freedom' (Baruch Spinoza, *Tractatus Theologico-Politicus* [Dover, New York 1951]).

19. Schmitt, *The Leviathan in the Political Theory of Thomas Hobbes*, p. 35.

20. Ibid., p. 79.

21. Carl Schmitt, *Politische Romantik* (Duncker & Humblot, Leipzig 1925), p. 115.

17 Diaspora, Utopia, Katechon

1. Valeriu Marcu, *Die Vertreibung der Juden aus Spanien* (Querido Verlag, Amsterdam 1934), p. 13.
2. Andreas Koenen, *Der Fall Carl Schmitt* (Wissenschaftliche Buchgesellschaft, Darmstadt 1995), p. 372. Originally living as a Communist in Germany, by the late 1920s Marcu was passing through the National Bolshevik circle around Niekisch. Jünger and Schmitt knew him from those years, and corresponded with him in France (Kiesel, p. 770).
3. Marcu, *Die Vertreibung der Juden aus Spanien*, p. 13.
4. Carl Schmitt, *Aufzeichnungen der Jahre 1947–1951* (Duncker & Humblot, Berlin 1991), p. 37.
5. Ibid., p. 154.
6. Marcu, *Die Vertreibung der Juden aus Spanien*, p. 202.
7. Ibid., p. 204.
8. Nicolaus Sombart, *Jugend in Berlin* (Carl Hanser Verlag, Munich 1984), p. 260.
9. Ibid., p. 264.
10. Thomas Hobbes, *Leviathan* (Hackett, Indianapolis, IN/Cambridge 1994), ch. XLIII, p. 407.
11. Barbara Nichtweiss, 'Apokolyptische Verfassungslehre', in *Die eigentlich katholische Verschärfung* (Wilhelm Fink Verlag, Munich 1994), p. 46. The words in quotation marks come from Schmitt, *Aufzeichnungen der Jahre 1947–1951*.
12. Heinrich Meier has claimed that such allusions demonstrate that Schmitt thought history was moving towards some final battle between Christ and the Antichrist. More surprisingly, he does not seem to think that attributing such absurd fundamentalist superstitions to Schmitt discredits him in any way (Heinrich Meier, *Die Lehre Carl Schmitts* [J.B. Metzler, Stuttgart 1994]).
13. Felix Grossheutschi, *Carl Schmitt und die Lehre von Katechon* (Duncker & Humblot, Berlin 1996) cites all the passages in which Schmitt used the term 'Katechon', making it easier to see the radical shifts in the significance it had for him.
14. Jacques Derrida, *The Politics of Friendship* (Verso, London and New York 1997), pp. 173–4.
15. In a 1942 essay entitled 'Beschleuniger wider Willen' (in Günter Maschke, ed., *Staat, Grossraum, Nomos: Arbeiten aus den Jahren 1916–1969* [Duncker & Humblot, Berlin 1995]), it is the force struggling to break through, not the force which restrains this, which is portrayed positively. Indeed, the term 'Katechon' is applied to those who would prop up an unsalvageable status quo: 'Historians and Philosophers should one day examine and describe the diverse figures and types of the world-historical restrainers and delayers.' In this capacity, Schmitt mentioned several individuals who represented unviable political structures doomed by world history: the old Kaiser Franz Josef, representing the European *ancien régime*; and Masaryk and Pilsudski, representing the ethnically unviable rump of this old order.

18 The International Order and World War

1. Günter Maschke, *Der Tod Carl Schmitts* (Karolinger, Vienna 1987), p. 352.
2. Carl Schmitt, 'Die Ära der integralen Politik' in ibid.
3. Carl Schmitt, *Die Wendung zum diskriminierenden Kriegsbegriff* (Duncker & Humblot, Berlin 1985), 2nd edn.
4. Ibid., p. 33.
5. Ibid., p. 52.
6. Carl Schmitt, *Theorie des Partisanen* (Duncker & Humblot, Berlin 1975, 2nd edn), p. 60.
7. There is a remarkably ambivalent footnote in *Die Wendung zum diskriminierenden Kriegsbegriff*, p. 43, where Schmitt writes of aerial bombardment of civilian populations:

   > That the transformation of 'war' into 'not war' does not just involve theoretical fine points is demonstrated by those authors who propose the airforce as a specific weapon of sanctions and civil war, in order to demonstrate the progress of military technology as simultaneously a world-historical progress in the transformation of war into a pacification action against rebellious or civilizationally backward populations, since it is obviously not war when bombs are dropped on such populations.

   This book was published not long after the Luftwaffe bombing of Guernica, and even if its political tendency is not entirely transparent, this passage at least cuts in different directions.
8. Andreas Koenen, *Der Fall Carl Schmitt* (Wissenschaftliche Buchgesellschaft, Darmstadt 1995), p. 786.
9. Ibid., p. 784.
10. Carl Schmitt, 'Über die zwei grossen "Dualismen" des heutigen Rechtssystems' (1939), in Schmitt, *Positionen und Begriffe* (Duncker & Humblot, Berlin 1940), pp. 261–71.
11. Max Weber, *Economy and society* (University of California Press, Berkeley 1978), p. 641.
12. Carl Schmitt, 'Führung oder Hegemonie', in Günter Maschke, ed., *Staat, Grossraum, Nomos: Arbeiten aus den Jahren 1916–1969* (Duncker & Humblot, Berlin 1995), p. 228.
13. Carl Schmitt, 'Raum und Grossraum im Völkerrecht' (1940), in ibid., p. 249.
14. Carl Schmitt, 'Über die zwei grossen "Dualismen" des heutigen Rechtssystems' (1939), in *Positionen und Begriffe*, p. 264.
15. Schmitt, 'Raum und Grossraum im Völkerrecht', p. 249.
16. Frank-Rutger Hausmann, *Frankfurter Allgemeine Zeitung* (13 March 1999, no. 61).
17. Schmitt, *Positionen und Begriffe*, Foreword.
18. Koenen, *Der Fall Carl Schmitt*, p. 823. We can take such references to Christ seriously only if we remember what meaning they have in Schmitt's idiomatic repertoire.
19. Joseph Bendersky, *Carl Schmitt: Theorist of the Reich* (Princeton University Press, Princeton, NJ 1983), p. 259.
20. For an extremely informative treatment of the political context behind Schmitt's conception of *Grossraum* and the Monroe Doctrine, see Lothar Gruchmann, *Nationalsozialistische Grossraumordnung* (Deutsche Verlags-Anstalt, Stuttgart 1962).

21. Schmitt to Jünger, 29 September 1940, in Helmut Kiesel, ed., *Ernst Jünger – Carl Schmitt Briefe 1930–1983* (Klett–Cotta, Stuttgart 1999), p. 104.
22. Schmitt, 'Die Formung des französischen Geistes durch den Legisten' (1940), in *Staat, Grossraum, Nomos*.
23. Carl Schmitt, *Völkerrechtliche Grossraumordnung* (Deutscher Rechtsverlag, Berlin–Leipzig–Vienna 1941), p. 308.
24. Cited from Gruchmann, *Nationalsozialistische Grossraumordnung*, p. 18.
25. Carl Schmitt, 'Der letze globale Linie' (1943), in Maschke, ed., *Staat, Grossraum, Nomos*, p. 447.
26. Schmitt, *Völkerrechtliche Grossraumordnung*, p. 270.
27. Nicolaus Sombart, *Jugend in Berlin* (Carl Hanser Verlag, Munich 1984), p. 266. It is probable that Schmitt was personally affected by at least one aspect of this 'race war': his wife was Serbian, and in the 1920s he had cultivated a sentimental attachment to the Orthodox culture of that country. It is hard to believe that the genocidal practices of the Catholic Croatian Ustasha were not deeply disturbing to him.
28. Carl Schmitt, *Land und Meer* (Reclam Verlag, Leipzig 1942).
29. Sombart, *Jugend in Berlin*, p. 266.
30. Schmitt, *Land und Meer*.
31. Ibid., pp. 47–8.
32. Thomas Hobbes, *Elements of Law* (Cambridge University Press, Cambridge 1928), I.13.3.
33. Schmitt saw in Melville's 'Benito Cereno' a vivid literary encapsulation of his own predicament in the European civil war: it is a short story about a Spanish aristocrat who, after a mutiny on a slave ship, is forced by the mutineers to act as the ship's captain in their dealings with the outside world. What comes across from this dubious analogy is his extraordinary capacity for self-aggrandizement (Carl Schmitt, *Glossarium* [Duncker & Humblot, Berlin 1991]).
34. Schmitt, *Land und Meer*, p. 29.
35. Ibid., p. 58.
36. Ibid., p. 49.
37. Ibid., p. 74.
38. Ibid., p. 76.
39. Ibid.
40. Ibid., p. 41.

19   The Law of the Earth

1. Carl Schmitt, 'Die geschichtliche Lage der europäischen Rechtswissenschaft' (1943–44), in Schmitt, *Verfassungsrechtliche Aufsätze aus den Jahren 1924–1954* (Duncker & Humblot, Berlin 1958).
2. Ibid., p. 398.
3. R.C. van Caenegem, *An Historical introduction to Private Law* (Cambridge University Press, Cambridge 1988), p. 46.
4. Schmitt, 'Die geschichtliche Lage der europäischen Rechtswissenschaft', p. 398.
5. This opposition appears in the work of both Hayek and Oakeshott; see Perry Anderson, 'The Intransigent Right at the End of the Century', *London Review of Books*, vol. 14, no. 18, 24 September 1992.

6. Van Caenegem, *An Historical Introduction*, p. 59.
7. Carl Schmitt, *Der Nomos der Erde* (Duncker & Humblot, Berlin 1988), 3rd edn.
8. Ibid., p. 16.
9. Jean-Jacques Rousseau, *The Social Contract* (Harper & Row, New York 1984), p. 86.

20 Finis Germania

1. Helmut Kiesel, ed., *Ernst Jünger – Carl Schmitt Briefe 1930–1983* (Klett–Cotta, Stuttgart 1999).
2. Carl Schmitt, *Das internationalrechtliche Verbrechen des Angriffskrieges und der Grundsatz 'Nullum crimen, nulla poena sine lege'*, edited with comments and an Afterword by Helmut Quaritsch (Duncker & Humblot, Berlin 1994).
3. Ibid., pp. 16, 23.
4. Schmitt, *Aufzeichnungen der Jahre 1947–1951*, (Duncker & Humblot, Berlin 1991), p. 264.
5. Ibid., p. 45.
6. Schmitt to Jünger, 20 July 1948, in Helmut Kiesel, ed., *Ernst Jünger – Carl Schmitt Briefe 1930–1983* (Klett–Cotta, Stuttgart 1999), p. 232.
7. Ibid., p. 190.
8. Robert Kempner, *Das Dritte Reich im Kreuzverhör* (Esslingen, Munich 1969), p. 298.
9. Carl Schmitt, *Ex Captivitate Salus* (Greven Verlag, Cologne 1950), p. 9.
10. Schmitt, *Aufzeichnungen*, p. 240. In his not yet de-Nazified lexicon 'Nazi' and 'Jew' were equivalent to 'Right' and 'Left', the ultimate enemies in a European civil war which had started in 1917 and had now, in his assessment, got way out of hand.
11. This is the subject of Dirk Van Laak's fascinating and extraordinarily well researched book *Gespräche in der Sicherheit des Schweigens* (Akademie Verlag, Berlin 1993).
12. Schmitt to Jünger, 10 June 1948, in Helmut Kiesel, ed., *Ernst Jünger – Carl Schmitt Briefe, 1930–1983* (Klett–Cotta, 1999), p. 228.
13. Schmitt, *Aufzeichnungen*, p. 109.
14. Ibid., p. 292.

Conclusion

1. Carl Schmitt, 1963 Preface to *Der Begriff des Politischen* (Duncker & Humblot, Berlin), p. 17.
2. Carl Schmitt, *Die Diktatur* (Duncker & Humblot, Leipzig 1921), p. 142.
3. Roberto Unger, *Democracy Realized* (Verso, London and New York 1998), p. 213.
4. Jürgen Habermas, *Die Einbeziehung des Anderen* (Suhrkamp, Frankfurt am Main 1996), p. 396.
5. In ibid.
6. Perry Anderson, *The Origins of Postmodernity* (Verso, London and New York 1999).

Bibliography

Books by Carl Schmitt

Über Schuld und Schuldarten: eine terminologische Untersuchung, Strassburger Inaugural-Dissertation (Breslau 1910).

Gesetz und Urteil: Eine Untersuchung zum Problem der Rechtspraxis: eine Untersuchung zum Problem der Rechtspraxis (C.H. Beck, Munich 1969).

Der Wert des Staates und die Bedeutung des Individuums (C.H. Beck, Munich 1969).

Politische Romantik (Duncker & Humblot, Munich 1925).

Die Diktatur (Duncker & Humblot, Leipzig 1921).

Politische Theologie (Duncker & Humblot, Leipzig 1922).

Römischer Katholizismus und politische Form (Jakob Hegner, Hellerau 1923).

Der Kernfrage des Völkerbundes (F. Dümmler, Berlin 1926).

Die geistesgeschichtliche Lage des heutigen Parlamentarismus (Duncker & Humblot, Munich 1926).

Volksentscheid und Volksbegehren (W. de Gruyter, Berlin Leipzig 1927).

Der Begriff des Politischen (Duncker & Humblot, Berlin 1932).

Carl Schmitt: Der Begriff des Politischen (Hanseatische Verlaganstalt, Hamburg 1933).

Verfassungslehre (Duncker & Humblot, Munich 1928).

Hugo Preuss – Sein Staatsbegriff und Seine Stellung in der deutschen Staatslehre (J.C.B. Mohr, Tübingen 1930).

Der Hüter der Verfassung (Duncker & Humblot, Berlin 1931).

Legalität und Legitimität (Duncker & Humblot, Berlin 1932).

Staat, Bewegung, Volk: Dreigliederung der politischen Einheit (HAVA, Hamburg 1933).

Über die drei Arten des rechtswissenschaftlichen Denkens (HAVA, Hamburg 1934).

Der Leviathan in der Staatslehre Thomas Hobbes (HAVA, Hamburg 1938)/ *The Leviathan in the Political Theory of Thomas Hobbes*, trans. George Schwab (Greenwood Press, Westpore, CT 1996).

Die Wendung zum diskriminierenden Kriegsbegriff (Duncker & Humblot, 1938).

Völkerrechtliche Grossraumordnung (Deutscher Rechtsverlag, Berlin–Leipzig–Vienna 1941).
Land und Meer (Reclam Verlag, Leipzig 1942).
Das internationalrechtliche Verbrechen des Angriffskrieges und der Grundsatz 'Nullum crimen, nulla poena sine lege' (Duncker & Humblot, Berlin 1994).
Ex Captivitate Salus (Greven Verlag, Cologne 1950).
Der Nomos der Erde (Duncker & Humblot, Berlin 1950).
Aufzeichnungen der Jahren 1947–1951 (Duncker & Humblot, Berlin 1991).
Glossarium (Duncker & Humblot, Berlin 1991).
Theorie des Partisanen (Duncker & Humblot, Berlin 1975).
Politische Theologie II: Die Legende der Erledigung jeder politischen Theologie (Duncker & Humblot, Berlin 1970).

Collections of essays written and edited by Carl Schmitt

Positionen und Begriffe (Duncker & Humblot, Berlin 1940).
Verfassungsrechtliche Aufsätze aus den Jahren 1924–1954 (Duncker & Humblot, Berlin 1958).

Collections of essays written by Carl Schmitt with a different editor

Staat, Grossraum, Nomos: Arbeiten aus den Jahren 1916–1969, ed. Günter Maschke (Duncker & Humblot, Berlin 1995).

Major Articles by Carl Schmitt

'Das Rheinland als Objekt internationaler Politik' (1928), in *Positionen und Begriffe.*
'Status Quo and Peace' (1925), in *Positionen und Begriffe.*
'Zu Friedrich Meineckes *Idee der Staatsräson*' (1926), in *Positionen und Begriffe.*
'Donoso Cortes in Berlin, 1849' (1927), in *Positionen und Begriffe.*
'Werden und Wesen des faschistischen Staates' (1929), in *Positionen und Begriffe.*
'Völkerrechtliche Probleme des Rheingebiets' (1928), in *Positionen und Begriffe.*
'Völkerbund und Europa' (1928), in *Positionen und Begriffe.*
'Der unbekannte Donoso Cortes' (1929), in *Positionen und Begriffe.*

'Das Zeitalter der Neutralisierungen und Entpolitisierungen' (1929), in *Positionen und Begriffe*.

'Der Führer schützt das Recht' (1934), in *Positionen und Begriffe*.

'Vergleichender Überblick über die neueste Entwicklung des Problems der gesetzgeberischen Ermächtigungen' (1936), in *Positionen und Begriffe*.

'Über die zwei grossen "Dualismen" des heutigen Rechtssystems' (1939), in *Positionen und Begriffe*.

'Absolutism' (1925), in *Staat, Grossraum, Nomos*.

'Der bürgerliche Rechtsstaat' (1928), in *Staat, Grossraum, Nomos*.

'Machiavelli' (1927), in *Staat, Grossraum, Nomos*.

'Die Formung des französischen Geistes durch den Legisten' (1940), in *Staat, Grossraum, Nomos*.

'Beschleuniger wider Willen' (1942), in *Staat, Grossraum, Nomos*.

'Führung oder Hegemonie' (1940) in *Staat, Grossraum, Nomos*.

'Raum und Grossraum in Völkerrecht' (1940), in *Staat, Grossraum, Nomos*.

'Die letzte globale Linie' (1943), in *Staat, Grossraum, Nomos*.

'Staat als konkreter an geschichtliche Epoche gebundener Begriff' (1941), in *Verfassungsrechtliche Aufsätze aus den Jahren 1924–1954*.

'Machtpositionen des modernen Staates' (1933), in *Verfassungsrechtliche Aufsätze*.

'Die Diktatur des Reichspräsidenten nach Artikel 48 der Weimarer Verfassung', reprinted with *Die Diktatur*, 1924 edn.

'Diktatur und Belagerungszustand. Eine Staatsrechtliche Studie', *Zeitschrift für die gesamte Staatsrechtswissenschaft*, vol. 38, 1916.

'Reichspräsident und Weimar Verfassung', *Kölnische Volkszeitung*, no. 198, (15 March 1925).

'Der Hüter der Verfassung', *Archiv des öffentlichen Rechts, Neue Folge* XVI, 1929, pp. 161–237.

'Das Reichsgericht als Hüter der Verfassung', in *Die Reichsgerichtspraxis im deutschen Rechtsleben. Festgabe der juristischen Fakultäten zum 50 jährigen Bestehen des Reichsgericht*, vol. 1. pp. 154–78.

'Eine Warnung vor falschen politischen Fragestellungen' *Der Ring*, Jg. 3, Heft 48 (30 November 1930), pp. 253–6.

'Gesunde Wirtschaft im starken Staat' *Mitteilungen des Vereins zur Wahrung der gemeinsamen wirtschaftlichen Interessen in Rheinland und Westphalen*', Heft 21 (23 November 1932), pp. 13–23.

'Der Missbrauch der Legalität', *Tägliche Rundschau*, 19 July 1932.

'Das Gesetz zur Behebung der Not von Volk und Reich', *Deutsche Juristen-Zeitung*, Jg. 38, Heft 7 (1 April 1933), pp. 455–8.

'Die deutschen Intellektuellen', *Westdeutscher Beobachter*, Jg. 9, Heft 126 (31 May 1933).

'Die Bedeutung des neuen Straatsrats', *Westdeutscher Beobachter*, 17 July 1933.

'Das Gespräch über die Macht und den Zugang zum Machthaber', *Gemeinschaft und Politik*, Jg. 2, Heft 10 (1954), pp. 9–15.

'Die Ära der integralen Politik', *Lo Stato. Rivista di Scienza politiche, guiridiche ed economiche*, April 1936, pp. 191–6. Translated from Italian by Günter Maschke.

'Nationalsozialismus und Rechtsstaat', *Juristische Wochenschrift* 63, 1934, pp. 713–18.

'Neue Leitsätze für die Rechtspraxis', *Juristiche Wochenschrift*, Jg. 62, 1933, p. 2793.

'Der Neubau des Staats und Verwaltungsrecht', *Deutscher Juristentag*, pp. 242–51.

'Können wir uns vor Justizirrtum schützen?', *Der Angriff*, 1 September 1936.

'Das Judentum in der deutschen Rechtswissenschaft' in 'Die deutsche Rechtswissenschaft im Kampf gegen den judischen Geist', *Deutsche Juristen-Zeitung*, Jg. 41, Heft 20 (15 October 1936), pp. 1193–9.

Other Cited Works

Anderson, Perry, 'The Intransigent Right at the End of the Century', *London Review of Books*, vol. 14, no. 18, 24 September 1992.

Anderson, Perry, *The Origins of Postmodernity*, Verso, London and New York 1999.

Anschütz, Gerhard, *Verfassung des deutschen Reiches* (George Stilken, Berlin 1924).

Aristotle, *Politics* (Penguin, Harmondsworth 1975).

Barker, Rodney, *Political Legitimacy and the State* (Clarendon Press, Oxford 1991).

Beckerath, Erwin von, *Wesen und Werden des faschistischen Staates* (Springer, Berlin 1927).

Bendersky, Joseph, *Carl Schmitt: Theorist of the Reich* (Princeton University Press, Princeton, NJ 1983).

Beneyto, Jose Maria, *Apokolypse der Moderne* (Klett–Cotta, Stuttgart 1987).

Benjamin, Walter, *Geschichtsphilosophische Thesen* (Suhrkamp, Frankfurt am Main 1995).

Benjamin, Walter, *Gesammelte Briefe* (Suhrkamp, Frankfurt am Main 1997).

Bentin, Arwed, *Johannes Popitz und Carl Schmitt: Zur wirtschaftlichen Theorie des totalen Staates in Deutschland* (C.H. Beck, Munich 1972).

Bobbio, Norberto, *Democracy and Dictatorship* (University of Minneapolis Press, Minnesota 1988).

Bobbio, Norberto, *Thomas Hobbes and the Natural Law Tradition* (University of Chicago Press, Chicago 1993).

Bodin, Jean, *Six Books of the Republic*, cited in Norberto Bobbio, *Democracy and Dictatorship* (University of Minneapolis Press, Minnesota 1989).

Breuer, Stefan, *Anatomie der Konservativen-Revolution* (Wissenschaftliche Buchgesellschaft, Darmstadt 1993).

Caenegem, R.C. van, *An Historical Introduction to Private Law* (Cambridge University Press, Cambridge 1988).

Caldwell, Peter, *Popular Sovereignty and the Crisis of German Constitutional Law* (Duke University Press, Durham, NC 1997).

Chace, William, *The Political Identities of T.S. Eliot and Ezra Pound* (Stanford University Press, Palo Alto, CA 1973).

Cicero, *De Officiis* (Heinemann, London 1975).

Cortes, Donoso, 'Discours sur la Dictature', in *Oeuvres de Donoso Cortes*, vol. 1 (Briday, Lyon 1877).

Cortes, Donoso, *Der Staat Gottes* (F.A. & Co. Verlag, Leipzig 1933).

Curtius, Ernst Robertus, *Der Syndikalismus der Geistarbeiter* (Mohr, Bonn 1921).

Curtius, Ernst Robertus, 'Briefe von E.R. Curtius an Carl Schmitt (1921–22)', *Archiv für das Studium der neureren Sprachen und Literaturen.*

Curtius, Ernst Robertus, *Der Deutsche Geist in Gefahr* (Deutsche Verlags-Anstalt, Stuttgart/Berlin 1932).

Dahlheimer, Manfred, *Der deutsche Katholizismus 1888–1936* (Verlag Ferdinand Schöningh, Paderborn, 1999).

Derrida, Jacques, *The Politics of Friendship* (Verso, London and New York 1997).

Dieckmann, Hildemarie, *Johannes Popitz – Entwicklung und Wirksamkeit in der Zeit der Weimarer Republik* (Lutz, Berlin 1960).

Dyson, Kenneth, *The State Tradition* (Oxford University Press, Oxford 1987).

Dyzenhaus, David, *Legality and Legitimacy* (Oxford University Press, Oxford 1997).

Eagleton, Terry, *The Ideology of the Aesthetic* (Blackwell, London 1990).

Ebach, Jürgen, *Leviathan und Behemoth* (F. Schöningh, Paderborn 1984).

Eley, Geoff, 'Conservatives and Radical Nationalists in Germany', in Martin Blinkhorn, ed., *Fascists and Conservatives* (Unwin Hyman, Boston, MA 1990).

Eliot, T.S., 'Make it New', *Criterion* 7 (1924).

Eliot, T.S., *After Strange Gods* (Harcourt & Brace, New York 1934).

Flickinger, Haris-Georg, ed., *Die Autonomie des Politischen* (VCH Verlags-gesellschaft, Weinheim 1990).

Gramsci, Antonio, 'The Modern Prince', in *Selections from the Prison Notebooks* (International Publishers, New York 1980).

Grimm, Dieter, *Deutsche Verfassungsgeschichte, 1776–1866* (Suhrkamp, Frankfurt am Main 1988).

Grossheutschi, Felix, *Carl Schmitt und die Lehre von Katechon* (Duncker & Humblot, Berlin 1996).

Gruchmann, Lothar, *Nationalsozialistische Grossraumordnung* (Deutsche Verlags-Anstalt, Stuttgart 1962).

Guizot, M., *The History of the Origin of Representative Government in Europe* (Henry G. Bohn, London 1852).

Gurian, Waldemar, *Um des Reiches Zukunft: Nationale Wiedergeburt oder politische Reaktion?* (Herder & Co., Freiburg 1932).

Gurian, Waldemar, 'Entscheidung und Ordnung', *Schweizerische Rund-schau*, Jg. 34, 1934, pp. 566–76.

Habermas, Jürgen, *Between Facts and Norms* (MIT Press, Cambridge, MA 1995).

Hart, H.L.A., *The Concept of Law* (Oxford University Press, Oxford 1979).

Hauriou, Maurice, *Précis du Droit universel* (Librairie du Recueil Sirey, Paris 1929).

Hegel, G.W.F., *Philosophy of Right* (Cambridge, Cambridge University Press 1987).

Heller, Hermann, *Gesammelte Schriften* (Sijthoff, Leiden 1971).

Hermens, Ferdinand, *Zwischen Politik und Vernunft: Gesammelte Aufsätze aus drei Welten* (Duncker & Humblot, Berlin 1969).

Hobbes, Thomas, *Elements of Law* (Cambridge University Press, Cam-bridge 1928).

Hobbes, Thomas, *Dialogue between a Philosopher and a Student of the Common Law* (University of Chicago Press, Chicago 1987).

Hobbes, Thomas, *Leviathan* (Hackett, Indianapolis, IN/Cambridge 1994).

Hoeges, Dirk, *Kontroverse am Abgrund* (S. Fischer, Frankfurt am Main 1994).

Hoepke, Klaus-Peter, *Die deutsche Rechte und der italienische Faschismus* (Droste Verlag, Düsseldorf).

Holmes, Stephen, *The Anatomy of Antiliberalism* (Harvard University Press, Cambridge, MA 1994).

Hürten, Heinz, *Reichswehr und Ausnahmezustand: ein Beitrag zur verfassungs-problematik der Weimarer Republik in ihrem ersten Jahrfünft* in Rheinisch-Westfälische Akademie der Wissenschaften, Vorträge G222.

Jung, Otmar, *Direkte Demokratie in der Weimarer Republik* (Campus Verlag, Frankfurt/New York 1989).

Jünger, Ernst, *Der Krieg als inneres Erlebnis* (Velhagen & Klasing, Bielefeld 1933).

Jünger, Ernst, *Die totale Mobilmachung* (Junker & Dunnhaupt, Berlin 1934).

Kelsen, Hans, *Allgemeine Staatslehre* (Berlin, Junius Springer Verlag 1925).

Kelsen, Hans, *Problem der Souveränität und die Theorie des Völkerrechts* (Mohr, Tübingen 1928).

Kelsen, Hans, 'Wer soll der Hüter der Verfassung sein?', in *Die Wiener rechtstheoretische Schule* (Pustet, Munich 1968).

Kelsen, Hans, 'The Idea of Natural Law (1928)', reprinted in Hans Kelsen, *Essays in Legal and Moral Philosophy* (Reidel, Boston, MA 1974).

Kelsen, Hans, *Introduction to Problems of Legal Theory* (Clarendon Press, Oxford 1992).

Kempner, Robert, *Das Dritte Reich im Kreuzverhör* (Esslingen, Munich 1969).

Kennedy, Ellen, 'Carl Schmitt and the Frankfurt School', *Telos* 71, Spring 1987, pp. 37–67.

Kiesel, Helmut, ed., *Ernst Jünger – Carl Schmitt Briefe 1930–1983* (Klett–Cotta, Stuttgart 1999).

Koenen, Andreas, *Der Fall Carl Schmitt* (Wissenschaftliche Buchgesellschaft, Darmstadt 1995).

Lacqueur, Walter, *Weimar* (Putnam, New York 1974).

Leutszch, Martin, 'Der Bezug auf die Bibel und ihre Wirkungsgeschichte', in *Die eigentlich katholische Verschärfung* (Wilhem Fink Verlag, Munich, 1994).

Lewis, Wyndham, *The Art of Being Ruled* (Black Sparrow Press, Santa Rosa 1989).

Löwy, Michael, *Georg Lukács: From Romanticism to Revolution* (New Left Books, London 1979).

Lukács, Georg, review of *Politische Romantik*, *Archiv für die Geschichte des Sozialismus und der Arbeiterbewegung*, 8, 1928, pp. 307–8.

Lukács, Georg, *The Destruction of Reason* (Merlin, London 1980).

Niccolò Machiavelli, *The Prince and the Discourses* (Carlton House, New York 1962).

Mann, Thomas, 'Von deutscher Republik', in *Gesammelte Werke*, vol. XI (S. Fischer, Frankfurt am Main 1960).

Mannheim, Karl, *Ideologie und Utopie* (F. Cohen, Bonn 1929).

Mannheim, Karl, *Konservatismus* (Suhrkamp, Frankfurt am Main 1994).

Marcu, Valeriu, *Die Vertreibung der Juden aus Spanien* (Querido Verlag, Amsterdam 1934).

Marx, Karl, *The Eighteenth Brumaire of Louis Napoleon* (Progress, New York 1963).

Maschke, Günter, *Der Tod Carl Schmitts* (Karolinger, Vienna 1987).

Maurras, Charles, *Romantisme et Révolution* (Nouvelle Libraire National, Paris 1925).

Mauss, Ingeborg, 'Volk und Nation im Denken des Aufklärung, *Blätter für deutsche und internationale Politik* 5, 1994.

Meier, Heinrich, *Die Lehre Carl Schmitts* (J.B. Metzler, Stuttgart 1994).

Meier, Heinrich, *Carl Schmitt and Leo Strauss: The Hidden Dialogue* (University of Chicago Press, Chicago 1995).

Mommsen, Hans, *The Rise and Fall of Weimar Democracy* (University of North Carolina Press, Chapel Hill 1996).

Münkler, Herfried, *Im Namen des Staates: die Begründung der Staatsräson in der frühen Neuzeit* (S. Fischer, Frankfurt am Main 1987).

Muth, Heinrich, 'Carl Schmitt in der deutschen Innenpolitik des Sommers 1932', *Historische Zeitschrift*, Beiheft 1, Beiträge zur Geschichte der Weimarer Republik (1971), pp. 75–147.

Neumann, Friedrich, *The Rule of Law under Siege* (University of Chicago Press, Chicago 1996).

Netanyahu, B., *Abravanel* (Jewish Publication Society of America, Philadelphia 1968).

Nichtweiss, Barbara, 'Apokolyptische Verfassungslehre', in *Die eigentlich katholische Verschärfung* (Wilhelm Fink Verlag, Munich 1994).

Noack, Paul, *Carl Schmitt: eine Biographie* (Propyläen Verlag, Berlin 1993).

Nolte, Ernst, *Der Faschismus in seiner Epoche* (R. Piper Verlag, Munich 1963).

Peterson, Erik, 'Was ist Theologie?', in *Theologische Traktate* (Kösel Verlag, Munich 1950).

Plato, *Collected Dialogues* (Princeton University Press, Princeton, NJ 1973).

Quaritsch, Helmut, ed., *Complexio Oppositorum* (Duncker & Humblot, Berlin 1988).

Quaritsch, Helmut, *Positionen und Begriffe* (Duncker & Humblot, Berlin 1989).

Roth, Jack, *The Cult of Violence* (University of California Press, Berkeley 1980).

Rousseau, J.-J., *The Social Contract* (Harper & Row, New York 1984).

Rüthers, Bernd, *Wissenschaft als Zeitgeist–Verstärkung?* (C.H. Beck, Munich 1989).

Schar, J.H., *Legitimacy in the Modern State* (Transaction Books, New Brunswick 1981).

Sombart, Nicolaus, *Jugend in Berlin* (Carl Hanser Verlag, Munich 1984).

Sontheimer, Kurt, *Antidemokratisches Denken in der Weimarer Republik* (Nymphenberger Verlagshandlung, Munich 1962).

Sorel, Georges, *Reflections on Violence* (Collier Books, New York 1950).

Spinoza, Baruch, *Political Works* (Clarendon Press, Oxford 1958).

Staff, Ilse, *Staatsdenken im Italien des 20 Jahrhunderts Beitrag zur Schmitt-Rezeption in Italien* (Nomos, Baden 1991).

Sternhell, Zeev, *Neither Right nor Left: Fascist Ideology in France* (Princeton University Press, Princeton, NJ 1996).

Strauss, Leo, *The Political Philosophy of Thomas Hobbes* (Oxford University Press, Oxford 1936).

Strauss, Leo, *Isaac Abravanel: Six Lectures* (Cambridge University Press, Cambridge 1937).

Strauss, Leo, *Natural Right and History* (University of Chicago Press, Chicago 1953).

Strauss, Leo, *On Tyranny* (Cornell University Press, Ithaca, NY 1968).

Strauss, Leo, 'Comments on *The Concept of the Political*', reprinted in J. Heinrich Meier, *Carl Schmitt and Leo Strauss: The Hidden Dialogue* (University of Chicago Press, Chicago 1995).

Tocqueville, Alexis de, *Democracy in America* (Vintage, New York 1958).

Toepner, Kurt, 'Der deutsche Katholizismus zurischen 1918 und 1933', in Hans Joachim Schoeps, ed., *Die Zeitgeist der Weimarer Republik* (Stuttgart 1968).

Ulmen, Gary, *Politischer Mehrwert* (Weinheim 1991).

Van Laak, Dirk, *Gespräche in der Sicherheit des Schweigens* (Akademie Verlag, Berlin 1993).

Von Bruch 'Deutsche Hochschullehrer als Elite', in Hans Joachim Schoeps, ed., *Zeitgeist der Weimarer Republik* (E. Klett, Stuttgart, 1968).

Weber, Max, *Economy and Society* (University of California Press, Berkeley 1978).

Index